OXFORD STUDIES IN AFRICAN AFFAIRS

General Editors
JOHN D. HARGREAVES *and* GEORGE SHEPPERSON

FRENCH COLONIAL RULE
AND THE
BAULE PEOPLES

Pacification atrocity in Ivory Coast, 1910

FRENCH COLONIAL RULE AND THE BAULE PEOPLES: RESISTANCE AND COLLABORATION, 1889-1911

BY

TIMOTHY C. WEISKEL

CLARENDON PRESS · OXFORD
1980

Oxford University Press, Walton Street, Oxford OX2 6DP

OXFORD LONDON GLASGOW
NEW YORK TORONTO MELBOURNE WELLINGTON
KUALA LUMPUR SINGAPORE JAKARTA HONG KONG TOKYO
DELHI BOMBAY CALCUTTA MADRAS KARACHI
NAIROBI DAR ES SALAAM CAPE TOWN

Published in the United States
by Oxford University Press, New York

British Library in Publication Cataloguing Data
Weiskel, Timothy C
    French colonial rule and Baule peoples. –
    (Oxford studies in African affairs).
    1. Ivory Coast – Colonization   2. Baoulé
    I. Title   II. Series
    966.6'8   DT545.7   79–40886
    ISBN 0–19–822715–9

Printed in Great Britain by
Lowe & Brydone Printers Limited, Thetford, Norfolk

To My Parents
for their unfailing inspiration and support

The conquest of the earth, which mostly means the taking it away from those who have a different complexion or slightly flatter noses than ourselves, is not a pretty thing when you look into it too much.

Joseph Conrad
Heart of Darkness, 1902.

Avec nos meilleurs compliments

Institut Historique Allemand
9, rue Maspéro
75016 Paris

Tel. 870-95-55

Mit verbindlichen Empfehlungen

Deutsches Historisches Institut
9, rue Maspéro
75016 Paris

Tel. Nr. 870-25-55

Contents

List of Illustrations x

List of Maps xi

Abbreviations xii

Acknowledgements xiv

Preface xvii

Introduction 1

I. The Pre-colonial Baule: An Economic and Socio-Political Outline 5

II. French Penetration and the First Baule 'Revolt', 1889-1895 33

III. Military Withdrawal and Baule Prosperity, 1895-1898 66

IV. Slave Emancipation, Taxation, and Renewed Resistance, 1898-1902 99

V. Governor Clozel's Peace Strategy and the Politics of Collaboration, 1903-1907 142

VI. Governor Angoulvant's Development Plans and the Final Phase of Baule Resistance, 1908-1911 172

VII. Patterns of Resistance and Collaboration 211

VIII. French Conquest and Baule Resistance in Historical Perspective 231

NOTES 245

BIBLIOGRAPHY 285

INDEX 309

List of Illustrations

Pacification atrocity in Ivory Coast, 1910. (Photo
Harlingue-Viollet)   *frontispiece*

1. a. Captain Marchand (*c.* 1893), first European explorer
   among Baule.
   b. Commander Monteil (*c.* 1894), commander of Kong
   Expedition, 1894–5.
   c. Albert Nebout (*c.* 1892), first civilian administrator
   among Baule.
   d. Maurice Delafosse (*c.* 1897), early administrator and
   first ethnographer of Baule peoples.

2. Officers outside the military outpost at Bouaké,
   established in 1898. (Photo Harlingue-Viollet)

3. Akafou 'Bulare' (Akafou, the man of 'iron'), chief of the
   southern Ngban, d. July 1902.

4. a. Governor General Ernest Roume, first Governor
   General to establish economic planning for French West
   Africa as a whole. (Bodleian Library Oxford)
   b. Governor François-Joseph Clozel (*c.* 1906), author
   of collaboration policy with Baule. (Bodleian Library
   Oxford)
   c. Governor General William Ponty, who authorized use
   of *tirailleurs sénégalais* for final suppression of Baule
   resistance, 1910–11. (Bodleian Library Oxford)
   d. Governor Gabriel Angoulvant, author of strong-arm
   tactics for complete suppression of Baule resistance
   after 1908. (Photo Harlingue-Viollet)

5. Commander Noguès, commander of troops sent to defeat
   Baule resistance among the Akoué and Nanafoué, 1910–11.

6. Senegalese troops about to begin operations against
   Baule resisters, *c.* 1910. (Photo Harlingue-Viollet)

7. Yao Guié, captured 13 June 1910, and died in captivity.

8. Baule warriors submit arms as part of conditions imposed
   for peace with French colonial administration. (Photo
   Harlingue-Viollet)

List of Maps

1. Eighteenth-Century Trade and Migration 7
2. Detail of Bowdich Map (1817) 10
3. Principal Baule Groups and their Southern Migrations in the Nineteenth Century 12
4. The Baule Peoples: Western Frontier of the Akan 14
5. Baule Late Nineteenth-Century Trade Patterns 16
6. Trade between the Sudan and the Gulf of Guinea according to Binger, c. 1889 18
7. Southern Baule and Lower Bandama Rival Trading Chains, c. 1890 29

Abbreviations

Alm. Ann. Mars. – Almanach Annuaire du Marsouin.
ANRCI – Archives Nationales de la République de la Côte d'Ivoire (Abidjan)
ANRM – Archives Nationales de la République du Mali (Bamako)
ANRS – Archives Nationales de la République du Sénégal (Dakar)
ANSOM – Archives Nationales (France), Section d'Outre-Mer (Paris)
A.O.F. – Afrique Occidentale Française
AUA – Annales de l'Université d'Abidjan.
Bat. – Bataillon.
BCAF – Bulletin du Comité de l'Afrique Française.
BCAF–RCD – Bulletin du Comité de l'Afrique Française-Renseignements Coloniaux et Documents.
BIFAN – Bulletin de l'Institut Français de l'Afrique Noire – série B, Sciences Humaines.
BOCI – Bulletin Officiel de la Côte d'Ivoire.
Cah. ORSTOM – Cahiers de l'Office de la Recherche Scientifique et Technique d'Outre-Mer, série Sciences Humaines.
C.E.N.W.P. – Cahiers de l'École Normale William Ponty
C.F.A.O. – Compagnie Française de l'Afrique Occidentale
D.P. – Delafosse Papers
ÉRB – Étude Régionale de Bouaké (Abidjan, Ministère du Plan, 1962)
ÉRSE – Étude Régionale du Sud-Est (Abidjan, Ministère du Plan, 1967)
Ét. Éb. – Études Éburnéennes
Gov. Gen. p.i. – Governor General *par interim* (acting)
Gov. p.i. – Governor *par interim* (acting)
IFAN – Institut Français de l'Afrique Noire
JAH – Journal of African History

JO, Déb. Parl. – *Journal Officiel* (France), *Débats Parlementaires, Chambre des Députés*

JOAOF – *Journal Officiel de l'Afrique Occidentale Française.*

JOCI – *Journal Officiel de la Côte d'Ivoire*

M.C. – Ministre des Colonies

M.M.C. – Ministre de la Marine et des Colonies

NA–IFAN – *Notes Africaines-Institut Français de l'Afrique Noire*

P. – Pièce (item)

RTC – *Revue des Troupes Coloniales*

SEMC – Secrétaire d'État chargé de la Marine et des Colonies

Acknowledgements

The research for the following study has been conducted from 1970 to 1976 in Oxford, Paris, Abidjan, Bamako, Dakar, and Baule country itself. I owe particular thanks to Dr Colin W. Newbury who supervised my thesis work, demonstrating a patient and thoughtful concern for the problems I have encountered along the way. In addition I am grateful to Dr Edwin Ardener of the Institute of Social Anthropology, Oxford, who as my adviser during 1969–70 initially encouraged me to pursue research combining the disciplines of Social Anthropology and History.

In Paris I owe thanks to Mme Denise Paulme of the École des Hautes Études en Sciences Sociales (É.H.É.S.S.) whose guidance was particularly helpful in preparation for field work in the Ivory Coast. I am also grateful to Claude Meillassoux (É.H.É.S.S.) for the chance to attend his seminar during 1971–2 on pre-colonial slavery in West Africa. In addition, Marc Augé, Jean Copans, and François Pouillon deserve special thanks for their instruction and advice as the directors of the programme 'Formation à la Recherche en Afrique Noire' (F.R.A.N.) during 1971–2. I also wish to thank Mme Louise Delafosse for her kind permission to consult her father's private correspondence.

In the Ivory Coast I was grateful for the cordial welcome and assistance of Dr Claude Pairault, former Directeur de l'Institut d'Ethno-Sociologie and that of the current Director, Dr Georges Niangoran-Bouah. In addition Dr Joachim Bony, Directeur de l'Institut d'Histoire d'Art et d'Archéologie Africaine, was helpful. I am grateful to both these Institutes for including me as a 'Chercheur Associé' within their programmes and to the Ministry of Scientific Research for its permission to undertake archival and field research. In the archives themselves, I owe particular thanks to M. Guy Cangah, Director, and to his staff for their patience and efficiency.

In Bamako I owe thanks to M. Mamadou Sarr, Chef de la Division Recherche Scientifique of the Ministère de l'Enseignement Supérieur, for permission to consult the Archives Nationales de la République du Mali. In Dakar I was grateful to M. Jean-François Maurel for permission to consult the Archives Nationales de la République du Sénégal.

It would be impossible to present a full list of colleagues who have helped in one way or another throughout the past six years, but I would nevertheless like to thank MM. Christophe Wondji, Simon Mbra Ekanza, and Jean-Louis Triaud of the Faculté d'Histoire at the Université d'Abidjan as well as David Groff, Richard Horovitz, Philip Ravenhill, Judith Timyan, Susan Vogel, Jean-Pierre Chauveau and Michel Pescay, all of whom have provided helpful insights and encouragement throughout my field research. Finally, I wish to record my special debt to the late Pierre Étienne whose writings provide the core of contemporary Baule studies and who was kind enough to encourage my research from 1971 onwards.

In addition I wish to thank the Trustees of the Danforth Foundation (U.S.A.) for the Danforth Graduate Fellowship which enabled me to undertake field work, and the Trustees of the Rhodes Trust (Oxford), and in particular Sir Edgar T. Williams whose interest in and support of my work has been unfailing.

It is always difficult to account for the origin of ideas, but for me it is often the case that they emerge from argument with able adversaries. In this connection, I am indebted to Professor Ronald Robinson and to the members of the Oxford Commonwealth History Seminar for their particular kind of resistance and collaboration in the formulation of my ideas on this and many other subjects in imperial and African history.

Finally, I am forever indebted to Kathryn Kasch without whom this work would not have been attempted and could not have been completed.

Preface

This book is a case study of one of the most enduring and most brutally repressed resistance struggles in West African history. The work analyses the encounter between the Baule peoples of the central Ivory Coast and the French in the early years of colonial rule in order to examine the patterns of resistance and collaboration in an African stateless society and the motive forces behind French colonial conquest. Particular attention is given to the sequence of individual incidents and decisions in the belief that broader interpretive questions can only be discussed meaningfully when an accurate chronology has been established. In this respect the present account is a deliberate 'micro-history' – a single chapter in the larger story of the West African colonial experience.

As an exercise in micro-history the Baule case provides a particular challenge to the historian because of the nature of the source material. The Baule themselves do not have a written tradition; nor did any of the early French administrators concern themselves with recording in detail the Baule perception of events at the time. What we can know of the period is limited to the available European documentation and whatever can be reconstructed from conducting personal interviews and collecting oral traditions about the events. The present study is based on written European sources. It is hoped that it can serve as a point of departure for the new generation of Ivory Coast scholars who can extend and complete our understanding of Baule resistance with the systematic use of oral traditions.

The documentary evidence itself poses numerous problems. Summary reports of resistance activity and government policy were written at the time and sent from the Ivory Coast to Dakar and Paris, and they are preserved in the archives in these locations. Frequently, however, these reports were inaccurate or vague on specific points of detail, and sometimes they were deliberately misleading. Their intention was either to assure administrative superiors that everything was under control or alternatively to argue in favour of a particular line of policy. As a result the image they project of Baule resistance is often fanciful in the extreme, and it would be gullible historiography indeed to write an account from these sources alone.

To arrive at a more accurate understanding of the resistance phenomena it is necessary to penetrate several successive layers of official correspondence down to the level of the field notes, account books, monthly reports, and daily journals of the local administrators and military officers in the Baule village outposts. These documents, preserved in the Ivory Coast archives, contain the spontaneous and undigested observations of the participants and eyewitnesses involved in the early French encounter with the Baule, and they form the basis for the present study. Sources from other manuscript collections in Paris, Dakar, and Bamako are used when appropriate. In addition, the private papers of Maurice Delafosse, one of the first administrators among the Baule, were of particular assistance in completing this study, and I am grateful to Mme Louise Delafosse for granting me access to them.

Even with this rich variety of detailed information two problems remain. In the first place the record is highly fragmentary. Many reports known to have been written simply no longer survive. Some were destroyed in the resistance clashes at the time; others have since been mislaid or lost before the creation of the present-day archive collections. Beyond this common difficulty for colonial historians lies a second, more challenging problem: the issue of the underlying bias and distortion inherent in the existing sources themselves. Contemporary observers frequently offered explanations for the meaning of what they experienced, but in retrospect their judgements often appear strangely beside the point. Critical historians proceed on the assumption that events have meanings that may well have eluded those who witnessed them. The task at hand is to reveal those meanings by reading not only between the lines but through and beyond the lines of existing documentation to the point where an entire picture of events can be accurately and empathetically reconstructed. To get the story straight with only warped sources is not a simple task; but it is not impossible. African history can be written from even the most partial colonial sources if an analytical perspective is kept clearly in mind.

To furnish the necessary background for studying French conquest and Baule resistance, this account starts with a brief description of the pre-colonial evolution of the Baule peoples in the eighteenth and nineteenth centuries. Chapter II follows with a detailed presentation of the early stages of French inland penetration including the explorations of Captain Marchand, the Monteil expedition, and the first Baule revolt. Chapter III describes the period of Baule prosperity from 1895 to 1898, following the French military retreat to the coast. Chapter IV examines the origins and character of the second phase of Baule resistance, while Chapter V elaborates Governor Clozel's attempts to restore collaborative arrangements with Baule chiefs after the failure of initial military operations. Chapter VI details the collapse of collaboration and the development and eventual defeat of the third phase of Baule resistance in the face of Governor Angoulvant's new economic and military initiatives. In Chapter VII an attempt is made to take a retrospective look at the general patterns of Baule resistance activity to highlight its characteristic features. The study concludes by considering Baule resistance in historical perspective in order to interpret the significance of the diverse phenomena and evaluate the Baule case in the wider context of West African colonial history.

T. C. Weiskel
Balliol College
Oxford
August 1978

Introduction

Resistance movements constitute the Rosetta stone of modern African history. By examining their features historians can translate the complexities of pre-colonial polities into the politics of colonial rule, and decipher the rhetoric of national independence in the light of the initial imperial conquest. As the key to both the enduring grammar and changing vocabulary of African history, resistance studies have understandably become the object of interest for several different historical schools. Nationalist historians study early resistance phenomena as an important prelude to the independence struggles of the 1950s and 1960s. Imperial historians regard these 'proto-nationalist' movements as vital in understanding the timing and character of European expansion. Pre-colonial historians and historically minded anthropologists examine them for clues to the pre-colonial economic and social structures as they reveal themselves under stress. Historians of the colonial period see in resistance studies the starting-point for assessing the impact of colonial rule in Africa. Whether as starting-point or terminus, essence or aberration, resistance movements have become a central theme in recent African historiography.

In West Africa the encounter between African rulers and the French has attracted the particular attention of historians in this regard. In this region the French directed their efforts in the late nineteenth century to subduing numerous Islamic reform movements which swept Senegal and the western Sudan. African political leaders including Lat Dior, Mamadou Lamine, Amadu Seku, and Samory opposed French imperial ambitions with organized armies, and in contending with these forms of opposition the French developed what might be regarded as a classic example of European military imperialism.[1] Conquest was frequently undertaken with very little direct initiative from Paris. Instead, the entire enterprise has been depicted as a series of effective *faits accomplis* engineered by ambitious young military officers obsessed with strategic concerns on the spot.

In Paris the politicians had had enough. In 1891 and 1893 they called a halt to the soldiers . . . but the colonels, with one hand on their Maxims and the other on their next set of proofs, were bent on routing out Muslim resistance . . . step by step the army eventually involved Paris in the economics of development.[2]

Beneath all of the blood and furore it appears that, in the western Sudan at least, there was no well-conceived economic rationale for French colonial conquest.

In interpreting French imperialism, however, it may be misleading to focus too exclusively upon the western Sudan. While this region clearly constituted the major theatre of French operations until 1898, it was not the only area in West Africa where they established their authority by conquest. On the contrary, many of their bloodiest battles took place elsewhere. At the turn of the century the French officers were only in the initial stages of conquest of the central Ivory Coast. Campaigns in this region were to last for more than another decade. It would appear that the same dynamic of military imperialism had extended itself southwards into this area long after the time when the era of military conquest was thought to be definitely closed. Just when the officers seemed to have been restrained in the western Sudan, they appear to have run amuck in the forest regions of the Ivory Coast.

Reflecting upon the course of French colonial expansion in West Africa, Commandant Chailley drew attention to this anomaly in 1953: 'Il avait fallu vingt ans pour joindre le Sénégal au Tchad; il en couta trente pour dessiner et reconnaître la Côte d'Ivoire'.[3] If Chailley's observation is correct, it suggests that in the Ivory Coast the French faced even greater opposition than they had experienced in the military conquest of the Sudan. Other historians have made broadly similar observations. Writing in 1971 on the subject of West African resistance Michael Crowder commented: 'The longest war fought by the Europeans in West Africa after that against Samori was against the peoples of the southern Ivory Coast, in particular the Baule, who resisted occupation village by village . . .'.[4] Similarly, in his recent textbook on African history, Robin Hallett mentions the French conquest of the Baule and states that 'nowhere in West Africa except in the campaign against Samory was a colonial power faced with so exhausting a war . . .'.[5]

These summary assessments invite extended investigation, for they suggest that our understanding of French military imperialism remains incomplete if it is confined to events in the western Sudan alone. It is as if the saga of colonial conquest has been told without its concluding chapter.

A careful study of the relations between the French and the Baule during this period will help to complete the story, and for this reason the present study should be of interest to readers whose concerns lie well beyond Baule history or French administration *per se*. Students of other regions in Africa and for that matter non-Africanists with interests in the Third World generally should find themes here germain to their own fields of study. Colonial rule has been an experience common to many in the modern world, and the history presented here reveals the colonial encounter in its starkest form.

The Baule case provides evidence to help answer two thorny questions in the wider context of West African history: first, what was the fundamental motive behind French military conquest in the region? and second, to what extent did early colonial rule refashion African economic, social, and political institutions? The tendency to date has been to regard French colonial conquests in West Africa as if they were the result of an uncontrollable military élite whose impetuous exploits on the spot in West Africa committed civilian authorities to accept an empire they had not intended to create and were hesitant to administer. While this general pattern may adequately explain French expansion in much of the western Sudan during the 1880s and 1890s, the Baule case demonstrates that a decade later in its final phase an entirely different dynamic of colonial conquest was at work in the central Ivory Coast. Here the civilians were in control, and the motivation for conquest was explicitly economic. The officers and their *tirailleurs sénégalais* were summoned to execute a specific task in accord with civilian administrative imperatives. The object of conquest was neither land nor mineral wealth, but rather labour. The captains and colonels were unleashed by civilian authorities to subdue independent African farmers and transform them into a tractable labour force in the service of an embryonic colonial economy.

The answer to the second thorny issue concerning the impact of early colonial rule in West Africa is also readily apparent in the Baule case. Recent studies on the 'economic revolution' in West Africa have tended to minimize the importance of early European control for the transformation of rural social and economic life. Drawing their examples primarily from coastal areas and regions of British influence, scholars have suggested that by and large European paramountcy merely provided a thin veneer over a series of indigenous export economies, leaving local political and social structures to function in much the same way as they had in a pre-colonial context.

Once again the Baule case suggests a marked exception to this pattern. In this instance colonial rule brought with it the violent imposition of the 'economic revolution'. The Baule peoples were jolted from their position as producers of gold and cotton cloth in a persistently viable regional economy and forced into a new role as peasant producers for the world commodity markets. The economic transition was by no means smooth, and political and social institutions suffered significantly in the process. To be sure, the French were able to cultivate collaborators to assist them in engineering this transformation, but these new 'chiefs' found themselves acting increasingly as mere agents of the French administration, and in the process the entire institution of chieftaincy lost credibility among the Baule in a remarkably short period. Clearly then, in this case, early colonial rule involved a radical and abrupt change from pre-colonial patterns of economic, political, and social life. Even if the Baule case proves to be an exception in the broader West African context, it cannot be ignored, for its very particularities highlight the most striking contours of the European colonial enterprise and illumine the nature of 'traditional' African practices in the contemporary world.

CHAPTER I

The Pre-colonial Baule:
An Economic and Socio-Political Outline

THE SEVENTEENTH- AND EIGHTEENTH-CENTURY BACKGROUND:

For most of the seventeenth and eighteenth centuries the region corresponding to the eastern half of the present-day Republic of the Ivory Coast remained an area of marginal significance for European maritime traders. Known in the trading jargon at the time as the Quaqua Coast, this region proved inauspicious for large-scale European trading activity for both geographical and political reasons. Swift coastal currents and offshore whirlpools made approach from the sea a hazardous affair, and a series of lagoon formations separating the open sea from the mainland meant that it was impossible for ocean-going vessels to gain unimpeded access to sizeable trading communities.[1] Politically, the region represented a complex mosaic of petty chieftaincies, most of which had only recently established themselves as a result of migrations from the east and north. With relatively small amounts of arms and munitions these independent polities could control the intricate system of lagoon waterways, and they effectively prevented the Europeans from establishing onshore trading factories.[2] While numerous European fortifications became the focal point for an expanding trade system along the Gold Coast just to the east, the only attempt to establish an onshore trading fort on the Quaqua Coast aroused local hostilities and ended in disaster only a few years after its initial creation.[3]

The absence of permanent European trading forts on the Quaqua Coast had important implications for the pattern of economic activity in the hinterland during the late seventeenth and eighteenth centuries. Lacking a fixed and regular outlet on the coast directly to the south, trade from the interior tended to be diverted instead in an east–west direction, as these hinterland regions became integrated as peripheral areas of an expanding Akan commercial system. Slaves, gold, and woven cloth from the Quaqua Coast interior flowed eastwards towards

Kumasi and other Akan trading centres in return for guns, gunpowder, and European manufactures obtained initially from the trading factories on the Gold Coast. The entire region was intimately involved in a complex inter-regional trade in luxury goods, but for the time being the bulk of the trade tended to reinforce economic expansion in the Akan regions of the Gold Coast hinterland while circumventing the populations along the Quaqua Coast.

Migration and settlement accompanied and extended the westward expansion of the Akan trading network. The full dimensions of the migrations into the Quaqua Coast hinterland remain as yet imprecise, but available accounts of oral traditions from virtually all of the groups in the area record origin myths linking these groups with the Akan areas in and around the Ashanti kingdom.[4] The broad socio-political outline of these migrations is apparent. The influx of European guns and munitions in exchange for slaves from the mid-seventeenth century onwards heightened the internal rivalries and external warfare in the emerging Akan states.[5] Some of the victims of these wars were integrated into the enlarged political systems within the Gold Coast hinterland itself. Others were sold as slaves to Europeans in the Gold Coast forts. Still others were able to flee beyond the range of effective military control of the Ashanti and other Akan states, and these refugees dispersed themselves in the hinterland of the Quaqua coast. There they established themselves initially as pocket minority settlements, but gradually they gained ascendancy over the surrounding Gouro, southern Mandé, and Dida populations through a combination of outright conquest and manipulation of local marriage alliances and advantageous trading connections with the Akan commercial system.[6]

One of the polities to emerge from this pattern of westward Akan migration and trade was a group known as the Baule peoples. Oral traditions initially recorded in the early colonial period link Baule origins with the escape of a minority faction from Kumasi in the early eighteenth century following an unsuccessful bid for control of the Ashanti kingdom. Upon the death of the Ashantihene, Osei Tutu, a dispute emerged over the right of succession between two nephews, Dakon and Opoku Ware. Dakon was killed in the ensuing struggle, and according to the tradition recorded by Maurice Delafosse a large number of his partisans fled westwards under the leadership of his sister, Aura Poku.[7] As with the origin myths of other similar groups in the region, the Baule accounts emphasize the themes of royal origins, massive migration, miraculous escape, and resounding military conquest; but recent research indicates that these accounts probably represent more in the way of literary convention than they do in the way of reliable historical narrative.[8]

In reality, the number of immigrants was probably quite restricted, and they most likely arrived in several successive waves of piecemeal migration rather than in one dramatic epoch of conquest. Furthermore, while armed conquest may well have played some role in particular encounters between the Baule and the pre-existent inhabitants of the region, the rise of Baule hegemony in the area can be explained more convincingly as the result of a much more gradual process of economic change and social stratification following the progressive integration of the territory into the Akan commercial network (see Map 1).

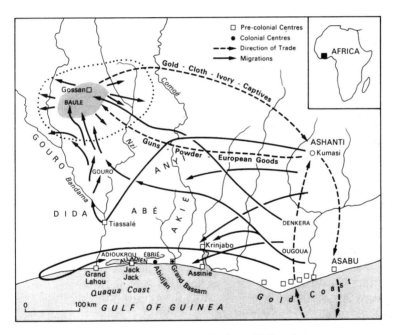

1. Eighteenth-Century Trade and Migration

Whatever the precise mechanisms were that assured Baule ascendancy in the area, it is clear that their initial presence did not stimulate trade in a north-south direction leading to an expansion of activity on the Quaqua coast. On the contrary, as Professor Yves Person has pointed out, their intrusion into the region may well have been responsible for eclipsing whatever north-south trade existed there up until their arrival.[9] Early sources refer to an African export trade in woven cloth from the Quaqua Coast, but this trade declines and virtually disappears at roughly the same time that the Baule emerge as important in the hinterland.[10]

Throughout the eighteenth century the trade arriving from the interior at Grand Lahou, the natural coastal outlet for the Baule southern trade, was never significant enough to attract sustained European interest. During the early 1760s, for example, when the French were secretly investigating the possibilities of expanding their influence on the coast, the observations of one agent on the spot were frankly discouraging concerning Grand Lahou: 'il y a quelquefois à traiter 100 captifs à la fois, peu d'or et de morfil, cela ne vaut point encore la peine d'un établissement'.[11] The slaves may have resulted from the sporadic warfare in the Baule region to the interior, but the trade was clearly not regular enough to justify an attempt to establish a fort, nor were the quantities of gold or ivory sufficiently abundant to attract French attention. Shortly afterwards, in 1786, the French resident at Whydah was instructed to investigate the possibility of expanding trade along the Quaqua Coast, and a treaty was in fact concluded with Lahou in 1787, granting the French permission to construct an onshore factory. In the event, however, the French never followed up this initiative, presumably, in part at least, because the volume of commodities offered never reached profitable levels. Whatever trade the Baule conducted most probably focused towards the east and not the south.

Given this pattern of external trade it is perhaps not surprising that Europeans first became aware of the existence of the Baule not from the coastal peoples but rather from the Ashanti themselves. In 1817, T. E. Bowdich recorded hearing of the Baule for the first time in the course of his mission to Kumasi:[12]

A powerful Kingdom called Bahooree, which has hitherto successfully resisted the Ashantees, was described to be westward, and expected to afford refuge to the King of Gaman [Abron] on the approaching invasion. [i.e. the Ashanti invasion of Gaman.]

On the basis of this information, Bowdich placed the Baule, or Bahooree, as he called them, to the north-west of Bondoukou, clearly beyond the sphere of Ashanti authority (see Map 2). European cartographers copied Bowdich's information faithfully, and subsequently the Bahooree are dutifully placed on European maps to the north-west of Bondoukou in published atlases throughout most of the mid-nineteenth century.[13] The very inaccuracies of these maps serve to underscore the central historical point that during this early period communications remained more developed in the east–west direction than in the north–south direction.[14]

NINETEENTH-CENTURY TRADE AND MIGRATION

The decline of the slave trade and the gradual shift to the production of palm products for export during the early nineteenth century profoundly altered both the production systems on the Quaqua Coast and the direction of trade in the Baule interior. In contrast to the earlier period the coastal region became an important focal point of European trading interest as local groups began to produce the commodities required by the European industrial economies. This trade, in turn, stimulated greatly expanded commercial contacts between the coastal peoples in the south and the Baule peoples to the north. As early as 1821 one British observer argued that his government should seek to establish a fort at Lahou in order to profit from the extensive interior trading connections emanating from this point.[15] Similarly, other agents pointed out that such an outpost would have immediate economic rewards, for as one of them put it, 'more business is done here than in the whole distance from Cape Mount to Saint Andrews; the quantity of gold and ivory sold annually is greater than at any of the European settlements, Cape Coast and Accra excepted'.[16]

As the nineteenth century progressed trading relations both on the coast and in the interior intensified, but the nature of the exchange in each region began to diverge in the process. On the coast, exports of gold and ivory, previously the main staples of the region's trade, declined in relative importance, while agricultural products became far more significant. During the second decade of the nineteenth century the luxury items still accounted for over three times the value of exported agricultural produce, but by the end of the 1830s – scarcely twenty years later – palm oil had become the region's dominant export commodity.[17]

Important social and political changes accompanied this fundamental

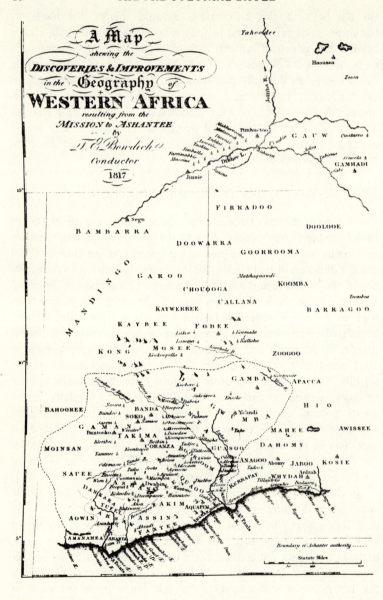

2. Detail of Bowdich Map (1817)

shift in economic activity along the coast. The overall quantity of bulk import goods increased markedly and so did the absolute number of trading agents. Because there were few barriers to entrance into the palm oil trade numerous petty chieftains began to take part, and in social terms the economic benefits of European trade became widely dispersed. Concomitantly the units of political power tended to fragment along the coast as local chiefs competed with one another for a dominant role in the European trade.[18]

Ultimately, the relative power of any particular coastal chief depended upon his economic success and this was based on two reciprocally related phenomena: first, the relative influence he could exercise with European traders in order to receive goods on credit; and second, the amount of palm oil he could deliver to repay his creditors and obtain further European goods for trade or distribution. Improvement in either one of these domains would tend to reinforce advantages in the other, and as a result trading communities on the coast became actively engaged in expanding the process of production. Land and trees were readily available, and the necessary tools could be easily obtained from Europeans; but the restricted supply of labour constituted a significant constraint upon increased production. Once the coastal groups had expanded their production by mobilizing all available domestic labour, they began to turn to their trading links with the interior to provide for their needs.[19]

In addition, coastal chiefs, seeking to consolidate and demonstrate their relative importance in the eyes of potential European trading partners, continued to require important quantities of gold jewellery and finely woven cloth as symbols of their chiefly estate. As more and more chiefs sought to affirm their status in this fashion, the aggregate demand for these luxury goods increased significantly. In effect, the economic 'revolution' on the coast had the result of perpetuating and indeed extending the pattern of 'royal' trade in the Baule interior. In exchange for a massive influx of European manufactures the Baule were encouraged to provide the same old staples of the eighteenth-century regional trade - slaves, gold, and finely woven cloth.

The available evidence suggests that the Baule responded to these intensified demands in a number of ways. To begin with, although there are no eyewitness accounts of Baule economic activity at the time, indirect sources indicate that Baule cloth production expanded considerably. By the mid-nineteenth century European agents on the coast began to receive details of interior regions north of Lahou for the first time, and the information they obtained emphasized the value of the cotton cloth trade with the Baule area. Similarly the evidence indicates that the gold trade expanded as well. During the 1860s a French naval officer, investigating the commercial potential of the area, related information he had heard, mentioning that the Baule themselves were in commercial contact with groups to their north. As he put it:

Le commerce de Baouré [*sic*] consiste en or, en riches pagnes de coton dont la souplesse et l'éclat rehaussent la valeur. Les Bambara viennent sur ce marché avec des chevaux; il ne leur est pas permis de dépasser.[20]

The picture that began to emerge at the time and that has subsequently been confirmed by recent research is one of intensified and extended production among the Baule in response to the opportunities available

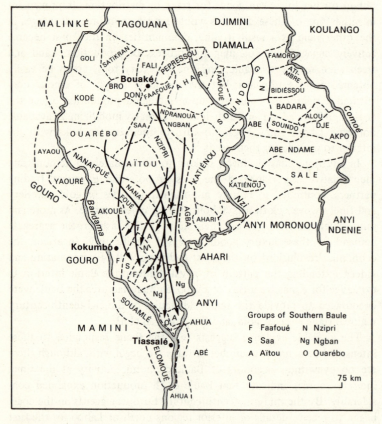

3. Principal Baule Groups and their Southern Migrations in the Nineteenth Century

for profitable trade with both their southern and their northern neighbours.[21]

As in the seventeenth and eighteenth centuries, the expansion of economic activity was accompanied and assisted by a series of interior migrations. Baule settlements in the north began to establish outpost settlements further south to enter into direct and sustained commercial relations with the coastal peoples (see Map 3). These southern colonies expanded during the course of the nineteenth century, and the pattern of southern migration received particular reinforcement towards the middle of the century with the discovery of rich gold deposits in the Kokumbo hills. Representatives from virtually every Baule group in the north sent labourers to work in the mines at Kokumbo in what amounted to a veritable gold rush.[22]

Some of the gold served to stimulate further exchanges with the coastal regions, and in the process the initial settlements that had started as tentative new outposts in an alien land became part of a well-integrated pattern of production and inter-regional trade. The southern colonies of the northern groups functioned simultaneously as new production centres and as relay stations for an increasingly important north–south trade. By the 1880s this pattern of internal migration had largely run its course, and the Baule groups were distributed in much the same way as they are today (see Map 4). At the time of European penetration in the early 1890s these groups had been in place for several decades, and they were competing with one another for favourable trade relations with their southern neighbours.

The economic expansion and accompanying southern migration that took place in the nineteenth century underscore two central features of Baule pre-colonial history that it is important to keep in mind in approaching the colonial era. In the first place, it must be emphasized that before their initial contact with Europeans, the Baule had become accustomed to a pattern of virtually unreversed expansion. At no time had they experienced an invasion. On the contrary, through the combined processes of military conquest, economic domination, and social assimilation the Baule had managed to extend their control over a wide variety of pre-existent groups in the interior. In this respect the first years of the colonial period can be said to have represented an encounter between two expanding cultures – the French on the one hand and the Baule on the other – each of which had to come to believe in its own capacity to conquer.

The second important point about the course of Baule nineteenth century history is that despite the remarkable change in the direction

4. The Baule Peoples: Western Frontier of the Akan

and intensity of trade, the structures of Baule production and the overall role of trade in the Baule economy remained much the same as in the eighteenth century. Whereas the coastal populations had adapted their economic and political structures to produce bulk agricultural products for the European commodity market, the Baule had not yet been integrated into this network of intercontinental exchange. Their economy was still based on the production and exchange of the classic commodities of the 'royal' or 'luxury trade' – that is, gold, ivory, richly woven cloth, and slaves. Trade in these commodities remained the prerogative of politically dominant chiefs, and a specialized commercial sector deriving its existence primarily from profit-making exchanges had not yet emerged. In this sense, pre-colonial exchange among the Baule can be characterized as trade without merchants.[23]

The resulting structure of the Baule economy was strangely archaic. Although gold dust and gold nuggets were universally recognized as a medium of exchange, and although virtually every Baule household produced something for export, economic activity remained embedded in a complex network of socio-political structures. Internal produce markets were non-existent within Baule country. Instead the major commercial transactions took place at what could be called 'transit markets' on the periphery of Baule territory. The importance of these villages derived from their position on an inter-ethnic frontier where they could function as relay points for transiting trade between two separate ethnic groups. Tiassalé emerged as a particularly important transit market on the southern Baule border. There dominant Baule chiefs or their personal representatives would meet with their counterparts from the neighbouring ethnic groups to the south to barter goods on favourable terms (see Map 5).[24]

Trade was seasonal, and it characteristically took the form of periodic expeditions. A Baule chief who had amassed enough gold, woven cloth, and captives to obtain the goods he wanted in the south, travelled to Tiassalé with an armed band of his dependants and slave porters. Along the way he would seek shelter and protection from allied groups to whom he was usually related by ties of common descent or marriage. In this respect the southern colonies of the northern Baule groups served a particularly useful role, and exchange between the parent settlements and the offshoot colonies was sustained by these trading practices.

Once the chief had arrived in Tiassalé he was put into contact with a trading partner from the south under the auspices of a resident intermediary with whom they both stayed. Known locally as *sikéfue* these men were figures of considerable local prestige, and they did derive a certain measure of advantage by facilitating exchange between others, for they were compensated for their services. The *sikéfue* were not, however, merchants in any conventional sense. On occasion they might agree to store goods for a client, but they did not generally stock merchandise on their own account for the explicit purpose of making profits on retail sales. Their role was more akin to that of an innkeeper than that of a merchant. Their main function was to provide the institutional framework within which an inter-regional house-trade could be conducted.[25]

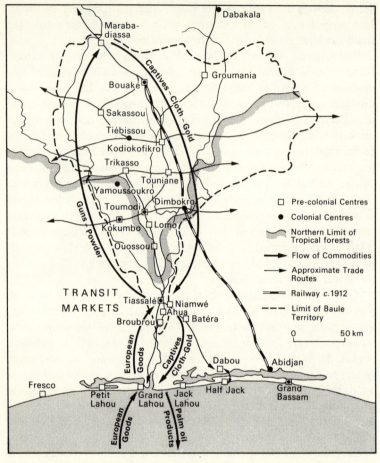

5. Baule Late Nineteenth-Century Trade Patterns

Given this pattern of exchange it is difficult to summarize the function of trade among the pre-colonial Baule. An independent class of commercially-minded agents with relative autonomy from the local political structure had not yet emerged among them, but trade cannot therefore be said to have been unimportant for that reason alone. On the contrary, trade occupied a very important role precisely because every chief had a stake in pursuing it to his best advantage. The way in which chiefs defined their advantage, however, did not resemble classical commercial profits. To be sure they sought to obtain goods at the cheapest possible barter rate and for this reason they journeyed to

Tiassalé, but generally they did not set out to purchase goods with the sole intention of deriving profit from their resale in the north. Most goods were obtained for local consumption or use within the productive industries in Baule country itself.

Ultimately it was control over indigenous production rather than middleman merchant activity that formed the basis of wealth and political power among the Baule. Individual Baule chiefs would obtain European manufactures from the coast and trade them to their neighbours to the north not so much to realize an immediate profit on this exchange alone, but rather to obtain at the best possible price the captives that they could then employ as labour within their own households. As Captain Binger's map of 1889 demonstrates, the products entering one end of the Baule region were not the same as those leaving the other end. Imports entered into local processes of production, and the products of these industries provided the major source of Baule wealth (see Map 6).

BAULE SOCIO-POLITICAL STRUCTURES

Two centuries of migration and exchange with non-Akan ethnic groups left their mark on Baule social and political life. Although Baule myths link them to the peoples of the Kumasi region in the Ashanti kingdom, it is clear that in their socio-political organization the Baule differed considerably from these heartland Akan. In general the Akan groups to the east were characterized by a kinship structure based upon identifiable matrilineages interrelated through regular patterns of preferred cross-cousin marriage, but the Baule lacked any of these socio-political structures.[26]

Among the Baule neither patri- nor matrilineages existed; instead the basic unit of social organization was a pragmatically determined cognatic descent group, or *awlô bô*. Moreover, marriage rules prohibited all forms of parallel marriage, and in particular cross-cousin marriage was considered a form of incest. The earliest record of Baule kin terms indicates that they were characterized by a broadly generational, or Hawaiian, pattern of kinship terminology in which fathers' and mothers' siblings are equated with 'father' and 'mother' with no distinction made for lateral difference. Similarly, special cousin terms were absent from Baule usage; both cross and parallel cousins were designated by the same term as sibling. The lack of terminological distinctions suggests a highly fluid kinship system in which a great deal of scope existed for the manipulation of multiple kin ties as social circumstance required.[27]

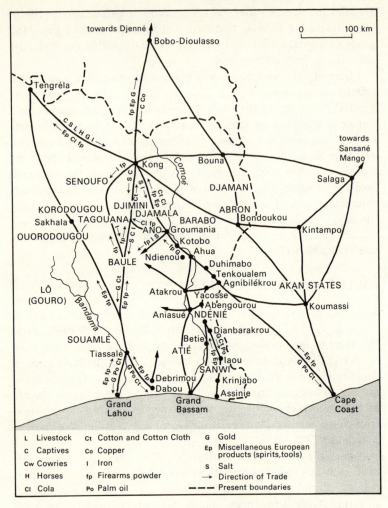

6. Trade between the Sudan and the Gulf of Guinea according to
Binger, *c.* 1889

The Baule *awlô bô*, or household, consisted in its simplest form of a
man, his wife or wives, their immediate children and any slave
dependants that the household head may have been able to acquire.
Over time as the children grew to maturity and established their own
families, they could choose to remain within the *awlô bô* in which they
grew up. In this fashion some *awlô bô* could become quite large, con-

taining an association of people of several different generations all of whom traced ties of descent or marriage to the household head, or *awlô kpenngben.*

As an exogamous unit the *awlô bô* became linked to other homologous units through ties of marriage alliance. Because of the prohibition on parallel marriages, however, these alliances could never repeat themselves between two groups. Thus, instead of being related through a limited nexus of strong alliances, these groups were linked in marriage in an extensive pattern of non-renewable alliances. As the French were to find out in the early years of colonial rule, this pattern of social organization had important implications for the capacity of the Baule to resist military conquest. While the Baule appeared to lack the social organization capable of mobilizing a strong and united alliance against an adversary, they none the less possessed a wide network of diffuse alliance ties that could prove ideal for organizing defensive retreat and dispersed guerilla activity.

The nature of pre-colonial political organization among the Baule is difficult to reconstruct in any degree of detail. In the early colonial accounts the tendency was to take the Baule origin myths at face value and write as if the eighteenth-century Baule were organized in a centralized kingdom under the control of Queen Aura Poku and the Ouarébo 'nobles'. Other immigrant groups including the Faafoué, the Nzipri, and the Sa were also reputed, like the Ouarébo, to be of royal origin in Kumasi. To these 'noble' groups were attached several subordinate groups including the Aïtu, the Nanafoué, the Ngban and the Agba. All of these peoples were said to have recognized the authority of Queen Poku at the time of the initial migration, and according to Maurice Delafosse, Queen Poku's first two successors, Queen Akwa Boni and Kouakou Guié, enjoyed a similar degree of absolute authority over the numerous disparate groups of Baule.[28]

The pattern of southern migration in the nineteenth century probably contributed to a general process of political fragmentation among the Baule, but it is impossible to know to what extent the eighteenth century Baule ever really constituted an organized state system. In any event by the end of the nineteenth century it was clear that the Baule were a stateless society, lacking the well-developed political institutions of centralized control typical of the Akan states to the east. Maurice Delafosse was the first colonial administrator among the Baule to study their institutions closely, and as he phrased it:

Il n'y a pas de chefs de tribus au sens que nous donnons au mot 'chef';
il n'y a même pas à proprement parler de chefs de villages: il n'y a que
des chefs de famille, au sens étendu de ce mot 'famille'. Le régime
politique se confond avec le régime social . . .[29]

On the most basic level, then, political influence was a function of
one's kinship position as a household head, or *awlô kpenngben*.[30] The
awlô kpenngben was the custodian of the household treasury, or
adya. This consisted principally of gold jewellery or gold dust and
richly woven cloth which was managed by the household head as a
form of capital on behalf of the household as a whole. The *adya*
accumulated from the pooling of individual production, and it was
from this household treasury that debts would be paid, trading ventures
would be financed, and captives would be bought. In short, by concentrating the most valued forms of wealth in the hands of the household head, the other members of the *awlô bô* were providing him a
quantity of social capital which they expected him to deploy in their
collective interest.

The performance of the household head was closely watched, and
retribution for squandering the household *adya* could extend beyond
the grave. Upon the death of the *awlô kpenngben* the household *adya*
was displayed during the funeral and transmitted intact to his successor.
One's position in the after-world was thought to be a function of the
memory which people retained of the deceased person, and this
memory was in turn directly related to both the absolute and the
relative size of the family treasury displayed at the funeral.[31] To the
extent that the deceased *awlô kpenngben* had succeeded in increasing
the household *adya* beyond the amount that had been left to him by
his predecessor, he was well remembered. Conversely, one's reputation
suffered if the relative size of the *adya* had diminished. Hence, the
whole structure of belief created a situation in which one of the most
compelling ambitions of any household head was to enlarge the household treasury entrusted to him.

In order to do this the *awlô kpenngben* needed to increase the
overall production of his household. During the nineteenth century the
technology of production remained relatively simple in the gold mining
and cotton producing sectors of the Baule economy, and land was still
comparatively abundant. The major restraint upon the productive
capacities of the Baule resided in the relative scarcity of labour.
Ultimately, those chiefs who could attract and retain the most manpower in their service emerged as the most wealthy and thus the most
influential political figures. For much of the nineteenth century, then,

household heads directed their attention to what might best be called the politics of manpower.

Given the cognatic nature of the Baule descent groups, a household head was not automatically guaranteed the loyalty of his close kin. If conditions in a given household became too unbearable a freeborn member might choose to take up residence in another *awlô bô* of which he was a potential member. Normally this did not often happen within the lifetime of a single household head, but his death might well occasion a major shift in the composition of the *awlô bô*, depending upon the popularity of the designated successor. The successor was obliged to some extent to solicit the loyalties of the members of the *awlô bô* by offering them conditions which were sufficiently attractive to dissuade them from taking up residence elsewhere.

This pattern of kin group recruitment had several implications for the style of political leadership which emerged among the Baule during the nineteenth century. In practice the skills of the negotiator became prerequisites for any household head who wished to maintain or extend his following. Skilful household heads could, for example, conclude advantageous marriage arrangements whereby their *awlô bô* would retain effective control over the children of in-marrying women, while at the same time, they would acquire control over those of out-marrying women. Similarly, skilful *awlô kpenngben* could obtain favorable barter terms for the goods their dependants produced, and with accumulated capital in gold and woven cloth they could further expand their productive output by purchasing more slaves and recuperating the fruits of their labour. All of these activities required deliberate and often prolonged negotiations.

If a household head successfully recruited enough dependent kin and slaves, he could seek to establish his own village.[32] He would thus assume the role of *klo kpenngben* - that is, village headman or chief. The pervasive diffusion of arms and munitions in the nineteenth century made it possible for smaller and smaller groups to establish their effective autonomy from one another. Under these conditions many men who under other circumstances would have been limited to the role of household head within a larger village, found themselves capable of becoming independent village chiefs. To the extent that they could attract other potential kinsmen to join them, they could increase their production. In short, wealth and influence were reciprocally related. Intelligently employed inherited wealth could be used to attract more dependants, and more dependants created still more wealth. On this level political leadership was essentially conservative in character, for a chief's concern was to maintain and gradually expand his following through the prudent allocation of available resources in the expectation of a calculated return.

A successful village chief could expect to extend his influence beyond his own village through a variety of means. By arranging marriage alliances for his junior kinsmen, a village chief entered into contact with other chiefs of varying importance from surrounding villages. As the importance of a particular village became recognized in a region, marriage exchanges between it and outlying villages could take on an asymmetrical character. Residence patterns among the Baule were ideally virilocal, but in practice they proved to be ambilocal, reflecting most closely the relative resources of the partners concerned. Wealthy chiefs could expect to attract sons-in-law to reside in their village, while at the same time gaining control over daughters-in-law. A *klo kpenngben* who managed to conclude these types of arrangements in several different directions, simultaneously swelled the ranks of his immediate following and extended the radius of his allies.[33]

Baule village chiefs were expected to defend the interests of their dependants if they became involved in disputes with neighbouring villages, and in his role as conciliator a chief could extend his influence beyond his own village. Disputes frequently arose over land rights, incomplete marriage payments, divorce indemnities, or debts incurred in trade. Village chiefs tried to reach an agreement between themselves for infractions which their dependants committed. In the event that the two village chiefs failed to agree upon a settlement, they could take their case to arbitration before a third village chief whose seniority, impartiality, and influence they both respected.[34] Chiefs in this position were usually elderly village chiefs of considerable substance who had achieved a regional reputation for their capacity to conciliate disputes. In some cases they claimed to be direct descendants from original leaders of the early migrations, but their role as arbitrators was something which they had acquired by virtue of their demonstrated abilities. In other words, although descent criteria played some part in determining who might most easily aspire to the role of senior or paramount chief in a given region, these criteria alone were not sufficient to qualify an individual for the task. One's descent position needed to be validated by widely recognized achievements.

Chiefs of this respected status were known as *nvle kpen* and addressed with the revered title of *famien*, but it appears that their position was not as fully crystallized as the institutions of *klo kpenngben* and *awlô kpenngben*. In this respect the position of *nvle kpen* or 'paramount chief' is perhaps better characterized as a role rather than an office. Individual village chiefs could gain considerable influence over a wide area, and in this sense they could be considered paramount chiefs, but their status was a function of their personal skill more than it was a feature of the role of *nvle kpen* itself. The evidence suggests that the formalized character of the role probably varied regionally. Broadly speaking, in the northern areas where settlements had been established on a stable basis for the longest period, the role of *nvle kpen* came closest to approximating a formalized office which could be inherited. Among the southern settlements, however, where migrant Baule groups had only established themselves since the middle of the nineteenth century, it seems that the institution was still in the process of formation and represented an achieved status or recognized role, rather than a formalized office. In either area the primary function of a paramount chief was essentially judicial.

Judicial procedures themselves generally served to increase the wealth and consolidate the importance of the paramount chief concerned.[35] Paramount chiefs received gifts in the first instance from each party in order to agree to hear the case. Subsequent proceedings cost money as well, and a paramount chief would often be paid for his pains in gold. More importantly, perhaps, the paramount chief would often emerge from the proceedings as the creditor to the losing party. Most disputes were settled by payment of compensation, but if the losing party was incapable of paying the fine at the end of the case, he would often place himself in debt directly to the paramount chief who would pay it on his behalf. In reality the paramount chief usually paid out very little to the winning party, because by custom the winning party was held responsible for the costs of the proceedings. Once these had been deducted by the paramount chief from the amount of the indemnity to be paid to the winning party, there was usually little left to be extended to the victor. On the other hand, the losing party was held to be in debt for the full amount of the settled indemnity to the paramount chief himself. In this fashion, paramount chiefs extended their influence beyond the range of their own kin, acquiring debtors as effective dependants from a wide geographic area.

An important village chief or a paramount chief could further extend his influence by concluding a special form of marriage arrangement with a similarly high-ranking chief from another region.[36] These alliances, known locally as *atonvle* marriages, conferred considerable prestige upon those who undertook them. The main reason for this was that these marriages were very expensive affairs. In addition to paying an inordinately high bride-price to the distant chief for his wife-to-be, a chief who concluded this type of alliance was required to finance public festivities accompanying the arrival of the bride in his village. Next to funeral ceremonies these occasions were the most expensive public events among the Baule, and those who had demonstrated their capacity to finance such events had given public proof of their wealth.

The marriage arrangement itself worked to the chief's long-term advantage, for in exchange for the unusually high bride-price he acquired undisputed rights over his wife's offspring. Children of such marriages were in effect uniquely dependent upon their father's *awlô bô* and were not permitted to return to their mother's kin group. Thus, by concluding an *atonvle* marriage, a chief was strengthening his political position by securing the unqualified allegiance of his future descendants. As a means of generating dependants this form of marriage was more advantageous than all others. Only the purchase of female slaves afforded the chief with the same structural guarantee of absolute control over his offspring.

In the absence of developed state structures among the precolonial Baule, the *atonvle* alliances provided important inter-regional political linkages.[37] Alliances of this kind could also serve as the basis for continuous commercial exchanges between distant groups, and there is evidence that some of the wealthy chiefs in the southern settlements concluded *atonvle* marriages with chiefs from the northern Baule groups.[38] Whether or not commercial motives were paramount in moving chiefs to establish these alliances remains obscure, but it is likely that once they were established these alliances served as channels for the flow of trade goods in the mutual interest of both allied parties. Hence in addition to its symbolic function as an index of wealth, the *atonvle* marrige conferred multiple advantages upon those who could afford to conclude them.

In terms of the pattern of political activity among the Baule, then, although it is accurate to say that the Baule were a stateless society, it would be misleading to suggest that political power among them was evenly distributed. On the contrary, marked hierarchies existed in local patterns of leadership.[39] In summary form, the gradation of leadership roles can be represented along these lines:

Paramount chief	*nvle kpen*
Village chief	*klo kpenngben*
Household head	*awlô kpenngben*

On each level, the respective role was more of an achieved status than it was an inherited office. One's chances of acquiring and maintaining the particular status depended upon the size of one's following, and this was related most directly to one's age, wealth, and personal skill in recruiting kinsmen and attracting other dependants.

This pattern of political activity created a situation in which a chief, in order to assert his authority at one level, was constantly trying to extend his influence beyond that level through the skilful manipulation of marriage alliances, credit and debt arrangements, and advantageous trade relations. In contrast to societies in which political office was hereditarily determined, and authority was a built-in feature of rank, the Baule political system was exceptionally fluid. Junior chiefs – that is, *awlô kpenngben* or *klo kpenngben* – were afforded considerable prospects for increasing their importance as they grew older and more wealthy, but the authority they achieved could not be transmitted intact to their successors or genealogical heirs. It was perhaps this feature of Baule politics which moved Delafosse to observe: 'la forme politique qui prédomine est l'anarchie.'[40]

In reality, although the Baule lacked a strong institutionalized framework of authority, Baule politics demonstrated a high degree of internal consistency. Political leadership, like the kin group upon which it ultimately depended, needed to be constantly regenerated. In this process the skills of negotiation and conciliation as well as the capacity for prudent calculation concerning the deployment of manpower and wealth proved to be the qualities most necessary for successful leadership.

PATTERNS OF CONFLICT ON THE EVE OF EUROPEAN PENETRATION

The non-ascriptive character of Baule kin groups established rivalry as an endemic feature of Baule social relations. Chiefs at all levels were engaged in muted competition for the effective support of mutually available kin. These rivalries existed between different *awlô bô* within a village, and if the animosity between two *awlô kpenngben* became too intense, the unity of the village could be jeopardized.

Under normal circumstances a gradual process of village fission was the regular result of the progressive displacement of populations as lands became exhausted around the immediate environs of a particular settlement. Villages were generally surrounded by a series of agricultural encampments, or *niamwe*. Each household within a village would create one or more *niamwe* close to its fields, and as the farmland in the vicinity of the village became less and less productive the *niamwe* could be located at a considerable distance from the village itself. The encampment consisted initially of temporary habitations capable of housing the members of a household near to the fields during the period of intense agricultural activity from February through April and August through October. Over a period of years the makeshift accommodations in a *naimwe* could be transformed gradually into more permanent dwellings, and the *niamwe* itself would thus take on the appearance of a small village in which the members of a household would spend increasing amounts of time.

When tensions between two *awlô bô* in a village became pronounced, the normally gradual process of transforming a *niamwe* into a place of permanent settlement tended to accelerate. One or both of the *awlô bô* would effectively split off from the parent village to form an independent village out of its respective *niamwe*. Thus, the existence of the *niamwe* provided the Baule with a mechanism for coping with the potentially dangerous conflicts which could flare up from the inherent rivalry between cognatic descent groups.

This means of dealing with social tensions had several important implications for the total pattern of social relations throughout Baule country. In the first place, the entire process helped to contribute to the generally weak pattern of Baule chiefly authority. The centrifugal tendencies of swidden agriculture combined with the flexible definition of Baule kin groups imposed practical limits on the exercise of arbitrary authority by *awlô kpenngben* and *klo kpenngben* with respect to their dependants. If demands became too intense, junior kinsmen or dissident villagers could simply hive off with their families to transform their *niamwe* into permanent settlements.

Perhaps more important, the process of social fission never really resolved conflicts: instead it merely projected them on to a different plane. Tensions between *awlô bô* became rivalries between villages as each household group transformed its *niamwe* into a permanent settlement. Thus, localized disputes tended to project themselves outwards over time, and relatively minor incidents, although never provoking overt hostility, could take on the proportions of enduring feuds, sometimes lasting in varied forms for generations. Often the precise cause of the original friction would have been forgotten, but a residual feeling of mistrust persisted between villages that were historically related.

Among the Baule, then, geographic proximity was not necessarily a reliable index of political solidarity, as it frequently was in segmentary lineage societies. A village which was commonly recognized as being the parent settlement in a particular area could not simply count upon its seniority to assure its political pre-eminence. The Baule had a great respect for seniority, but an even greater respect for achievement. Thus, a Baule household head who could establish his own village and success-fully attract subordinate kin, acquire dependent slaves and build up an autonomous unit of production was widely acknowledged in his own right.

Since Baule village chiefs were constantly trying to extend the scope of their influence on a regional level, inter-village animosities could be projected on an ever wider scale. Feuding villages sought out relations with other feuding villages at a greater distance, and tentative lines of co-operation and hostility could be extended beyond the territorial scope of any one chief's authority, forming a network of rival ties across an entire region. Indeed, rival groups often linked up along their borders with corresponding factions within the socio-political structure of a neighbouring ethnic group, and in this fashion opposing networks of rival villages could transcend ethnic boundaries.

This pattern of rival village linkage became particularly pronounced among the Baule during the late nineteenth century as the different resources available along the Baule northern and southern borders stimulated the development of inter-regional exchange. Since commer-cial relations among the Baule remained embedded in the general nexus of socio-political relations, enduring political conflicts were simul-taneously expressed as commercial rivalries. Every chief had an interest in engaging in commerce, for to the extent that he succeeded in obtaining a secure source of captives from the north and European trade goods from the south, he could consolidate his autonomy and gain a relative productive advantage over his local political rivals. Com-peting chiefs would therefore seek to extend the range of their socio-political alliances in a north–south direction in the expectation that these relations would serve as a channel for the circulation of trade goods to their advantage. Collectively these strategies led to the development of what could be called parallel 'trading chains' – that is, several parallel series of villages linked to one another in a north–south direction through multiple levels of kinship, political, and commercial alliances.

The result was that fixed trade routes, in the sense of universally recognized and widely employed highways of regular and secure commerce, did not exist among the Baule. Instead the territory was transected by numerous alternate trails, serving as networks for the competing trading chains. On a map a 'trade route' could only sketch a general axis along which the more particular competition of trading chains took place. Within Baule country it is not yet clear what the precise linkages in the networks of co-operation and exchange were. In most cases the trading chains developed on the basis of the infra-structure of related communities formed in the process of the directed southern migrations of the mid-nineteenth century, but trading chains were not limited to groups of common origin. In any event trade focused towards two terminuses along the northern Baule frontier, Marabadiassa in the west and Groumania in the east. The dividing point for the two branches of the trade seems to have been in the vicinity of Toumodi, where the northern flow of trade was intersected by a west-east trade route from Kokumbo towards the Anyi territories. The general area around Toumodi was referred to by the Baule as *ngonda*, or the 'crossroads', reflecting the pivotal position of that settlement for the patterns of exchange within Baule country.[41]

Although little is known about the trading chains in northern or central Baule territory, evidence from the lower Bandama region reveals the emergence of two distinct trading chains beginning on the coast and extending northwards to well within the southern Baule groups.[42] On the one hand the villages of Grand Lahou, Broubrou, Tiassalé, Sindréssou, Éliassou, Brimbo, Singrobo, and Lomo (or Domo) formed one trading chain. Those of Half Jack, Jack Lahou, Tiakba, Tamabo, Ahuem, Ahuacré, Ahua, Niamwé, Nianda, N'Zianou, Ahuakro, Ouossou, and Kpouébo formed a rival axis of commercial alliance (see Map 7). Schematically the two parallel trading chains can be represented in this manner:

(NORTH)

(Baule peoples)	Lomo (Ouarébo)		Kpouébo (Ngban)
	Singrobo	versus	Ouossou
	Brimbo		Ahuakro
			N'Zianou
	Éliassou		Nianda
	Sindréssou		Niamwé
(Élomoué peoples)	Tiassalé	versus	Ahua
	Broubrou		Ahuacré
			Ahuem
			Tamabo
(Avikam peoples)	Grand Lahou	versus	Tiakpa
			Jack Lahou and Half Jack
			(Alladian peoples)

(COAST)

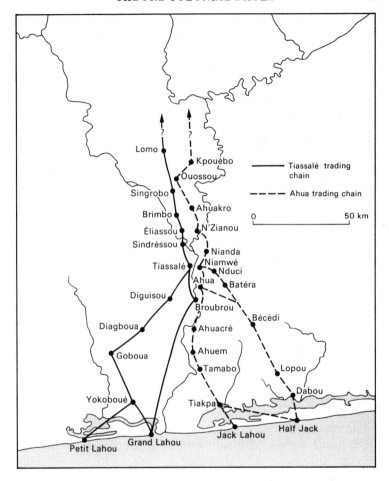

7. Southern Baule and Lower Bandama Rival Trading Chains, *c.* 1890

Historically, the Grand Lahou-Tiassalé-Lomo trading chain seems to have been the oldest, and the Half Jack-Ahua-Kpouébo alliance appears to have emerged more recently, largely as a consequence of the conversion of coastal commerce from the trade in ivory and gold to the export of palm produce. In the eighteenth and early nineteenth centuries Grand Lahou dominated coastal commerce during the era of the luxury trade. Its position at the south of the Bandama river enabled it to serve as the natural outlet for the interior groups that produced the gold and collected the ivory in the Bandama basin.

By the mid-nineteenth century, however, the availability of palm oil along the entire length of the coast between Grand Lahou and Assini effectively deprived Grand Lahou of its former commercial pre-eminence. Palm oil was produced by the Adioukrou and Ébrié peoples along the interior lagoons and exported by the Alladian peoples situated on the thin band of land separating the ocean from the fresh-water lagoons. In their capacity as produce brokers in this expanding commerce, the Alladian, known to the Europeans as the Jack-Jacks, became quite prosperous and attracted the major portion of the European trade.[43]

The ascendancy of the Jack-Jack continued throughout the latter part of the nineteenth century, and by 1885, when the French Resident reported on the advisability of establishing customs posts along the coast, he indicated that the only significant points to control would be the Jack-Jack villages of Grand Jack and Half Jack. Grand Lahou had fallen into comparative commercial decline.[44]

In the interior a corresponding displacement of commercial activity seems to have taken place, as dissident groups split off from Tiassalé and established themselves on the opposite bank of the Bandama. The villages of Ahua and Niamwé, whose oral traditions indicate that they originated from Tiassalé, set themselves up as commercial rivals to Tiassalé, founding further trading settlements to the south (Ahuacré and Ahuem).[45] It is difficult to date the schism which led to the development of commercial rivalry in this region. Some accounts indicate that the initial disputes between Tiassalé and Ahua occurred shortly after the arrival of the populations in the region, presumably in the eighteenth century.[46] Whether or not this is true, it seems that it was not until the development of the palm oil trade on the Alladian coast that this dispute could become a full-scale rivalry between distinct trading chains. Ahua, Niamwé, and their allies gained increasing autonomy as the Alladian linked up with them to acquire slaves, gold, and woven cloth from the Baule in the interior.[47]

Within the southern Baule region itself, an analogous rivalry developed between the Ouarébo and the Ngban. Once again the precise chronology involved remains obscure. Some accounts suggest that the northern Ouarébo dispatched warriors to the southern Baule area some-time after 1830 to subdue the Ngban, who were disrupting (i.e. diverting) trade between Tiassalé and the northern Ouarébo groups.[48] This would suggest that Ngban settlement in the area preceded Ouarébo intrusion in the south, and that the Ouarébo communities were relatively recent, established only in the wake of the alleged military expedition.[49]

Other oral traditions collected in the early colonial period outline the process in reverse, emphasizing the pre-eminence of the Ouarébo in the region and suggesting that the Ngban under the leadership of a chief, named Akafou, challenged Ouarébo domination only twenty years prior to the arrival of the French.

La région d'Ouossou a été occupé par les Baoulés au XVIII siècle . . . . Les Ouarébos qui dirigeaient le movement se seraient établis dans la région de Bouaké, mais tenant à conserver une ligne de ravitaillement avec la côte, ils ont établi une véritable ligne de postes depuis Bouaké jusqu'à Bouroubourou sur le Bandama. C'est ainsi que Tiassalé, Mbrimbo, Singrobo, Ouossou, Lomo, Domikro, Assomwé, Toumodi, etc. étaient Ouarébo. Grace à cette ligne d'étapes les Ouarébos du nord avaient de la côte la poudre, les fusils, et le sel dont ils avaient besoin.
Les Ouarébos qui devaient à cette epoque représenter la caste militaire abusaient de leurs avantages. C'est ainsi qu'à Ouossou ils percevaient un droit de piège sur les convois. Akafou, né à Moronou, et marié à Kakoubla, s'étant établi à Ayrémou au sud de Ouossou . . . mécontent des exactions des Ouarébos, il réussit à grouper entre 1860 et 1870 les Ngbans dont il était le chef et les Assabous qui obéissaient à Kakoubla, et après une série de guerres meurtrières, il réussit à chasser les Ouarébos de la région d'Ouossou. Ceux-ci se réfugiaient à Singrobo et Mbrimbo et Akafou devint le chef incontesté d'Ouossou où il s'établit.[50]

More research is needed on the oral traditions of this area before the sequence of Ouarébo and Ngban settlement can be established with certainty, but two important aspects of the area's history seem beyond dispute. In the first place, there was some kind of armed conflict between the Ouarébo and Ngban over their respective commercial influence in the area in the period just prior to French colonial rule. Secondly, it is clear that the Ouarébo associated themselves with the Tiassalé-Grand Lahou trading chain whereas the Ngban linked themselves through Nzianou to the Niamwé-Ahua-Half Jack trading chain. Fatou Aka, the chief of Naimwé on the eve of French penetration, was the son of a Baule woman, and he was known to have pursued commercial relations with the Ngban through his maternal kin in open competition with his rival, Etien Komenan, the chief of Tiassalé, whose allies were among the Ouarébo Baule.[51]

It would be inaccurate to conclude that the rise of the palm oil commerce along the Alladian coast directly caused the conflicts in the Tiassalé area and the southern Baule interior, but it would not be misleading to suggest that these phenomena were closely related. The dispersal of economic and political power on the coast following the rise of the palm oil economy created conditions which favoured the development of multiple trading linkages towards the interior, thereby providing rival groups there the opportunity to forge competing commercial alliances towards the coast. The process was a reciprocal and cumulative one, giving rise to patterns of intra-ethnic conflict and inter-ethnic co-operation extending beyond the range of particular chieftaincies. Events on the coast reverberated far to the interior, and in this respect the predisposition of various Baule groups towards the French could be said to have been prefigured long before the French actually confronted the Baule. To the extent that French activities on the coast seemed to favour a particular trading chain, its rival could be expected to be reticent towards, if not overtly hostile to, the French presence. Similarly, by intervening to the disadvantage of a particular coastal trading centre, the French were bound to animate lines of potential resistance and collaboration far beyond the range of their immediate endeavour. The character of initial Baule response to the French would thus depend heavily upon the particular nature of the French intrusion on the coast.

CHAPTER II

French Penetration and the First Baule 'Revolt', 1889-1895

PRELUDE TO PENETRATION – THE COASTAL CUSTOMS REVOLTS AND TIASSALÉ RESISTANCE, 1889-1892

For the most of the nineteenth century French governmental attitudes toward their Ivory Coast possessions alternated between fits of mild concern and prolonged periods of frank indifference.[1] In 1843 the French fortified Grand Bassam and Assini in an attempt to check an anticipated British expansion westwards from the Gold Coast. The government hoped that its presence would encourage the development of French commerce on this section of the coast, but the response of French trading firms proved disappointing. The complexity of local politics among the lagoon populations led to repeated conflicts between merchants and African palm oil producers and middlemen. When the French government showed itself reluctant to back up French commerce with consistent armed force, Victor Régis, the largest single French trading concern on the Ivory Coast, closed up his operations in 1854 and turned his attention to areas further down the coast.[2] In the 1860s and after, Arthur Verdier continued as the sole French merchant in the area, but his intrigues inspired an abiding mistrust in official circles and encouraged Ministry officials to think of the Ivory Coast as a liability rather than an asset.[3]

The departure of Régis in 1854 and the slump in palm oil prices in Europe starting in 1862 meant that the trading factories were of little intrinsic value to French overseas commerce. With this in mind Governor Faidherbe drew up a report in 1863 outlining the condition of France's West African possessions in which he suggested that France should consolidate its interests in Senegal and secure its trade with the Senegambia interior by acquiring from the British the territory of the Gambia. 'In exchange for the Gambia', he wrote, 'the English might be offered Gabon, Assinie . . . Grand Bassam and Dabou . . . '.[4] For Faidherbe the Ivory Coast possessions were clearly dispensable.

Proposals for exchanging the Ivory Coast outposts for the Gambia continued to be forwarded at various points for the next twenty years.[5] As late as December 1887 the Undersecretary for the Colonies, Eugène Étienne, a well-known advocate of imperial expansion, still indicated his willingness to consider ceding the Ivory Coast possessions if an acceptable exchange could be arranged. At this point, however, the British hesitated on the proposals, and in the event they lost their chance forever. By the time they agreed to undertake frontier negotiations in March 1889, Étienne had changed his mind, and 'Assinie and Grand Bassam were not for sale'.[6]

The reasons for this abrupt shift in the official thinking about the Ivory Coast are to be found in the changing character of French expansion in the Sudan from 1886 onwards.[7] In the previous years from 1883 to 1885 Sudanese expansion by way of Senegal had suffered setbacks, and it was apparent that the railroad schemes upon which so much initial hope had been based were proving far too expensive in the eyes of the French Chambre des Députés. Railway funds which had provided most of the financing for military expansion in the Sudan were cut, and the military found it difficult to maintain its position and secure its supply lines on its reduced budget. Recognizing the difficulties which a continued dependence upon the Senegal railway scheme implied, General Gallieni proposed that the French advance by way of the Senegal should be abandoned in favour of developing potential lines of access to the coast through the Futa Jallon and the south. Gallieni felt that the territory south of the Niger and even the Ivory Coast deserved more attention in this respect.[8] The new focus of attention away from the Upper Senegal had two simultaneous consequences: the relative importance of the Gambia in French imperial strategy was depreciated, while that of the previously neglected Ivory Coast possessions was correspondingly enhanced.

By 1889 the combined explorations of Captain Louis-Gustave Binger and Marcel Treich–Laplène traced a potential route of access from the coast to Kong and the Niger river, and Ministry officials began to regard the Ivory Coast as a potentially important colony to provide support for the Sudan.[9] In addition, local observers began to be concerned about British imperial designs on the territory to the northwest of the Gold Coast possessions, and for this reason as well the French began to consider the Ivory Coast possessions as an essential part of their West African empire.[10]

There was to be no further talk of abandoning the outposts to the British. On the contrary, by an administrative decree of 1 August 1889

Eugène Étienne consolidated the French holdings into a colony known collectively as 'Les établissements Français de la Côte d'Or' under the direction of a governmental 'Résident'. The Resident was placed under the authority of the Lieutenant Governor of the Southern Rivers, but he retained the prerogative of corresponding directly with the Under-secretary for the Colonies in Paris. The Anglo-French accord of 10 August 1889 granted international recognition to the French claims on the coast, and with this issue momentarily resolved, the adminis-tration was free to turn its attention to the task of regulating coastal commerce. Articles 11 and 12 of the 1 August 1889 decree established the fiscal autonomy of the colony and provided for a local budget to be raised from customs duties levied on imports and exports. Treich-Laplène became the first Resident, and Eugène Étienne gave him instructions to establish customs posts along the coast between Assini and Grand Lahou.[11] Thus, in principle at least, the framework of colonial administration was clearly established. It remained to be seen how the coastal populations would react to the customs duties that the French intended to impose to finance their new colonial venture.

At Grand Bassam and Assini the installation of customs personnel occurred without particular incident, but further west at Half Jack on the Alladian coast and at Grand Lahou at the mouth of the Bandama river, events took a more violent turn, as local populations resisted French attempts to interfere with the established patterns of commerce. Along this section of the coast French presence had been slight throughout the nineteenth century. Indeed, Europeans as a rule had not established themselves onshore. The characteristic exchange took place between African 'traitants' and European 'super-cargoes' or trading hulks, anchored offshore. The supercargoes, for the most part, received their provisions from and sold their palm oil to English vessels from London, Liverpool, or Bristol. The trading language was English and the African merchants often explicitly asked for English manu-factures because, over time, their trading partners to the interior had developed a marked preference for British trade goods. Even under the best of circumstances it would not have been easy for the French to install customs stations in this area where they were considered to be aliens to the local trading tradition.[12]

What is more, the trade conditions themselves were steadily worsening. Because of the falling price of palm oil, the coastal popu-lations were experiencing a progressive deterioration in the barter terms of trade. The average price of palm oil between 1886 and 1890 dropped on European markets to £20 per ton. This represented the lowest price since the earliest days of the trade and a full 50 per cent decline from the price of twenty-five years earlier.[13] European merchants responded to this decrease by lowering the prices they paid for oil along the coast or increasing the price of their trade goods or both, but one way or another the barter terms of trade moved against the coastal middlemen and the inland producer. In some cases the changes caused the English offshore merchants to restrict credit, and at times coastal populations frankly wanted the French merchants to come in and replace the English, in the hope that the French would reinstitute the 'old' prices.[14]

It is possible that the French administration benefited at first from this naïve belief, when they received permission to create their first customs post at Half Jack in December 1889. Nevertheless, they did not want to risk failure, and they took care to pay Bony, the wealthiest local merchant, 5,700 francs for the use of one of his concessions.[15] It is perhaps understandable that Bony expressed no opposition to the customs proposal.

When it became generally apparent, however, that the customs post was not simply a new merchant's store, and further, that the French agents wanted to exact an 80 per cent *ad valorem* duty on everyone's future imports, other African merchants, if not Bony himself, became enraged. Given the local pattern of trade between Europeans offshore and African merchants onshore, the creation of a customs post on land affected the African merchant in a more immediate and demonstrative manner than the Europeans in their floating hulks offshore. In Grand Bassam and Assini where European merchants had traded onshore for nearly fifty years, customs officers dealt directly and primarily with European agents, but in Half Jack where African merchants had jealously guarded their control of the onshore trade, the creation of a customs bureau dealt a direct blow to indigenous merchants, and it is not surprising that their reaction came quickly.

In early January 1890 skirmishes broke out between the customs officers and the local population who refused to sell food supplies to the newly created outposts. Treich-Laplène visited Half Jack on 12 January and tried to arrest the alleged leader of the local boycott, but the man escaped to the neighbouring village of Grand Jack. Attempts to negotiate his return through Bony failed, and Treich-Laplène wrote to Lieutenant-Governor Bayol in Conakry requesting the support of a gunboat. The incident, according to Treich-Laplène, called for an emphatic demonstration of French force.

Jamais les noirs de ces régions n'avaient commis une attaque aussi formelle et aussi lâche contre les Européens. Je le répète encore il faut un exemple sanglant ou des faits semblables se renouvelleront.[16]

Treich-Laplène received a gunboat, and on 28 January he anchored off Half Jack to dictate his terms. He held Half Jack and Grand Jack collectively responsible for the incident and demanded that they pay a combined fine of 25,000 f. Half Jack paid a substantial part of its share, but Grand Jack would not reply and refused to relinquish the alleged resistance leader. The gunboat opened fire on the village, causing only minor damage, but on 8 February Treich-Laplène landed forces and set fire to Grand Jack and its subordinate settlements on the lagoon, killing eighteen people and wounding others. Eventually the leader of the resistance movement was captured in a surprise night raid, and he was dispatched to exile in Dakar. Smarting under the impact of the attack, the inhabitants agreed to pay the imposed fine.

Before leaving the area the gunboat assisted in the installation of yet another customs station a few miles westward, this time at Grand Lahou. On 16 February 1890 Octave Péan, the French customs officer, informed the offshore trading hulks of his intentions and then negotiated an agreement onshore with a local notable named John Niaba. Despite signs of reticence among the local population, there was no open violence, and on 19 February the gunboat departed for Senegal, leaving behind twenty armed troops to ensure the security of the customs bureau. On the surface at least it appeared that French gunboat diplomacy was a success.

In the following months, however, it became apparent that the customs principle was no more acceptable to the population at Grand Lahou than it had been to the people of Half Jack and Grand Jack. In August 1890 an African merchant named Dabree refused to pay the customs tariff on a barrel of rum, and in addition he ordered his followers to cease providing food supplies to the French agents. An attempt by one of the French agents to seize the provisions forcibly erupted in a violent incident in which one sergeant was killed and another severely wounded. The French responded immediately by opening fire on the population, killing fifteen Africans and seriously injuring twelve others. Their counter-attack culminated in setting fire to the dissident section of the village.

Subsequent French demands were equally severe. Octave Péan had assumed the post of Resident since Treich-Laplène's death in March 1890, and when he arrived at Grand Lahou after the incident, he acted in much the same way as his predecessor had earlier in the face of the

Half Jack revolt. He insisted upon the payment of a fine of 750 ounces of gold (71,000 f.)[17] and the surrender of those alleged to be responsible for the uprising. When the gunboat *Ardent* arrived on 30 August the villagers acceded to the demands, paid the fine, and turned over those accused of instigating the incident.[18] Péan, like Treich-Laplène, evidently felt that the use or threatened use of force would be sufficient to squelch African resistance to the new colonial regime.

In part Péan's assessment was accurate. Coastal villages offered no further armed resistance to the creation of additional customs posts. In another respect, however, the French repression of the coastal customs revolts marked only the beginning in a prolonged series of African resistance movements to the interior. The existence of trading chains linking the coastal villages with commercial partners far to the interior meant that the unsuccessful coastal revolts and the new customs measures were bound to have reverberations far beyond the immediate purview of the customs installations themselves. In February 1891, five months after the Grand Lahou revolt, Péan came under a full-scale attack from the Adioukrou palm oil producers on the north of the lagoons near Dabou, and it was only with the help of Lieutenant Armand that he was able to repress this inland revolt. Once again the repression was severe: nine villages were burned to the ground, twenty-seven Africans were killed and forty-two others were wounded. In addition, Péan collected heavy fines from the population, totalling 35,000 f., including payments in the local trade currency known as 'manillas' and 7.2 kg. of pure gold.[19]

Further indications of African determination to resist French intrusion became apparent when the French tried to explore the inland course of the Bandama river.[20] In February and March 1891 two teams of explorers converged upon Grand Lahou to launch expeditions towards the interior. The first, under the direction of Lieutenants Armand and de Tavernost, had been sent out by the Undersecretary of the Colonies, Eugène Étienne. The second, led by two commercial explorers named Voituret and Papillon, was sponsored by the Société d'Études de l'Ouest Africain. Both groups intended to make their way up the Bandama, stop at Tiassalé, and then proceed northwards through Baule country towards the Sudan. In February the Armand–de Tavernost expedition succeeded in reaching Tiassalé, but they were unable to find an interpreter willing to take them further north, and they returned to Grand Lahou to try to recruit a guide on the coast. While they were still making their preparations at Grand Lahou, the other team of explorers set out on 18 March towards Tiassalé where they intended to await the arrival of Armand and de Tavernost before proceeding north through Baule country together.

In the event, the plans of the explorers were brought to an abrupt halt by Etien Komenan, the chief of Tiassalé.[21] He was reportedly irritated by the conduct of the expedition under the military leadership of Lieutenants Armand and de Tavernost, and he was determined not to let them get beyond Tiassalé. It was for this reason that they were unable to find a willing interpreter in Tiassalé itself and were obliged to return to Grand Lahou in February 1891. When the two commercial explorers, Voituret and Papillon, set out in March 1891 from Grand Lahou towards Tiassalé, they were assumed to be part of the same French expedition, and they were attacked and drowned, apparently on Etien Komenan's orders, as they made their way through the rapids near Broubrou. After de Tavernost's departure from Tiassalé in late February, Etien Komenan had mobilized warriors from surrounding villages with the intention of resisting further French intrusion, and since Voituret and Papillon appeared to be the forerunners of a new French initiative, Etien Komenan had them assassinated before they could reach Tiassalé.[22]

The French tried to retaliate by launching a military expedition to defeat Tiassalé. The Resident sent for troops from Conakry and in early May 1891 a company of Senegalese soldiers under the command of Lieutenant Staup set out from the coast to conquer Tiassalé. The results were disastrous for the French. On 4 May 1891 they occupied Dabou and then proceeded inland over the trade route between Dabou and Tiassalé. On 11 May Etien Komenan's forces attacked the company between the villages of Batéra and Nduci (see Map 7), and after a four-hour battle Lieutenant Staup, wounded and unable to walk, ordered his troops to withdraw to Dabou.[23]

Staup's own account of the affair indicated his general unpreparedness for fighting in the tropical forest. He seemed surprised that the usual Sudanese military tactics to which he was accustomed were of no use in the dense underbrush. The armaments of the Africans included modern Remingtons as well as the traditional Dane guns, and Staup admitted that in combat they demonstrated a discipline and courage worthy of the best trained troops. As for their numbers, the accounts are not consistent. The first report to the Resident spoke of 800 armed attackers, but Staup's final report mentioned the figure of 1,500.[24] In either case Etien Komenan had mobilized a sizeable force, including several Baule warriors from the region to the north of Tiassalé.[25] In the following weeks when Lieutenant Staup withdrew completely from the

Ivory Coast, with no attempt to launch the expected counter-attack, the French looked particularly weak. The grand military expedition which they had hoped would teach all inland chiefs a salutary lesson ended in what appared to be an unqualified French retreat.

The murder of Voituret and Papillon and Staup's ignominious defeat dealt a blow to French plans to penetrate Baule territory from the coast. Subsequent attempts to traverse Baule country from the north met with no more success. In June 1892 Binger tried to return to the coast from the Kong region by way of Baule country, but he was obliged to abandon his effort when his porters deserted him.[26] The French resident on the coast attributed Binger's difficulty directly to an alleged 'alliance faite entre les gens du Baoulé et ceux de Tiassalé . . . .'[27]

Throughout 1892 the French at Grand Lahou and Half Jack (known by this time to the French as Jack-ville or Jacqueville) tried to negotiate a treaty with Tiassalé to terminate hostilities and open the way for peaceful penetration of the Baule region. Éloi Bricard, the administrator at Grand Lahou and later the acting Resident of the colony, succeeded in opening discussions through Bony, the influential chief of Jacqueville and John Niaba, the recognized chief of Grand Lahou. Emphasizing the commercial advantages of a potential agreement, Bricard appears to have played upon the traditional trading rivalry between the Grand Lahou–Tiassalé trading chain on the one hand and the Half Jack–Ahua–Niamwé trading chain on the other, and eventually he succeeded in coaxing representatives from both Tiassalé and Niamwé into signing a treaty on 29 December 1892.[28]

Precisely what the Africans thought they would gain from the treaty remains unclear, for the text itself appears inexplicably one-sided. Tiassalé had succeeded in fending off the French military assault and there was no ostensible reason why they should have felt compelled to pay a tribute of 100 ounces of gold (9,600 f.) 'en signe de paix et de soumission' in addition to returning the remains of Voituret and Papillon and agreeing to deliver the 'son' of Etien Komenan as a hostage to the French.

It is likely that the phrase which interested the Africans most was the one which emphasized that 'le pays de Thiassalé . . . commercera librement à l'avenir avec les indigènes de la Côte et les Européens'. Bricard had stressed the future commercial advantages which the treaty would entail and these potential advantages may well have outweighed the concessions in the minds of the signators. The representatives of Tiassalé and Niamwé may well have felt that the word 'librement' meant that the French intended to alter their customs policy, and it is perhaps for this reason that each of the rival trading chains was willing to come forward. In anticipation of expanded trade and preferential tariff concessions neither party wished to be left out of an agreement with the French that would guarantee them an ascendant position over their longstanding rivals.

More research needs to be done on the precise linkages that existed between Grand Lahou and Tiassalé on the one hand and Half Jack and Niamwé on the other before the local significance of the Tiassalé treaty can be fully understood, but there is no doubt that the French felt it entitled them to free access to the interior. As Bricard reached the final stages of his negotiations with Tiassalé, the Ministry of Colonies began to examine a new proposal for renewed exploration of the Ivory Coast hinterland. The author of the proposal was Jean-Baptiste Marchand, a veteran of military campaigns in the Sudan, whose sense of patriotism and considerable personal ambition inspired him to search out a viable and secure route from the coast to the Sudan.[29] Marchand was confident that he could succeed where others had failed, and the news of Bricard's treaty with Tiassalé focused his attention on the Bandama valley. His plan received Ministry support and he arrived in the Ivory Coast in March 1893 to launch what became the first exploratory mission to penetrate Baule territory.

CAPTAIN MARCHAND, AHUA, AND THE DEFEAT OF TIASSALÉ, 1893

When Jean-Baptiste Marchand began to draw up his proposal for linking the Ivory Coast with the Sudan in late 1892, the idea of military expansion was receiving severe criticism in Paris. Parliamentarians were losing patience with what they considered to be the excessively expensive Sudanese military campaigns – manœuvres which they felt to be of less immediate utility to France as a nation than they were to the individual careers of the ambitious officers concerned.

After the Undersecretary of the Colonies, Jean de la Porte, appointed Colonel Louis Archinard as Commandant Supérieur of the Sudan in 1888, he instructed him specifically to avoid further conquests and concentrate instead upon consolidating French positions and developing agriculture and commerce in the interior. Archinard initially complied with these instructions, but when circumstances permitted, he abandoned them in favour of a more personal and assertive policy. Between 1889 and 1891 he launched a series of campaigns explicitly to destroy the Tokolor Empire to the north and Samory to the south-east, largely, without the prior knowledge or consent of his superiors in Paris. In effect he presented them with a *fait accompli*.[30]

The campaigns needed to be paid for, and when the government presented the Chambre with the bill in the autumn of 1891, the *députés* began to express their full sense of outrage. They called for an immediate halt to military expansion and emphasized instead the advantages of commercial and diplomatic means of extending French influence. Both Undersecretary Étienne and his successor Émile Jamais affirmed that the government had no intention of pursuing a policy of military expansion, but their assurances to the *députés* did not check the Sudanese military. The junior officers continued their exploits throughout 1892 and the mounting costs stirred up renewed criticism of military expansion in late 1892 and early 1893, forcing the new Undersecretary for the Colonies, Théophile Delcassé, to pledge further restraint of the seemingly uncontrollable military in February 1893.[31]

In this atmosphere of heightened criticism it is perhaps not surprising that, in his proposal to the Ministry, Captain Marchand made no mention of military objectives. Instead, he chose to emphasize the commercial and diplomatic rationale for his exploration plans. According to Marchand, merchants from London, Manchester, and Liverpool were urging Lord Salisbury to construct a railway from the Gold Coast northwards. If the British merchants were to prevail, they would be in a position to drain the lucrative trade of the Niger bend area to the coast and the French would be deprived of the proverbial riches of her Sudanese empire. France, Marchand argued, needed to forge viable commercial routes from the coast to the Sudan, and since railways were too expensive, the most economical means of achieving this was to use the natural river systems to best advantage.

Marchand's plan was to explore the nagivational possibilities of one of the coastal rivers with the intention of developing a short overland linkage between its headwaters and those of an upper Niger tributary. From his experience at Mopti and Sikasso, Marchand had chosen the Bagoé river as the most suitable affluent of the Niger for his purposes, and from what he could discern from Binger's sketchy maps, either the Cavally or the Bandama looked promising for penetration from the coast. The mission itself would be inexpensive, Marchand reasoned, for he intended to travel lightly, depending upon personal diplomacy with local chiefs rather than a demonstration of force to gain access to the interior.[32]

Had the Ministry officials reflected upon Marchand's proposal with great care they might have recognized its weaknesses. Marchand had never been on the coast, and his acquaintance with commercial questions there or, for that matter, anywhere else, was slight and limited to what he had read in Binger's published travel journals. While these volumes were full of copious detail about Sudanese trade, they were sketchy in the extreme concerning the coastal trade, and for the most part Binger merely repeated the traders' tales of the 1860s.[33] Although Binger's accounts were optmistic about potential trade from the coast inland in 1889, there was scarcely enough hard information upon which to build real expectations, and the disastrous exploration attempts of Voituret, Papillon, Armand, and de Tavernost in 1891 should have served as sobering reminders of the difficulties which lay ahead in Baule country.

As for diplomacy, Marchand's performance in the Sudan hardly recommended him. Archinard had dispatched Marchand to Tiéba in Sikasso to secure Tiéba's support against Samory, but far from attaining this, Marchand succeeded only in permanently alienating Tiéba from the French cause. Clearly Marchand was no diplomat; he was a soldier through and through, by training, experience, and temperament, and like many young officers of the Archinard era he was propelled by acute ambition. None the less, despite these negative features the Ministry gave its approval to Marchand's mission, perhaps on the assumption that the treaty which Bricard had concluded with Tiassalé in December 1892 guaranteed Marchand's unimpeded access to the upper reaches of the Bandama.

If successful, the mission would undoubtedly have pleased those who had been calling for a more explicitly commercial emphasis to French expansion. In March of 1893, as Marchand reached Grand Bassam, the Undersecretary for the Colonies, Delcassé, transformed the Ivory Coast into a fully autonomous colony and named Louis-Gustave Binger its first governor.[34] Binger had been a long-time proponent of commercial expansion from the coast, and under his governorship the colony, it was hoped, would provide the kind of commercial success for which the critics of military expansion had been clamouring for several years. On the face of it, the prospect of Binger's civilian control and Marchand's peaceful penetration looked most promising indeed.

Binger clearly advocated a policy of coastal consolidation and prudent inland advance, but although he had been appointed in March, he did not arrive on the coast until the autumn of 1893. By this time Marchand had already been in the colony for six months and his activities had altered the situation considerably. Binger wrote to

Marchand in June from France, appealing to him to remain on the coast until he arrived, but Marchand felt that too much hesitation would compromise his own mission. By the time the governor finally came, Marchand had departed for the interior, and he was well on his way through Baule country. Even before he received Binger's appeal, Marchand had already reached Tiassalé.[35]

The treaty with Tiassalé gave Marchand reason to hope that he could proceed freely up the Bandama valley, and he began to make preparations for this as soon as he arrived on the coast. In April 1893 the acting governor, de Beeckman, had begun making overtures to Etien Komenan through Bricard, the administrator of Grand Lahou, in order to clear the way for Marchand's expedition. He authorized Bricard to distribute gifts if necessary and told him to emphasize to Etien Komenan how important the success of the mission would be for his own prosperity. Bricard was to make it clear that if Etien Komenan co-operated, he could expect to receive French support to liberate himself from his commercial dependence upon the chiefs of Lahou.[36]

Just prior to these overtures, however, de Beeckman moved to establish greater control over the coastal trade which had been ignoring the customs regulations. The customs posts which the French had created were not fully effective because traders could circumvent these specific towns. African merchants could exchange goods with European vessels offshore without paying duty, provided that they remained a safe distance away from the customs bureaux at Grand Lahou and Jacqueville. In early April de Beeckman tried to halt these practices by outlawing all offshore trade not conducted at towns with customs officials.[37] This move to tighten control over coastal commerce threatened Etien Komenan's commercial position, for he had significant trade links with Petit Lahou against which the new measures were directed. De Beeckman's manœuvre probably appeared to Etien Komenan as a flagrant violation of the 'free trade' clause contained in the treaty of 29 December 1892.

When Marchand and Bricard began their penetration up the Bandama river in late April, they encountered Etien Komenan's opposition, and they were unable to get beyond Ahouem, a river village less than half-way to Tiassalé itself. Further overtures to Tiassalé were unfruitful, and according to Marchand, Etien Komenan affirmed defiantly that 'no white man would pass through Tiassalé'.[38] Marchand's peaceful penetration had come to a standstill. He withdrew to Grand Lahou on the coast on 2 May, and there he apparently considered abandoning the Bandama route in favour of an attempt by way of the Comoé valley and Kong.[39]

The French, however, were not without friends on the lower Bandama. As a principal participant in the 1892 negotiations with Tiassalé, Bricard was well aware which villages were traditional trading rivals. France could expect to find potential allies among Tiassalé's competitors.[40] The French considered Ahuem 'neutral' or even 'friendly' during the 1891 hostilities between Tiassalé and the French. Etien Komenan had tried, apparently without enduring success, to intimidate the village into opposing the French at the time.[41] To the north of Ahuem and related to it stood Ahua, another riverbank village just fifteen kilometres south of Tiassalé. Ahua contained a large settlement of Nzima traders, and for years it had been a commercial rival of Tiassalé. After the battle of Batéra in May 1891, Etien Komenan extended his control to villages along the Dabou route and this left Ahua in a relatively unfavourable commercial position. Ahua's major overland route through Niamwé towards the Baule interior had been cut off when Etien Komenan extended his influence as far south as Batéra on the way to Dabou. By 1893 the formerly prosperous route from Ahua to Niamwé had fallen into disuse, and the population of Ahua were embittered by the commercial eclipse which Tiassalé had imposed upon them. 'Je connaissais cette situation', Marchand wrote in retrospect, '. . . et [je] comptais sur cet antogonisme latent pour trouver dans Ahua une excellent base d'opérations contre Thiassalé.'[42]

Marchand decided to ally himself with Ahua and subdue Tiassalé by force. In doing so he thought he would be supported as well by the Baule groups north of Tiassalé. As he explained his decision:

J'étais d'ailleurs encouragé . . . par l'attitude du grand pays de Baoulé, qui se separait complètement de Thiassalé et n'était pas hostile, au contraire! à l'entrée des blancs sur son territoire.[43]

With assistance from acting Governor de Beeckman, Marchand assembled a force of 120 men and set out for Tiassalé from Grand Lahou on 18 May 1893. On 21 May he occupied Broubrou, Tiassalé's most important ally on the lower Bandama, without firing a shot. The inhabitants of Broubrou had deserted the village and assembled at Tiassalé. On 23 May Marchand received word that Tiassalé's forces were grouped near Ahua, and he sent Captain Manet with fifty troops to help assure the defence of the village. In return, Nzi Aka, the chief of Ahua, sent thirty porters to assist in transporting the munitions and supplies from Broubrou to Ahua. The following day the movement of the troops to Ahua was completed, and the village became the 'quartier général des Français'.[44]

On 25 May Marchand launched his attack on Tiassalé, approaching the village from the opposite side of the Bandama by the overland route between Ahua and Niamwé. Both sides opened fire at each other across the river, but Marchand waited on the left bank of the river, largely out of range of Tiassalé's muskets, until the Tiassalé forces had expended much of their powder and shot. Only then did he cross the river and occupy Tiassalé itself. Etien Komenan and his war leader, Komenan Buen, fled before the occupying troops along with a large portion of the population.[45]

Having occupied Tiassalé and ousted Etien Komenan, Marchand recognized Fatou Aka, whom he described as the 'second chief of Tiassalé',[46] as the new chief of the region. As he explained it later, 'j'ai mis un roi de notre choix . . .'.[47] Fatou Aka was in fact the chief of Niamwé prior to French arrival. Niamwé was the village just opposite from Tiassalé on the left bank of the Bandama, and although it was within the Tiassalé sphere of influence since the 1891 incidents, traditionally it was a major village along Tiassalé's rival trade route from Ahua to Nzianou. By recognizing Fatou Aka as the new chief, Marchand did far more than reshuffle the lines of authority within a single village. Although he did not realize it, Marchand had in effect committed the full weight of French military forces to support the re-emergence of the Ahua-Niamwé-Nzianou trading chain. It is not surprising that, as the traditional chief of Niamwé, Fatou Aka was willing to collaborate with Marchand and delighted to accept his newly constituted authority over Tiassalé, his former trading rival.[48]

Clearly, the capture of Tiassalé signified different things to different people. The rapid and seemingly decisive nature of the capture pleased those officials in Paris who tended to view the move as a just and long overdue punishment dealt to a traditional foe of French advancement inland. Marchand in effect presented the Ministry with another military *fait accompli* so characteristic of the younger officers of his generation, but there was no public uproar. The manœuvre had not been too costly and the expenses were shouldered by the local administration, requiring no additional budgetary allocations from Paris. In addition, Marchand reported the incident in terms of a decisive gesture – a move which, once executed, would require no long-standing military presence. On the contrary, he thought it would open up the avenues of trade to the interior.[49] Perhaps for these reasons, Marchand was generally applauded, not condemned, for the success of his commando-style intervention.

Marchand himself believed that the capture of Tiassalé would guarantee access to the Sudan and the total support of the Baule peoples. When Tiassalé fell, representatives from Baule groups arrived in the village and expressed their desire to make an alliance with the French, emphasizing that they had always regarded Tiassalé as an obstacle to their free trade with the coast.[50] Furthermore, Marchand thought that by appointing Fatou Aka as chief, he was securing Baule allegiance, and he urged Governor Binger to support Fatou Aka fully for precisely this reason:

Fatou Aka, par sa famille, appartient au Baoulé *où il a toute influence.* Si donc vous voulez ouvrir ou plutôt tenir ouvert le Baoulé, car il l'est aujourd'hui, à l'influence française, maintenez énergiquement Fatou Aka à Thiassalé.[51]

It seems likely that Fatou Aka did indeed have kinsmen among the Baule, especially given the marital strategies of telegamy which the Baule frequently employed along vital trade routes, but Marchand sorely misread the extent of Fatou Aka's influence and clearly underestimated the importance of Tiassalé's Baule allies. It was not until later that the seriousness of Marchand's miscalculations became evident, and in the following years the French paid dearly for his mistakes in judgement.

For the Baule and their neighbours the fall of Tiassalé signified the intrusion of the French as an important new element in local power rivalries, but the meaning of this was not immediately apparent. Some hastened to make friends with the French in hopes of obtaining a potentially powerful ally for their cause. Generally these people represented those who had been the victims of Tiassalé's expansion since 1891 and they included the chiefs of Ahua, and Niamwé and their Baule trading partners north of Tiassalé. For their part, Etien Komenan and Komenan Buen and their supporters maintained their hostility, but for the time being they remained at a distance. Meanwhile the inhabitants of Tiassalé and most Baule to the north adopted an attitude of wait-and-see. After all, maybe Marchand would lose patience like de Tavernost and Armand, and after a transient occupation perhaps he too would return to Lahou as they had in 1891.

It was by no means self-evident what Marchand wanted to do in Tiassalé. Etien Komenan and his followers were still at large and could easily strike at Fatou Aka if the French withdrew. Fatou Aka realized how vulnerable his position was, and it worried him considerably.[52] In local political terms the capture of Tiassalé still lacked the definitive symbolic character which it had acquired in Marchand's own mind. Everything depended upon what the French chose to do next with their momentary advantage. Most of the population waited expectantly in apparent submission. The ambiguity of the situation no doubt increased when Marchand placed Tiassalé under the control of Captain Manet and returned to the coast in early June.

In Grand Bassam Marchand made final preparations for his exploratory mission, but before he could return to Tiassalé he became ill. During his absence, Manet made the first preliminary trips into Baule country north of Tiassalé, penetrating as far as Singrobo. The administration continued to give its full support to Fatou Aka,[53] and upon Marchand's recommendation they sent a civil administrator, Charles Pobéguin, to assist Manet in Tiassalé. It was not until mid-August that Marchand left Grand Bassam for Tiassalé, and after passing via Grand Lahou, he arrived in Tiassalé on 3 September 1893, determined to begin his long-awaited Baule explorations.

MARCHAND'S BAULE EXPLORATIONS AND SAMORY IN THE NORTH, 1893–1894

In retrospect it is difficult to sift Marchand's material for the elements of historical fact. When facts about the Baule appear, they are usually embedded in tangential argumentation, and the arguments are hopelessly intermingled with questions of judgement, preconception, misconception and just wishful thinking, all glued together with the pervasive adhesive of ambition. Basically, in Marchand's writings, whatever was reported was, *ipso facto*, a success.

Taking the cue from Marchand's own glowing accounts, historians and admirers ever since have tended to perpetuate the myth of Marchand's unqualified success among the Baule during 1893 and 1894. In later years Marchand went on to greater glory in several successive missions for the French colonial cause, and the popular success of these later ventures retrospectively conferred a measure of lustre to his first mission among the Baule. In the biographical literature on Marchand the Baule mission is generally portrayed as a brilliant prelude to an even more brilliant career.[54]

There emerges as a result of numerous secondary repetitions what one might call the 'official version' of Marchand among the Baule. In outline form it runs something like this: the capture of Tiassalé inspired fear and respect in the hearts of all Baule. Because he had eliminated the traditional obstacle to their trade with the coast, they welcomed Marchand warmly and without reservation. He was able to travel wherever he wished, and as a result conducted a thorough reconnaissance of all of Baule country, winning friends for the French cause wherever he went. His rapid and unpredictable itinerary earned him the name of '*kpakibo*' - a respectful title meaning 'he who creates new paths', and the mere mention of the name was sufficient to inspire silence and submission. The valuable information which he obtained about local customs and politics served as the basis for the success of later French penetration in the area. Such is the 'official version' of Marchand among the Baule.

For the purposes of administrative history or for surveys of French colonial expansion, the gap between the myth and the reality of Marchand's travels has not been very important. In this tradition of writing the most important fact about the mission was that Marchand emerged as the first European to travel through Baule country and come out alive. This was no mean achievement in itself, and when one remembers that numerous others had unsuccessfully attempted the same feat before him, and that three other Europeans had even died in the process, it is not difficult to understand why this achievement alone could give rise to the heroic myths in subsequent writing. So far, most of the historical writing on the Ivory Coast remains on the level of administrative history, and it is perhaps for this reason that historians have not yet penetrated the historiographical problem at hand.

When we leave the level of survey history and turn to an examination of the precise encounters among the Baule, the inadequacy of the 'official version' of Marchand's explorations becomes readily apparent. As with most myths, the discrepancy between the 'official version' and reality is rather large, and a close reading of Marchand's own letters makes this quite clear.[55]

The incongruities in Marchand's accounts are striking from the outset. On the one hand he reports: 'le Baoulé dans son entier, ne demande qu'une chose, me voir filer chez les Bambaras le plus vite possible, et m'y aider de tout son pouvoir . . .'.[56] Yet in the same letter, he tells Binger that it is virtually impossible to obtain reliable information from the Baule concerning the best routes of penetration:

quant à me donner des renseignements . . . bernique – ni Pobéguin, ni moi, ni vous n'y réusira *qu'en allant voir*. Ils ne s'opposent pas à ce que nous allions partout, oh mais là pas du tout! seulement . . . Ils n'ouvrent pas la bouche. Quand on n'a pas une silence insurmontable ou même une négation énergique, ils vous répondent: Ah oui peut-être . . . Impossible rien obtenir de plus.[57]

Even around Tiassalé itself the French encountered this form of passive non-cooperation:

Pobéguin, l'administrateur actuel de Tiassalé, depuis 3 mois en fonctions, ne peut pas savoir si une route partant de Tiassalé va à une plantation ou à un village voisin, les noirs disent et soutiennent, *jusqu'à ce que le contraire de ce qu'ils disent leur ait été montré*, le contraire de la vérité.[58]

The Baule were well-informed about various trade routes to the north, and it is likely that this kind of wilful obfuscation on their part illustrated something less than full enthusiasm for Marchand's presence or purpose.

The Mission experienced more serious setbacks almost immediately. On 9 September 1893, the day before the planned departure, Captain Manet drowned in the rapids north of Tiassalé while he was on his way to recruit porters. The official accounts of the death treat it as an accident, but the similarity between Manet's drowning and the earlier deaths of Voituret and Papillon inspired a certain measure of fear on the part of remaining porters, and 130 of them abandoned their charges and fled. Marchand later described the mood at the time in ominous terms: 'la province elle-même qui n'acceptait notre passage que grace à la crainte inspirée par la chute de Thiassalé commence à se soulever.'[59] Nevertheless, Marchand was determined to proceed, and on 13 September he set out from Tiassalé for the north by way of Eliassou, Brimbo, and Singrobo.

At the village of Ouossou, just north of Singrobo, Marchand was encouraged by the warm welcome he received from Akafou, chief of the Ngban. At the time of French penetration Akafou had become a leader of considerable importance in the southern Baule region. Through several strategic marriages he had acquired extensive influence over a series of villages east of Ouossou as far as the right bank of the Nzi river. In this geographic location, Akafou had emerged as the major Baule trading partner of the pre-1891 Ahua–Niamwé–Nzianou trading chain to the south. To the extent that this trade route constituted a rival trading alliance to that dominated by Tiassalé, Akafou can be said to have been at least potentially hostile to Tiassalé prior to 1891.

His hostility no doubt increased when Tiassalé, under Etien Komenan, severed the Ahua–Niamwé–Nzianou network by bringing Niamwé and the left bank of the Bandama under his control after 1891. The mutual trading relationship between the Ngban to the north of Tiassalé and Ahua to the south-east had been cut as a result of the eastward extension of Tiassalé's control. In the region above Tiassalé, Akafou became known as the inveterate enemy of Tiassalé's commercial allies who resented his repeated harassments of their trading convoys *en route* to Tiassalé. As a traditional adversary of Etien Komenan, then, it is perhaps understandable that Akafou initially greeted Marchand with open arms. For his part, Marchand was pleased with his reception at Ouossou and he recommended that Akafou receive a ceremonial staff as an official expression of French gratitude.[60]

Beyond Ouossou, however, Marchand encountered his first explicit resistance from a Baule chief. Kouadio Okou, chief of the Ouarébo village of Lomo, was a long-standing opponent of Akafou and an ally of Etien Komenan. While Marchand was still in Ouossou, Kouadio Okou made it clear that he would oppose Marchand's further advance northwards. As Marchand described it, 'un petit roi du nom de Kouadio Okou . . . m'avait, comme ami de Thiassalé, envoyé un déclaration de guerre . . .'[61] Nearly a week of negotiations followed during which Marchand sent gifts to Lomo to help persuade Kouadio Okou to receive him. During his wait, Marchand launched exploratory side trips westwards to visit the Souamlé peoples on the west bank of the Bandama, and he began to appreciate the degree of political fragmentation of the Baule peoples. Upon his return, Kouadio Okou had agreed to let him proceed, and Marchand once again turned northwards, arriving at Toumodi on 28 September. Initially Marchand had hoped to be in Sakhala by the end of September;[62] clearly his progress was much slower than he had anticipated.

During the next few weeks Marchand's pace quickened. In October he explored west of Toumodi as far as Kokumbo, the most important gold mining centre among the Baule, and after returning once more to Toumodi, he again turned northwards and travelled to Touniniané among the Nanafoué. From there he launched a third westward reconnaissance, travelling as far as the banks of the Bandama by way of the western Nanfoué and Akoué groups. Returning to Touniniané he then turned northwards once again and reached Kodiokofikro on 3 November 1893. Perhaps because of his quickened pace, the information in Marchand's writings about these regions becomes extremely scanty and incomplete.[63]

On 11 November Marchand reached the northern Baule village of Gossa or Gbuèkékro, and there the entire Mission began to change its character. Gbuèkékro, or Bouaké as it became known to the French, was, as Marchand described it, the 'capitale d'une forte colonie Achanti [e.g. Akan] à la frontière nord du Baoulé aux confins des contrées païennes Senoufos du Soudan'.[64] Traditionally, Bouaké had not been a particularly notable settlement. It received no mention at all in Binger's accounts of his travels through the north, suggesting that its reputation as a trading centre in 1888 was not very widespread. By late 1893, however, it had become a major centre in the armament trade between the Baule and Samory's troops.

Since Marchand's departure from the Sudan in 1892 the campaigns against Samory had continued and indeed intensified, largely on the personal initiative of officers like himself who acted independently of directives from the Ministry of the Colonies. Archinard, who since August 1892 was once again in charge of the Sudanese military, was the architect of the renewed campaign against Samory. He ordered Colonel Combes to attack and pursue Samory from the west, to cut off his supply lines of armaments from Sierra Leone. Combes executed his orders and chased Samory as far eastwards as the Baoulé River. In addition, Commandant Briquelot captured Erimakono in the early months of 1893, sealing off any further direct access of Samory to the armament sources in Sierra Leone.[65]

The combined effect of these operations had a considerable impact on conditions in the northern Ivory Coast. Samory's agents began to advance along the headwaters of the Sassandra and Bandama rivers in search of new sources of arms through commercial exchanges with the southern peoples of the Ivory Coast. When he arrived at Bouaké, Marchand stumbled upon the eastward advance of Samory's influence, and he became quite alarmed. While serving as an officer in the French Sudan, Marchand had come to regard Samory as an implacable enemy of French colonialism, and he realized that Samory's presence dashed all hopes of his cherished plans for linking the coast with the Sudan. Samory's advance, according to Marchand, needed to be halted at all costs. Fortunately, thought Marchand, this would be possible because the French could count on the combined effectiveness of the treaty which Binger had concluded with Kong and the fidelity of Kouassi Gbueké, the Baule chief of Bouaké. As Marchand wrote from Bouaké, 'le chef m'est complètement acquis maintenant'.[66]

In both of these estimations, Marchand proved to be over-optimistic. After a series of reconnaissances around Bouaké in early December 1893, Marchand returned to Bouaké itself, but this time he was greeted with something less than enthusiasm. During this stay in Bouaké, as he later explained, 'le roi me déclarait qu'il recevrait Samori . . . et qu'il était loin de considérer l'arrivée de ce chef comme désastre pour le Baoulé.'[67] In the last week of December an attempt was made to poison Marchand, and he took several days to recover. When he tried to leave Bouaké and seek refuge further east in early January, he was attacked at the Baule village of Boungué. He escaped unhurt, but it was clear that in the Bouaké region his safety was by no means guaranteed and that France was not likely to find an eager ally against Samory in Kouassi Gbueké.

The inhabitants of Kong proved equally hostile towards Marchand, although for different reasons. Once again, the activities of the French military in the Sudan were the immediate cause of their hostility. In April of 1893 Archinard had personally directed a campaign against Amadu along the Niger river, capturing Djenné, Mopti, and Bandiagara. These towns on the Niger were the traditional terminal points on the north for much of the long-distance Dyula trade, which originated in the region of Kong. Their capture by the French led to the collapse of this commerce.

When Binger visited it in 1888, Kong was a thriving commercial centre, but when Marchand approached the town in April 1894 the whole area was experiencing the disastrous effects of a prolonged famine and a near total eclipse of trade. As Marchand reported, 'La croyance en France à la richesse des pays Dioula est un erreur; il n'y a pas de contrée plus pauvre, plus déshérité de la nature que le pays de Kong . . .'.[68] In addition to the general trade depression many of the inhabitants of Kong had turned against the French because several Dyula merchants from the Kong region had been killed during Archinard's siege of Djenné. Marchand's first emissaries to Kong were refused a reception, and he was told that he would not be able to enter Kong alive.

In early May the attitude of some inhabitants softened and on 11 May he was finally granted an audience with the elders. Even after entering Kong, however, Marchand was not warmly received. He was given no food and little hospitality, and his own porters threatened to abandon him. His assistant, Baillay, was publicly insulted in the market, and Marchand could do nothing to command respect. The cordial treaties which Binger and Treich-Laplène had concluded in 1888 seemed to have little meaning in 1894.[69] Marchand eventually convinced some of the Kong merchants to send caravans southwards through Baule country as a gesture of goodwill, but even this marginal achievement had little enduring impact when the envoys of Samory began to arrive in June 1894, announcing that one of Samory's sons and 200 *sofas* intended to worship in the mosque at Kong.

In addition to Samory's expansion and Kong's hostility, a third element worried Marchand. For several months he had been preoccupied with the seemingly pervasive influence of the British in zones of traditional French concern. While still among the Baule Marchand reported that the commerce of that area was 'tout entier entre les mains des trafiquants noirs de la colonie anglaise de Cap-Coast arrivant du l'Est en tournant Grand Bassam par le Nord'.[70] Furthermore, directly to the east of Baule country, along the Comoé river, French influence suffered serious setbacks in March 1894 when Kasai Dihié, king of the Anyi of Indénié, killed a French official named Poulle and the administration was able to do nothing to avenge his death. Marchand heard of the incident during his travels in the Anno region, and he reported that the French were considered to have been defeated.[71] French influence was particularly weak in the areas closest to the British Gold Coast, and Marchand feared that the British would profit from this by extending control westwards.

Marchand's fears were aggravated in Kong. There he was joined on 17 May by Moskowitz, an explorer who had been charged with the mission of establishing French influence southwards from the Sudan, along the northern fringe of the Gold Coast territories. The frontiers between the French and British possessions were as yet unsettled and still open to dispute. Moskowitz had hoped to extend French influence to Bole and Bouna, but he had been preceded in this by only a few days when George Ferguson, a Fanti agent from Cape Coast, signed a treaty with Bouna on 16 April 1894.[72] Once again the British seemed to be enlarging their territory to the detriment of French claims.

After hearing about this encounter from Moskowitz, Marchand began to regard his presence in Kong as a symbol of future French commercial claims along the entire middle Niger. On 18 May 1894, Marchand, Moskowitz, and Baillay organized a 'French market' in Kong to emphasize the importance of French presence in the face of the reputed British advance. As Marchand explained the gesture:

c'était surtout le premier acte offensif de la lutte au Niger central contre l'envahissante exportation britannique, lutte qui doit devenir bien autrement vive dans un avenir très prochain . . .[73]

Marchand's solution to the crisis of dwindling French influence was simple. It consisted of concluding a direct alliance between the French and the Dyula of the Kong region in the hope of simultaneously excluding the English from the Dyula markets and stemming the eastward expansion of Samory. In order to cement this alliance, the French, Marchand argued, needed to send a military expedition to the aid of Kong immediately. In July 1894 Marchand descended rapidly to the coast and cabled his views to the Ministry. Not to act, he argued, could mean the potential junction of Samory's forces with the Gold Coast and the perpetual separation of the French coastal colony from her possessions in the Sudan.

In assessing Marchand's statements about the Baule, we must keep these events clearly in mind. After 11 November 1893, when Marchand reached Bouaké for the first time, his attention shifted markedly from Baule questions to a threefold preoccupation with the advance of Samory eastwards, the indifference and even hostility of Kong, and the alleged expansion of British agents from the Gold Coast. Marchand gave up his initial project for joining the coast with the Sudan by the river systems, but in its place he elaborated a new strategy to protect French influence and salvage a measure of personal recognition. According to Marchand, the French had to come to Kong's defence and grant the Dyula access through Baule country to French traders on the coast. Loaded down with French manufactures the Dyula would subsequently traverse Baule areas once again and disseminate the articles of French industrial production throughout their traditional trading networks of the Niger Bend area, winning the Sudan for the French commercial empire. As Marchand summarized it: 'le Dioula est fait pour répandre nos produits dans la boucle et en drainer les productions . . .'.[74]

In Marchand's new plan Baule country became the corridor through which French-Dyula relations would develop to full fruition. A few surveillance posts would be all that was necessary to assure the safety of the trading caravans, and these would provoke no resistance whatsoever from the Baule:

Il n'y a absolument rien à redouter comme conséquences de cette mesure qui ne présente que des avantages – les populations ne feront et ne peuvent faire aucune espèce d'oppostion, au contraire; 4 ou 5 miliciens et un commis indigène suffiront largement.[75]

Such an affirmation was, to say the least, optimistic. Marchand knew that commercial disputes often caused internal feuding and warfare between Baule groups. In addition he was aware that the Baule traditionally opposed any Dyula penetration of their territory and that the Dyula were openly sceptical about their own safety among the Baule. Furthermore, he had witnessed the thriving commerce in guns and powder which the Baule were conducting at great profit to themselves with agents of Samory in the north. Clearly his new proposals, if successful, threatened to antagonize the Baule by upsetting virtually every level of their existing economic organization, and yet Marchand chose to characterize the Baule as completely receptive to his plans.

Perhaps by the time Marchand returned to Grand Bassam in July 1894 he had honestly lost touch with Baule sentiment. He had been travelling since September 1893, but during those ten months only slightly more than three months had been spent in Baule country itself, and that time had come at the very outset of the mission. His rapid descent through Baule territory in early July hardly permitted him enough time to assess the Baule mood thoroughly. In effect, his impressions of the Baule in July 1894 were derived from vague memories of the situation six months earlier.

Even in this respect Marchand seems to have suffered from a mild amnesia. All recollections of his difficulties among the Baule seemed to be erased from his mind in the sweeping optimism of his new vision. Tiassalé's resistance, Kouadio Okou's opposition, and Kouassi Gbueke's open sympathies with Samory all disappeared from Marchand's calculations. It is possible that the urgency which he felt towards the situation in northern Ivory Coast blinded him to the full implications of his own proposals among the Baule. It is equally possible, however, that in order to encourage ministerial support for his plans, he consciously sought to minimize the risk of Baule opposition. In any case, whether Marchand was simply forgetful or consciously deceptive, his message to the Governor was unambiguous 'Le Baoulé *tout entier* est soumis et attend notre occupation. Nous n'avons dans cette immense province que des amis.'[76] His explorations may have rectified many of the French misconceptions about the north, but in the process he had generated a new set of illusions about the Baule. Marchand's plans for Kong were predicated upon the myth of Baule passivity.

THE KONG EXPEDITION AND THE FIRST BAULE 'REVOLT' 1894–1895

Marchand's early warnings about Samory's advance did not stimulate immediate response from Paris. In January 1894 Governor Binger doubted that Samory would attack Kong, and Albert Grodet, the new civilian governor of the Sudan, reported that Samory seemed receptive to the idea of coming to a new settlement with the French.[77] With the failure of the Moskowitz mission and the arrival of Samory's emissaries in Kong by June of 1894, the situation grew more serious, and when the news of possible British advances in the region reached Paris, Delcassé considered the issue with renewed concern. Binger, by this time in France on leave, changed his earlier opinion and recommended that an expedition be sent to defend Kong. The Minister concurred and began to formulate plans for a military campaign. The Chambre was still generally reluctant to authorize new military expenditures, but by a fortunate coincidence the Franco-Congolese Agreement of 14 August meant that the military expedition under Colonel Parfait-Louis Monteil, initially intended for the Congo, was no longer urgently required there, and Delcassé diverted it instead to the Ivory Coast without necessitating any new cost.[78] On 21 August 1894 Monteil received the order to redirect his expedition to the Ivory Coast. He left Loango on 3 September and arrived in Grand Bassam on 12 September to go to the aid of Kong.

Delcassé's instructions to Monteil made it clear that the political objectives of the mission were, as far as he was concerned, its most important aspect. He wanted Monteil to defend Kong from Samory's advance, but ordered him not to destroy Samory's forces, proposing instead a measure of recognized autonomy to Samory if he were to remain in the border area near Sierra Leone and Liberia. More important than this, however, Delcassé wanted envoys from Monteil's mission to reach the French posts in the Niger Bend and complete the linkage between similar treaty-making missions which were to make their way northwards from Dahomey. His intention was to encircle both the Germans in Togo and the British on the Gold Coast and thus complete the task which Moskowitz had tried unsuccessfully to accomplish six months earlier.[79] The defence of the residents of Kong no doubt had some intrinsic urgency to it, especially since Binger had signed and Marchand had affirmed a formal French alliance with the Kong chiefs, but in the 'official mind' questions of imperial rivalry with Germany and Britain were still more important than the sanctity of any particular treaty with African chiefs. Basically Delcassé hoped that the Monteil expedition would be able to accomplish three things at once: stop Samory, maintain the alliance with Kong, and contain France's colonial rivals. Of these three objectives the last dominated Delcassé's thinking.

When he arrived in Grand Bassam, Monteil was faced with the problem of which route to choose to reach Kong. He had basically two alternatives: the Camoé valley by way of the Anyi kingdoms which Binger had visited in 1888, or the Bandama and Baule country. Binger favoured penetration by way of the Comoé,[80] but eventually, upon the advice of Marchand, Monteil decided to proceed through Baule country. After cabling Paris in July, Marchand launched a second quick trip through Baule territory during August and early September. In preparation for the coming military expedition Marchand placed civilian administrators in Toumodi and Kodiokofikro, with instructions to assess the possibilities of recruiting porters among the Baule. When he returned to Grand Bassam on 21 September, Marchand convinced Monteil that the Baule route looked the most promising, and Monteil informed Paris of his decision.[81]

From the outset the expedition was plagued with logistical problems. Because of transportation difficulties from the Congo, Monteil was obliged to leave several contingents of his troops either in the Congo itself or in Dahomey along the way, in the hope that they could join him as soon as possible. Although he arrived with the first company on 12 September, it was not until 28 October that the 4th Hausa Company reached Grand Bassam from Dahomey. Other contingents of Senegalese troops came on 14 October and 4 November from Senegal, but the rations and materials for the expedition were still lacking and did not all arrive in Grand Bassam until 13 December 1894. Monteil blamed Paris for these difficulties, and implied that they were intentional expressions of the Ministry's dissatisfaction with his choice of the Baule route. 'Ce plan ne fut jamais accepté qu'à contre gré par les bureaux du ministère des Colonies; tous les obstacles furent mis à son exécution.'[82] Binger was still on leave in France and it is possible that he hoped that Monteil would remain on the coast until he returned to Grand Bassam to discuss his preferred plan of penetration by way of the Comoé.

Locally, the movement of troops and supplies provoked further difficulties. The central problem involved the question of porterage. Even before Monteil had arrived in Grand Bassam, Albert Nebout, the administrator whom Marchand had placed in charge of Kodiokofikro in Baule territory, reported that porterage would pose a serious problem among the Baule.

j'ai prévu la population du passage de la colonne, avec toutes les précautions possibles. On ne se resignera pas à porter tant de charges; j'en ai peur; il faudra employer l'intimidation, la force peut-être. Dans ce cas, qu'arrivera-t-il? une fuite générale des esclaves . . .[83]

In the south it became apparent that porters who had been recruited were unwilling to carry their loads for more than a few kilometres from their villages of origin. Porterage was for the most part the work of captives and slave dependants. Slaves from the Abidji villages between Dabou and Tiassalé were unwilling to carry their loads very far into Baule country for fear of being held in ransom by the Baule with whom Abidji had had several disputes prior to European arrival. Several southern villages were reluctant to provide porters at all, particularly Lopou, a major Adioukrou village on the overland road from Dabou towards Tiassalé.[84]

Eventually Lieutenant Desperles devised a relay system to overcome these problems. Essentially, porters would be expected to carry their loads only to the limits of the territory controlled by their own chiefs. There, they would depose the provisions, and new porters from the next area would take them to the northern frontier of their own recognized territory. Desperles hoped that this system of relay connections would ensure the orderly transport of goods steadily northwards. Clearly such a system was cumbersome and time-consuming, and it required thorough co-ordination between French officers and the respective Baule chiefs.[85]

In time the system collapsed for complex reasons involving the structure of authority among the Baule and the nature of slave labour. The intrusion of scores of porters into Baule country required the provision of food. The customary diet was one of plantain bananas and yams, and since these were too heavy to carry profitably, the Baule villages along the way were requisitioned for provisions. The Baule were unaccustomed to provide food simply upon demand, and the slave porters had no money to pay for it since they were not compensated until their porterage was finished, if at all. Disputes arose on multiple levels over petty debts. Normally the French compensated the chiefs for the porters they provided, but the slave porters were not always compensated in turn and could thus not pay for their food. Indeed chiefs almost never *paid* their slave porters, for by definition, slaves were those whose labour the chief could control without payment. Payment in such cases would be tantamount to a recognition of the slave's liberty, something which the chiefs were not willing to accord, no matter what the French wanted. Nevertheless, the Baule expected compensation for the provisions which the slaves of other chiefs had consumed, and when it was not forthcoming, their own slaves, acting as porters in the relay linkages above Tiassalé, began to pillage the supplies of the caravans. Lieutenant Desperles provided a clear account of the process:

En partant de Ouossou, les porteurs marchent avec une rapidité extraordinaire de façon à s'éloigner là plus possible de l'Européen et de quelques hommes qui les escortent; lorsqu'ils sont à une distance convenable ils entrent dans la brousse, défoncent les caisses, se restaurent, cachent une partie du contenu de façon à la retrouver au retour, puis reprennent leur marche très allègre.[86]

All evidence suggests that the major Baule chiefs who acted as inter-mediaries with the French disapproved of this pillaging. As Desperles observed with respect to the chief of the Ngbans, 'Je ne crois pas qu'on puisse rendre responsable Akafou de tous ces actes qui se commettent à son insu . . . Ce sont les voleurs eux-mêmes qu'il faut châtier . . .'.[87] To blame the slave porters uniquely, however, was also misguided, for it seems that these slaves acted with the support if not upon the instigation of their own masters. These masters were not paramount chiefs, like Akafou, but they were nevertheless free men over whom Akafou had nominal authority. It was upon these freemen that the expedition to a virtual standstill. According to Monteil, 80 per cent of turn to them to supply provisions and porters. Yet they were not receiving visible compensation, and when Akafou proved incapable of obtaining what they desired from the French, these men were willing to help themselves.

The pillaging of the caravans brought the northern progress of the expedition to a virtual standstill. According to Monteil 80 per cent of the caravans' supplies were lost in some cases between Tiassalé and Toumodi, and the movements had to be halted in mid-November until the full force of the expedition could be concentrated at Tiassalé and assure the safety of the supply lines with armed escorts.[88] Monteil left Grand Bassam for Tiassalé on 24 October to supervise the operations personally.

As if these problems were not sufficient, Monteil soon found himself embroiled in others. Shortly after his departure from Grand Bassam the Abouré inhabitants of Akaplass near Bassam challenged the French in open revolt. Commander Pineau attempted to take Akaplass by force, but he failed, suffering heavy losses. He notified Monteil, who then returned to Grand Bassam to take charge of a punitive expedition. On 16 November 1894 he occupied Akaplass, and in the following days he restored security to the region around Grand Bassam.[89] This un-expected diversion was costly in time, men, and materials, and it was not until mid-December that Monteil could once again return to Tiassalé with the bulk of his troops to resume his proposed penetration through Baule country towards Kong.

During Monteil's absence the mood of the Baule hardened signifi-cantly. Fatou Aka, formerly one of France's strongest allies, was openly disturbed about the mistreatment of one of the porters which he had provided and the alleged rape of a woman by five Senegalese soldiers. He sent messages to other Baule chiefs in the north expressing his dis-pleasure.[90] Commandant Caudrelier, who had been placed in charge of Tiassalé during Monteil's absence reported the mood succinctly:

Il n'y a ici, pour le moment, aucune menace d'insurrection, mais des preuves constantes d'insoumission . . . Je crois que nous ne pouvons rien faire de sérieux dans ce pays-ci tant que nous n'en avons pas maté les populations à coup de fusil.[91]

The situation deteriorated irretrievably when it became apparent that as a result of French presence slaves were beginning to elude the authority of their Baule masters. In effect, the problems of porterage and pillaging touched off a generalized crisis of authority between the Baule and their slaves. While some slaves pillaged French caravans with the tacit support of their masters, others did so hoping to obtain goods with which to purchase their own freedom. Still others refrained entirely from pilfering French supplies, but they began to regard service for the French as the means of obtaining a protected passage back to their freedom in the north. Slaves received encouragement in this expectation when Captain Desperles refused to return a fugitive slave who sought refuge in the French post at Toumodi. Recently arrived from the north, the slave spoke only Bambara and encouraged by a Senegalese soldier who spoke a related dialect, the slave fled from his Baule master in Broukro and offered to work as Desperles's personal valet. Despite a formal request for the slave's return from Niango Kouassi, the chief of Toumodi, and a strong warning from Nebout that the Baule would be very displeased if the slave were not returned, Desperles persisted in his intention to 'liberate' the slave.[92]

Desperles's conduct had the most profound symbolic impact, for he was the officer in charge of recruiting porters from Baule villages. As far as the Baule were concerned, Desperles's behaviour undermined their own authority by demonstrating that slaves could flee from their masters with impunity and expect French protection. The number of attempts to escape remained limited, but a generalized mood of slave insubordination became manifest. As Nebout reported: 'Les chefs ont peu d'autorité . . . sur leurs propres esclaves qui depuis notre occupation n'obéissent plus guère que par déférence ou bonne volonté.'[93]

After Monteil suspended the movement of caravans in mid-November, the tension abated slightly as the need for porters declined. But this measure did not solve the problem; it only postponed it, for if the French renewed their attempts to recruit porters, slave insubordination was bound to erupt once again. Nebout had already predicted several months previously that in the north the conscription of porters might well provoke what he called 'une fuite générale des esclaves . . .'.[94] The Baule were not prepared to tolerate this.

Even in the absence of new demands for porters the situation grew steadily worse. Attempts by the French military to punish guilty porters for pillaging caravans only aggravated the crisis of authority among the Baule. The military reasoned that severe punishment would serve as a salutary example to discourage further incidents.[95] Independent of its effect on future pillaging, however, the policy had unanticipated implications for relations between the Baule and their slaves. The punishments gave some slaves even greater incentive to escape their conditions of servitude, and villages along the main route of French advance began to witness the exodus of their captive populations. Most of these renegade slaves remained within Baule country, but they took every available opportunity to move away from the Tiassalé-Toumodi axis by seeking out new relationships of dependence and protection in villages to the east or to the west of the major line of French penetration.[96]

By the time Monteil returned to Tiassalé with plans to march northwards, a crisis of major proportions began to take shape. Latent Baule hostility congealed in an explicit form when Asmaret, the chief of the Adioukrou village of Lopou, undertook a diplomatic mission through the southern Baule villages to Sakassou itself. The village of Lopou had refused to provide porters for Monteil's troops on their way from Dabou to Tiassalé, and as punishment, the French publicly humiliated the village chief.[97] Asmaret realized that alone he could do little to halt French penetration, but by travelling to Sakassou and meeting with village chiefs along the way he hoped to enlist Baule support in a concerted movement to resist further French intrusion. The proposed alliance was only partially concluded because the French learned of the plot in time to dissuade certain Baule chiefs from lending it their support. Akafou and Fatou Aka apparently refused to join the conspiracy, but Kouadio Okou was reported to be openly sympathetic to the idea.[98] By mid-December 1894 plans for armed resistance were a matter of open discussion among the Baule.

Violence erupted when Monteil began to move his troops from Tiassalé towards Toumodi in late December.[99] On 22 December Monteil sent a contingent of engineers to work on the road between Brimbo and Ouossou and inform the Baule chiefs that he wished to convene them all in Ouossou to settle the problem of porterage once and for all. On 24 December Monteil sent Commander Caudrelier ahead with a company of troops, and he intended to follow in a few days. Hostilities broke out north of Ouossou on 25 December 1894 when a convoy was pillaged near Moronou. Violence occurred simultaneously below Ouossou when a group of engineers was greeted with gunfire on their way to Pokosiabo; without returning fire they went back to Ouossou. Within a few hours a small convoy which formed part of Caudrelier's advance arrived in Ouossou from the south, but along the way they had been forced to abandon many of their munitions because their porters had fled. In trying to recuperate them, Sergeant Ventzel was also met with gunfire south of Ouossou and he returned to the village without the supplies. Ouossou had in effect been cut off from both the north and the south.

For the next several days French troops and supplies remained in the village under a state of siege. Monteil, still in Tiassalé, was as yet unaware of the situation, and on 26 December he dispatched three companies of troops northwards as initially planned. The move, although not intended as a defensive strategy, proved fortunate for those in Ouossou, for on 27 December French troops in the village came under a full-scale attack from three sides. They were able to ward off the attack only when Caudrelier arrived from the south with a portion of his company. In his hurry to come to the aid of those in Ouossou, Caudrelier was obliged to leave part of his contingent in Pokosiabo under the command of Sergeant Dufour, but this group was also attacked. Sergeant Dufour and four soldiers were wounded and barely reached Ouossou alive. Simultaneously, a munitions convoy which had been following Caudrelier's contingent came under Ngban attack.

Meanwhile in Ahuakro, a village to the east of the main convoy route, a contingent of twenty-five soldiers which had been conducting a reconnaissance mission in the area, under Lieutenant Haye, came under severe fire from the Ngban. Two soldiers were killed and fourteen wounded, and Haye and his wounded troops were forced to barricade themselves in self-defence in a village hut. Two of the envoys they sent for help were killed and a third succeeded only under cover of night in reaching the main body of French troops. It was not until the next day that reinforcements under Lieutenant Baratier were able to liberate Haye and his demoralized troops.[100]

As part of the same series of attacks the eight Senegalese troops in charge of French supplies at Moronou were besieged on the night of 27 December. Two were killed, and the others straggled south to Ouossou, arriving days later. The scattered yet simultaneous attacks by the Ngban on 27 December caught the French completely by surprise and showed every sign of being part of a well co-ordinated revolt.

Other groups beyond the Ngban also manifested their open hostility. While the Ngban were harrassing the French convoys in the south on

27 December, Kouadio Okou, chief of Lomo, stopped two armed envoys who were headed from Toumodi towards the troops in the south. The envoys were killed and decapitated, and their remains were sent throughout the other villages around Toumodi in an attempt to invite other Baule groups to join in revolt.[101] On 28 December Kouadio Okou led a group of 500 armed Baule to occupy the residence of the civilian administrator in Toumodi. Charles Monteil, the brother of Lieutenant-Colonel Monteil, was the administrator in charge and apparently he avoided an outbreak of violence only by declining to call out the troops in the nearby garrison.[102] North of Toumodi the administrator at Kodiokofikro subsequently reported that other groups in that area were sympathetic with the Ngban uprising, and that some had actually sent several hundred warriors to assist the Ngban.[103]

When Lieutenant-Colonel Monteil had studied the incidents leading up to the siege of Ouossou, the attack at Ahuakro, the interception of the Toumodi envoys and the threats to the civilian administrator in Toumodi, he realized that the situation was serious. By early January the French forces had had six killed and thirty wounded in these attacks, and so far they had done little to retaliate. Monteil felt that a demonstration of force would be necessary, but before he undertook this, he cabled Paris describing the situation:

La colonne, avec peine en mouvement, s'est trouvée subitement devant une insurrection générale de tout le Baoulé entre Bandama et Toumodi. D'abord le convoi libre a été pillé, puis l'attaque s'est produite de tous côtés . . . nos troupes . . . ont été absolument surprises par ces attaques . . . j'espère bientôt vaincre cette insurrection.[104]

In Paris, changes in the Ministry of the Colonies delayed a decisive response. Delcassé, the Minister who had authorized the Monteil expedition, was still in charge when the news of the Baule uprising arrived, but on 26 January he was replaced by Émile Chautemps. The new Minister was alarmed by the news and cabled Governor Binger for advice. The difficulties which the expedition had encountered among the Abouré near Grand Bassam and the expensive and time-consuming engagements with the Baule made it apparent that Monteil's expedition was going to be a costly affair with marginal results. Chautemps wanted to avoid unnecessary military commitments of the kind which had plagued the Ministry in the Sudan for so many years. When it became evident that Monteil's mission would probably not be able to achieve its major political objectives for a while to come, Chautemps instructed the Sudan to undertake the diplomatic expeditions necessary in the area north of the Gold Coast, and upon the advice of Binger he cabled

Monteil on 18 February instructing him to dissolve the expedition and return to the coast.[105]

The prospect of protracted warfare with the Baule sufficiently discouraged Chautemps from committing any more resources to Monteil's expedition. Monteil's recall is often attributed to his disastrous engagements with Samory's troops, but careful attention to chronology reveals that Chautemps ordered him to dissolve the expedition *before* he made contact with Samory's *sofas*.[106] The recall was a direct function of Baule resistance, not Samory's strength. Because of the long lapse in time between Chautemps's dispatch and Monteil's reception of the recall telegram, several more battles took place between the French and the Baule,[107] but in a sense Chautemps's telegram of 18 February already granted the Baule an assured victory over Monteil. No matter how much damage he tried to inflict upon the Baule, Monteil was destined to withdraw from the battle.

CHAPTER III

Military Withdrawal and Baule Prosperity, 1895-1898

MONTEIL'S DEPARTURE AND ITS REPERCUSSIONS

The ministerial telegrams of 18 and 21 February made it clear that not only was the expedition to be abandoned, but Monteil himself was to hand over command to his subordinate officer, Commander P. C. Caudrelier. Monteil's military leadership had thus been called into question. As one of his lieutenants wrote later about the Minister's telegram, 'Le dépêche ne visait pas une expédition, elle visait un homme. Pour atteindre l'homme, on déclarait la colonne dissoute.'[1]

The news that he had been relieved of his command came as a particularly heavy blow to Monteil when he received it from his brother, Charles, upon reaching Satama on 17 March, for he had just returned from two weeks of harrowing engagements with Samory's *sofas*. In these encounters twelve of his troops had been killed and forty-two others injured, and he himself had received a shot in the arm on 14 March. Weakened by his wound and exhausted from the rapid and prolonged march, Monteil had to be carried in a hammock as the expedition retreated before Samory's bands. In Satama he had hoped to recuperate, and with troops advancing northwards from Baule country he planned to establish a solid base of operations for a renewed campaign against Samory. From Satama he also planned to dispatch Lieutenant Baratier eastwards to fulfil the initial political aim of his mission by establishing French treaties with African chiefs north of the Gold Coast as far as northern Dahomey.[2] But Monteil's plans came too late. Dissatisfied with his performance among the Baule, the Minister had terminated his command and adjourned the mission, and Monteil realized with considerable bitterness on 17 March that his costly encounters with Samory's *sofas* had all been in vain.

If the idea of disobeying the Minister's orders occurred to Monteil, it must have been apparent to him that he was in no position to act on his own initiative. Unlike his fellow military officers in the Sudan who had often disregarded ministerial directives with impunity, Monteil lacked the forces to attempt such a move. Commander Caudrelier, still in Baule country, controlled the bulk of the expedition, and he could not provide Monteil with additional troops or supplies without contravening orders from the Ministry, something which he was not likely to risk, since the Minister had in effect promoted him. Monteil felt victimized by civilian intrigues and a ministerial mistake, but given the conditions in which he found himself he could neither contest nor disregard the decision. As he acknowledged, 'à distance, il n'y avait pas à essayer de dissiper un malentendu probable ou à déjouer des manœuvres coupables, il y avait à s'incliner.'[3] Rather than the stronghold which Monteil had initially envisaged it to be, Satama was to become the starting point of a long and humiliating withdrawal to the coast.

The return itself proved to be more problematic than initially supposed, for Monteil was again to encounter renewed Baule hostility. Some of the hostility was a direct extension of the troubles which Monteil had had with the Ngban below Toumodi in January. The southern Ngban in this region were related by ties of kinship and migration to the larger parent group of Ngban in the north, along the main caravan route from Kodiokofikro to Satama. As early as 22 Janaury, a month before Monteil attempted to travel from Kodiokofikro to Satama, Captain Marchand, after a rapid reconnaissance in the north, warned that there might be difficulties along the route because of the mutual sympathies of the two related groups.[4] When Monteil set out northwards from Kodiokofikro, he met with resistance as Marchand had predicted, and he dealt with it in a brutal fashion. From the village of Attiégoua onwards volunteer porters were scarce, prompting Monteil to obtain them by force. When villagers at Simbo refused to supply porters on 24 February, Monteil seized the chief and the elders and burned the village to the ground.[5] Monteil obtained his porters, but the Ngban harboured their resentment. In addition, the Baule were all the more enraged when, in departing from Kodiokofikro, the troops killed a woman reputed to be a cult priestess in the region.[6]

To these particular grievances was added the generalized antagonism of the northern Baule towards the entire purpose of Monteil's expedition. Monteil, and Marchand before him, had announced far and wide that they intended to put an end to the marauding bands of Samory's *sofas* who were capturing large numbers of Djimini and Djamala inhabitants and selling them as captives to the Baule. Baule opposition to Monteil in the north was inspired by his expressed intention to put an end to their lucrative commerce with Samory. Monteil himself was aware of this:

les populations avaient vu d'un mauvais œil le passage de la colonne
allant opérer contre Samory, parce que, pendant tout le temps du
séjour de ce dernier dans le Djimini, les esclaves étaient à vil prix . . .
La colonne était donc mal vue par eux à l'aller; elle l'était bien
davantage au retour . . . [7]

In addition to putting a stop to this trade, Monteil's continued
demand for porters amounted to an enforced liberation of the captives
already in Baule service before his arrival. Porters were by definition
captives among the northern Baule, and by requesting porters, Monteil
was in effect demanding that the Baule release their captives to
accompany him under armed French protection to their areas of origin,
north of Satama. Since the provisions and supplies they were expected
to carry were consumable goods, the porters would not be needed on
the return trip, and in any case, once they had found their way to their
respective villages of origin, they were not likely to return voluntarily
to servitude among the Baule. Thus, for the northern Baule, Monteil's
expedition posed a double threat to their economic privilege as it
progressed northwards, and they waited expectantly for its return to
take their revenge. As early as 2 March 1895, the day before Monteil
had actually made his first contact with Samory's *sofas*, Lieutenant
Bourrat at Kodiokofikro warned him that the Ngbans and the Assabous
wished to attack the expedition when it returned, and meanwhile these
groups did everything they could to interrupt communications between
Kodiokofikro and Monteil in the north.[8]

Monteil's return through northern Baule country from Satama to
Kodiokofikro exceeded the Baule's expectations. The expedition itself
was so weak that it could hardly defend an orderly retreat, and in
addition it was accompanied by an estimated 10,000 refugees from the
Djamala region[9] who, rather than submitting themselves to almost
certain servitude and perhaps death at the hands of Samory's *sofas*,
chose instead to cling to the remnants of the French expedition, for
what meagre protection it might afford.[10] The troops and refugees set
out from Satama on 24 March and were harassed by Samory's *sofas*
until they reached the banks of Nzi river, the norther frontier of Baule
territory. The Baule began to attack the group on 26 March and battles
continued on 27 March as the expedition and the refugees passed near
Marékro, N'Drikro and Temérébré. When Monteil had made his way
through Ngban country, he expected to receive better treatment from
the Nzipri, the Baule group occupying the area around Kodiokofikro.
But in this too he was disappointed, for they joined in the attack
despite the opposition of their paramount chief, Kouadio Koffi, a

faithful collaborator with the French. It was not until Monteil reached the friendly village of Atté on 28 March that he was finally out of danger.

The engagements with the Baule had swelled the numbers of dead and wounded,[11] and although there is no reliable way of estimating the number of refugees who were captured, it is probable that within a few days several thousand Djamala men, women, and children were enslaved by the Baule in this fashion.[12] What the Minister no doubt intended to be an orderly change of command and a reduction of troop strength, rapidly took on the proportions of one of the most notorious routs in French colonial history.[13]

Monteil was furious, for he realized that he was being held personally responsible for his expedition's miserable performance, and he did not feel that its failure was his fault. As early as January he had expressed his dissatisfaction with Marchand's misleading intelligence reports concerning the alleged docility of the Baule peoples. When Monteil threatened to discipline him, Marchand was insulted and demanded an apology, indicating that if Monteil did not withdraw his threat, he would take the affair to the Minister himself.[14] Monteil did not pursue the matter, perhaps because Marchand was a fellow officer. Instead, Monteil increasingly focused his growing rage upon the civilian administrators in Baule territory, and when he returned to Kodiokofikro after his disastrous encounters with Samory and the northern Baule, he could contain his anger no longer. Immediately upon arriving on 29 March 1895, he rebuked Albert Nebout, the civil administrator, chiding him for the way in which he had handled the administration of his post and impugning his patriotism. Nebout was a Chevalier de la Légion d'Honneur and was not likely to suffer an insult to his patriotism lightly. The following day he replied that since Monteil was a wounded man, he would not seek immediate personal redress from him for the severe insult, but Nebout warned him that he was taking the liberty of informing his own administrative superiors of the incident. Nebout was confident that, as he phrased it, 'Ils apprécieront si . . . j'ai merité d'être insulté, et si, correct et calme, devant un blessé qui m'injurait je suis resté digne de la Croix et de leur estime'.[15]

Monteil was not intimidated. On the contrary, in an immediate retaliatory note he reiterated his initial insult and went on to imply that Nebout through his manner of reporting on the expedition's progress, was personally responsible for the recall of the entire mission:

Il est parfaitement exact que dans un moment d'indignation je vous ai taxé de mauvais français et que j'ai traité de misérables les procédés que vous avez employés depuis six mois vis-à-vis des fautes et gestes de la colonne dont j'avais le commandement.

Je vous accuse Monsieur, et cela de manière formelle, d'être la cause première du malentendu qui s'est produit au sujet des opérations de la colonne de Kong par vos rapports haineux et faux . . .[16]

The persistent antagonism between civilian and military authority which had for so long been endemic in the Sudan began to erupt on a local level in the Ivory Coast. For several months already the tension had been mounting. In November Monteil indicated that he regarded the local civilian administrators as incompetent obstacles to his mission and he had complained about them to the Minister. The trouble derived in part from the fact that Governor Binger was on leave in France for the first several months of the Mission's presence in the Ivory Coast. Monteil looked forward to Binger's return to regularize the administration within the colony:

Il est grand temps qu'il revienne; ses remplaçants sont peut-être de bons chefs de bureau mais n'ont fait preuve d'aucune des qualités qui sont nécessaires à la conduite des hommes, Européens ou indigènes. Ils n'ont aucun sens politique.[17]

When Binger returned, however, it became apparent that he supported his civilian administrators, and the fundamental problem of conflicting military and civilian authority was thrown into sharp relief. Monteil suspected the civilian administration of having used Samory's presence in the northern Ivory Coast merely as a pretext for obtaining the military troops needed for the pacification of the entire colony.[18] He was angered by the administration's requests to quell the insurrection among the Abouré at Bonoua and frustrated by the civil administrators' inability (he even suspected unwillingness) to recruit porters among the Baule. Armed as he was with ministerial instructions to reach and defend Kong, he felt the civil administrators were to be placed at his command to achieve that primary goal. Indeed, since it was Marchand who first placed the administrators at the Baule posts, Monteil tended to regard the civilians in the area as mere auxiliaries to his purpose.

The administrators, for their part, were new in their posts, particularly in Baule territory, and they had not yet established sufficiently stable relations with local chiefs to be able to recruit porters on demand, especially since the problem of porters touched the very heart of the system of Baule domestic slavery. Furthermore, the civil administrators resented being told how to do their jobs by military officers, none of whom had had any experience in the coastal colonies and most of whom tended mistakenly to think that the peoples of the forest ethnic groups could be intimidated into submission by demonstrations of force as in the Sudan. The Ivory Coast was, after all, a colony under a civilian governor which depended entirely upon customs receipts for its financial security. Far from assisting in the business of administration, the presence of more than 1,000 troops in Monteil's expedition made things more difficult by stifling trade and straining relations between the administrators and their subjects. By early February 1895 the position of the civilian administration had become so untenable as a result of the military's presence among the Baule that Nebout indicated he was tempted to resign.

si je n'avais pas la crainte de déplaire à M. le Gouverneur, je demanderai à descendre à la côte, convaincu que dans la situation actuelle l'administration civile n'a plus rien à faire, ne pouvant rien . . .[19]

With this swelling undercurrent of tension it is perhaps not surprising that Monteil suspected the civil administration to be the source of his failures and the instigator of his recall. Not content to leave the blame with Nebout alone, Monteil penned a similarly vituperative letter to Governor Binger on the same day that he relinquished control of the expedition to Caudrelier. In it he accused him of engineering the Minister's decision and squarely blamed Binger for any unfortunate repercussions which might be forthcoming after his departure: 'Les ordres que vous avez provoqués, je vous en laisse la responsabilité avec ses conséquences.'[20]

In the event, the consequences of Monteil's departure proved to be even more explosive in Paris than locally. Throughout the first six months of 1895 the failure of the Kong expedition and the justifications for its recall, as well as the alternate solutions proposed to remedy the situation in the Ivory Coast became subjects of heated debates in the Chambre and in the popular press. In the uproar, parliament and the French public alike rapidly lost sight of the precise reasons for the Baule revolt and Monteil's consequent recall. Indeed from the outset the most profound confusion characterized the popular accounts of what actually happened. Samory and the Baule peoples were linked in the popular press in the most improbable of conspiracies, and the Baule revolt of late December 1894 was depicted as being directly inspired by Samory's troops. L'Afrique Française, for example, reported in its February issue that 'en sortant de la forêt, un peu au nord de Singrobo, la colonne trouva le Baoulé soulevé par les bandes de Samory . . .'.[21] In reality, the nearest of Samory's troops could have been no closer than 200 kilometres from Singrobo. Furthermore, the

Baule clearly had their own grievances against Monteil's expedition, and it was these that inspired their revolt.

As for Monteil's recall, various parties fabricated their own fanciful versions of what had motivated the government's decision. Once again, the autonomy of the Baule revolt, and its determinant role in provoking Chautemps's decision was completely lost from view in the public debate. For those who considered Baule resistance as merely an instance of Samory's influence, the recall became a symbol of retreat before France's most hated adversary, and this precipitated a public scandal. The press attacked the government's decision,[22] and in the Chambre the Minister of the Colonies, Chautemps, came under a blistering attack from the right-wing deputies led by Le Herissé.[23] According to them and their pro-militarist sympathizers, Chautemps's recall of Monteil was a cowardly abandonment of military initiative and a withdrawal from the battle at precisely the moment when victory was in sight.[24] The staggering gap between this version of events and what had actually occurred, did not deter its proponents. Indeed, they may not have even perceived the discrepancy because for them the important feature of the Monteil affair was that it represented yet another instance of military officers falling victim to civilian judgements. In Paris, as in the Ivory Coast, the Monteil recall became the touchstone of an escalating controversy over civilian versus military control of the colonies.

From Chautemps's reply to his critics in the Chambre on 1 March, it was clear that his main concern was not Samory in the north, but rather the prospect of having to commit additional troops and resources to a stop-gap campaign against the Baule peoples in the south. In this respect, perhaps the most alarming news from Monteil which Chautemps found on his desk when he took office was the telegram received on 16 January 1895 in which Monteil stated: 'après diverses reconnaissances et opérations la situation tend à s'améliorer sans qu'il soit cependant question de soumission; une opération importante sera nécessaire encore.'[25] Difficulties in reaching Kong were no doubt to be expected, and it is probable that the Ministry was willing to accept a certain number of these incidents as a matter of course, but Monteil's suggestion that 'une opération importante sera nécessaire . . .' was more than the Minister was prepared to tolerate.

To understand just why this was so it is necessary to place Monteil's recall within the context of the colonial issues of the day. The vicissitudes of the official thinking become intelligible only when the broader stage of events is kept clearly in view. When the Ministry received

Monteil's foreboding assessment, it had already been engaged for over a year in a protracted and acrimonious debate between civilian and military authorities in the Sudan. At the end of 1893 it looked as though the proponents of civilian control had finally subordinated the unruly military commanders in the Sudan. By dismissing Archinard and appointing Albert Grodet as the first civilian governor of the Sudan in late 1893, Delcassé hoped to inaugurate a new era of commercial expansion undisturbed by the military excesses of the previous years. In his instructions to Grodet, Delcassé declared quite emphatically that 'the period of conquest and territorial expansion must be considered as definitely over . . . all your efforts must be aimed at consolidation and exploitation'.[26] The policy of commercial development remained, however, largely a dead letter. Grodet was prevented from effectively implementing it because the military officers under his authority continued to ignore his attempts to bridle their exploits. With an undisguised contempt for civilian authority they acted on their own initiative and presented the government with costly military *faits accomplis*. In Paris as well, Grodet's opponents sustained their criticism of his civilian administration. When Lieutenant-Colonel Étienne Bonnier led an unauthorized expedition to capture Timbuktu and met with disaster, the pro-militarist press tried to blame Grodet for the massacre, suggesting that the troops had been killed while returning from Timbuktu on Grodet's orders.[27] The charges were spurious, for Grodet had in fact forbidden the expedition from the outset. The mission was destroyed through its own military unpreparedness, but none of these facts prevented the pro-militarists from trying to use the incident to discredit Grodet and the principle of civilian administration.[28]

In late 1894 circumstances surrounding the Monteil expedition began to look ominously similar to what had occurred earlier that year in the Sudan. The Ivory Coast, like the Sudan, was ostensibly controlled by a civilian governor, but since the arrival of Monteil's expedition, the military had taken over the leadership in local affairs. When it became apparent that Monteil's expedition generated a state of war wherever it went, the crisis of authority came into the open. Predictably, Monteil's response to the deteriorating situation was to suggest that an important new offensive would be needed in the south to subdue the Baule, but the mere suggestion of such an operation triggered governmental hostility, for experience in the Sudan amply illustrated that local military initiatives rapidly got out of hand. From the Minister's perspective it was urgent to recall Monteil before he embroiled the French in a new theatre of military operations. Referring to Monteil's engagements with the Abouré in Bonoua and with the Baule above Tiassalé, Chautemps declared to the Chambre on 1 March 1895:

nous guerroyons là assez inutilement dans des contrées d'habitudes troublées par des querelles de chef à chef et que la présence d'une forte colonne a surexcitées davantage. Les renseignements que nous avons reçus . . . du Gouverneur Binger, nous ont confirmés dans cette opinion . . . qu'il y avait lieu de ramener d'urgence l'entreprise à ses proportions normales.[29]

In the exchange that followed the Minister's explanation, lines of controversy in the Chambre were thrown into dramatic relief:

M. le Ministre: La colonne ainsi réduite, n'exigeant plus la présence d'un officier d'un grade aussi élevé, M. le Lieutenant-Colonel Monteil et son état major seront rappelés.

M. Le Herissé: Encore un de lâché!

M. le Ministre: Monsieur Le Herissé, je ne puis accepter ce mot.

M. Le Herissé: Je dis que vous lâchez le Colonel Monteil comme vous avez abandonné beaucoup d'officiers. C'est toujours la même chose.

M. le Président: Monsieur Le Herrissé, n'interrompez pas. Vous avez la tribune pour vous expliquer; vous êtes inscrit.

M. le Ministre: Messieurs, en toute circonstance, je saluerai l'héroisme et le dévouement patriotique du Colonel Monteil . . . [mais] les colonies ne sont pas faites pour les militaires, elles sont faites pour le pays que le gouvernement administre sous le contrôle et la haute direction du Parlement (applaudissements). Voilà la verité exacte. Il ne peut pas y avoir d'autre situation pour un officier, si digne soit-il de notre admiration, et c'est le cas du Colonel Monteil (nouveaux applaudissement).

La Direction des troupes est confiée à M. le Commandant Caudrelier que nous plaçons – contrairement à ce qui a été fait à l'égard du Colonel Monteil – sous l'autorité immédiate du gouverneur de la colonie. (Très bien! très bien! à gauche) . . .[30]

In this round of the controversy the case for civilian control seems to have won the day. The Ivory Coast, at least for the time being, came under the full control of its civilian governor and plans for military reductions proceeded. The debate, however, was not yet closed. Indeed, in the following weeks the militarists were to win what was for them a far more significant prize than the control of initiative in the Ivory Coast.

The new round of controversy began just three days later, on 4 March 1895, in the context of the Chambre debate on the colonial budget. Le Herissé, with the unofficial support of Archinard, made a renewed attack on Grodet's civilian administration in the Sudan. To the list of familiar accusations Le Herissé added a new charge. Grodet, he alleged, was partially responsible for the failure of the Monteil mission because he refused to send troops to Monteil's aid.[31] As part of the initial plan for the Monteil expedition, the Minister intended to deploy troops from the Sudan to move southwards and join Monteil's forces coming up from the coast towards Kong. Grodet argued, however, that Kong was too distant from the base camps of the Sudan to allow for effective manœuvres. Grodet's primary worry was that Commander Dargélos at Bougouni might use the occasion of the Kong expedition to engage the French forces in further unsanctioned offensives, and to keep the military under control, Grodet ordered Dargélos not to take part in the Kong campaign. As a result, while Monteil faced difficulties at first among the Baule and subsequently with Samory's *sofas*, 3,000 French troops who might have come to his assistance remained idle in the Sudan.[32]

Whether or not the Sudan troops could have made an effective contribution was perhaps debatable,[33] but in any case Grodet's inaction provided fuel for his militarist opponents. Le Herissé called for a thorough investigation of Grodet's administration. Strictly speaking, Grodet had done nothing irregular; indeed his order to Dargélos not to move was perfectly consistent with the Ministry's intentions of restraining the military in the West African colonies. Nevertheless, following the uproar over his decision to recall Monteil, Chautemps was unwilling to risk further criticism by coming to Grodet's defence. Within a few weeks the militarists had won their case. Grodet was recalled, and civilian administration in the Sudan came to an end.[34]

The repercussions of the Monteil affair did not stop here, however, for the whole incident revealed a gaping deficiency in the structure of French control over the West African colonies. Up until this point the officers in the Sudan and the merchants and governors on the coast had operated independently of each other. But as explorations from the coast began to meet the Sudanese officers moving southwards in pursuit of Samory, the necessities of administration began to change. The Monteil expedition underscored that a continued lack of co-ordination between colonies could prove costly. To avoid further embarrassments of this kind, and to prevent the possibility of disputes between those colonies under civilian control and those under military leadership, Chautemps created the new office of Governor General of French West Africa. As he explained it in June 1895, the primary function of the new administrative machinery was to co-ordinate policy between the various colonies, particularly in military affairs.[35]

The departure of Monteil's mission in the face of the first Baule revolt clearly crystallized a number of unresolved issues in French colonial circles. In the process, civilian authorities regained leadership in the Ivory Coast, and the Colonels reasserted their control in the Sudan. More importantly, however, by the end of June 1895, both of these territories had been transformed into subordinate colonies within the broader federation of French West Africa. Within just six months of the first Ngban attacks, the Baule faced an entirely new administrative structure on the French side of the colonial equation.

CIVILIAN ADMINISTRATION AND COASTAL COMMERCE

The long-range implications of the changes were not apparent to either the French or the Baule at the time, but a definite shift in the character of French control could be perceived immediately. When Governor Binger returned from his leave, he met with members of the commercial community, and in March 1895 he formed a Conseil d'Administration, designed largely to facilitate continuous consultation between the administration and the commercial interests.[36] The major complaint of the trading houses was that the Monteil expedition interfered with commerce, particularly the trade in guns and powder. In his absence, Binger's replacement, Lemarie, severely restricted the sale of armaments in an effort to reduce possible friction between Monteil's expedition and the local populations. As a result of the prohibition on arms sales Binger estimated that local traders were losing nearly 300,000 f. annually in potential trade, and he could not afford to ignore their concern, because the colony's budget depended upon customs duties levied on this commerce. If commerce stagnated for long, the budget of the colony itself would be in danger of running a deficit. Such considerations may have influenced Binger to recommend Monteil's recall in February 1895, although there is no direct evidence to prove this.[37] In any case, as soon as Binger learned of Monteil's recall he re-opened the trade in guns and powder, even before Monteil himself had received his new orders. In a related move Binger also rejected a proposal from the British authorities, designed to guarantee the suspension of armament sales in both the Ivory Coast and the Gold Coast.[38] Commercial houses were given permission to meet the rising African demand for more arms and munitions.

Both Binger and the commercial community attributed the colony's difficulties to Monteil's expedition. As he reported to the Minister in

April 1895, 'La situation actuelle est loin d'être brillante pour la colonie. Toutes les pertes qu'elle a subies du fait de cette guerre n'ont servi à rien. Notre prestige est plutôt amoindri . . .'.[39] According to Binger the civilian administration would be able to rectify the damage done and re-establish French control: 'J'ai heureusement d'excellents administrateurs qui par leur influence et le prestige qu'ils ont acquis pourront tenir le pays.'[40]

Binger's confidence was not misplaced; the administrators among the Baule were indeed men of exceptional ability. Charles Monteil had proved his capacity to deal with difficult negotiating situations during the attacks on the expedition. With tact and personal calm he averted a violent engagement with Kouadio Okou and his followers when they appeared prepared to attack the post at Toumodi. Albert Nebout came to the Ivory Coast with experience as an explorer in Central Africa. As the sole surviving member of the ill-fated Crampel mission and a veteran of the Dybowski expedition, he was well aware of the hazards of hasty and imprudent dealings with Africans. Marchand placed him in charge of an administrative outpost at Kodiokofikro in September 1894, and from the beginning Nebout's reports demonstrated a keen awareness of the local political situation. He had a well-developed sense of his task as a civil administrator, and he refused to be intimidated by Lieutenant-Colonel P. L. Monteil's pre-emptive style.[41]

Perhaps the most promising of Binger's auxiliaries was a young *commis des affaires indigènes* named Maurice Delafosse. When he arrived in the Ivory Coast, Delafosse was only twenty-three years old, but already he had an exceptional preparation for service in Africa. As a student at the École des Langues Orientales in Paris, Delafosse initially studied Arabic under Professor Houdas, but he soon focused his linguistic abilities on the study of African languages. Even before leaving Paris he wrote an analysis of Dahomeyan languages on the basis of informants he interviewed in France. Interested in the customs and history of the peoples of the Ivory Coast, Delafosse carefully read the travel accounts of the Ivory Coast interior before he arrived in the colony.[42] After a brief period of military service in Algeria, Delafosse came to the Ivory Coast and joined the ranks of the civilian personnel in Baule country. He witnessed the first Baule revolt against Monteil, and like Nebout he developed a strong sense of the potential role of a civilian administrator. Inspired by a profound humanism, Delafosse began to study the Baule language and their customs, and within a few years he achieved a fluency in the language and a familiarity with the customs that has rarely been equalled by any European since his time.[43]

The major task that faced the civilian administrators was to distinguish themselves from the remaining military forces in the eyes of the Baule peoples. This was not a simple matter, for although Monteil and a large portion of the expedition had departed, a significant number of military personnel remained in Baule country, ostensibly to protect the civilian authorities and the Dyula refugees grouped around the administrative posts among the Baule.[44] Already before Monteil departed, some of the civilians succeeded in projecting a different image to the Baule than that of their more assertive compatriots. At the same time that the expedition was experiencing trouble with the Baule, Delafosse succeeded in negotiating the safe passage through Baule-Agba territory of two envoys dispatched by Governor Binger towards Bondoukou. The mission failed because the inhabitants of Bondoukou refused to receive them, but their safe return illustrated that even at this early stage the Baule were willing to accept civilian administrators on terms different from those on which the military were accepted.[45]

In a move to maintain Baule tranquillity after the departure of the bulk of the Monteil forces, the civilians continued their efforts to detach themselves from any association with the soldiers:

Partout où il y a un administrateur, il s'attache à la déconsidération des militaires vis à vis des indigènes disant que les tirailleurs sont des bandes de pillards, que ce sont les militaires qui ont amené la révolte des N'Gbans et qui seuls sont responsables des obligations de portage imposée aux habitants.[46]

The remaining officers resented this, and Commander Pineau complained that civilian-military relations were worse in Baule country than he had witnessed in any other context, adding, somewhat caustically, 'il semble que nous ne défendrons pas ici les mêmes intérêts de la France'.[47] The solution, Pineau thought, was to transform Baule country into a full-fledged military territory, and when he returned to France, he compiled a 'Projet d'occupation du Baoulé', formally proposing the idea.[48] The plan was never pursued, perhaps because of ministerial changes in Paris. Locally the issue smouldered somewhat inconclusively until André Lebon, the new Minister of Colonies, finally recalled the remaining troops in mid-1896.[49] As of September 1896 three civil administrators and a handful of local militia were all that remained of the French presence among the Baule.

The colony's commercial statistics demonstrate a resurgence of trade as the civilian administration took control. In 1894 the total value of recorded imports and exports was 7,193,452 f. This figure dipped in 1895 to 6,706,047 f., largely as a result of the disturbances caused by the Monteil expedition. In 1896, however, the trade bounded to an unprecedented record of 9,339,553 f. The increase reflected an expansion of both imports and exports; but of the two sectors, imports expanded more rapidly than exports, indicating that the consumption of European trade goods rose more sharply than the production of export commodities.[50] This was a signal to the European merchant that the vast untapped consumer market in the interior was beginning to express its demand for European goods.

The items which the Europeans offered in increasing quantities were for the most part the same goods that had been traded on the coast since the 1860s. These included manufactured textiles, primarily Manchester cottons, rifles, trade muskets, gunpowder, alcohol (gin and 'trade' rum), leaf tobacco, salt, iron tools, and a miscellaneous collection of trade curiosities known collectively as *la pacotille* in French, consisting of perfume, mirrors, trade beads, ceremonial umbrellas, and the like.[51] In the coastal and lagoon areas these items were either advanced on credit against a calculated return in palm products (palm kernels or palm oil), or purchased with *manilles* - a special-purpose currency which the European merchants had introduced to facilitate bargaining in palm products during the previous decades.[52]

The introduction of these trade goods was not without deleterious effects. As one might expect, while the military officers remained, they objected strenuously to the resumption of the trade in guns and powder, arguing that it would make the country ungovernable. The merchants were not deterred by these protestations, and after 1895 the government adopted an attitude of benign indifference to the armaments trade, realizing perhaps that effective restrictions would only alienate the commerce it was trying to attract and in case would prove too difficult to enforce. The trade in spirits also had undesirable effects. As one observer recorded:

Les indigènes ne s'abonnent que trop à l'alcool, et c'est à tel point que le décor de la forêt tropical est souvent gâté pour l'Européen remontant les fleuves, par la vue de bouteilles de gin carrées, flottant vides au fil de l'eau.[53]

Aside from its aesthetic impact on the scenic beauty of the tropical forest, alcoholism took its toll on the African populations, particularly among the chiefs for whom the consumption of European gin became an attribute, indeed almost a necessity, of office. Though some of its more unseemly aspects were perhaps regrettable, Europeans had little difficulty in justifying the trade: 'Pour permettre aux blancs de s'implanter dans de tels pays, d'y commercer, il faut évidemment créer à l'indigène des besoins nouveaux. L'alcool est là un auxiliaire énergique mais sûr.'[54]

Since the 1840s coastal populations had produced palm oil and kernels in exchange for these European goods, but by the 1890s some important structural changes were taking place in the coastal commerce. Two trends are apparent in retrospect. First, the declining price of palm products on European markets led some Africans to increase their production in order to maintain their income. Secondly, in addition to the rising output of those engaged in the trade of palm products, during the 1890s the colony's trade as a whole experienced a commodity shift towards the export of wild rubber and tropical timber, in response to increased European demand for these items. It is useful to outline briefly some of the features of these changes, because both trends implied new kinds of economic possibilities for the Baule in the interior.

From 1886 onwards the price for palm oil dropped in European commodity markets. Between 1886 and 1890 its price averaged only £20 per ton, a figure which represented a decline of 50 per cent from the price paid twenty-five years earlier. The prices of some of the European manufactures decreased as well, but not sharply enough to offset the decline in the world price of palm products. As a result, the barter terms of trade of the primary producer declined.[55] This was generally true for palm oil producers throughout West Africa, but responses to the situation differed from area to area depending upon local circumstances. In the Ivory Coast production initially decreased in the mid-1880s,[56] but output increased significantly from 1890 to 1892 as producers struggled to maintain their income in the face of the declining barter terms of trade and the new customs duties. The volume of exported palm oil rose from 1,885 tons in 1890 to 4,671 tons in 1892, and palm kernel exports increased from 162 tons to 731 tons over the same period.[57]

Production during this period remained largely in the hands of the Adioukrou, the Ébrié, and the Abouré, the ethnic groups traditionally engaged in this activity.[58] The increased volume of exports was not due to any technical innovations in the collection or preparation of the palm produce, but rather to an increase in labour input. No doubt part of the increase in the labour supply came from groups such as the Alladian or the Brignan who, having been deprived by the Europeans of their former role as exclusive middlemen, turned instead to palm oil production to maintain their incomes. The most important source of new labour, however, came from captives purchased by the coastal populations from the Baule and other groups to the interior.[59] This commerce with the interior for slaves was not new, but the decline in the price of palm products from 1886 onwards gave it renewed importance, for it was only through increasing his production that a coastal chief could maintain his income. In the absence of technical improvements the only way to increase production was to obtain more producers as dependants.

Lieutenant Armand reported that slaves arrived in the Tiassalé area either as the result of initiatives by individual merchants who purchased them in the interior and brought them directly southwards or as a result of a more gradual process of displacement through repeated sales from village to village. Around Tiassalé they were quite numerous, and in some instances constituted entire villages. The captives involved were evidently not Baule, but came instead from groups further north. In Tiassalé Armand encountered one individual who had been enslaved during a war with Ahmadou, presumably near the Niger River, and along the coastal lagoons Armand reported that one frequently met slaves of Bambara origin.[60] Clearly, the sustained decline of European prices for palm produce affected more than just the coastal peoples.[61]

Faced with a discouraging return on their labour for palm products, not all African producers tried to increase their output in this sector. In some areas emphasis shifted towards other exports which were more profitable. On the Gold Coast these included wild rubber, timber, and cocoa.[62] Interest in the first two commodities spread westwards from the Gold Coast into the Ivory Coast in the 1890s as a result of several concomitant developments. In the case of rubber, the underlying reason for its expanded trade derived from the rising prices Europeans were prepared to pay for it. Unlike palm products European prices for wild rubber rose constantly throughout the 1890s. A kilogram was worth 2.60 f. in 1890, but by 1900 it fetched 6.10 or even 6.50 f.[63] The enthusiasm for rubber in Ghana led to careless tapping practices which killed the vines, and as a rubber 'boom' progressed, traders were obliged to go further and further inland to locate producing vines and trees. Some moved westwards in search of the latex, and when the Anglo-Ashanti war of 1896 interrupted the collection of rubber in the Ashanti forest, production in the Ivory Coast became increasingly important.

Tropical timber also emerged as important among the Ivory Coast's exports during the 1890s for analogous reasons. Because of their bulk, mahogany and other tropical woods could only be exported profitably from areas close to the coast or accessible to water transport. The coastal areas were rapidly denuded of their timber in western Ghana, and attention shifted to the Ivory Coast lagoons during the 1890s, particularly after 1895 when a period of drought in southern Ghana rendered the Ankobra river useless for the transport of logs from the interior to the coast.[64] By 1896 the value of tropical woods exported from the Ivory Coast was second only to the value of the palm products, accounting for over 20 per cent of the total value of the colony's exports. Third on the list, behind palm products and timber, was wild rubber. Between 1896 and 1900 the commodity shift that began earlier in the decade became even more dramatic. The value of wild rubber exports rose tenfold in just five years from 440,190 f. in 1896 to 4,734,014 f. in 1900. Rubber became the Ivory Coast's largest export, and its earnings in 1900 were greater than the value of all the other exports combined.[65]

The shift towards different export commodities occurred in the Ivory Coast as new groups were drawn into the network of export production. The mode of production of those engaged in palm oil exports remained unaltered; it had not been transformed or abandoned, it was simply by-passed. Those who went out to collect wild rubber were not the same people who would otherwise have been engaged in palm oil production. Similarly the exportation of timber did not concern the traditional palm oil producers. In short, while the economy as a whole had demonstrated its capacity to adapt to the changing demands of the world market, individual producers, and indeed entire ethnic groups, were perhaps less flexible than the highly variable export figures would suggest at first glance. Changes in these figures reflected an extension of the circle of exchange, but not necessarily a modification of productive capacities on the part of those already committed to export production.

Groups who had not previously been engaged in the production of primary products for European markets became integrated into the export network as the result of the initiatives of a small class of English-speaking African entrepreneurs. Known locally as 'Nsoko' or 'les Apollonien' or more derisively as 'les Esquires',[66] these African traders originated from Nzima and Fanti communities in the eastern Ivory Coast and western portions of the Gold Coast. With capital which they had accumulated during the eighteenth century in trade along the Gold Coast, these traders extended their influence over petty commerce on the Ivory Coast as the palm oil production began in earnest during the early years of the nineteenth century.[67] In 1811 a small group of

Apollonien are reputed to have established themselves at Grand Bassam, and when the French installed their outpost at Grand Bassam in 1842, they concluded one of the necessary treaties with 'Le Roi Peter', chief of the Apollonien community.[68] Disputes frequently arose between the Apollonien and the palm oil producers over control of the trade. Although the Apollonien were never capable of establishing a monopoly over the export commerce, they began to dominate the import trade. Their ability to speak English made them a valuable asset to trading chiefs along the coast who employed them as intermediaries with the offshore English cargo vessels. By the 1880s small colonies of Apollonien were installed at every major trading point along the coast, where they assisted local chiefs in their trading ventures.

A number of them had been sufficiently successful to accumulate enough capital to finance their own trading expeditions to the interior, and by the time the French annexed the area as a colony, the Apollonien had completely displaced the 'Bambara' traders, previously reputed to be the primary intermediaries between the coast and the inland peoples.[69] Prevented from dominating the export commerce in palm produce, these entrepreneurs focused their attention instead upon profits to be gained from distributing European imports to various groups along the lagoons and in the interior. Initially, the Apollonien were paid in gold for these imported goods,[70] but when Europeans began to express an interest in rubber and tropical timber, these traders were in an ideal position to mobilize their traditional commercial partners in the interior to produce these new commodities for export. This they did, beginning in the early 1890s, and within a decade their initiatives culminated in a dramatic transformation of the colony's export structure.

French attitudes towards the Apollonien varied as their relations with them evolved. Arthur Verdier was hostile towards them as his commercial competitors, but he employed several as agents.[71] The French were willing to use them as potential allies against hostile inhabitants when they installed their customs posts in the coastal trading towns, but as the extent of Apollonien commercial influence in the interior became evident, the French began to resent their presence. There were two reasons for this. In the first place, the administration began to recognize that so long as they remained auton-omous, the Apollonien were potential obstacles to the expansion of French commerce in the interior. Their knowledge of the country, their familiarity with its languages, and their willingness to carry on trade with a very low overhead, meant that even with much less capital at their disposal, these indigenous traders could effectively undersell European brokers for a long time to come. In order to provide a more open field for French merchants, the administration began to consider that one of its tasks was to break the commercial power of what one observer referred to, significantly, as 'ces juifs de la côte'.[72]

The second reason for official antagonism towards this African entrepreneurial class was more explicitly political. The Apollonien, and especially the more prominent 'Esquires' among them, spoke English, traded exclusively with English ships, transacted their business in English pounds and shillings, and maintained intimate contact with their relations in the neighbouring Gold Coast. Considering their dominant role, the Ivory Coast appeared to be French only on paper. One French visitor to the colony openly conceded: 'On peut avouer que notre colonie nouvelle est tout au moins aussi anglaise que française, si elle ne l'est même pas davantage.'[73] In the context of heightened imperial rivalry during the 1890s this was an alarming situation, and French officials ceased to be amused by 'les indigènes . . . qui baragouinent la langue de Shakespeare'.[74] The alleged role of English-speaking rubber merchants from the Gold Coast in the Assikasso revolt of 1898 strengthened French feelings of Anglophobia, and the Apollonien came to be regarded as potentially subversive.[75] In 1898 the administration implemented measures expressly designed to eliminate this entrepreneurial class by making it increasingly difficult for it to do business in the colony.

French measures included placing a heavy tax on exported timber and a similar tax on all rubber exports destined for England. Those Apollonien who refused to pay these taxes were dealt with by a system of summary justice, while those who paid them soon found themselves operating in uncompetitive conditions. The autonomy of this African trader class diminished immediately on the coast, particularly when the English merchants Swanzy Ltd., with which many of the Apollonien conducted their business, sold its holdings to the Compagnie Française de l'Afrique Occidentale (CFAO) in 1898. The Apollonien continued to retain a measure of influence in the interior, and the English still controlled the shipping lines to Europe, but on the coast itself the administration did its best to carve out a new niche for French import–export firms.[76] In this outpost of the colonial empire, French commerce followed the flag. It was only after the administration crippled their competitors that French commercial interests began to take hold.

TRADE, PRODUCTION AND SOCIAL CHANGE AMONG THE BAULE, 1895-1898

Monteil's retreat opened an era of unprecedented prosperity for the Baule peoples. The relaxation of restrictions on trade in guns and powder coupled with the mounting demand for captive labour in the palm producing areas on the coast encouraged an impressive expansion of Baule commerce. As in the Sudan, one of the major results of French military intervention had been to stimulate a local commerce in captive slaves, and in the years between 1895 and 1898 the Baule peoples exploited their privileged position as primary purveyors of armaments to Samory to turn this trade to their best advantage.

Samory became increasingly dependent on the Baule for armaments after he began to move eastwards into the northern Ivory Coast before the advancing French forces from the Sudan. His most stable source of munitions had traditionally been Freetown, but as a result of Commander Briquelot's capture of Erimakono in 1893, Samory's supplies were interrupted, and by September 1893 British officials in Freetown agreed to outlaw further sale of munitions to Samory's men.[77] Similarly, in 1894 Monrovia ceased to provide a source of supplies.[78] King Prempeh I of Ashanti seemed willing to furnish some arms to Samory and he proposed an alliance to Samory in 1895, but Samory never agreed to the alliance because he was unwilling to antagonize the British, who were preparing to invade Ashanti at the time.[79] From mid-1894 Samory depended almost entirely upon Baule commerce to supply his needed armaments, and he was forced to accept the conditions of exchange and the terms of trade that they imposed.

Previously, Samory had been accustomed to obtaining his arms directly through agents acting on his behalf at Freetown or Monrovia, but with the Baule the situation was not the same.[80] Samory could purchase his supplies from them on the northern fringe of their territory, but his agents were not allowed direct access to southern sources of supply.[81] The Baule bought the guns and powder at Tiassalé and transported them northwards to Gbuèkékro or Katiakofikro. There they met Samory's agents and conducted their transactions.

The munitions consisted for the most part of Belgian-made trade muskets and barrels of powder. Comparatively few rapid-fire, breech-loading rifles entered through Baule territory. Accurate figures on the volume of the trade are not available, but estimates in August 1895 suggest that 1,300 barrels of powder and several hundred muskets transited Tiassalé's three European trading houses every month. Two of these trading establishments, Swanzy and Rider & Son, were English; the third was French, managed by an agent of Arthur Verdier; and a fourth was in the process of setting up operations in August 1895. The volume of commerce in the hands of the Apollonien was not calculated at the time, but it may well have exceeded that of the European firms. Some care was taken to conceal the trade by transporting the goods over devious routes and packing the powder in gin cases, so it seems likely that the total amount of munitions entering the area exceeded the amount which European firms declared for customs purposes on the coast.[82]

The administration was not alarmed about the expansion of commerce in munitions. Indeed, they looked upon the trade with a certain measure of satisfaction, since it added to the colony's revenues and stimulated French trading houses to extend their operations at least as far inland as Tiassalé.[83] French commerce in southern Baule territory was so dominated by the armament trade that one inspector warned of serious consequences if restrictions were ever to be re-imposed:

si malheureusement une nouvelle mesure d'interdiction du commerce des armes et de la poudre survenait, ce serait la stagnation complète des affaires et nous priverions la Métropole d'un débouché possible.[84]

Samory was accustomed to paying for his armament supplies with gold, ivory, cattle, or wild rubber, but in this respect as well, his relations with the Baule differed from his previous experience. Samory lost control over the gold producing areas of the Sudan in 1893 as he began to move eastwards, and his gold reserves were depleted when he traded with the Baule. Furthermore, the Baule were unlikely to be impressed with whatever gold he had to offer, since they produced it themselves. Similarly, an epidemic reduced Samory's livestock herds in 1892, and those that remained were less resistant to trypanosomiasis than the breeds which the Baule already possessed, which made them relatively less attractive as objects of exchange against Baule supplies in munitions. There is some evidence that the Baule accepted ivory and rubber in exchange for arms, but as the rubber trade had not yet penetrated Baule country and as they already obtained most of their ivory from their Gouro neighbours to the west, these items did not interest them to a great extent.[85]

Prior to Samory's arrival the Baule conducted a lucrative trade for slaves with a Hausa merchant-warrior named Mory Touré at the town of Marabadiassa on the Bandama river, and they were well aware of the profits to be obtained by purchasing captives in the north and reselling them in the south where the demand for labour in palm producing areas was high. Mory Touré also recognized the value of this commerce, and according to some sources he personally convinced Samory that the best way to deal with the Baule was to expand this trade.[86] Whether or not Mory Touré played a decisive role in determining the terms of trade remains obscure, but it is clear that from 1894 Samory began to offer slaves to the Baule on a massive scale. He had not introduced the trade to the area, but from 1893 to 1898, while he was in the north, the trade in slaves with the Baule took on unprecedented proportions.

Reliable figures on the volume of slave imports and the price of sale and resale are even more elusive than statistics on the arms trade. Nevertheless the information available suggests that tens of thousands of people may have been reduced to slavery during this period, as entire ethnic groups were rounded up and dispatched for sale to the south. Not all the slaves went to the Baule. Some were sold to the Gouro in the west, and still others went to various Anyi groups in the east, but because of their strategic position, the Baule received the greatest portion of the trade. Profit margins were at all times attractive. At the slave market in Katiakofikro a Baule could expect to pay the equivalent of 60 f. for a slave under normal circumstances, and in the forest area the same slave would sell for 150 f. For a time in 1895 the terms of trade were even more favourable for the Baule. Monteil's troops had not inflicted many losses on Samory's forces, but before leaving the area in March 1895 Monteil burned Samory's store houses at Sokola-Dioulassou, and at the end of the dry season that year, Samory was forced to exchange slaves for chickens, goats, and even yams or manioc just in order to stave off famine within his ranks.[87]

Never before had slaves been so cheap. If in previous years slaves were primarily regarded as the prerogative of important chiefs, during the period from 1894 to 1898, the influx of captives was so great that virtually every Baule household could expect to obtain several slaves. Concentrations of slaves among the northern Baule reached staggering proportions. In one instance a village of 200 or 300 people was alleged to contain only one household (awlô bô) of Baule freemen; all the other inhabitants were reputed to be captives.[88] Although this was perhaps an extreme case, other sources suggested that in the north the number of captives perhaps exceeded the number of Baule freemen.[89] Some of these captives remained in the north,[90] but many were destined to be sold or exchanged with southern Baule villages in return for guns, powder, or other European goods. The Baule economy experienced the biggest trading boom in its history, and in the process the north regained the relative economic importance which it had lost over the years since the discovery of gold at Kokumbo and the development of the coastal palm oil trade in the 1840s.

Despite this remarkable upsurge in the slave and munitions trade on the northern and southern borders of Baule territory, it would be a mistake to assume that Baule prosperity during the period from 1895 to 1898 derived uniquely or even primarily from profit margins on this transiting commerce. If this had been the case, one would expect that a specialized merchant class might have emerged during this period – a recognizable group of Baule entrepreneurs whose existence depended uniquely upon their capacity to buy goods cheaply in one area and sell them dearly in another. But such a class did not appear among the Baule. Long-distance commerce remained the prerogative of chiefs, and the characteristic mechanism of transaction was not the open market of generalized exchange, but rather the particularistic relationship between established trading clients. In short, despite the expansion in the scale of Baule commerce, the structure of exchange remained largely as it was during the pre-colonial period. As in an earlier age, trade was not so much the origin of wealth as an index of wealth.

The normal trading venture took the familiar form of a periodic expedition to Tiassalé, organized by an individual Baule who had amassed enough surplus resources to offer in exchange for the goods he desired.

Le tempérament personnel et indépendant des Baoulé empêche la formation de grosses caravanes . . . Chaque individu va vers Tiassalé, accompagné de sa famille et de ses captifs, par petites troupes; ils partent de tous les points du Baoulé . . .[91]

The object of these expeditions was to obtain provisions on the best possible terms. In this respect the intention was not commercial gain in the conventional sense. The Baule concerned did not buy goods in the south primarily with an eye to the profit margin he could realize by reselling these same goods in the north. Instead, the supplies he obtained, with the possible exception of some armaments, were destined primarily for use or consumption in his own household. Even in the case of munitions, most of the guns purchased at Tiassalé remained in Baule hands, and large amounts of powder were consumed locally to mark the importance of festive occasions.[92] Only a fraction of the armaments sold at Tiassalé found their way to Samory, especially after he was compelled by circumstance to purchase foodstuffs with his captives.[93] Similarly, only a small portion of the slaves obtained in the north were sold eventually to neighbouring ethnic groups in the south; most were dispersed throughout Baule territory and integrated as supplementary sources of labour into the Baule households.

It was not the sale of slaves, but rather the labour of slaves that provided the fundamental basis of Baule prosperity. The major source of Baule wealth came from marketing an increased output of traditional commodities which were produced by their newly acquired labour supply. Slaves contributed to Baule productivity in a number of ways. Some were put to work for their master's benefit on the various goldfields at Kporéssou and Kokumbo among the Faafoué-Baule, Zaakro among the Nzipri, Sikanzué among the Nanafoué, Kossou among the Akoué, and Kami among the Yaouré.[94] Others assisted in the production of woven cloth for sale within Baule country or for export. Slaves contributed either by planting, tending, and harvesting the raw cotton or by spinning, dyeing, and weaving it into the finished cloth. In this latter industry, particularly in the final stages of preparation, the Baule dominated production, but they were able to devote more time exclusively to textile production precisely because the captive labour began to produce the necessary subsistence crops for the consumption of the household as a whole. Similarly, the fabrication of gold jewellery by specialized artisans expanded as more gold became available from the increased productivity of Baule goldfields, and more labour time could be devoted uniquely to this activity.

Near Kokumbo labour specialization developed to the point where entire villages devoted themselves primarily to the production of foodstuffs for sale to the mine workers, and in some cases yams were sold for gold dust.[95] The population of Kokumbo in 1896 was reported to have reached 1500 or 1800 people, most of whom were engaged in the multiple tasks of mining itself.[96] Many of those who worked in Kokumbo came from other areas of Baule country during the dry season, and the seasonal character of their activity meant that they would not have planted crops in the area to supply their own needs. Under these circumstances it is understandable how the local trade in foodstuffs developed, for the miners, by purchasing food with gold dust, were in effect prepared to pay enormously inflated prices for commodities which were formerly only produced within the household for subsistence needs. The inflated prices stimulated agriculatural output and the distinction dissolved between subsistence and market production as the entire Baule economy became increasingly monetarized. In the Kokumbo area at least, a Baule household could embark on agricultural production with the reasonable expectation of acquiring gold dust in return for their labour investment. To a limited extent the same process occurred in the areas around the French administrative posts, especially between 1895 and September 1896 when each centre still contained a garrison of Senegalese troops who were prepared to pay for provisions. In each case, it was the labour of the newly acquired slaves that provided the basis for profits derived from agricultural production.

In addition to gold mining, cloth manufacture, and agricultural production, slaves contributed to Baule prosperity in a number of other minor pursuits. Slaves assisted in the production of palm wine and tobacco,[97] and these commodities could be marketed or exchanged for profit locally. Captives sometimes hunted for their masters, and the products of the hunt could be distributed advantageously by the Baule master. By 1898 the Apollonien traders began to purchase wild rubber in Tiassalé, and it is probable that the slaves were among those most heavily employed in the collection of this new export commodity.[98] In terms of commerce itself, trusted slaves were sometimes dispatched to Tiassalé to buy provisions for their masters, and when the Baule conducted these expeditions themselves the slaves carried the supplies as porters. In all of these minor sectors of the Baule economy, as well as in the major realms of gold, cloth, and agricultural production, the only significant restraint on growth had been the relative scarcity of labour, not of land. The new abundance of slaves from Samory lifted the traditional barrier to production, and as a result the years from 1894 to 1898 constituted a period of unparalleled expansion within all sectors of the Baule economy.

The influx of a large number of slaves within a relatively short time had important repercussions on Baule social structure as well. As in the pre-colonial period, the Baule sought to incorporate their new slaves as thoroughly as possible into their own kinship structures through marriage alliances and fictive filiation. The increased number of slaves made it possible, and indeed preferable, for freeborn Baule to conclude marriages with slaves, and the Baule began to do this on a massive scale.

The reasons for preferring slave marriages were inherent in the labour needs of the Baule household and the logic of Baule kinship practice. Traditionally one of the main concerns of a Baule household head was to maintain and if possible expand the number of dependent kin in his own *awlô bô*. Only in this way could he be assured of increasing the manpower at his disposal.[99] To avoid losing control over his own children and to retain his accumulated wealth within the household from one generation to the next, a freeborn Baule male in pre-colonial times could conclude an *atonvle* marriage alliance. From this type of marriage he would obtain exclusive authority over his children and they in turn could inherit from him.[100] In practice this form of marriage alliance was the preserve of a privileged few, for the inordinately high bride-price required for an *atonvle* marriage placed it beyond the means of most freeborn Baule men. Nevertheless, for those who could afford it, there were long-term economic advantages to be derived from concluding these marriages, despite the exorbitant initial expense of the bride-price itself. Furthermore, by linking prominent territorial chiefs in alliance with one another this institution enhanced the local influence of each chief involved and served as a mechanism of political unification with Baule society as a whole.

At first glance one might expect that the period of Baule prosperity beginning in 1894 would have led to an expansion of *atonvle* marriages, because greater numbers of Baule men could afford the required bride-price. In reality, however, the intrusion of a large quantity of slave women dealt a fatal blow to this prestigious form of political marriage alliance. The reason for this was simple. Structurally the *atonvle* marriage and slave marriage were almost identical from the perspective of the freeborn Baule man. Marriage between a Baule and a slave woman afforded virtually all the advantages to be acquired from the traditional *atonvle* marriage alliance at only a fraction of the cost. Instead of spending an enormous sum in an inflated bride-price to obtain exclusive rights over their children, Baule chiefs began to employ the same capital to purchase several female slaves. The children which these slave wives bore for their masters would necessarily be subject to these men's control, for by definition the woman slave had no kin relations to contest their authority.

In short, slave marriage provided nearly all the advantages to be derived from an *atonvle* marriage, but unlike the *atonvle* arrangement, it required only a minimal investment. Important chiefs turned increasingly to this form of marriage, and within a relatively short period the traditional *atonvle* alliance had been virtually eclipsed.[101]

In addition to displacing *atonvle* marriage among the well-to-do Baule, unions with slave women became so widely practised that the entire structure of marriage exchange within Baule society began to acquire a new shape. Traditionally, the household was an exogamous unit. Men could not marry women within it without committing incest, and as a result they were obliged to choose their wives from other groups usually outside their own village of origin. Furthermore, men were forbidden to marry women in groups from which any other of their siblings had already married. These marriage prohibitions produced an extremely diffuse exchange system in Baule society as a whole. In defining parallel marriage as incestuous, Baule marriage rules assured that no new marriage would be allowed to replicate an alliance which already existed by virtue of an earlier marriage between members of two given households. By favouring the maximum spread of marriage alliances in a great number of different directions, the traditional system as a whole was perhaps best characterized as a highly extroverted form of generalized marriage exchange. After 1894 this system changed radically. Marriages between Baule men and slave women transformed the previously extroverted pattern of Baule exchange into a highly introverted system based essentially on household endogamy. Baule men no longer needed to search far and wide for wives outside their own villages. Without contravening incest taboos they could engage in a form of quasi-endogamy by marrying women within their own household. Similarly, Baule women no longer needed to be given in marriage to Baule men from neighbouring villages, for they too could marry male slaves from within the household. Slave marriages provided the Baule household with a legitimate means of reproducing itself demographically without recourse to the exchange of marriageable members with outside groups. To the extent that slave ownership became a widespread phenomenon after 1894, household endogamy became a generalized practice. Whenever possible a household head would prefer this form of marriage as part of a strategy to obtain the maximum control over an enlarged number of dependants.

Politically, the transformations of Baule marriage patterns implied two related changes in the effective structure of power throughout Baule country. Household endogamy simultaneously strengthened the individual residential group as a political unit and decreased the extent of inter-group marriage exchange. The overall political effect was to increase local political autonomy and diminish the prospects for inter-group alliance. In the absence of centralized state structures, marriage alliances constituted the major means of achieving a measure of supra-village political unity, but the rise in household endogamy as a function of Baule slave marriages after 1894 effectively stunted the prospects for developing extended inter-regional or even inter-village alliances.

At the time the need for inter-group alliances may not have appeared particularly urgent to the Baule, especially since the French withdrew their military forces, but in later years the state of political fragmentation resulting from the decline of inter-group marriage placed the

Baule at a distinct disadvantage in their attempts to resist further French penetration. Inter-group marriages formerly helped to mitigate the danger of open armed conflict between Baule groups, but as these alliances declined and the strength of individual groups increased, there remained few mechanisms that could function effectively to prevent petty disputes from developing into armed confrontation between different Baule groups. We have no way of assessing accurately whether the number of disputes between Baule groups over questions of debt collection, trade rivalries and the like actually increased during this period, but it is clear that disputes of this kind were potentially far more divisive to the fabric of Baule society after 1894. The individual group's capacity for waging war increased considerably with the introduction of new manpower and weapons, and at the same time the social institutions which had traditionally served to avert armed confrontation were no longer being created. In effect, the transformation of Baule marriage patterns and the consequent political fragmentation provided the French with the potential elements for pursuing a classic policy of divide and rule.

Although the French never fully realized the fundamental reasons for Baule internal divisiveness, they were quick to recognize its value for their own purposes. Intelligence reports written at the time of the Monteil mission revealed numerous armed conflicts between rival Baule groups. In some cases particular groups invited the French to join them as allies in defeating potential rivals. The Faafoué-Baule of Kokumbo promised the French 400-500 porters if the French would help them conclude their war with the Saafoué-Baule.[102] In other cases, individual Baule groups offered themselves as allies to the French, should the French want to conduct punitive expeditions against their traditional enemies. The Nzipri-Baule, for example, indicated their willingness to join the French in an attack on the Agba-Baule, should the French wish to launch such an offensive.[103] Beyond the immediate tactical advantages to be obtained from these kinds of alliances Nebout suggested that the French should consider exploiting internal Baule antagonisms as a matter of policy in order to secure the loyalty of specific groups: 'il serait bon peut-être de profiter des haines qui existent entre certaines peuplades; les unes compromises nous resteraient sûrement fidèles.'[104]

Despite its apparent advantages this policy proved difficult to pursue after 1895 for the Monteil expedition and the subsequent pattern of civilian administration significantly altered the social geography of Baule country. The French had trouble in establishing continuous relations with Baule chiefs because the engagements between Monteil and the Baule inspired many of the Baule chiefs to move their villages away from the major route of French penetration.[105] The result was that several formerly prosperous villages became virtual ghost towns. The French tried to encourage the Baule to reoccupy their abandoned villages, but the Baule proved reluctant for the most part to do so, fearing renewed French demands for porters and provisions.

In the absence of continuous contact with the Baule population, the French depended more and more heavily upon the communities of Dyula refugees who had fled the Djimini area in the wake of the Monteil retreat. These refugees followed the French forces southwards through Baule country, and those who avoided being captured as slaves by the Baule huddled in clusters around the French outposts establishing enclave communities in a fundamentally hostile Baule environment. By 1897 the Dyula population at Toumodi outnumbered the Baule population by two to one.[106] At Kodiokofikro where the Baule population was estimated to be only 200 inhabitants, the Dyula population reached an estimated figure of 5,000.[107] For the first time, Dyula established themselves at Tiassalé, and when Akafou proved reluctant to reoccupy his village of Ouossou along the Tiassalé–Toumodi route, the French considered transforming it into an entirely Dyula town simply by installing a sizeable Dyula community in place of the absent Baule.[108]

From 1895 to 1898 the French and the Dyula developed a mutually supportive symbiotic relationship to the virtual exclusion of the surrounding Baule. The French depended upon the resident Dyula for porters, provisions, and manpower for construction tasks, etc., and the Dyula enjoyed the security afforded by French protection. Households of Dyula agriculturalists, artisans, and traders began to prosper under the aegis of French control, and by 1897 the Dyula had virtually replaced the Apollonien merchants north of Tiassalé. The emerging pattern of quasi-urban centres dominated by Dyula populations and linked in sustained communication by Dyula merchants began to approximate the early visions of Marchand.[109]

By favouring the creation of Dyula settlements in close association with the administrative centres, the French effectively imported their initial collaborators into Baule country. For a time this looked like an ideal solution for all parties concerned. In exchange for security the Dyula were willing to provide the services the French required; the French were pleased to obtain Dyula porters and employ Dyula labourers; and the Baule seemed content to leave both communities alone, devoting themselves instead to expanding their own village production and regional trade. It is important to note, however, that the entire arrangement was predicated upon a strangely distant relationship between the French and the Baule, a relationship which one might legitimately call a 'working misunderstanding'. Neither the French nor the Baule understood what the other intended, but for the time being that did not seem to matter. The Dyula as a group served to mediate the impact of colonial rule, allowing the French to obtain what they wished without requiring them to extract it from the local population. Thus, although the French did not in any meaningful sense control the Baule peoples, nevertheless with Dyula help they succeeded in erecting at least the framework of colonial administration in the midst of Baule territory.

If the Dyula presence facilitated French administration in the immediate context of the post-Monteil retreat, in the long-term the development of Dyula enclaves within Baule territory introduced important constraints on the evolution of French-Baule relations. The Baule, it will be recalled, considered the Dyula to be slaves, or at least potential slaves. The close relationship between the Dyula populations and the French administration led the Baule to associate any kind of work for the Whites as a form of labour appropriate only for slaves. The Dyula and not the Baule were the first to respond to French demands for wage labourers; and once they did so, the Baule came to regard employment for wages as an index of slave status.[110] Indeed, the Baule generally sought to distance themselves from the areas of European concentration (known locally as *blôfue-klo*, or 'white men's villages'), and similarly they avoided the areas which became known as *dyula-klo*, or Dyula villages, situated in close proximity to the French installations. As one present-day anthropologist has observed about this period: '. . . les milieux non-traditionnels qui s'édifiaient autour des postes militaires ou des postes d'administration constituèrent pendant longtemps des pôles de répulsion.'[111]

Given this pattern of development, it is perhaps not surprising that after 1895 French assessments of the Baule began to change radically. In 1893 Marchand characterized the Baule as '. . . relativement douces, et hospitalières . . .',[112] but the Monteil expedition proved that this was not the case when the French interfered internally with Baule slave populations. Similarly, before 1895 the Baule had a reputation in French circles of being extremely industrious, capable of producing large amounts of gold and valuable trade cloth.[113] This production, far from declining, actually expanded from 1895 to 1898, but because the Baule tended increasingly to avoid European centres, and because they appeared to disdain opportunities for wage employment, the French began to formulate a markedly unsympathetic image of the Baule peoples, assigning them a measure of stupidity, lethargy and moral degeneration which had been totally absent from their earlier appreciations. Albert Nebout, for example, a capable administrator and usually a sympathetic observer, wrote of the Baule character in 1900:

Les qualités morales leur font entièrement défaut: ils n'ont ni dignité, ni courage, ni énergie; nous ne parlerons pas de la vertu . . .
Ils n'ont aucune aptitude particulière et sont médiocres en tout; pour le commerce, les cultures, les travaux manuels, etc., ils ont à peu près perdu les instincts primitifs des peuples plus sauvages.[114]

Perhaps not unexpectedly, the Baule suffered even greater abuse when they were compared in the eyes of the French to the Dyula:

Dans le Baoulé sont en présence deux populations: la population indigène fétichiste, sauvage, guerrière, pillarde et insolente, et les dioulas, ces commerçants musulmans de Kong, du Djimini, du Diammala . . . d'une civilisation bien supérieure.[115]

While much of this attitude can be traced directly to the bitterness which the French felt towards the Baule after their humiliating defeat in 1895, popular pseudo-scientific theories of racial hierarchy contributed to this perspective as well. The Baule, according to this point of view were taken to represent one of the most 'primitive' and consequently least 'intelligent' peoples in all of West Africa.

On ne saurait dire que tous les Baoulé sont stupides, mais ils sont en général peu intelligents, bien inférieurs aux familles Mandé-Dioula, aux Zemma de la Côte de l'Or, aux Haoussas, et à tant d'autres familles du Sénégal et du Soudan.[116]

It is instructive to examine the reasoning behind such statements, for although they have no basis in fact, they nevertheless reveal important myths which conditioned French perceptions and guided official policy towards the Baule throughout the subsequent colonial period. The central assumption was that Africans could be considered 'civilized' only to the degree that they had experienced some measure of domination by an external 'white' culture. The Zemma or Apollonien communities of the Gold Coast were judged to be partially 'civilized' because of their centuries of contact with white traders and their evident commercial experience. Sudanese populations, the Dyula, and the Hausa may not have had extensive contact with Europeans on the coast, but their state of civilization was attributed to 'contact' with another, historically more remote, 'white' influence – Muslim North

Africa. Islam, while still considered to be inferior to Christianity, was thought to represent a superior form of spiritual development to that found among non-Muslim groups in Africa, and some observers described Dyula traits specifically with reference to Muslim culture. Thus, after a trip through Baule country in 1896, Dr Lasnet observed:

les Dioula sont infiniment supérieurs aux Agnis [Baule], la civilisation musulmane les a façonnés, ils sont industrieux, très commerçants, durs à la fatigue, [et], une qualité très rare chez les noirs, très travailleurs . . . de la population agni nous n'avons rien de semblable à espérer.[117]

Dr Lasnet's comparison between Muslim and non-Muslim populations is in itself indicative of a broader shift in attitude as the civilian administrators took progressive control from military commanders. Traditionally, French officers in the Sudan were convinced that Muslim leaders with their jihad-like military movements were the single biggest obstacle to French control in West Africa, and they were not above making alliances with subordinate animist populations to defeat the Muslim communities. The tasks of administration, however, differed from those of military conquest, and when Chautemps appointed Jean-Baptiste Chaudié as the first Governor General, he advised him to work through the Muslim populations, whom he regarded as more enlightened and advanced than the non-Muslim Africans.[118] In the era of civilian administration Muslims were to become France's strongest allies in West Africa.

As Dr Lasnet's statement suggests, however, the reasons for Dyula superiority as far as the French were concerned were only partially related to spiritual matters. In reality, the most reliable index of a group's degree of 'civilization' was to be found in its willingness to integrate itself within the colonial economic structures either by trading or consuming European manufactured goods or by responding to European demands for agricultural commodities, porters, and wage labourers. It was this willingness that the Dyula and the Hausa of the Sudan had in common with the Apollonien of the Gold Coast and it was why all three of these peoples, as well as others under French control in the Sudan and Senegal, were presumed to be more 'intelligent' than the Baule. The French felt themselves to be offering a superior economic, political, and moral order to the African peoples. Those who accommodated themselves to this new order were by definition on the road to civlization. Those who, on the contrary, failed to recognize the seemingly self-evident superiority of the new order were described by the French as 'peu intelligent' and their autonomous development outside the purview of the colonial economy was taken as yet another indication of their hopelessly savage condition.

Only by understanding this curiously twisted line of reasoning is it possible to appreciate the irony of the unfolding situation. While the Baule enjoyed the most prosperous period in their entire history, the French became convinced that they were among the most primitive peoples they had ever encountered in Africa. Dr Lasnet voiced the thoughts of many of his French contemporaries in the colony when he summed up the Baule character in these terms:

Les Baoulés sont peu intelligents; ils sont sans industrie, sans commerce, rien ne les intéresse. La vue d'objets qu'ils ne connaissent pas incite leur frayeur, rarement leur curiosité. Ils sont très paresseux et travaillent fort peu, ayant tous des captifs. Ils sont guerriers comme tous les peuples primitifs et sans cesse en lutte de tribu à tribu; leurs croyances sont enfantines et leur fétichisme est des plus grossières. Il faudra bien longtemps à notre sens pour donner l'essor à ce pays et l'ouvrir efficacement à la civilisation.[119]

The tranquillity of Baule country between 1895 and 1898 emanated on the one hand from the expanding economic possibilities for the Baule, and on the other, from a policy of minimal administrative interference from the French. If either of these conditions were to be reversed, the tenuous peace between the Baule and the French would be seriously compromised, for clearly neither group had yet developed a serious respect for the other.

CHAPTER IV

Slave Emancipation, Taxation, and Renewed Resistance, 1898-1902

SAMORY'S RETREAT AND THE SIEGE OF BOUAKÉ, 1898

While the civilian administration maintained a somewhat distant relationship with its nominal subjects in the Baule area, the Sudanese military command enjoyed its final hours of glory in the north. Although the administrative reforms stemming from the Monteil retreat led to the creation of a civilian Governor General who was to oversee military activities after 1895, effective control in the Sudan passed back into the hands of the colonels. For a while it looked as though the area south of the Niger Bend might become the scene of a major confrontation between competing imperial forces, each attempting to establish its claim along the upper reaches of the Comoé and Volta rivers, but the Anglo-French agreement of 14 June 1898 delineated the areas of respective control, and imperial rivals shifted their interest increasingly to the upper Nile instead.[1] Free from competition with Britain concerning their respective limits of imperial control, the Sudanese military could focus its attention upon an all-out conquest of their long-standing enemy – Samory.

After Monteil's retreat the French had attempted unsuccessfully to come to terms with Samory through some kind of negotiated settlement, but the military became convinced that only a total military defeat of Samory would resolve the situation.[2] Their attitude hardened in August 1897 when Captain Braulot was massacred on the outskirts of Bouna at the hands of Sarantyeni Mori, one of Samory's sons. Plans were drawn up for a concerted campaign against the Imam, and in September 1897 Commander Caudrelier led an expedition south from the Sudan to occupy Bobo-Dioulasso. From there Lieutenant Demars was dispatched to establish an outpost on the upper Comoé river and threaten Samory's north-eastern front. Shortly thereafter Clozel occupied Bondoukou by advancing northwards from the coast, and when Sarantyeni Mori and his troops abandoned Bouna, the English forces occupied it in November 1897. With his eastern and northern frontiers occupied by French and British forces, Samory's expansion came to an end. He was forced back upon the territories he had already occupied, and by late 1897 he was confined to the Dabakala-Kong area just north of the Baule.

To deliver the *coup de grâce* to their arch-enemy the French sought to win the support of Babemba of Sikasso, the leader of the Senufo kingdom of Kenedougou, situated along Samory's northern flank. Samory and King Tiéba, Babemba's brother and predecessor, were long-standing enemies, and there was some reason to suppose that Babemba might agree to an alliance with the French, for Samory's long and ultimately unsuccessful siege of Sikasso in 1888 created a feeling of enduring enmity between the two empires. By the end of 1897, however, the French became concerned by the seeming neutrality of Babemba and alarmed by reports that he was supplying horses to Samory's forces, and they dispatched Captain Morisson to Sikasso in January 1898 to secure Babemba's alliance. Morisson's mission was a failure, and in leaving Sikasso his troops were ambushed and massacred. In retaliation Lieutenant Colonel Audéoud made plans for a heavily armed expedition to storm Sikasso and take it by force.

Meanwhile, learning that only a small garrison of Samory's *sofas* was protecting Kong and that the English at Bouna were entertaining the idea of capturing the town, Lieutenants Demars and Mechet of the Volta regiment under Commander Caudrelier launched a pre-emptive attack on Kong and captured it by surprise on 25 January 1898. Their move proved to be premature, however, for their supply lines with the rest of Caudrelier's forces were cut. In mid-February the *sofas* surrounded Kong and held the officers in a state of siege without food or water. It was not until 27 February that Commander Caudrelier could finally relieve the dying garrison in Kong, chasing some of Samory's bands as far west as the Bandama. Samory himself had by this time removed his camp from Dabakala to Bori-Bani on the right bank of the Bandama, and there he vowed to remain, and take his stand against the French.

In the Sudan plans proceeded for the siege of Sikasso, and Lieutenant-Colonel Audéoud ordered Caudrelier to establish a string of outposts westwards from Kong to the Bandama river to cut off a potential retreat of Sikasso's population and prevent them from joining forces with Samory. Caudrelier reached a point just seventy kilometres south of Sikasso on the Bandama and Sikasso's southern retreat was sealed off. Audéoud arrived in front of Sikasso on 15 April 1898 and by 1 May the town had fallen into French hands. Having subdued Samory's only potential ally, the French forces focused their attention on the Imam and his marauding bands of mobile *sofas*.

Samory was quite shaken by the capture of Kong and the siege of Sikasso. Despite a heavy attack on Kong on 30 April, his *sofas* failed to recapture the town, and when news of the fall of Sikasso reached him, his situation began to look desperate. Conditions deteriorated further when on 20 May a regiment under Commander Pineau headed south from the Sudan to provision Kong and rid the area of Samory's remaining forces. In early June Pineau's troops defeated Bilali, one of Samory's commanders, in a surprise night battle at Tiémou on the Bandama and in the following days he pursued Samory's forces to within thirty kilometres of Bori-Bani itself. Then, after joining forces with Captain Benoît from the Volta regiment, Pineau made his way to Kong and there began to draw up plans for the subsequent administration of the conquered territory.

Demoralized by the rapid collapse of his defences in the east and north, Samory apparently abandoned plans for a defensive stand at Bori-Bandi and began to envisage retreat. His intentions were not at first clear to the French and at one point Nebout warned of the possibility of Samory invading Baule country. When Governor Mouttet heard this news, he requested the Minister of Colonies to place Senegalese troops on the alert.[3] In the event, Samory made no move on Baule country, perhaps for two reasons. In the first place, he was well aware that the Baule were heavily armed, and on terrain where horses were of little use he would doubtless suffer heavy losses and perhaps defeat from the Baule themselves. In addition, it seems that he began to fear an imaginary French expedition reputed to be making its way northwards through Baule country. As Nebout reported:

la nouvelle d'une colonne montant par le Baoulé l'a achevé: cette colonne imaginaire était terrifiante, les éléphants remplacaient les chevaux et les canons marchaient seuls sur les routes. . . . les bruits sont venus jusqu'à Samory qui, alors, a declaré qu'il ne se défendrait plus, parlant même de se jeter dans une rivière pour y mourir.[4]

Whether Samory ever really contemplated suicide, or what precise role this imaginary expedition played in determining his action, will perhaps never be known, but as Nebout observed, 'Ce qui est certain, c'est que Samory est parti rapidement – désespéré.'[5] After calling his Dyula troops to his side, he began a long and desperate retreat westwards towards the distant border with Liberia on 12 June 1898. The French pursued him and eventually captured him in a surprise attack at Guélémou on 29 September 1898, thus terminating the longest series of campaigns against a single enemy in the history of French Sudanese conquest.

In the wake of Samory's retreat, the French sought to create the framework of stable colonial administration along the northern Baule border, and their attention focused on Bouaké. The idea of establishing an outpost at Bouaké was not a new one. Ever since Marchand visited the town in 1893 the prospect had been entertained as a possibility. In 1893 and 1894 it was clear that Kouassi Gbuéké himself and the Baule in the north were openly opposed to the idea of French presence, and the French did not pursue the issue at that time.[6] Kouassi Gbuéké's opposition to the idea of having the French in or near his village continued after the Monteil retreat, for during most of 1895 he did not want the French to interfere with his profitable trade in slaves with Samory. As one observer noted, 'il sera toujours heureux de nous sentir loin de son village, car il comprend bien que notre présence chez lui ou près de lui serait la ruine de son commerce.'[7]

By the end of October 1895, however, there was an indication that difficulties were emerging between Kouassi Gbuéké and Samory's forces.[8] The *sofas* had by this point captured Bondoukou, and it is likely that prices for slaves increased as Samory's plight became less desperate than it had been in the earlier months of 1895. By mid-1896 Kouassi Gbuéké showed signs of resenting the presence of Samory's forces in the area, and Delafosse reported that he would have given his approval to the creation of a French outpost at Bouaké, were it not for the fact that he feared reprisals from Samory if he did so.[9] When the Braulot mission departed from Bouaké, representatives from Samory came and installed themselves in the town, and Kouassi Gbuéké, wanting to rid himself of them, threatened to call upon the French for assistance.[10] In February 1897 when Kouassi Gbuéké died, his brother and successor, Kouassi Blé, warmly welcomed Albert Nebout, leaving the French with the impression that there was hope for an alliance with him against Samory. Governor Mouttet subsequently instructed Nebout to look into the possibility of creating an administrative post at Bouaké, and prospects looked favourable in this regard when it became apparent to Nebout and Bonhoure that populations throughout the northern Baule area wished to rid themselves of Samory's troops.[11]

It is important to note that in the north the Baule attitude of growing openness towards the French was predicated upon a particular image of what French presence might achieve for them. All of the exchanges about eventual French installation were conducted from late

1895 through 1897 with civilian administrators to the south, in the context of a possible alliance against Samory. It seems likely that in the face of increasingly heavy exactions from Samory, the northern Baule began to regard the French as potential allies to help them regain a measure of autonomy from Samory's *sofas*. If this was their goal, their essential aim would have been to reassert the favourable trading terms for slaves which they first enjoyed with Samory early in 1895. So long as the French could aid them in achieving this goal, their presence would not be resented; indeed administrators like Delafosse or Nebout might prove an asset. Both of these men were literate in Arabic and they could serve as useful negotiators between the Baule and Samory. Furthermore, administrators of this character clearly posed no military threat to the Baule, for there were no French troops in the south to come to their assistance. As long as French presence meant the support of civilian administrators from the south in developing a co-operative stance against Samory, such a proposition had everything to recommend itself to the Baule at the end of 1897.

By mid-1898 the situation had changed dramatically. When it became apparent to the Baule that French presence meant the intrusion of authoritarian military officers from the Sudan, *after* Samory was no longer a threat, they were clearly less than enthusiastic about developing further relations with the French. By this time, however, the French no longer thought it necessary to consult the Baule on the matter. In June 1898 when Commander Pineau drew up a programme to administer the territory acquired from Samory, he included plans for establishing a permanent military garrison at Bouaké, apparently without concerning himself with Baule attitudes.[12] Construction of the post began in August 1898 under the direction of Captain Benoît, and for the first time it looked as though the French would be able to maintain sustained communications between the civilian administration of the Ivory Coast and the Sudanese Command in the interior.[13] The long-awaited junction between the coastal colony and the Niger river was finally complete – or at least so it appeared on the map.

Blinded by their victory over Samory, in the Bouaké area the officers seemed incapable of foreseeing the difficulties which lay in store for them in relating to the Baule. Attempts to recruit labourers for the construction of the first Bouaké post proved surprisingly successful at first – indeed entirely too successful. Many of the newly acquired slaves among the Baule presented themselves at the post, willing to undertake any labour the French required in exchange for their liberty from their Baule masters. The French obliged by creating at Bouaké a 'village de liberté', in the same way they had done in the areas they conquered militarily in the Sudan.[14] The settlement, established in close proximity to the post, constituted a pool of man-power which the French could draw upon as they had in the case of the 'Dyula-kro' at Toumodi, Kodiokofikro, and Tiassalé. Captain Benoît seemed to regard the area around Bouaké as newly-conquered territory and he proceeded to liberate slaves in the fashion to which he had become accustomed in Sudanese campaigns.[15]

Predictably, this practice did not endear him to the Baule. Relations deteriorated further when Kasso, a brother of Kouassi Blé, the chief of Bouaké, was wounded accidentally at the post while Captain Benoît was demonstrating the use of his revolver to the assembled chiefs in late August 1898. The Baule began to refuse to have any further relations with the French. Nevertheless, their slaves continued to escape and seek French protection. In early October Baule hostility became overt when a Senegalese soldier, sent out to recruit labourers, was killed in the village of Tiéplé. Benoît arrested and temporarily imprisoned Kouassi Blé and sent for troop reinforcements from Dabakala. When additional troops arrived, the French took a more aggressive initiative. On 14 November 1898 they captured Katia Kofi, chief of Katiakofikro, the formerly prosperous slave market just north of Bouaké, and they executed him the following morning for allegedly fomenting anti-French sentiment in the Bouaké area.[16] With this gesture the French clearly demonstrated their willingness to deal brutally with Baule who wished to see them leave.

The situation developed into a crisis in December when Kasso allegedly committed an act of plunder against the French post. It is not clear what the exact crime was, but it is likely that Kasso attempted to repossess an escaped slave who had sought refuge in the French post.[17] Benoît ordered Kasso to appear before him, but Kasso refused. Benoît then summoned Kouassi Blé and ordered him to deliver his brother, but Kouassi Blé, perhaps remembering his first imprisonment and the more unfortunate fate of Katia Kofi, also refused to acknowledge Benoît's command. Instead, during the night of 19–20 December Kouassi Blé evacuated the village of Bouaké, securing all women and livestock well out of reach of the French forces. On 20 December the Baule surrounded the post and shouted insults at the French until Captain Benoît dispersed them with a bayonet charge executed by Lieutenant Pruneau. As yet no shots had been fired, but the atmosphere was fraught with tension. On the following day the Baule attempted to block the arrival of a supply caravan, allowing it to pass only after

Lieutenant Pruneau came to its assistance with an armed detachment. Still no shots were fired.

On 22 December Captain Benoît lost all patience with the situation and acted impetuously. He dispatched Pruneau to surprise the Baule warriors and capture hostages. The Baule were vigilant enough to escape, but in doing so they opened fire on Pruneau's detachment. Benoît was furious, and in retaliation he ordered his forces to pillage and burn the village of Bouaké. As the inhabitants had already evacuated the village, no Baule were injured, but the French confiscated several tons of rice in the raid and left Kouassi Blé and his followers with only the smouldering remains of their huts.

In return the Baule unleashed full-scale counter-attack the following day, assaulting the French garrison from three sides simultaneously. Benoît estimated that between 2,000-3,000 Baule took part in the siege, and fighting was long and heavy. Fearing the possibility of a renewed attack, he sent for reinforcements from Dabakala. For the first time since the campaigns against the Monteil expedition in 1895, the Baule launched a co-ordinated offensive against the French presence in their midst.[18] The link between the coast and the Sudan was severed once again, only four months after it had been established. This time, however, it was not Samory and his *sofas* who frustrated French designs to unite their empire, but rather the Baule themselves.

ADMINISTRATIVE AMBIGUITY AND THE ECONOMIC BASIS OF RENEWED RESISTANCE, 1899

The Bouaké attack underscored the residual ambiguities of French control in West Africa. Despite the creation of the Government General to unify colonial administration, the French continued to pursue two quite different policies on the ground. In the Sudan French authorities continued to consider colonial rule as an extension of military conquest. Accordingly, the Captains in charge tended to relate to the Baule around Bouaké as subjugated peoples from whom they expected to collect taxes and liberate slaves. To the south, French colonial rule had come to mean something considerably more restrained, less assertive. The question of collecting taxes had not yet arisen, and the disaster of the Monteil expedition reminded the remaining civilian administrators of the consequences of trying to interfere with Baule control over their slaves.

These two different styles of colonial rule confronted one another along the northern Baule frontier, and predictably the spokesmen for each approach advocated different solutions for the crisis precipitated by the Bouaké attack. 'J'estime', wrote Benoît to Nebout, 'qu'une forte colonne s'impose en pays baoulé . . .'.[19] Outlining what the French could hope to achieve by such a move, Benoît continued:

les conséquences les plus imposantes en seront:
1) le désarmement presque général de ces populations;
2) leur soumission définitive à la force;
3) la possibilité de l'établissement d'un impôt annuel;
4) la suppression du commerce trop libre de la poudre et des armes;
5) la fin du cauchemar dont souffrent les malheureuses populations Djiminis, Katiolas, ou Tagouanos, sequestrées, achetées ou vendues par les Baoulé.[20]

In conclusion he emphasized that only 'une colonne rapide et efficace' would resolve the situation, and he indicated that he was forwarding this opinion to his military superiors in the Sudan.

Nebout disagreed. In the letter in which he forwarded Captain Benoît's assessment to the Governor at Grand Bassam, Nebout countered Benoît's opinion with his own: 'mon avis formel', he wrote, 'est qu'une colonne rapide serait absolument inefficace: du sang et des dépenses pour rien. Pour obtenir ce que demande M. Benoît il faudrait occuper très fortement le Baoulé . . .'.[21] Nebout estimated that a full-scale occupation of Baule country would require nine squadrons of forty to sixty troops placed at strategic outposts through the country for a period of two or three years. This was clearly more than even the most avid militarists were prepared to commit, and in the absence of such a commitment Nebout advocated a more cautious approach towards the Baule. To use force in a 'colonne rapide' as Benoît had suggested would only serve to provoke heightened Baule resistance and Nebout argued that this would leave the civilian administration all the more vulnerable to Baule attack: 'nous ne pouvons employer la force pour obliger les Baoulé à l'obéissance; on pourrait se heurter à une résistance armée et les garrisons sont trop faibles.'[22] Nebout recognized perhaps more clearly than anyone else at this point that the Bouaké revolt was indicative of a pervasive feeling of discontent among the Baule, and any hasty French attempt to retaliate militarily could touch off a resistance struggle on a scale previously unknown in the Ivory Coast.

Penel, the acting Governor in Roberdeau's absence, forwarded both Captain Benoît's and Nebout's observations to the Minister of Colonies, highlighting what he thought to be the essential problem in administering the Baule area. 'Les difficultés présentées tiennent pour une bonne part à la dualité de politique suivie dans . . . le Baoulé . . .'.[23] According to Penel the juxtaposition of military rule in the north alongside a more conciliatory civilian authority in the south created a situation which would lead inevitably towards social disruption.

Les dangers de cette dualité, au sein d'un même peuple, sautent aux yeux. On peut craindre notamment si l'action militaire se développe, que les tribus du Nord émigrent vers le Sud et cherchent à s'y établir de vive force.[24]

Fearing the possibility of these disruptive migrations, Penel seconded Nebout's opinion that for the time being a punitive expedition of the kind Benoît suggested would provoke more Baule hostility than the colony could cope with. The immediate course of action would be to let things settle by ignoring Benoît's appeal for an expedition.

Penel realized, however, that such a programme was only a make-shift solution. Even if the captains did not get their expedition, they remained installed at Bouaké, and the duality of French policy towards the Baule persisted. According to Penel, this ambiguity could not be allowed to last for long. Addressing his comments to the Minister of Colonies, Penel put the case quite simply: 'il devient nécessaire qu'une entente s'établisse entre les deux colonies pour arrêter, s'il est possible, une politique commune et déterminer nos limites d'influence respectives.'[25]

For reasons independent of the Bouaké revolt, colonial officials in Paris also became convinced of the necessity to clarify lines of civilian and military rule in the West African empire. Moreover, by this time, critics of military rule in the Sudan once again were gaining the upper hand. Lieutenant-Colonel Audéoud, the military Lieutenant-Governor of the Sudan, never worked co-operatively with Governor General Chaudié, and the confusion of the Sudan's finances after the costly Sikasso siege and Samory campaign of 1898 persuaded many that the time had come for an end to the era of military rule. The Minister's instructions to Colonel Trentinian, Audéoud's successor, made it clear as early as November 1898 that preparations should be made for the transition to civilian authority in the Sudan.[26] The Anglo-French agreement of June 1898 combined with the capture of Sikasso and the defeat of Samory in September of the same year, alleviated the need for continued military activity in the area – or at least so it seemed in Paris. In December 1898, just as the Baule were preparing to attack the post at Bouaké, the Minister assured the Chambre confidently that 'the era of conquest is definitely closed'.[27]

Benoît's appeal for an immediate expedition came to naught, then, not so much because of the opposition of local civilian officials in the Ivory Coast, but because Parliament and the Ministry had grown tired of military insubordination and excessive expenditure. As far as they were concerned, the military had had its day, and they were determined to bring it to heel. In the spring of 1899 Governor General Chaudié put forward a specific proposal for terminating military rule in the Sudan, and in September the Minister appointed him to a special commission to decide upon the fate of the area. When the commission reported in favour of dismembering the Sudan and dividing the territory between the neighbouring colonies under civilian administration, the Minister accepted its suggestions. Military rule came to an end by the terms of the ministerial decree of 17 October 1899.[28]

The issue of military influence was not so neatly settled, however, for although the resistance movements in the Sudan had been crushed by December 1898, the Baule had only begun to fight. Within a year of Samory's defeat the French found themselves being drawn into military commitments in a new theatre of operations on a scale for which they were not prepared and under conditions that made the Sudanese campaigns look simple by comparison. The French had hardly finished congratulating themselves on their victory over Samory before they found themselves humiliated at the hands of the Baule, and once again local conditions would revive the debate between the Captaines d'Infanterie and the Commis d'Administration.

In effect, the attack on Bouaké marked the beginning of a new phase in French-Baule relations – a phase dominated increasingly by military commanders. Benoît's request for an expedition was initially ignored, but by July 1900 the civilian administration handed over formal control in Baule country to the military officers, and in the following months French troops engaged in campaigns every bit as costly as those characteristic of the heyday of Sudanese conquest. Samory's defeat may well have hastened the demise of military control in the Sudan, but it simultaneously heralded an era of military ascendancy in Baule country.

It would be tempting to account for the rise of military influence among the Baule as an effort on the part of the Sudanese military clique to assert a measure of control in a new region, to compensate for the power which they had lost in the Sudan. From this perspective the intrusion of the military into Baule country could be interpreted as merely an additional chapter in the continuing feud between civilian and military authority in French colonial circles. Having been removed from the Sudan, the militarists were down but not out, and once they had mustered their forces, the officers re-established their autonomy further south among the Baule.

Upon closer examination it becomes apparent that such an explanation is misleading, for it ignores that military rule among the Baule was ushered in at the request of the civilians themselves, albeit somewhat reluctantly. Despite their aversion to the principle of military rule, civilian administrators found themselves in late 1899 appealing to the Minister of Colonies to send an expedition against the Baule. Similarly, in spite of reluctance in Paris to become engaged in this manner, the Minister authorized the requested expedition. What accounted for this curious reversal on the part of both the local administration and the Ministry itself?

The answer is to be found in the changed conditions among the Baule. Samory's departure and French military intrusion dealt a resounding blow to the Baule economy. Fugitive slaves in the north sought protection from the French at Bouaké, and as we have seen, Benoît's willingness to encourage slave emancipation provoked the Baule attack on the post in December 1898. With assistance from thirty-five troops from Dabakala, Benoît restored a measure of order during January 1899, but the situation was perhaps best characterized as a qualified stand-off between the Baule and French forces. Although a semblance of calm persisted on the surface, conditions continued to deteriorate as far as the Baule were concerned. During January alone, 2,500 more slaves sought refuge in the Bouaké post.[29]

Benoît returned to France in February 1899, but his successors were no more successful in coming to an enduring understanding with the Baule. Indeed, their policies seemed designed expressly to antagonize not only the Baule around Bouaké but those to the south as well. During March, Captains Mordocq, Mleneck, and Pelletier assembled 4,000 'refugees' from the French posts at Toumodi and Kodiokofikro and escorted them under armed guard back to their region of origin in the north.[30] These populations were ostensibly the 'free' inhabitants of the Dyula-kro that had grown up around each of the French administrative posts in Baule country, but among them were escaped Baule slaves who had been living in the *villages de liberté*. Moreover, the Baule looked upon even those who had always been 'free' as potential slaves – men, women, and children whom the Baule fully expected to assimilate as dependants as soon as the French departed. In this context it is perhaps understandable that when these convoys set out for the north, the Baule attempted to ambush them at several points along the way.

The Baule began to recognize that French presence constituted a permanent threat to their control over their dependent labour force, not only in the Bouaké area but throughout the southern regions as well.

While the nature of French intervention disturbed Baule relations with their slaves, Samory's departure simultaneously affected Baule trade structures. In the years before Samory's retreat the Baule had oriented their primary trade in a north-south direction, taking advantage of their intervening position between the coastal groups and those of the interior. During the 1890s the intensity of the trade had increased dramatically, but with Samory's retreat in June 1898 the whole structure of trade abruptly collapsed. Internal as well as external commerce ground to a halt among the Baule.

The reason for this was inherent within the mechanisms of Baule trade. The major problem derived from outstanding debts which under the new circumstances could not be repaid. Throughout the 1890s Baule from southern settlements had in effect 'invested' considerable amounts of capital in the north in the expectation of a return in slaves. In most cases the 'investments' involved southern Baule chiefs who had extended credit to their northern trading partners in the form of European trade goods, guns and powder on the understanding that they would receive captive labourers in return. As long as Samory provided captives and the northern Baule relayed them to their southern partners, trade flourished with relatively few internal constraints. The crisis began after August 1898 when the arrival of the French at Bouaké made it impossible for the northern Baule to obtain new captives and increasingly difficult for them to control the ones they already owned. The flow of trade had been blocked at its northern source, and northern Baule were unable to repay their southern creditors with the captives they demanded. The indebtedness of the northern chiefs increased when they hastened to obtain still more guns and powder during the Bouaké siege and its aftermath. In the process, credit had been stretched to its limits, and southern chiefs were increasingly tempted to foreclose on their northern partners, particularly after the exodus of some of their own captives in the convoys of March 1899.

Debt collection between Baule of the same region was normally accomplished through the mediation of a third party respected by each of the other two contracting partners.[31] Sometimes the debt would be shouldered directly by the intervening person. Although debt was not cancelled in this manner, an impoverished person could often rid himself of a persistent creditor by shifting the burden of his debt to the intervening party to whom he would in turn become indebted. The whole process contributed to the growing power base of those who could afford to pay debts on behalf of others, for by intervening in this manner, a given chief would in effect have added another dependant to his entourage. Locally, at least, this kind of practice effectively resolved the problem of debt collection.

Over long distances, however, difficulties arose, for in the absence of centralized political or judicial institutions it was often impossible to find a mutually respected third party to intervene. Furthermore, the debts involved could be considerable, involving the equivalent value of several caravans of trade goods. A third party could only liquidate such a debt by placing his own trading ventures in jeopardy, and this he would be reluctant to do. The ultimate means of debt collection over long distances took the form of seizure. The creditor simply captured and held in ransom any goods or persons belonging to or related to the debtor until the debtor could redeem them by paying the outstanding debt. During the late months of 1898 and throughout 1899 this practice became rampant as southern Baule chiefs sought to collect debts from their northern trading partners. Caravans of goods heading northwards were halted in the southern villages and the slave porters were seized and retained in ransom. If the northern chiefs could not pay their debts, the southern chiefs simply acted as if the goods and slaves in fact belonged to them.

While some of the civilian administrators clearly understood the mechanisms involved, their assessment of the situation differed significantly from that of the Baule themselves. For the Baule, a Dyula of the Djamala or Djimini region represented an actual or potential source of captive labour. By retaining a slave porter of a northern Baule chief, a southern chief was often merely obtaining, albeit coercively, the slave which his indebted northern partner owed to him. From the French perspective, however, things looked different. For them the distinguishing feature of those who were seized in this manner was not so much that they were *slaves*, but that they were *porters*. In short, while the Baule focused upon the element of domestic labour power involved, the French devoted their attention to the potential commercial role of the Dyula who had been seized in this fashion. As the practice of stopping caravans and seizing porters became more widespread during 1899, the civilian administrators became increasingly alarmed by what they regarded as the lack of security for trade.

It would not be an exaggeration to suggest that the issue at stake involved two alternate strategies for economic recovery in the post-

Samory era. The southern Baule were intent upon collecting their debts, consolidating the domestic unit of production and expanding their productive output (in gold mining and cloth weaving) with the labour of their newly acquired slaves. The French on the other hand, were determined to expand the colony's import-export trade by re-populating the devastated areas in the north with 'liberated' captives and encouraging the uninhibited flow of commerce across Baule territory between the coast and the Sudan. To the extent that the Baule and the French each sought to pursue these separate strategies, conflict seemed, if not inevitable, at least highly probable, for each strategy was based upon fundamentally different conceptions concerning the potential role of Dyula labour power and the importance of external trade.

MAURICE DELAFOSSE, KOUADIO OKOU, AND THE LOMO REVOLT, 1899

Relations between the Baule and the French at Bouaké reached a stale-mate situation during the early months of 1899. Kouassi Blé of the Faafoué-Baule and Kouamé Dié of the Ouarébo-Baule, both of whose warriors participated in the attack on Bouaké, indicated their willing-ness to come to terms with the military officers at Bouaké, but they were slow in executing the conditions of submission, and sought, apparently without success, to obtain the intercession of the civilian administrators at Kodiokofikro and Toumodi.[32] The civilian adminis-tration itself was in the midst of change. Albert Nebout who had been in charge of the Baule territory for more than two years, was preparing to go on leave, and Maurice Delafosse returned to the Ivory Coast from a tour of duty in Liberia to assume control of the area in Nebout's absence. The two men conferred on the coast in the last days of March, and by 6 April Delafosse was once again in Toumodi, where he had begun his administrative career four years earlier, in the aftermath of the Monteil expedition.[33]

On the face of it Delafosse seemed to be ideally suited for the delicate task of administering Baule territory. By temperament and experience he opposed the extension of military rule in the colonies. Instead he advocated the expansion of trade and considered the administration's role to be that of a relatively benign mediator in local disputes. In this his view coincided perfectly with those which the Ministry held in mid-1899. Despite the relatively restrained role which he envisaged for his administration from an official point of view,

Delafosse did not distance himself from his Baule subjects on a daily basis. On the contrary, after eighteen months of boredom as the French Consul in Monrovia, he looked forward with enthusiasm to re-establishing a close relationship with the Baule whom he had grown to admire. His earlier experience provided him with a basic understanding of Baule customs, and when he returned to Toumodi, he renewed personal friendships with local Baule chiefs and began seriously to pursue ethnographic and linguistic studies in the Toumodi area. If it were to be possible to win the confidence of the Baule in the post-Samory period, it certainly looked as though Delafosse was the man for the job.

Delafosse's major disadvantage, however, was that he had been absent from Baule territory for two years and during that time the political situation had changed significantly. It is probable that he discussed the Bouaké revolt with Nebout upon arriving in March 1899, but in subsequent reports he demonstrated little understanding of the broader implications of Samory's retreat and the wide-scale escape of Baule slaves. There is no mention at all in either his personal or official correspondence of the exodus under French protection of an estimated 4,000 Dyula from the Toumodi and Kodiokofikro environs. This move was undertaken at the very end of Nebout's administration in the area, and it provided the immediate backdrop to Delafosse's arrival.

Delafosse undertook a series of survey trips throughout Baule country in June and July 1899 to inform himself of the conditions in the area, but although his reports contain detailed descriptions of the economic potential of various areas (from the point of view of French commerce), their political content is thin indeed. After returning from a visit to the Ouarébo area in the north, for example, he limited his political comments to an absolute minimum: 'J'ai l'honneur de vous rendre compte que la situation politique du Baoulé est toujours la même, c'est à dire satisfaisante . . .'.[34] The Ouarébo groups had only a few months previously participated in the attack on Bouaké, and military authorities were still experiencing considerable difficulty in entering into negotiations with Toto Dibi and Kouamé Dié, the two major Ouarébo chiefs. It is possible that Delafosse knew nothing of this situation. It is more likely, however, that he was aware of it, but since Bouaké was under military administration, and strictly speaking beyond his domain of authority, he did not concern himself directly with the political situation there and did not recognize the broader implications of continued difficulty around Bouaké. Instead he focused his concern exclusively upon the southern Baule peoples.

His message to them was clear enough. As he recounted it to the Governor:

j'ai essayé d'expliquer la raison de notre présence dans le pays et ce que nous exigeons des indigènes: la liberté du commerce et des routes, le respect des caravanes; j'ai dit que nous respections les coutumes des indigènes, que nous ne portions atteinte ni à leurs droits ni à l'autorité de leurs chefs, mais que nous nous opposerions énergiquement à ce que des hommes ou des marchandises soient arrêtés sous prétexte de dettes impayées, comme cela se faisait d'une façon générale avant notre venue dans le pays.[35]

Throughout his various administrative tours of inspection Delafosse insisted upon this theme again and again. So long as the southern Baule continued to seize caravans and porters in order to settle outstanding debts with their northern partners, the Baule and Delafosse seemed to be on a collision course.

Deteriorating conditions on the coast did not strengthen Delafosse's position in relation to the Baule. By August 1899 a combined epidemic of bubonic plague and yellow fever had devastated both the European and African populations of Grand Bassam.[36] Communications from the coast were virtually non-existent,[37] and ships refused to put into the colony's ports because of the epidemic. These developments had a profound effect upon conditions inland. According to the Governor one rumour current in Baule country was that 'tous les blancs étaient morts à Grand Bassam au cours de l'épidémie et que les Français étaient décidés à abandonner la colonie'.[38] A certain amount of credence may have been lent to this rumour when the French administrator at Tiassalé, M. Dautier, died in mid-August. Delafosse himself was suffering from an infected sore on his left leg, making it difficult for him to walk, and it may well be that the visibly feeble condition of the civilian authorities in the colony encouraged the Baule to think that they too would soon withdraw, just as Monteil had departed in 1895.

Delafosse, however, had no intention of withdrawing at this point. Indeed when he travelled to Tiassalé to deal with oustanding administrative matters after Dautier's death, he received instructions which gave him a new sense of confidence and heightened his enthusiasm for his work among the Baule. Nebout met with Ministry officials upon returning to Paris, and in conjunction with Binger he had begun to draw up new plans for the administration of Baule territory. In Tiassalé Delafosse received directions from the Minister of Colonies, forwarded to him by the Governor, to undertake the necessary preliminary study of the Baule territory in order to identify Baule chiefs to serve as native authorities, with an eye towards introducing a head tax. This was a new departure for French policy towards the Baule, and Delafosse was keenly aware of its importance, both for the future development of Baule country and for his own prospects of career advancement. As he confided to his parents in a letter of 20 August, 'si ce travail réussit, comme je l'espère, ce sera une bonne note pour moi'.[39] Despite the difficulties of the immediate situation Delafosse returned to Toumodi, confident that the Ministry had plans for expanded activity among the Baule and aware that his own achievements would constitute the decisive ground-work for future colonial administration in the area. As an idealist imbued with a strong desire to shape the course of French contact with African society, Delafosse could hardly have asked for more. Necessity required what ambition desired, and Delafosse was doubly eager to succeed.

At the time, however, there was not much occasion for long-range planning. The mundane matters of daily administration demanded his attention as he returned from Tiassalé to Toumodi at the end of August 1899. Earlier that month three caravans of trade goods had been seized by Baule along the Tiassalé–Toumodi route in what had become a familiar pattern to Delafosse. He reported the incidents to the Governor, commenting somewhat routinely, 'Les causes sont toujours les mêmes: dettes impayées remontant à plusieurs générations, histoires de fétiches, etc.'.[40]

After the chance for lofty reflection in Tiassalé upon the future of French administration and the possibilities in store for his own career, it is not unlikely that Delafosse encountered these petty disputes with a sense of weary impatience. He was determined to settle these differences as decisively as possible in order to open the way for uninhibited commerce – something which he regarded as a necessary pre-condition for the realization of the Ministry's new administrative plans for the Baule territory.

On 30 August Delafosse was able to resolve two of the disputes in a meeting with chiefs at Ouossou, but the third proved to be more difficult. The problem involved Kouadio Okou, the Baule chief of the village of Lomo whom Delafosse had grown to dislike from his earlier tour of duty in Baule country. Kouadio Okou had been the first Baule chief to refuse to receive Marchand after the defeat of Tiassalé in 1893, and during the attacks on the Monteil expedition he had ordered the assassination of two Senegalese couriers and organized a march on the French post at Toumodi.[41] During August 1899 Kouadio Okou allegedly stopped a caravan carrying sixteen barrels of powder destined for the north, and when Delafosse tried to meet with him to settle the dispute during his return trip to Toumodi, Kouadio Okou fled, refusing to respond to Delafosse's convocation.[42]

Delafosse interpreted Kouadio Okou's escape as a challenge to his own jurisdiction in settling disputes of this nature, and he felt that to let such an incident pass unnoticed would seriously compromise his chances of resolving similar disputes in the future. Upon reaching Toumodi, Delafosse was convinced that an authoritative gesture was necessary. On 6 September he dispatched Sergeant Sissé Diallo and six troops to summon Kouadio Okou to Toumodi. If after three warnings the Baule chief refused to come to Toumodi, Diallo had instructions to set fire to Kouadio Okou's compound in the village of Lomo and then return to Toumodi. Kouadio Okou apparently considered the possibility of meeting Delafosse's demands, but an Ngban chief from Kpouébo named Yao Guié, convinced him to hold his ground. The two chiefs ultimately refused to comply with Delafosse's requests, and Sissé Diallo duly executed his instructions, burning Lomo to the ground.[43]

On the following day, 7 September, Kouadio Okou seized two other caravans passing along the route, demonstrating a further defiance of Delafosse's injunctions. In an effort to prevent the situation from deteriorating any further Delafosse sent Kouadio Okou a second appeal on 7 September, this time by way of intermediary Baule chiefs of the Toumodi region. Their mission proved no more successful than that of Sergeant Diallo in bringing Kouadio Okou to account. On 8 September they returned with his refusal and the news that he had sworn to attack the post at Toumodi.[44]

Delafosse did not seem to take the possibility of an attack seriously, but he immediately dispatched two notes, one to Tiassalé and one to Kodiokofikro informing the administrators there of the situation. In his message to Kodiokofikro he appealed to M. Seigland to come to Toumodi with four soldiers from his post in order to help him capture Kouadio Okou. As far as Delafosse was concerned the issue at hand still involved nothing more than subduing a single obstreperous chief. As he explained it to Seigland: 'Kouadio Okou est un obstacle à la paix et à la prosperité du Baoulé . . . il a été d'ailleurs renié par les autres Ouarébo et . . . sa suppression sera un soulagement pour tout le monde.'[45]

Before Seigland could arrive events took a more dramatic turn. At about 2.00 a.m. during the night of 8-9 September, less than twenty-four hours after Delafosse had first heard of Kouadio Okou's threat to attack Toumodi, Delafosse awoke to the smell of thick smoke. Two of

Kouadio Okou's men had penetrated the compound and set fire to the straw roof. The entire post was ablaze. The incident seemed strikingly parallel to Delafosse's burning of Lomo except in one particular: whereas Sissé Diallo had been instructed to make sure that the huts in Lomo were evacuated before he set them alight, Kouadio Okou apparently wished Delafosse to perish in the Toumodi fire. Delafosse escaped just in time, but he was able to save only a fraction of the armaments and administrative papers before the roof caved in. Three thousand rounds of ammunition exploded in the fire and Delafosse lost all his clothes and personal possessions, including five years of accumulated ethnographic notes and records on the Baule.[46]

Delafosse was embarrassed and enraged. As his daughter, Mme Louise Delafosse has suggested: 'il a tombé de haut et . . . le choc a été rude'.[47] In the days immediately following the fire Delafosse mustered support from the remaining Djimini refugees still resident at Toumodi. In addition he received the assistance of some Baule chiefs in the immediate environs of the post, most notably Niango Kouassi of Toumodi itself and Eoussou, the chief of the village of Abli, an Aïtu-Baule village nine kilometres north of Toumodi. On 12 September Seigland arrived with eight soldiers from Kodiokofikro, but it was not until Captain Le Magnen arrived from Bouaké on 18 September with fifty troops from the Sudan that it became possible for Delafosse to take the initiative against Kouadio Okou. By this time the element of surprise had been lost, and although Captain Le Magnen led several punitive raids on seemingly uncooperative villages between Toumodi and Tiassalé, he was unable to capture either Kouadio Okou or Yao Guié. By October the situation in Toumodi began to resemble the stalemate in Bouaké.[48]

To further complicate matters, the lines of military and civilian authority were in the process of reorganization in the Sudan just when Delafosse needed immediate support. Le Magnen judged that a full-scale military operation requiring two Sudanese companies would be required to subdue the area, but his own superiors in the Sudan ordered him to return to Bouaké in mid-October. As of 17 October military rule in the Sudan officially came to an end, and Le Magnen's superiors did not want to become committed to pursuing a new military campaign in the Ivory Coast at the very moment that they were expected to wind down their own operations. Future support for Toumodi and indeed Bouaké itself would most probably have to come from the coast and not from the Sudan. Bouaké and Kong, as well as much of the former Sudan, were expected to come under the jurisdiction of the Ivory Coast administration, in accordance with the reorganization measures of 17 October, and henceforth the Governor of the Ivory Coast would have to request troops from the Governor General. Only he could authorize new campaigns.[49] This was a long and cumbersome process and one which would have necessitated delays even if the Ivory Coast governor had been an avid proponent of military intervention.

In the event, the Ivory Coast administration was in a more profound state of confusion than that which characterized the Ministry, the Sudan, and the Government General, and it failed to act immediately upon Delafosse's requests. The epidemics of 1899 had taken their toll on the orderly functioning of the colony's administration, and everything it attempted had a makeshift quality to it. Governor Roberdeau who had been appointed to govern the colony in September 1898 still had not arrived by 1 October 1899. In his stead M. Capest, the colony's Secretary General, acted as temporary governor. Unfortunately Capest became ill towards the end of September 1899 and from 1–15 October he handed over the effective administration of the colony to M. Ribes, a subordinate administrator. It would have been during this time that Delafosse's request for two Sudanese companies would have arrived in Grand Bassam.[50] In these uncertain conditions no one acted decisively on the request. Governor Roberdeau finally arrived to take control of the colony on 15 October, but as he was new to the position and indeed to Africa in general, his approach was cautious and bureaucratic. He did not wish under any circumstances to overstep the bounds of the role ascribed to him by the Ministry, and he was well aware that the mood in Paris was against new military adventures.

In addition, it is clear from a close reading of the documents available that Delafosse's superiors in Grand Bassam basically disapproved of the way in which he had handled relations with Kouadio Okou. They were particularly alarmed by the fact that Delafosse appeared to have initiated the hostilities by burning Lomo to the ground. From this perspective it looked as though the burning of the post at Toumodi was merely a reprisal in direct retaliation for Delafosse's initial provocative action at Lomo.[51] Pencilled into the margin of Delafosse's first detailed description of the Toumodi fire were the following condemnatory observations:

M. Delafosse n'avait pas parlé de l'incendie [de Lomo]. C'est là une grave imprudence et il y a lieu à blamer sévèrement son auteur. M. Delafosse savait que nous ne disposons d'aucune force et qu'en cas de complication il nous serait impossible d'y faire face. Sa légèreté est donc inexplicable; elle pouvait en tout cas entrainer les plus graves conséquences.   . . . Il faudra déplacer M. Delafosse dès qu'il sera possible de lui donner un successeur.[52]

Not surprisingly, then, in his instructions to Delafosse, Governor Roberdeau warned him to limit the scope of his offensive against the Baule:

Les mesures de répression doivent être réduites au minimum indispensable, nous n'avons pas en ce moment à prendre sérieusement en main les nombreuses populations du Baoulé, mais seulement à maintenir une position. . . . Le seul but immédiat que nous devions nous proposer est d'assurer notre ligne de communication de Bouaké à Tiassalé.[53]

These instructions are revealing, for they underscore the differences which existed between the priorities of Delafosse as a local administrator, on the one hand, and Roberdeau as the colony's governor, on the other. Delafosse probably did not know that Bouaké and the entire northern region had come under the jurisdiction of Grand Bassam, for this only occurred on 17 October. As a result, for Delafosse the necessity of sustaining communications with Bouaké remained a relatively minor concern compared with the prospect of capturing Kouadio Okou. For Roberdeau, however, the priorities were reversed. The pursuit of Kouadio Okou needed at all times to remain subordinate to the dominant concern of maintaining communications with Bouaké. In the coming months Roberdeau would be expected to provision the troops at Bouaké, Kong, Odiénné, etc., by way of the Baule trade routes. He could not afford to let a local administrator carry on a private vendetta against a petty chief if by doing so he endangered the security of the vital supply routes to the north.

In the final analysis, then, Delafosse did not get his requested companies for a combination of three reasons involving, first, the reorganization measures of 17 October 1899, designed to tone down military initiatives throughout French West Africa; second, the state of confusion which existed in Grand Bassam in the wake of the 1899 epidemics, and third, the personal reticence of Governor Roberdeau, who was reluctant to let a local dispute compromise the fragile framework of his newly-enlarged colony. Embittered by the total pattern of governmental inaction, Delafosse began to see himself as a victim of an administrative bungle. In a letter to his parents, he complained specifically of Capest's bureaucratic attitude which he said 'paralysed' any chances of taking a firm initiative against Kouadio Okou in September and October 1899.[54]

Although Delafosse's antipathy towards Capest was understandable, it was none the less misdirected. The problem was larger than the personalities involved, and under different circumstances Delafosse might have recognized this himself. The Lomo revolt once again resurrected the age-old debate between military and civilian approaches to colonial administration. The irony of the situation was that during October 1899, when the cause of civilian administration gained its decisive ascendancy over the military, Delafosse, himself a long-standing advocate of the pacific approach, threw the entire weight of his convictions behind an appeal for military intervention. The attempt upon his life destroyed his confidence in the validity of restrained administration among the Baule, and overnight he became an avid proponent of direct and forceful repression. As Mme Delafosse has aptly expressed it: 'Le voilà devenu aussi "militaristé" que les militaires qu'il a cependant assez critiqués'.[55]

Delafosse's bitterness towards the Baule was as great as that towards his administrative superiors, particularly when it became apparent that the revolt was not confined to Lomo alone.[56] At the outset Delafosse's plans were limited to capturing Kouadio Okou, but after the intervention of Captain Le Magnen from Bouaké in the last days of September the revolt appeared to be spreading.[57] Over the following days Delafosse became convinced that Akafou was the hidden force behind the revolt:

il est certain qu'Akafou . . . a excité Kouadio Okou à la révolte, lui a prêté de son appui moral, a mis des guerriers à sa disposition et l'a averti du mouvement préparé par le Capitaine Le Magnen. . . . Je dirai plus: je suis moralement certain que Kouadio Okou n'aurait pas ouvert les hostilités s'il n'avait compté sur le concours d'Akafou . . .[58]

Faced with the evidence of spreading discontent Delafosse began to broaden the scope of his proposals for repressing the revolt. The solution, according to him, lay in capturing the key chiefs in the area, particularly Yao Guié and Kouadio Okou. As for Akafou himself, Delafosse wrote, 'Je crois qu'il faudrait profiter de cette occasion pour nous débarrasser de ce chef qui pourrait devenir pour nous dans la suite un obstacle sérieux.'[59] What Delafosse intended by the word 'débarrasser' was not made clear, but his strategy for dealing with the revolt was apparent. By eliminating the trouble-makers, Delafosse thought the trouble would disappear.

Once again the difficulty with Delafosse's analysis lay in his attempt to personalize the blame for the situation at hand. Just as he focused his resentment towards his administrative superiors upon Capest as an individual, he sought to explain the spread of the Baule revolt in terms of a conspiracy between discontented chiefs who were misleading their subjects. If anything, the pattern of events suggests just the reverse. Kouadio Okou and Akafou were bitter rivals and it was not likely that they would have conspired together to embarrass Delafosse as part of some prearranged plan.

The spread of the revolt is more satisfactorily explained by a broadly-based reaction against the initial steps taken to repress it. Captain Le Magnen arrived with fifty soldiers from Bouaké without provisions, and by early October he was feeding his troops from the fields of the Baule. The problem persisted even after he left, for within a few days Lieutenant Laforgue came to Delafosse's aid from Assikasso with thirty Senegalese soldiers and seventy-eight irregulars, and in addition, sub-Lieutenant Lauderoin arrived with fifty troops from the Tabou area. In all Delafosse had 158 men to feed and as he indicated in early November, 'nous vivons . . . depuis un mois, sur les plantations des rebelles qui, sûrement, ne se figuraient pas travailler pour nous lorsqu'ils plantaient leurs ignames.'[60] If the populations in the area were not confirmed 'rebels' before the arrival of these troops, many of them became so when they witnessed the pillaging of their own plantations by the occupying forces.

Initially, on 19 September 1899, Akafou swore his fidelity to the French cause to Captain Le Magnen at Ouossou, but when the effects of French presence became apparent to his followers, after the forceful French occupation of the village of Assakra, Akafou was under increasing pressure to join the rebellion. If he were not to declare himself against the French, Akafou ran the risk of losing the support of his own dependants who were rapidly defecting to the ranks of the more militant chiefs, Kouadio Okou and Yao Guié. Oddly enough, it was not the reputed alliance but rather the long-standing rivalry between Kouadio Okou and Akafou which finally moved Akafou towards revolt. Akafou was in effect competing with Kouadio Okou for the support of an increasingly enraged population. The pattern of opposition to the French looked strikingly similar to that which characterized the first Baule revolt against the Monteil expedition. Akafou was threatened with the loss of his local support unless he too joined in the resistance, and it was perhaps not surprising that in the following weeks his attitude towards the French became more expressly hostile.[61]

Delafosse continued to proceed as if there were a conspiracy involved. Rather than devote his efforts to alleviating the specific conditions which inspired revolt, he focused his attention upon enlisting the support of counter-conspirators – chiefs who, if not truly faithful to the French cause, could at least be described as united in their hatred of either Kouadio Okou or Akafou. Delafosse had no trouble in finding chiefs who were willing to collaborate with him in pursuing Kouadio Okou and fighting Akafou. Such men had been valuable auxiliaries ever since Nebout began to administer the Baule territory in 1894. As Nebout himself indicated upon first hearing of Delafosse's difficulties, 'M. Delafosse pourrait employer comme auxiliaires les Warébos de Tiassalé et les Atoutous, qui détestent les Ngbans depuis longtemps - l'espoir du pillage suffira pour obtenir leur concours.'[62] Delafosse employed this technique with considerable skill, enlisting the support of Baule from the Ouarébo of Toumodi itself and the Aïtu of the Abli region. When French troops were not forthcoming, Delafosse marshalled his Baule allies in an offensive against Kouadio Okou, pursuing him westwards to the right bank of the Bandama during November and December 1899.[63] Delafosse failed to capture Kouadio Okou, but he was successful in keeping him away from the Tiassalé-Toumodi route. An uneasy calm returned to the area.

On the surface it appeared that little had been lost and little gained. On a more fundamental level, however, the Lomo revolt marked a decisive shift in the character of Baule resistance. The lines of conflict were sharply drawn, but they were no longer uniquely between the French and the Baule. Rather they reflected more closely the classic lines of rivalry between local Baule chiefdoms. Delafosse sought deliberately to exacerbate these rivalries, and at his invitation Baule chiefs took up arms against their traditional enemies. The French, who had come to the area to elevate the Baule towards 'civilization', soon found themselves sinking irretrievably into the quagmire of local politics. On the spot, France's colonial empire was no stronger than its local allies; to champion the French cause meant in practical terms to further the interests of particular partisans. Delafosse wedded the French cause to that of particular chiefs, and in doing so he insured that if Baule resistance against the French were to continue it would inevitably express itself locally at least in part as a civil war between rival Baule groups.

MILITARY OCCUPATION, REQUISITIONS, AND GENERALIZED RESISTANCE, 1900-1902

Albert Nebout returned from his leave and took charge of Baule territory from Delafosse at Ouossou on 14 December 1899. In the following weeks his major effort was directed at trying to dissuade

Akafou from openly joining forces with Kouadio Okou. A close alliance between the two chiefs was improbable, given their history of conflict prior to French arrival, but Akafou risked losing the support of several Ngban villages if he appeared to be siding with the French. Yao Guié, himself an Ngban chief from the Kpouébo area, had been instrumental in encouraging Kouadio Okou to defy Delafosse, and in the following weeks he rallied a fraction of the Ngbans to Kouadio Okou's cause. Faced with the possible decline of his influence if he associated too closely with Nebout, Akafou withdrew from direct contact with the French and waited expectantly to see what initiatives the French were going to take. Despite rumours of an imminent attack in January 1900, nothing happened. Nebout avoided doing anything to provoke hostilities, and when the Ngban killed an itinerant Apollonien merchant, the French let the incident pass virtually unnoticed. Without sufficient troops all Nebout could do was to exhort Kouadio Okou's traditional enemies to separate themselves from the revolt, threatening eventual reprisals against those who joined Kouadio Okou.[64]

Nebout hoped that reinforcements would arrive before the Baule would call his bluff. Several months earlier, while still in France on leave, he had obtained authorization for a company of troops to assist him in implementing the newly-drawn-up plans for collecting taxes and conducting a census in the Baule territory, but these troops had not arrived when he resumed control from Delafosse. He had only a militia force of about forty men at his disposal, and he rapidly realized that this was insufficient for the task at hand. By the end of December he urgently requested three companies of Senegalese troops from his superiors.[65]

Delafosse's request for two companies had come to naught just three months earlier, partially as a result of the administrative reorganizations stemming from the measures of 17 October 1899.[66] By December, however, the lines of administrative procedure were more clearly defined, and the renewed appeal from Nebout convinced Governor Roberdeau that there was more at stake than a simple misunderstanding with a troublesome chief. The Governor planned to combine some of the troops operating in the Assikasso area with other contingents from the Cavally region to form the equivalent of one company within the colony itself. For the remaining two companies he dispatched an urgent request to Governor General Chaudié in St. Louis, emphasizing that two companies would be the absolute minimum to assert French control among the southern Baule.[67]

The response from St. Louis was disappointing. Governor General

Chaudié indicated that only one company would be forthcoming.[68] Furthermore, Colonel Combes, the supreme military commander of French West Africa, had persuaded Chaudié that the operation should be under the complete control of military personnel and not the local civilian administration.[69] The well-worn debate between civilian and military authority had not been completely laid to rest by the measures of 17 October 1899; the military commanders might have lost their autonomy in the Sudan, but they were about to reassert it in the Ivory Coast – this time with the full support of the civilian Governor General.

Governor Roberdeau objected strenuously to these conditions, both to the Governor General and to the Minister, arguing that Nebout should retain control of Baule administration while deploying military force simply as an auxiliary means of persuading the Baule to come to terms.[70] Roberdeau predicted that full military control would be disastrous, and he absolved himself of all responsibility for the forth-coming operations:

Je crains, tout en souhaitant fort me tromper, que les résultats de ce plan soient fâcheux et n'aboutissent qu'à troubler plus profondément le pays; je vous prie donc de ne pas trouver mauvais que je ne prenne aucune responsabilité dans un programme qui n'est pas celui que j'avais proposé . . .[71]

In the event, the lines of authority remained ambiguous for several months to come. The company of troops arrived from the Sudan under the direction of Commander Donnat, during February and March 1900, and Donnat and Nebout worked out a tentative basis for co-operation.[72] The results were not entirely satisfactory, however, and the military officers continued to press for complete control.[73] In July 1900, in the face of growing Baule resistance, Governor Roberdeau finally acceded to their request, and transformed the Baule region into a military territory, conferring full administrative responsibility upon the military officers under Commander Donnat's direction.[74]

Over the following months and years, Roberdeau's pessimistic predictions proved to be accurate. Military intervention generated further Baule resistance and revolt spread to groups with no previous contact with the French. Trading partners and allies by marriage were mobilized throughout Baule country, making it impossible for the French to localize the scope of the revolt.

The crux of the problem lay in the poor provisioning and insufficient support alloted to the occupying troops from the outset. The troops were not supplied with their usual rations of rice from Senegal or the Sudan, nor were they accompanied by porters to carry food, munitions, and medical supplies. This was an attempt at an economy drive, for rations of rice from Senegal and paid porters would have inflated the cost of the military manœuvres beyond the bounds which the Governor General and the administration in Paris were prepared to tolerate. The Minister had gone on record indicating that the era of military conquest needed to be terminated in West Africa.[75] Samory had been captured and the costly military campaigns of the Sudan were thought to be a thing of the past. In these circumstances it was unrealistic to expect the government to go on financing an expensive new military initiative.

Locally, the result was that the occupying troops depended entirely upon the Baule to supply their needs. Colonel Combes expected Commander Donnat to obtain both provisions and porters from the Baule. In trying to do so Donnat antagonized the Baule upon whom the French might otherwise have counted for support. The civilian administration had not attempted previously to collect taxes among the Baule, but in August 1900 the military commanders imposed an obligatory tax to be paid in kind and labour. Each household was expected to provide annually: one porter to transport supplies for two days; three days of work to clear roads; ten yams; and 100 to 150 grams of raw rubber. In addition every group of thirty households was required to provide one goat and one chicken.[76]

Some of the Baule groups immediately surrounding the French posts provided the required goods, hoping that the troops would not remain long in the area.[77] The military commanders also minimized their demands at first, realizing that foodstuffs were in short supply until the harvests of September and October became available. Their plan was to increase their exactions once the harvest was collected, and they intended then to launch their offensive against Kouadio Okou who was still at large.[78]

The problem with this strategy was that as the military requisitions became more pronounced, the Baule, who had up until this point retained an uncommitted attitude towards the dispute between Kouadio Okou and the French, began to side more explicitly with Kouadio Okou and the Ngban faction under Yao Guié who were in open revolt. Nebout had succeeded in neutralizing Akafou in the southern Baule region during the early months of 1900, and Akafou appeared willing to pay the French a tribute in gold, thinking perhaps that this was what the French had come for.[79] Simultaneously, however, Akafou reinforced his alliance with the northern Ngban,[80] and Kouadio Okou sought an alliance with the northern Ouarébo.[81] Both chiefs were preparing their defences in case the French opened an offensive. In the meantime their followers deserted the vicinity of the French outposts, taking care to hide their stocks of food and valuables in forest encampments.

Given the reluctance of the Governor General to supply provisions for the troops, and given the increasing unwillingness of the Baule to provide foodstuffs for their uninvited guests, it was only a matter of time before the French felt obliged to confiscate provisions by force. To Nebout the situation looked critical shortly after he handed over control to the military authorities. As he observed to the Governor:

> J'estime que le Commandant du Baoulé militaire n'a pas les moyens suffisants pour soumettre le pays. Les vivres manquent. . . . A un moment donné, le chef militaire devra faire la guerre, piller, pour faire vivre la troupe . . .[82]

By the time Nebout described the dynamic of the confrontation, it had already begun to take place. In May 1900 Commander Donnat issued orders for the first explicit attack on the Baule since Delafosse's makeshift offensives in November 1899. He instructed Captain Le Magnen, based in Bouaké, to conduct a monitory expedition against the northern Ngban. The ostensible purpose of the exercise was to make a show of French military prowess in such a way as to discourage northern groups from lending support to the southern Baule in the forthcoming campaign against Kouadio Okou and the dissident Ngban. In the event, Le Magnen attacked several Nzipri villages. His troops inflicted few casualties upon the Baule warriors, for most of them fled after brief engagements, but the conduct of the troops left the Baule in no doubt as to what was at stake. Le Magnen recounted the events in his official report:

> Après quelques minutes, on n'entendait plus un coup de fusil, les chemins de sortie étaient reconnus et le pillage du village commencait sous la protection des patrouilles . . .
> Le détachment ramenait huit prisonniers baoulés, un homme, trois femmes, et 4 enfants; huit captifs évadés des villages d'Atiégouakrou et de Kougnanne Kouadiokro, sept fusils et un butin composé de poulets, de sel, pagnes, savons, etc.; ce butin a été reparti entre les tirailleurs ayant pris part à l'action. Les prisonniers baoulés sont gardés comme otages; un certificat de liberté est demandé pour les captifs évadés.[83]

The fact that the Nzipri of Atiégouakro who had done nothing explicit to provoke the French none the less suffered from this organized plundering campaign, while the French did nothing to pursue Kouadio Okou, must have given other Baule groups reason to wonder what lay in store for them if the French remained. Instead of discouraging the development of open revolt, Le Magnen's expedition had precisely the opposite effect. Resistance sentiment spread rapidly throughout the north, particularly when it became apparent that as a matter of policy the French intended to liberate slaves. Baule slaves had once again begun to seek refuge at French posts, and conditions around Bouaké began to resemble the situation of two years earlier when the exodus of captives after Samory's defeat led the Baule to attack the Bouaké post in December 1898.[84]

Kasso, the brother of Kouassi Blé, the chief of Bouaké, assembled a group of partisans and began to travel throughout the northern Baule region exhorting the Baule to resist. His strategy was simple: he advocated total abstention from all relations with the French. 'Quand les blancs n'auront plus à manger', he explained, 'ils partiront.'[85] Kasso threatened to burn villages which continued to supply the French with foodstuffs, and as a result of his persuasion and the exhortations of the northern Ngban, the prospects of open revolt were openly discussed among two major groups of Faafoué - one under the leadership of Kouassi Blé and the other under a chief named Mvlan.[86]

Despite this kind of pressure the Fahari, under Koffi Ottokou, continued to supply the French faithfully at Bouaké with provisions, perhaps because they remembered that the French had executed Kotia Koffi for his open opposition in 1898.[87] In addition the Don peoples under Bendé Kouassi remained faithful to the French, in the hope of using the French to establish their autonomy from the Ouarébo.[88] But beyond these groups the only partisans for peace and accommodation with French in the north were the followers of an elderly woman chief named Kano. She had first met Marchand in 1893 and in 1900 she tried to use her influence among the Faafoué to advocate moderation. When she died in November 1900, however, the proponents of revolt among the Faafoué were virtually unopposed.[89] The Ahari and the Ngban along with the two major Faafoué factions provided the core of the northern dissenters. The Ouarébo were not openly hostile, but the French expected them to become so if the movement gained further ground.[90]

The French were unprepared for this rapid extension of revolt sentiment, and the military commanders began to agree with the civilian administrators that more troops would be required. They had anticipated that their attention would be focused in the south, but by striking their first blow against a northern group, the French opened up an entirely different theatre of operations. When Commander Aymerich took over control of the troops from Donnat in October

1900, the situation was critical. Communications between Bouaké and Kodiokofikro were precarious, and the post at Bouaké had to be reinforced with a contingent of sixty troops under Lieutenant Buck from the south.[91] Initial French attempts to intimidate the Baule by destroying several Faafoué villages in early November had no effect, and towards the end of the month Commander Aymerich was prevented from reaching Bouaké from Kodiokofikro by armed bands of Ahari and Ngban warriors. Aymerich cabled the Governor, urgently requesting two more companies of reinforcements.[92]

Governor Roberdeau forwarded the requests to Governor General Ballay, but since Ballay was new in his post and generally reluctant to launch fresh military initiatives, he sent the request to the Minister of the Colonies before acting.[93] The process was a long and cumbersome one, and it was not until January 1901 that a decision was taken to send more troops. Meanwhile the situation deteriorated in the northern Baule region and Baule warriors besieged the Bouaké post during the night of 20-1 December. As with the earlier siege in December 1898 it proved unsuccessful, but the post remained cut off from the rest of the French forces until Commander Aymerich finally broke through the Baule lines and reached Bouaké with reinforcements from Kodiokofikro on 27 December 1900.[94]

Bendé Kouassi of the Don and Koffi Ottokou of the Fahari were the only chiefs among the northern Baule whom the French could continue to count upon for support, and their authority began to be eroded in the eyes of their following. Koffi Ottokou frequented the French post, but the majority of the Fahari began to refuse to supply provisions to the French.[95] When Bendé Kouassi asked the Commanders for a French flag as a symbol of his fidelity to the French cause, he was publicly ridiculed by surrounding chiefs for his willingness to collaborate.[96]

The French position strengthened in January 1901 with the arrival of troop reinforcements and the development of a new strategy drawn up in St. Louis by General Combes, Supreme Commander of Troops in French West Africa, Governor General Ballay and François-Joseph Clozel, Secretary General of the Ivory Coast colony. The experiences of the previous year of military activity had amply demonstrated that poorly planned military initiatives generated more problems than they resolved and that if the French were to succeed, they would have to cultivate the collaboration of particular Baule groups. As things were, the French presence weighed most heavily upon those whom they considered as allies, for it was from these groups that provisions were obtained and porters were recruited. In St. Louis, Combes, Ballay and

Clozel agreed that in the future the heaviest exactions should be placed upon the most hostile groups, while those who collaborated should be relieved of the burden of porterage labour and requisitions. In this manner they hoped to encourage more Baule to collaborate. Combes issued orders to Commander Aymerich in the Ivory Coast to create a series of secondary military posts, on the one hand to link Tiassalé, Toumodi, Kodiokofikro and Bouaké in secure communication, and on the other to spread the burden of provisioning more evenly throughout Baule territory.[97]

The arrival of troops in Bouaké and Toumodi began to encourage some groups to come to terms with the French during February 1901.[98] Kouassi Blé and Mvlan of the Faafoué inquired tentatively concerning the conditions the French would impose, but at first their inquiries were not immediately followed up with definite gestures of compliance.[99] Nevertheless the French position seemed marginally more secure than during the previous year. Groups around Ouossou and Toumodi in the south remained quiet in the early months of 1901, and in the north Aymerich reported that 'plusieurs chefs de village amis ont demandé des drapeaux . . .'.[100] The French strategy seemed to be working by gradually enlarging the circle of active or potential collaborators. In concentrating their own efforts on maintaining supply lines and by avoiding any head-on confrontation with dissident groups, the officers appeared to be making some headway in creating the context within which collaboration was an attractive strategy for Baule chiefs to pursue. Kasso's prediction of imminent French departure had proved wrong, and by March 1901 Mvlan, the leader of the important group of Pépréssou-Faafoué, agreed to the French terms for terminating hostilities.[101] After a series of minor battles between other Faafoué factions and a detachment under the command of Aymerich, most of the remaining Faafoué groups agreed to French demands. Mvlan offered to serve as an intermediary to help the French secure the personal submission of Kouassi Blé as well as the dissident Ouarébo, and by the time General Combes arrived in Baule territory in April 1901 for a tour of inspection, the strategy which he had inaugurated with Clozel and Ballay in January appeared to be enjoying a measure of success.

To crown success with glory General Combes devised a plan which he thought would crush Baule resistance once and for all – he proposed to capture Kokumbo, the principal centre of Baule gold-mining activity. The goldfields in the Kokumbo area had initially been taken over from the Gouro by migrant Faafoué groups from the north about 1840, but the Faafoué were not the only Baule to work the Kokumbo gold deposits. In exchange for a proportion of the gold mined, the Faafoué chiefs of Kokumbo and the surrounding villages allowed other groups of Baule to dig for gold and work the mountain streams in the area.[102] The result was that small colonies of workers – for the most part trusted slaves under the direction of individual freemen – came to Kokumbo and clustered in a series of settlements in and around the mountain of Kokum Boka to dig for gold on behalf of chiefs throughout Baule country.

Ever since Marchand had first seen Kokumbo in 1893 the French had been aware of the importance of this gold-mining centre in the eyes of the entire Baule population. Visits to the mining sites had been made by French observers in 1896 and 1897,[103] and after preliminary reconnaissance missions during 1900 Commander Donnat suggested that the capture of the town would have a widely felt impact throughout Baule country because of the numerous prospectors in Kokumbo from all of the Baule groups.[104] In the spring of 1901 General Combes felt the moment had come for just such a dramatic gesture. He ordered Colonel Colonna d'Istria to occupy Kokumbo, and Commander Aymerich was instructed to execute a simultaneous campaign to rout out pockets of dissident Baule among the northern groups. Combes intended the two initiatives to mark a decisive departure from the fitful approach that he felt had characterized French military intervention to date, and he ordered his subordinates to devastate the recalcitrant groups as thoroughly as possible.[105]

Preparations for both campaigns began in late May. By mid-June Aymerich had completed his operations against the northern groups. With the help of the Soundo group under the leadership of chief Mbaya, Aymerich subdued groups of Ngban, Ahari, and Agba, and having completed his mission he made plans for his departure from the Ivory Coast, on leave.[106] The Kokumbo campaign was more drawn out and required more elaborate preparation for the assault of the defended town. After preliminary troop movements from Toumodi and Ouossou the French set up headquarters at Kpoumboubo and began to solicit the support of Baule groups around Kokumbo to take part in the attack.[107] On 9 June shortly after sunrise, Colonna d'Istria launched the offensive. After several hours of intense fighting against an estimated 1,500 to 2,000 Baule warriors, the advance guard under Adjudant Tournois finally reached the centre clearing in Kokumbo. The Baule defence had fallen and fled. Kokumbo was under French control.[108]

As the French had expected, the news of the capture of Kokumbo reverberated throughout Baule country. Combined with the impact of Aymerich's campaign in the north, the fall of Kokumbo appeared to break the will of the Baule to resist – at least for the time being. Groups that had cut off all contact with the French in the Bouaké vicinity ever since the revolt of December 1898 began to appear once again and affirm their fidelity to the French cause. The Faafoué under Kouassi Blé and Mvlan protested their allegiance and agreed to pay the French indemnities. The southern Faafoué in the Kokumbo region under their chief Kumi followed suit. During June and early July groups of Bro, Don, Fahari, Ahari, Saa, and Ngban arrived in Bouaké to swear their allegiance and come to terms with the French.

The sentiment of capitulation spread to groups with whom the French had had no previous contact. Because Kokumbo was defended by partisans from throughout Baule country, its capture affected many groups beyond its immediate vicinity. In June, for example, Lieutenant Nodé-Langlois reported:

Le grand chef des Ouarébos, Kouamé Guié, un fat et un poltron tout à la fois, s'est trouvé tout à coup disposé à la paix. Il a envoyé des boys (l'un d'eux serait son fils, mais je n'ai pu vérifier le fait) proposer sa soumission et tâter le terrain. Tout porte à croire que le 7 juillet il sera à Bouaké.[109]

In the event, Kouamé Dié did not arrive to present his submission until August 1901, but when it finally occurred, the surrender turned out to be a major public event. Accompanied by his principal wives, a series of village and regional chiefs, and an entourage of 200 supporters, Kouamé Dié arrived in Bouaké on 4 August 1901, several weeks after he was announced. As the French administrator explained:

L'orgueil seul empêchait ce chef de venir ici, il considérait cette démarche comme humiliante pour lui, le roi du pays. Enfin il se mettait en route lentement, très lentement le 28 juillet pour arriver ici le 4 août (Sakasso est à 2 petites étapes de Bouaké). Il accepte notre autorité avec toutes ses conséquences: création de postes, liberté des routes, impôt annuel, etc.
Suivant l'habitude, j'ai fixé l'amende qui est plutôt un tribut de soumission à 20 tas d'or.[110]

Among the southern groups the initial impact of the fall of Kokumbo seemed equally impressive. Kouadio Okou, who had taken refuge at first among the Souamélé and then among the northern Ouarébo after the Lomo revolt of 1899, was no longer a welcomed guest. In mid-July the chief of the Souamélé village of Sinzénou delivered Kouadio Okou to Captain Bastard and he was dispatched to

Toumodi for official surrender before Colonna d'Istria. Encouraged by the fact that Kouadio Okou was not brutally treated, Akafou also came forward to come to terms with the French. Akafou's own role in the Lomo affair and the following months of unrest remained unclear, but he had refused open contact with the French since October 1899. After the Kokumbo defeat he apparently felt, like Kouadio Okou, that it was time to make peace with the French, even at the cost of paying a tribute if necessary. On 9 August 1901 in a public gathering at Ouossou both chiefs acceded to French demands. Commander Colonna d'Istria imposed a tribute of twenty *tas* of gold (the equivalent of 3,000 f.) to be paid by Akafou and a more severe fine of fifty *tas* (or 7,500 f.) to be paid by Kouadio Okou in recognition of his instrumental role in provoking the Lomo revolt.[111] Neither Kouadio Okou nor Akafou were overly enthusiastic about rendering these enormous sums,[112] and they apparently tried to evade paying them in full. Nevertheless the French were in dire need of money to buy local provisions for their troops, and they were determined to deal harshly with these important chiefs to set an example for others. Captain Bastard imprisoned both Kouadio Okou and Akafou until their payments were made in full in October.[113]

This humiliating experience, following upon the defeat of Kokumbo, seriously undermined the position of these chiefs. Kouadio Okou, impoverished, betrayed, and disgraced, lost his following and withdrew ignominiously to live among the Souamélé where he had relations through the marriage of his daughter.[114] Akafou's position was somewhat stronger, but still precarious. During the 1890s he had acquired the honorific title *Bulare* ('iron', 'the man of iron'), partially because of his victory over Kouadio Okou, his major local competitor,[115] and partially because it appeared to his following that his negotiations with Monteil in February 1895 were responsible for Monteil's departure during the following month.[116]

Many Baule had come to believe that Akafou's skill as a firm negotiator had kept the French from occupying the country in 1895, and similarly his potential strength appeared to keep them from openly attacking the Ngban villages in the south during 1900 and 1901. The French had focused their attention in the north and upon Kokumbo, and it looked as if by acceding to their demand for tribute Akafou had once again succeeded in keeping the French at bay. The tribute payment was heavy and humiliating in itself, but if it served to reduce the threat of future French intrusion, the payment of the tribute would help Akafou Bulare to retain the loyalty of his following. If, on the other hand, the French presence began to weigh ever more heavily

upon the Ngban, Akafou Bulare's position would be seriously compromised, for he would appear foolish to have paid so much for so
little in return. Thus, the strength of Akafou Bulare as a chief and his
usefulness to the French as a potential collaborator depended largely
upon what kinds of demands the French would make upon him in
the months immediately following his payment of the tribute. If
their demands were too heavy, or if their treatment of him and the
other major chiefs such as Kouamé Dié too brutal, the cause of collaboration was not likely to gain many adherents among the junior
chiefs, for few Baule would willingly submit themselves to such
humiliation.

In the southern regions as in the north, several chiefs with no
previous record of relations with the French came forward to swear
their fidelity after the fall of Kokumbo. Once again the fact that many
southern groups had sent warriors to defend Kokumbo appears to have
explained why its capture by the French had the impact it did. During
July 1901 Attiégoua, an important chief among the Nanafoué, travelled
to Toumodi to present his submission as did groups of Gouro, with
whom the French had had somewhat strained relations since an
unsuccessful exploration mission had been forced to abandon its
efforts in Gouro country in 1897.[117]

In addition, an influential woman by the name of Yabo Mousso,
whom the French described as the 'femme chef des Akoués' allegedly
dipatched two of her sons to affirm her loyalty to the French cause in
late June 1901. Simultaneously the French moved into Akoué country
northwards from Kokumbo. A detachment of French troops under Lt.
Schneiggans established a new outpost at Bonzi among the Akoué on
28 June 1901, and the Adjoint Tournois took charge of cultivating the
cordial relations which Yabo Mousso's envoys had promised would
ensue. Yabo Mousso herself arrived at Bonzi on 7 July 1901 and
publicly affirmed that the Akoué would not begin hostilities against the
French so long as the French, for their part, would not wage war on the
Akoué.[118]

By September 1901, then, it appeared that Combes's military
initiatives were finally bringing the Baule to heel. Buoyed up by the
success of their campaigns the officers began to make plans for a
systematic census of all Baule villages and the regular collection of a
head tax, which Clozel had formally introduced in his capacity as acting
Governor in May 1901.[119] Control over the entire Baule region was consolidated under Colonna d'Istria whom Clozel designated upon General
Combes's departure as the 'Commandant de la Région du Baoulé'.[120]

Clozel was confident that General Combes's intervention had provided Baule administration with the firm footing that it had lacked from the beginning of the colonial period. Ever since the ill-fated Monteil expedition in 1894-5, French military intrusion had been a series of fitful mistakes. Campaigns under Captain le Magnen (1899), Commander Donnat (1900), and Commander Aymerich (1900-1) left the Baule with no clear conviction that the French intended to remain amongst them permanently. Each offensive had been followed by an inconclusive lull in fighting and a more or less direct departure of a portion of the French forces. It is not surprising that the Baule came to anticipate that the French would withdraw whenever the rains made troop manœuvres difficult. General Combes's strategy had such a resounding impact partially because he pursued his offensive throughout the rainy season, and this time Clozel was determined to retain enough troops in Baule territory to prove that the French had come to stay.[121]

Clozel's decision as acting Governor to maintain troop strength and confide all administrative functions to military officers proved to be disastrous for the cause of peace. Within a year of the seemingly unequivocal surrenders of Kouamé Dié, Akafou Bulare, Kouadio Okou, Yabo Mousso, Kouassi Blé, and others in August 1901, Baule groups once again resorted to armed struggle to resist further exactions from the domineering intruders. The problem was that although in August 1901 the paramount chiefs thought it was in their interest to negotiate a peace settlement with the French, their motivation to do so was not born of a pervasive sense of defeat among the Baule at large. Rather it seems to have stemmed from a calculated gamble on the part of the paramount chiefs that the costs for them of collaboration would probably not be as great as those of further resistance.

If the French had been satisfied with the tribute payments and withdrawn their troops as they had done repeatedly in the past, the gamble of the paramount chiefs would have paid off. Indeed, the paramount chiefs would probably have acquired a measure of prestige in much the same way as Akafou had several years earlier when he became known as the 'man of iron' after Monteil's departure in 1895. Kouamé Dié in particular would have gained stature, for if the French withdrew, he would have succeeded in diverting them from creating an outpost in his own village of Sakassou - something which none of the other major paramount chiefs had succeeded in averting. The expectation of French departure was not entirely unrealistic on the part of the paramount chiefs, given their historical experience. Their past encounters with the

French had nurtured the idea that sooner or later the French withdrew, and it is possible that they felt that by paying the tribute they could hasten that process. The payment of war compensations was not in itself foreign to the Baule. Within Baule custom it was normal procedure for the loser in battle to pay indemnities to the victor, usually in gold. Since this is what the French seemed to be after in the conquest of Kokumbo, it is plausible that the chiefs calculated that by relinquishing some gold they could purchase the right to no further interference. This was, after all, the way in which Europeans seemed to act elsewhere. On the Gold Coast, the British seemed content to withdraw to Cape Coast once again in 1900 after they had tried in vain to obtain the Ashanti Golden Stool.[122]

During the last months of 1901 and the early months of 1902 it became abundantly apparent to all Baule that the calculated gamble of the paramount chiefs was not producing the desired result. Not only did the troops remain, but the officers whom Clozel had placed in charge of collecting the newly introduced taxes were increasingly assertive and demanding. The taxes themselves were irritating to the Baule. Whereas they were accustomed to the payment of war indemnities,[123] the idea of renewable annual tribute was largely foreign to them. Stable political hierarchies so often correlated with practices of annual tribute payments in other parts of West Africa were absent among the pre-colonial Baule, and as a consequence the French attempt to collect annual taxes was an unprecedented innovation among most of the Baule in a way in which it was not among other groups in the colony.[124] Moreover, the military officers became increasingly intolerant of Baule hesitation. Whereas the Baule had hoped that the tribute payments would attenuate the French demands, the officers regarded them as initial symbolic gestures which they fully expected to be followed by manifest subservience and a continuous willingness to accede to all demands for provisions and labour.

As part of Combes's strategy the burdens of provisioning troops at Bouaké, Toumodi, and Ouossou were to be spread more evenly among the outlying groups, and it was precisely within these groups that discontent began to ferment. In the southern region the Ngban from the village of Kpouébo began to manifest open hostility in late 1901 towards Captain Bastard in charge of the post at Ouossou. Akafou, protesting his continued fidelity to the French cause, tried to act as a go-between to conciliate the Kpouébo Ngban and Captain Bastard, but his efforts failed and the Kpouébo peoples remained estranged from the French.[125] Under these circumstances Akafou Bulare's own position

became precarious indeed. When he was not able to command the submission of the Kpouébo Ngban, Captain Bastard began to have serious
reservations about Akafou's utility as a collaborator. Indeed, despite
Akafou's repeated affirmations of fidelity, Captain Bastard began to
suspect Akafou of double sympathies and developed doubt about his
sincerity. Akafou, for his part, was caught in a dilemma similar to that
at the time of the first Ngban revolt in 1895 and Kouadio Okou's revolt
in 1899. Given that the French were not departing and that Yao Guié
of Kpouébo had become the open spokesman for opposition to the
French, Akafou risked losing his own following if the resistance movement were to gain more ground.[126]

In the north, the officers at Bouaké began to consider Kouamé
Dié, paramount chief of the Ouarébo, as an obstacle to their plans for
collecting taxes. Before the French arrival Kouamé Dié was one of the
exceptional paramount chiefs who had apparently succeeded in exacting
tribute from subordinate groups. Kouamé Dié originated from a group
known as the Ouarébo-Assabou, but in the late 1890s he had extended
his control over the groups of Ouarébo-Faafoué and the Ouarébo-
Linguira. In addition his influence among the Bros and the Don was
also steadily increasing. Initial French intelligence reports indicated that
both the Ouarébo-Faafoué and the Ouarébo-Linguira would rally to the
French cause if the French were to launch a campaign to capture
Kouamé Dié in Sakassou, and the French were already aware that the
Don under Bendé Kouassi welcomed French intrusion to rid themselves
of Kouamé Dié's dominance.[127] Later reconnaissance missions revealed
that the Ouarébo-Faafoué, under their chief Koffi Ossou, would remain
faithful to Kouamé Dié in an eventual attack, but the Ouarébo-Linguira
could be counted upon to lend their support to the French against
Kouamé Dié. As Lieutenant Nodé-Langlois reported:

Les Linguiras réclament l'occupation de leur tribu par un poste. Ils ont
subi tant de vexations de la part de Kouami Dié qu'ils nous acceptent
comme des sauveurs. L'impôt qu'on leur demandera, disent-ils, leur
coûtera toujours moins cher que les taxations auxquelles ils sont
astreints . . . La situation est donc bien nette. Nous pouvons compter
absolument sur les Linguiras.[128]

The French officers anticipated that Kouamé Dié would oppose
their alliance with dissident groups of Ouarébo under his control, and
they feared that he would seek revenge in one form or another in the
future. As a result they envisaged eliminating him from the outset. By
the end of September 1901, only a few days after Kouamé Dié had paid
his full tribute of twenty *tas* of gold and sworn his submission, French
officers were formulating plans for Kouamé Dié's 'disappearance'.

Kouami Dié est trop autoritaire pour admettre notre ingérence dans ses affaires. Il a fait sa soumission, il a accepté toutes nos conditions, il a payé son tribut de guerre, mais en occupant le pays les indigènes se détacheront de lui pour se ranger sous nos lois humanitaires.

Voyant alors son autorité s'amoindrir il aura peut-être recours aux grand moyens pour chercher à conserver la trône vermoulue sur lequel repose son prestige.

Sa disparition s'impose . . .[129]

The campaign against Sakassou began in February 1902. A four-pronged manœuvre under Captain Lambert, from Bouaké, Captain Privey from Kodiokofikro, Captain Moreau from Séguéla and Lieutenant Dessuze from Salékro converged on Sakassou. In a quickly executed surprise attack on 22 February 1902 the French captured the village and with it Kouamé Dié himself. Many of Kouamé Dié's supporters fled and the French were in the process of discussing the terms of formal surrender with Kouamé Dié when a band of Ouarébo warriors under the command of Dié Lonzo, Kouamé Dié's son, tried to improvise a counter-attack. In the exchange that followed between the French and the Ouarébo partisans, Kouamé Dié was shot and killed.[130] The first major paramount chief, reputed to be the direct descendant and heir of Queen Poku, had fallen.

The French congratulated themselves on their victory, but the capitulation of Baule forces was not as thorough as they had hoped. The Ouarébo-Linguira, led by Okou Boni and his brother Okou N'Gatta, lent their support to the French along with N'Gatta Blé Koffi, the chief of Niamiabo and the woman chief, Moya Ba, from the village of Andofoué, but in the following months Koffi Ossou, chief of the Ouarébo-Faafoué faction, continued the armed resistance to the French and the revolt spread to the Kodé, led by Yao Guié of Béoumi.[131] In short, instead of suppressing resistance in the north, the unprovoked murder of Kouamé Dié had the effect of generating dissidence on an even wider scale. The pre-emptive use of military force to solve political problems had proved disastrous.

Among the southern groups conditions continued to deteriorate, and the officers became more and more impatient with their incapacity to command the respect of the population. Captain Bastard failed to obtain the compliance of the Kpouébo-Ngban, and Akafou Bulare's position appeared to be increasingly compromised. During the early months of 1902 three concomitant events raised the level of tension in the area significantly. In the first place the news of Kouamé Dié's death had a sobering effect upon Akafou Bulare who redoubled his affirmation of allegiance to the French. Secondly, General Houry, General

Combes's replacement as the Supreme Commander of French West African troops, arrived to inspect the progress of military operations during March 1902. This too had the effect of muting local opposition in the south at least temporarily, for the memory of General Combes's visit at the same point during the previous year and the subsequent campaign against Kokumbo was still fresh in the memory of the southern groups. Baule chiefs waited to see if Houry's visit was to be a prelude to another major offensive before openly declaring their sympathies.

The third event served on the contrary to strengthen Baule resolve to resist. Returning to the Ivory Coast, Governor Roberdeau resumed control of the colony from acting Governor Clozel, and it appears as if he misread the political situation entirely. The confident tones of the military reports from Bouaké after the death of Kouamé Dié masked the extent of Baule resistance sentiment, and it is possible that Roberdeau was not aware of the seriousness of the internal situation. In any event he seemed more worried by the fact that the ban on the sale of gunpowder and guns in the Baule area was causing significant commercial damage to the trading houses on the coast and depriving the colony's budget of needed revenue. In a move which in retrospect can only be described as a monumental miscalculation, Roberdeau acceded to the demands of the commercial community to restore the free commerce in munitions, and on 8 March 1902 he authorized the sale of gunpowder and muskets in Baule territory.[132]

The impact was immediate. In April alone 1,241 barrels of gunpowder, amounting to a total of nearly 16 tons of explosives, were sold at Tiassalé along with 283 guns.[133] In May another 808 barrels or nearly 10 more tons were purchased along with 255 guns. By November a total of 776 guns and 45 tons of powder had been sold to the Baule at Tiassalé.[134] The Baule armed themselves on an unprecedented scale, creating a situation which was bound to make compliance impossible.

Throughout General Houry's presence in the Ivory Coast the military concentrated its efforts on pursuing Koffi Oussou among the Ouarébo, whom they captured at the end of May 1902.[135] During this period Captain Bastard at Ouossou was strictly forbidden to take any initiative against the increasingly hostile Kpouébo-Ngban in the south, for Commander Colonna d'Istria did not want to precipitate new and costly encounters while General Houry was on his tour of inspection.[136] General Houry left the Ivory Coast in early June, and no sooner had he departed than the situation among the southern Ngban took a turn for the worse.

On 28 June 1902 Akafou Bulare presented himself at the Ouossou post accompanied by sixty well-armed warriors with the intention of talking to Captain Bastard. Among the men were chiefs from the dissident village of Kpouébo, but not those known to be most hostile. It appears that Akafou Bulare was trying to make a show of force to negotiate some kind of settlement of grievances between the Kpouébo and the French, but before talks could get underway, the encounter took an unexpected twist. Bastard commanded the Baule to put down their arms; Akafou ordered them to retain them. Bastard then dispatched a French officer and several Senegalese troops to disarm the group - by force if necessary. In the mêlée that ensued, the majority of the warriors escaped, but the French succeeded in capturing 55 guns and Akafou Bulare himself. Akafou was imprisoned, and although Captain Bastard admitted that Akafou's role was not altogether clear in the incident, he was repeatedly beaten and eventually died in his cell on 8 July 1902.[137]

Akafou Bulare's death, following upon that of Kouamé Dié, and the massive Baule rearmament, triggered a widespread revolt among the entire Ngban population and beyond. Attacks on trading caravans along the major north-south axis began in July, spreading to the Agba and the southern Ouarébo as well.[138] A French offensive against the dissident Agba was so miserably ineffective that other groups were moved to the verge of revolt. The Akoué were reported to be encouraged by Agba successes against the French, and the administrator at the Bonzi post warned that his position was precarious: 'agir par la force ne donnerait comme résultat que le soulèvement général de la tribu ne demandant qu'un motif pour se soulever.'[139]

Confidence among the dissident groups was so high that a portion of the Akoué in consort with the Faafoué were making plans for the recapture of Kokumbo with the support of Nanafoué and Saafoué factions.[140] In September 1902 the Nanafoué attacked the French outpost at Salékro, cutting its supply lines with Kodiokofikro, and after several costly encounters with the Nanafoué the French evacuated the post, having sustained heavy losses.[141] Throughout October and November the French launched several minor initiatives against the southern Ngban, but by December 1902 they were forced to abandon their operations when they ran out of munitions. Militarily the French position had deteriorated seriously; politically the events of 1902 totally eclipsed the seeming gains which the French had been so proud to announce in August 1901.

Frustrated by the increasingly elusive movements of the Baule guerrillas and their own shortage of supplies, the military officers in the final months of 1902 opted for a strategy of total destruction against every dissident group within their range. What began as a limited operation by Delafosse against a single Baule chief, Kouadio Okou, in 1899, escalated to a full-scale 'search and destroy' policy against an entire population.[142] The pursuit of specific chiefs, or the capture of individual villages had proven futile. As one officer explained it:

Dans ce pays d'anarchie qu'est le Baoulé, l'objectif des colonnes n'est ni un roi à vaincre, ni une capitale à saisir, ni, en un mot un objectif géographique quelconque. Qu'il s'agisse d'un campement nouveau à conquérir, ou d'une tribu auparavant soumise mais révoltée à punir, le but à atteindre par la colonne est la réduction complète de cette tribu.[143]

To achieve victory in these circumstances pillage and destruction became the primary offensive weapons:

il faut avoir souvent recours à un système de réduction tout à fait spécial, en saisissant ou en détruisant . . . tout ce qui peut avoir le plus de prix aux yeux de l'adversaire . . . en ruinant méthodiquement tous ses biens, en capturant ses troupeaux, en libérant ses esclaves, en recherchant dans les cachettes les familles des combattants pour en retenir prisonniers les membres influents, voire même les femmes . . .[144]

Governor Roberdeau's pessimistic predictions of February 1900 had proved correct: by handing over control of the Baule territory exclusively to the military the only result after nearly three years of intermittent fighting had been to breed massive resistance on a scale previously unimaginable. What was worse, the situation showed no immediate signs of improving simply by continuing to use the same strategy. Indeed, the status quo had become completely untenable, for although the scope of resistance sentiment had expanded several-fold within a year, French troop strength had declined markedly from a total figure of 1,036 in June 1901[145] to only 637 by July 1902.[146] A dramatic change in policy was urgently required. Either the French would have to commit large amounts of additional personnel and materiel to launch a new and more extensive campaign against the Baule, or they would have to abandon hopes of military victory and seek instead to come to terms with them through more adroit political means. When Clozel assumed direction of the colony as acting Governor in November 1902, these were the stark alternatives confronting him.

The capture of Samory in 1898 signalled the beginning of the end for military rule in the French Sudan, but the same event engendered a series of reactions among the Baule, giving rise to a new theatre of

1 a. Captain Marchand (*c.* 1893),
first European explorer among Baule.

1 b. Commander Monteil (*c.* 1894),
commander of Kong Expedition, 1894–5

1 c. Albert Nebout (*c.* 1892),
first civilian administrator among Baule.

1 d. Maurice Delafosse (*c.* 1897),
early administrator and first ethnographer
of Baule peoples.

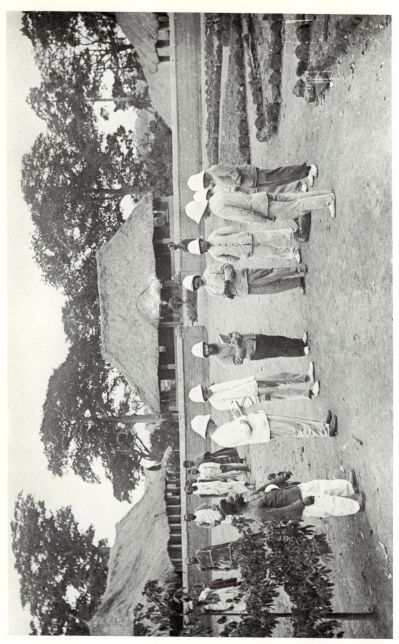

2. Officers outside the military outpost at Bouaké, established in 1898.

3. Akafou 'Bulare' (Akafou, the man of 'iron'), chief
of the southern Ngban, d. July 1902.

4 a. Governor General Ernest Roume,
first Governor General to establish
economic planning for French West
Africa as a whole.

4 b. Governor François-Joseph Clozel
(*c.* 1906), author of collaboration policy
with Baule.

4 c. Governor General William Ponty,
who authorized use of *tirailleurs sénégalais*
for final suppression of Baule resistance,
1910–11.

4 d. Governor Gabriel Angoulvant,
author of strong-arm tactics
for complete suppression of
Baule resistance after 1908.

COLONIE FRANÇAISE – COTE D'IVOIRE

Le Chef de Bataillon NOGUÈS, commandant

Coll. E.T-W.C.

5. Commander Noguès, commander of troops sent to defeat Baule resistance among the Akoué and Nanafoué, 1910–11.

6. Senegalese troops about to begin operations
against Rabih's 'army', 1910

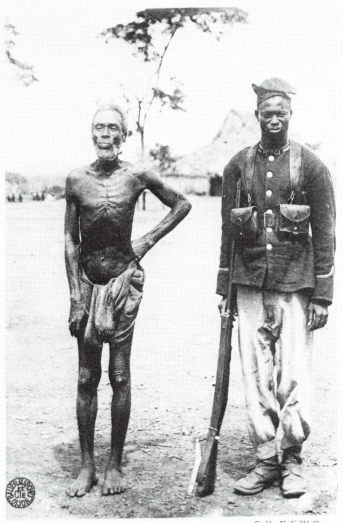

COLONIE FRANÇAISE   COTE D'IVOIRE

Coll. E.T.W.C.

Chef de tribu N'gbans prisonnier de guerre

7. Yao Guié, captured 13 June 1910, and died in captivity.

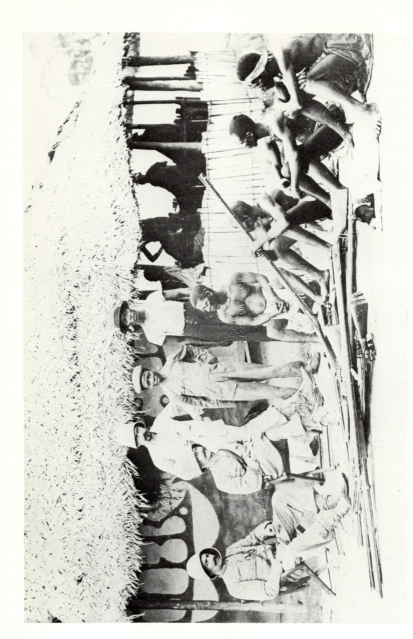

8. Baule warriors submit arms as part of conditions imposed for peace with French colonial administration

escalating military operations from 1898 to 1902. As so often happened in the Sudan, the consequences were costly and inconclusive. Impetuous young officers clamoured for more troops and supplies and requested authorization to extend their operations to crush Baule resistance once and for all.[147] In their zeal, however, the officers had overshot the mark. By dealing brutally with the paramount chiefs and allowing their strategy to degenerate to the level of unrestrained plunder and destruction, the officers diminished the possibility of achieving an imminent political settlement. It remained to be seen whether the civilian authorities would allow the military officers to run their course as they had in the Sudan, or whether they would seek to create a new atmosphere of political collaboration.

CHAPTER V

Governor Clozel's Peace Strategy and the Politics of Collaboration, 1903-1907

THE ORIGINS AND CHARACTER OF CLOZEL'S NEW POLICY

By the time Françoise-Joseph Clozel took control of the colony as acting governor in late 1902 he had already acquired considerable experience in the African colonies.[1] Born in 1860, Clozel became interested in colonial matters while completing his *service militaire* in Algeria. When his military obligation had been completed, he entered the Algerian administration in 1885 as a *Secrétaire de commune mixte*, and he began to cultivate an avid interest in Muslim society, religion, culture, and customs, under the continued guidance of Professor Octave Houdas at the *Faculté des lettres* in Algiers. In 1891 he joined an exploration mission to Tchad and continued explorations in the Congo in 1893. Through his mentor and teacher Houdas, Clozel met Binger after his return from the Congo, and in 1896 he came to the Ivory Coast for the first time to join the talented group of young administrators whom Governor Binger had assembled to assume the difficult task of establishing civilian administration in the colony in the wake of the disastrous Monteil expedition. Like Charles Monteil, Albert Nebout, and Maurice Delafosse whom he joined, Clozel was imbued with the conviction that the era of unrestrained military expansion was drawing to a close and that the colony could only proceed on a stable basis under the prudent administration of civilian authorities.

Clozel's experiences during his first few years of duty in the Ivory Coast severely tested these convictions. Placed in charge of the Anyi-Indiéné region, he succeeded in extending French control as far north as Bondoukou in a well-executed move to cut off Samory's eastward advance, but shortly thereafter he was seriously wounded in an assault led by Anyi warriors at Assikasso. He recuperated from his injuries in France, and returned to his post with a more sober appreciation of the difficult task of local administration.[2] In 1899 when Governor Roberdeau arrived to assume the direction of the colony, Clozel was promoted to Secretary General, and as Roberdeau was new to Africa and frequently absent from the colony itself, Clozel virtually ran the colony's affairs for the next three years - or at least this is how it looked in Grand Bassam.

In the interior the political situation deteriorated in Baule country from 1899 to 1902, and the military officers gained more and more independence from the direct control of the civilian administration. Clozel's attitude to these events remains rather obscure. By inclination, it would seem that Clozel, like Roberdeau, would have mistrusted the military, and it is possible that Roberdeau's strong and principled objection to the escalating military role as early as 1900 was inspired by Clozel, his closest adviser. On the other hand, Clozel's own experiences among the Anyi may have been sufficient to alter his earlier views on the necessity of military presence in much the same way that Delafosse after September 1899 became the advocate of strong military intervention.

Historians will have to await further research on Clozel's biography before anything can be said with assurance, but there are at least two major indices that Clozel became convinced of the necessity of firm military initiative. In the first place, Clozel, in his capacity as acting governor during January 1901, developed the plans in co-ordination with Governor General Ballay and General Combes for the major offensive campaigns of early 1901.[3] Secondly, once these campaigns had been executed by Aymerich and Colonna d'Istria, Clozel praised General Combes and made it clear to the Minister of Colonies that troop strength needed to be maintained among the Baule.[4] Both these actions were hardly consistent with a programme of limited civilian administration, and they suggest that under the pressure of events, Clozel had abandoned his earlier convictions concerning the limited character of proper colonial administration.

If this was the case, it is apparent that Clozel changed his mind once again in late 1902, for from November 1902 onwards Clozel became the outspoken exponent of peaceful accommodation with the Baule resisters. Here too several interpretations are possible. On the one hand, it is possible that Clozel was driven to this conclusion by the evident failure of the military to achieve decisive and enduring results. The euphoria and self-confidence which accompanied the symbolic submission of Kouassi Dié, Akafou Bulare, and Kouadio Okou in August 1901 faded quickly during the following year when it became evident that the military officers were incapable of transforming their military victories into a basis for stable and continuous administration in Baule country. The murder of Kouamé Dié in February 1902 and the death of Akafou Bulare in French hands in July of the same year removed two of the potentially most influential collaborators within Baule country, and the officers responsible for these deaths were clearly not able to control the repercussions of their own impetuous mistakes.

In this perspective, then, it would be possible to suggest that Clozel forsook the military approach on the basis of purely local calculations. As he admitted, it was probable that the French had sustained greater losses in fighting the Baule than they had been able to inflict upon the Baule, and under these circumstances to continue fighting would be sheer folly.[5] In this light, Clozel's policy was tantamount to an admission of military stalemate if not outright defeat. The Baule had won in battle, but perhaps, thought Clozel, it would be possible to subordinate them gradually by means of negotiation.

Without denying the validity of this perspective, it is none the less possible to highlight other less parochial considerations which may have been equally determinant in inspiring Clozel's new approach. To do this it is useful to glance back over the months leading up to Clozel's new policy. In January 1902 Ernest Roume, formerly a *Directeur* within the Colonial Ministry, was appointed as the Governor General of French West Africa. When he arrived to take up his functions in St. Louis in March, he learned of the deteriorating military situation among the Baule. As a long-standing opponent of military excesses,[6] it is probable that Roume was not pleased with the escalation of military operations. When in June he received the report of General Houry summarizing the result of Houry's military inspection among the Baule, he recognized how serious the situation had become.[7]

At the end of June 1902 Roume travelled to France for consultations with Gaston Doumergue, the newly appointed Minister of Colonies, and in October he returned with a new package of reforms designed to give the Governor General added power over the disparate territories in the federated structure of French West Africa.[8] Roume let it be known that he expected to exercise more control than his predecessors in order to strengthen the federal government structures.[9] As Colin Newbury has pointed out, 'Roume, intended to subordinate the territorial authorities as far as the 1902 Decree would allow – and further'.[10]

Clozel was summoned to Dakar, the new administrative capital of the Federation, in early November and there he was informed of Roume's plans for the administration of the Federation. This series of consultations and decisions culminating in Clozel's personal meetings with Roume in early November was perhaps as much responsible as the local military situation for the new turn in Clozel's policy when he returned to the Ivory Coast on 25 November 1902. Clozel may well have felt uneasy about the direction which events were taking in the colony throughout 1902, but it was not until he returned from meeting with Roume that he began to do something decisive to change the situation. As had happened earlier with the Monteil affair in 1895 and the Lomo revolt in 1899, deteriorating local circumstances combined with changing priorities in Paris and Dakar to determine the unfolding pattern of policy on the spot.

Whatever the ultimate origins of the policy were, its character became apparent within a few days of Clozel's return from Dakar. Commander Betsellère replaced Commander Colonna d'Istria in Baule country, and Lieutenant-Colonel Vimont, based in Grand Lahou, became the senior military commander for the entire Ivory Coast. Clozel instructed Betsellère to proceed in a negotiative manner, separating resisters from potential collaborators in an effort to forestall the possibility of a united Baule movement against the French - a spectre which began to worry the officers after the rumours about a combined assault on Kokumbo began to circulate.[11]

It would be an overstatement to characterize this policy as a strategy of 'divide and conquer', for the French had little hope of conquering the Baule in the immediate future. Nevertheless, Clozel clearly hoped to use Baule disunity to the administration's long-range advantage by making the option of collaboration attractive to at least some chiefs. In effect Clozel's 'new' policy represented the revival of the strategy that Albert Nebout had articulated as early as 1895: 'Il serait bon peut-être de profiter des haines qui existent entre certains peuplades; les unes compromises nous resteraient surement fidèles.'[12] Delafosse employed this approach in recruiting Baule partisans to pursue Kouadio Okou in 1899, and it met with a measure of success until the arrival of the occupying troops changed the entire character of the encounter between the French and the Baule from 1900 through 1902. Nebout, Delafosse, and Clozel had matured in their African experience together and they had become close personal friends, sharing a common approach to the problems of local administration. From late 1902 until the end of Clozel's tenure as governor these three men were to work co-operatively to repair the damages inflicted by military intervention and cultivate the politics of collabbration.[13]

The first step was to tone down the military pressure on the Baule and halt the search-and-destroy campaigns which the military had resorted to in desperation in the closing months of 1902. Clozel instructed Betsellère to take even the slightest expression of submission as a gesture of peace: 'J'estime . . . d'une manière générale que toute offre de soumissions partielles, si infime que soit la fraction ou le village qui en est l'auteur, doit être acceuillie et examinée.'[14]

As for the conditions of submission, and the collection of taxes, Betsellère was told to be indulgent. As Clozel explained it to the Governor General:

comme je ne voulais pas que la perception de l'impôt fut un obstacle à la prompte pacification du pays, j'ai donné à cet égard les instructions les plus élastiques à M. le chef de Bataillon Betsellère.
. . . Je lui ai dit notamment d'en ajourner totalement la perception là où il croirait qu'elle pourrait soulever la moindre difficulté.[15]

Clearly, such a policy represented a dramatic reversal of the one pursued by the military officers only a few months previously.

Clozel's reforms went further to remove the basis for Baule hostility. General Houry's inspection tour of 1902 revealed that Baule resistance sentiment was inspired principally by the question of labour recruitment for the porterage needs of the occupying troops. The demands for porters had been too excessive for the Baule to meet with their slaves alone. Freeborn Baule had been forced to undertake porterage labour for the French, and this was something they were prepared to resist, for such work was a symbol of slave status. As Houry pointed out, it was difficult enough to convince the Baule to send their slaves to do such work:

mais les conséquences furent tout autres et plus graves lorsque pour satisfaire à nos demandes, les chefs Baoulés durent faire appel aux hommes libres . . . c'est bien là la principale et presque la seule raison de leur attitude.[16]

Clozel concurred with Houry's opinion, emphasizing: 'C'est là qu'il faut chercher la cause préponderante de la rebellion: tout le reste, même les brutalités et les maladresses de certains chefs de poste n'est qu'accessoire et occasionnel'.[17] To alleviate the situation, Clozel created several companies of professional porters to be recruited among the Dyula populations from the Kong region.[18] This gesture he hoped would go a long way to quell Baule discontent.

Simultaneously, Clozel terminated the sale of guns and powder in Baule country, reversing the ill-advised decision which Governor Roberdeau had taken in March 1902.[19] In doing so Clozel hoped that he could achieve an effective cease-fire even on the part of those groups that remained explicitly hostile to the French presence. In the event, Baule armament supplies were diminished but not toally cut off, for the Baule simply purchased them from other neighbouring groups among whom the sale of munitions remained legal. As General Houry was to point out, the partial ban on arms sales within the colony as a whole had little effect on the Baule will to resist.[20]

To remove another major area of contention between the Baule and the French, Clozel made it clear that he did not intend to proceed towards a full-scale liberation of Baule captives. This had been a tactic which military officers openly advocated as a means of subduing the Baule,[21] but Commander Betsellère and Clozel both realized that this policy would seriously compromise the prospects of peace among the Baule, and he proceeded very cautiously in this realm.[22] After the famous slavery scandal in Senegal during 1904 involving the son of Émile Chautemps, the former minister of Colonies, pressure was brought to bear upon Clozel to liberate all domestic slaves in the colony.[23] This Clozel did in an official decree in 1905, but it was clear from the instructions given to administrators that the measures were designed more for metropolitan consumption than for local reform. Local officials were advised:

Il serait donc impolitique et imprudent de proclamer à grand bruit la nouvelle du décret.
Vous n'avez pas à vous occuper du passé; j'entends que vous n'avez pas à ordonner aux maîtres le renvoi des captifs de case pas plus que vous n'avez à conseiller à ces derniers de saisir une liberté dont ils seraient d'ailleurs embarrassés.[24]

In terms of positive policies designed to attract collaborators Clozel sought to implement the provisions of the 1901 head tax regulations whereby the chiefs were to be allocated 25 per cent of the revenue which they were able to collect and turn over to the French.[25] Here was a straightforward monetary incentive for chiefs to align themselves with the French. In the pre-colonial context few chiefs had sufficient power to exact a tribute from other groups in surrounding areas, but as a result of this policy chiefs who succeeded in presenting themselves as legitimate spokesmen in French eyes could intercede in the tax collection procedures in such a way as to procure significant advantages for themselves. After a year of exercising this policy, Clozel officially reduced the allocations to chiefs from 25 per cent to 10 per cent, but it appears that this lower figure represented a minimum.[26] The administrators actually awarded returns to the chiefs on a differential basis reflecting the zeal of the chief himself. As Clozel later explained the policy to the Governor General:

Je ne veux pas . . . me lier les mains en réglant d'une manière fixe les remises à payer aux chefs. Je tiens à ce que ces remises soient considérées par ceux-ci plutôt comme une gratification pour le zèle qu'ils mettent à faire rentrer l'impôt, que comme un traitement qui leur est servi.[27]

In addition, a category of expense referred to as 'les fonds pour cadeaux politiques' began to appear in official usage, and Clozel made direct payments to chiefs he considered to have demonstrated exemplary fidelity.[28] In a similar fashion the ban on munitions sales was at times selectively lifted to accommodate co-operative chiefs 'pour des services et travaux particuliers méritant une récompense'.[29] Indeed, the administration sought on virtually all occasions to favour those chiefs and their families who had opted for open collaboration. In 1906 they made it possible for the son of their closest Ouarébo collaborator to travel to France as a participant in the Marseille *Exposition Coloniale*.[30] The French had not demonstrated such largesse towards one of their Baule subjects since 1895 when Delafosse had taken Kouassi Amané, son of his personal friend and Ouarébo chief of Toumodi, Niango Kouassi, to France during his annual leave.[31]

In addition to receiving tax rebates and political favours collaborating chiefs could hope to be nominated to regional judicial tribunals with the authority to settle local disputes and impose fines on offenders. Clozel established a series of tribunals within Baule country on the basis of Delafosse's description of pre-colonial judicial procedures among the Baule, and he employed these structures specifically to reward the chiefs who had remained loyal throughout the 1900-2 period of resistance activity. Thus, during Clozel's tenure as Governor, Niango Kouadio (of the Toumodi Ouarébo), Kouamé Akafou (of the Nzipri at Kodiokofikro), M'Bahia (of the Soundo at M'Bahiakro), Toto (of the Satikran), Bendé Kouassi (of the Don), Kouassi Blé and Mvlan (Faafoué), and Okou N'Gatta and N'Gatta Blé Koffi (of the Ourébo-Linguira near Sakassou) all found themselves elevated to important tribunal positions to administer justice under close French super-vision.[32] It remains unclear whether these chiefs were rewarded monetarily for their judicial functions. Delafosse indicated clearly in commenting upon pre-colonial practice that:

La justice n'est pas gratuite au Baoulé. . . . Les présidents de conseil de village ou de tribu, et surtout les arbitres se font toujours et quelquefois largement payer leur peine et, s'il y a lieu, leur déplacement . . .[33]

It is likely that the French administration continued this tradition in an attempt to make the new judicial procedures attractive enough to inspire these chiefs to take an active part in them. It would have been easy for the French to recompense the chiefs for their efforts without imposing high fines on guilty parties simply by compensating the chiefs out of the political funds at their disposal. There is some evidence that the administration tried to keep the fines low with the effect of encouraging all parties to bring their grievances before these tribunals.[34]

Once the procedures were established the judicial apparatus provided the cornerstone of Clozel's collaborative policies. Following Delafosse's blueprint, Clozel had succeeded in erecting a system in which all parties appeared to gain some advantage. Those who suspected they would have to pay dearly to have their case heard sympathetically before an important chief in a traditional context clearly saw that it was to their advantage to place their grievance before the newly-constituted tribunal instead, where their costs were minimal and, more important, the potential fines relatively low. Even those who were judged to be in the wrong had an interest in submitting themselves to these new forms of judicial procedure. Indeed, they perhaps saw the advantages of French 'justice' before all others. For them the new arrangements were accepted with such alacrity not because the settlements were just in any abstract sense, but rather because justice was comparatively cheap.

Those judged to be guilty were not the only ones to gain by the system. Clearly those who had been aggrieved benefited from the relative efficiency of the judicial proceedings as well. In the pre-colonial context those judged to be in the right were often held responsible for the burden of compensation to be paid to the adjudicating chiefs.[35] Under the newly instituted French procedures their costs were greatly reduced. In addition they could expect that if they received a favourable judgement, the French administrator would act on their behalf to procure the necessary compensation from the guilty party. Once again, then, the French system of justice administered by the collaborative chiefs recommended itself on the grounds of its palpable compensations rather than its abstract principles of law.

For the collaborating chiefs, of course, there were manifold advantages in the new system. Monetary compensation was perhaps the least important. From the perspective of these chiefs, the main virtue of the judicial system was that it made it possible for them to project their influence and authority on a scale to which they probably could not have aspired in a pre-colonial context. This, in turn, served to consolidate their position as powerful chiefs in the extra-legal context.

Henceforth few of their direct subordinates would seek to challenge or evade their authority if it became clear that by doing so they ran the risk of being taken before a regional tribunal where their insubordination would be brought to the attention of the French.

Because the judicial role was such an important constituent of chiefly power in the pre-colonial context, the French, by placing the legal process in the hands of collaborative chiefs, effectively armed these chiefs with a powerful weapon which they could use to the detriment of their traditional political rivals. It soon became apparent even to those chiefs who had resisted the French militarily that it was in their best interests to be named as members of one of the judicial tribunals. Once the advantages of collaboration were so clearly set forth, it was only a matter of time before competing chiefs tried to outdo one another to associate themselves with the French. These chiefs had not invented the system, nor had they necessarily invited the French to set it up; but once it was established they saw no reason why they should not make use of it to their best advantage. In this respect, the politics of collaboration remained a subset of the politics of local influence among the Baule. The judicial procedures and tax regulations introduced by the French were new elements in an old game, and they had to be manipulated for all they were worth as long as they lasted.

Local administrators began to observe that the Baule came to them in increasing numbers to put their disputes before the newly-established tribunals, or simply to have them judged summarily by the administrator himself.[36] Indeed by 1907 near the end of Clozel's tenure, Commander Charles, Betsellère's successor as head of the Baule region, reported: 'Les tribunéaux indigènes sont encombrés de plaideurs'.[37] Given the advantages afforded to all parties concerned this was not improbable.

For the most part, however, the French misread the significance of the Baule receptivity to the judicial procedures. In the first place they attributed the popularity of the judicial system to what they had come to believe were the universally valid principles of French 'justice'. From this perspective the fact that the Baule eagerly accepted the system served as an affirmation to the French that the Baule had come to recognize the innate superiority of French culture.[38] In reality, of course, the reasons for Baule enthusiasm were most probably altogether unrelated to judgements on this plane. The nature of Baule pre-colonial social structure was such that the settlement of disputes was a costly and drawn-out affair. French intrusion simply provided the structures within which this no longer needed to be the case, and there need be little wonder why this aspect of French presence became attractive to the Baule.

A more serious misunderstanding on the part of the French stemmed from their assumption that Baule acceptance of judicial procedures was in itself an index of their total submission to the colonial regime.[39] The roots of this mistaken assessment were to be found in their initial misreading of the significance of Baule enthusiasm. The French, confident that the Baule had finally come to recognize the superiority of their civilization, assumed that compliance would follow – perhaps only gradually, but none the less inevitably. If the administrators had been more fully cognizant of how the Baule were manipulating the judicial structures to their own ends, perhaps they would have been less confident about the future. For the Baule it was still perfectly possible to accept some features of French colonial rule without necessarily acceding to others. Clozel may have conceived of his colonial policy as a total package, but there was no reason why the Baule should have perceived it in these terms at this early stage. Even those who had no intention of paying taxes saw that there was advantage to be gained in the new judicial arrangements. With this aspect of the colonial bargain they could co-operate without necessarily feeling themselves to have succumbed totally to French control. For much of Baule country it remained an open question as to who was manipulating whom. Throughout most of Clozel's tenure as Governor it would have been accurate to say that the administration depended more heavily upon the collaborating chiefs than these chiefs did upon the administration.

Much of Clozel's approach echoed the themes prevalent in British colonial policy at the time. There is no doubt that French colonial circles were strongly influenced by developments in British West Africa, and both Delafosse and Clozel were in the forefront of the intercolonial dialogue.[40] During this period French colonial policy experienced a profound alteration in its orientations as governors and local administrators began to talk increasingly of pursuing a programme of 'association' rather than the previous policy of 'assimilation'.[41] Within the Ivory Coast local practice often seemed to embody some of the tenets of 'indirect rule', particularly with respect to dealing with local chiefs and tolerating religious customs. At one stage the French even went so far in this direction as to discuss seriously the possibility of placing local fetish priests on the administration's payroll. The idea was ultimately dropped partially because the fetish priests were thought to have little collective impact as leaders and partially because employing them would have necessitated a considerable expense, but the fact that it was suggested as an idea illustrates the extent to which the French administration had become prepared to accommodate themselves to local customs.[42]

It would, however, be misleading to read into these policies a whole-hearted attempt to implement a system of 'indirect rule'. In particular Baule country was still heavily garrisoned with troops, and the memory of the painful years of fighting had still not completely subsided among the Baule. Similarly, although taxes were not always collected from outlying groups, the burden upon those close to the French posts was considerable. Moreover, Clozel's attempt to cover the tax system with a thin veil of legitimacy by channelling it through the chiefs did not mislead local villagers. There were few illusions, even among the most self-important of the collaborating chiefs, as to where ultimate power resided.

In this respect, French presence among the Baule was best typified not as 'indirect rule', but as 'direct rule gone native'.[43] With the guidance of the published manuals and monographs of veterans like Maurice Delafosse, other administrators began to become accustomed to their unfamiliar environs. Clozel specifically required them to conduct their own ethnographic researches as part of an attempt to help them understand local customs more thoroughly.[44]

So long as colonial circles in Paris and Dakar were talking increasingly in terms of 'association' rather than 'assimilation' it gradually became respectable as well as enjoyable to taste the flavour of local customs. Delafosse himself had taken a Baule wife, and others were encouraged to do the same by Dr Barot's *Guide pratique de l'Européen dans l'Afrique Occidentale*, published in 1902. Readers were informed of the advantages of locally arranged marriages:

A marriage contracted with an influential chief's daughter may serve to tighten the bonds of sympathy which bind the Negro to the European and to facilitate the administration of the country. Among certain peoples, the Baoulé for example, the women, who are all-powerful, come readily to us, and will be one of our strongest instruments of pacification.[45]

Clearly, duty required what the flesh desired. The justification was complete. During Clozel's tenure of office the civilian administrators proved themselves to be every bit as capable in performing their patriotic duties through this form of *conquête* as their military predecessors had been with their more conventional military strategies. Indeed, so thorough was their success that towards the end of his period in office Clozel felt compelled to caution his subordinates about the dangers of extending excessive 'hospitality' towards Baule women.[46]

On this level the contrast with the principles of 'indirect rule' was striking. The French administrator did not rule through local chiefs; he became a local chief.[47] Structurally he succeeded in inserting himself at the apex of the local socio-political hierarchy. Above the *chef de case* (*awlô kpenngben* in Baule) came the *chef de village* (*klo kpenngben*) and above him came the *chef de canton* (*nvle kpen*); but above them all came the *chef de poste* - the local administrator. In French language usage the progression was complete. Furthermore the French strove to establish the equation in Baule linguistic usage as well. Delafosse explicitly urged local administrators to insist upon being addressed by their subjects with the respectful phrases reserved for traditional chiefs of considerable rank.[48]

In military circles Clozel's policies came in for heated criticism. In Baule country itself one captain submitted his resignation to Commander Betsellère after having been disciplined for overstepping the bounds of Clozel's new directives.[49] Another captain was relieved of his command for similarly refusing to tone down his authoritarian style with the Baule. Both officers were supported in their objections to Clozel's approach by Lieutenant-Colonel Vimont in opposition to their immediate superior Commander Betsellère. Betsellère remained faithful to Clozel's directives throughout the controversy even at the expense of defying his own immediate superior, Vimont. Clozel defended Betsellère before the Governor General and eventually succeeded in replacing Vimont with Lieutenant-Colonel Bruchet, an officer who appeared to be more clearly sympathetic to Clozel's new policy.[50]

The debate, however, did not stop there. In France the time-worn controversy over civilian and military approaches to colonial problems flared up once again with respect to the Ivory Coast. In the pages of the *Revue des Troupes Coloniales* Clozel's policy came under open attack from the veteran officers of the Baule campaigns. Captain Privey, who had taken part in the combined assault of Sakassou leading to the death of Kouamé Dié in 1902, wrote a blistering critique of Clozel's 'politique des races'. Drawing upon the experiences of Lieutenant-Colonel Pennequin in Tonkin and Colonel Lyautey in Madagascar, Privey argued that a thoroughgoing conquest was called for in Baule country, and he deplored the fact that Clozel had abandoned the task apparently in response to what he referred to as 'la nervosité métropolitaine'.[51] The basic fallacy of Clozel's policy, according to Privey, lay in its premature pretentions: 'On a voulu administrer avant de conquérir . . .'.[52] Privey contended that this was a fundamental mistake: 'on a dû se rendre compte, en un mot, que la conquête pacifique de ces populations, incapables d'apprécier nos sentiments d'humanité et de civilisation à leur juste valeur, n'était qu'une pure chimère.'[53]

Other articles aired similar critiques, but for the remainder of Clozel's tenure they appeared to have little effect on policy in the Ivory Coast.[54] Clozel and Nebout, who acted as Clozel's replacement whenever he was absent from the colony on leave, continued to pursue the policies of collaboration with the skilful assistance of Commander Betsellère and his eventual replacement, Commander Charles.[55]

EUROPEAN COMMERCIAL PENETRATION AMONG THE BAULE

Although many of the veteran military officers remained disgruntled with Clozel's new policies among the Baule, the commercial community had good reason to be pleased. Clozel recognized that the Ivory Coast was not destined to become a settler colony. Consequently, the economic viability of the colony would in the future depend largely upon the prosperity of the import-export sector. According to Clozel it was the business of the administration to assist the expansion of commerce. More direct intervention would run the risk of antagonizing the local population. For the foreseeable future Clozel envisaged a programme of extending the means of communications towards the interior to facilitate the expansion of the European commercial frontier. As he phrased it:

Je serais plutôt porté à croire à l'inefficacité des mesures administratives sur le développement économique d'un pays. En dehors des grands travaux, chemins de fer, ports, routes, canaux, qui, intelligemment conçus, doivent exercer une action directe et immédiate sur la pacification et le mouvement commercial d'une contrée neuve, ce que nous pouvons est peu de chose.[56]

For the colony as a whole Clozel's plans included the development of landing facilities for ocean vessels at Grand Bassam and Port Bouet, the amelioration of lagoon transport to improve communications along the coast, the extension of telegraph communications inland, and the construction of a railway from Abidjan on the Ébrié lagoon northwards toward Bouaké.[57] These programmes necessitated massive new capital investment. In 1903 legislation in Paris made it possible for the Government General to raise metropolitan loans for the development of public works in the Federation, and with this money full-scale construction on the railway began. The loans needed to be repaid from the federal budget of the Government General in Dakar, and to give this budget a more solid financial footing, further reforms were introduced in October 1904.[58] Henceforth the entire amount of customs duties collected on imports and exports within each colony were handed over to Dakar. From there a portion went to servicing the metropolitan debt and the rest was redistributed throughout the Federation for projects or expenses which received the approval of the Governor General.

The effect of these reforms was, on the one hand, to reduce the capacity of the local administration to pursue any independent military initiative, and on the other, to increase its overall dependence upon the prosperity of the import-export sector. The amount of capital which Clozel could expect to receive from Governor General Roume to implement his ambitious programmes for infra-structure extension depended entirely upon his ability to collect customs duties. To tax import-export firms too severely would only serve to discourage their efforts, but by giving them an enlarged scope to expand their operations inland Clozel hoped to raise increasing amounts of revenue from an overall rise in the volume of commercial activity.

It is perhaps not surprising that the most clear-cut statement of Clozel's dilemma came from the military officers who were by and large the victims of his new measures. In addition to their criticism of what they called 'la nervosité métropolitaine' these officers tended to portray the local situation as if the administration were being held to ransom by the colony's commercial interests. As one officer described it:

La colonie de la Côte d'Ivoire a toujours été une colonie d'administration essentiellement civile. Elle n'a accepté l'action militaire qu'à son corps défendant. . . . Elle aspire à redevenir entièrement civil. Ses ressources sont bâties seulement sur le commerce, c'est à dire les droits de douanes. Pour ne pas diminuer ces droits, elle tient à la liberté de la route, d'où défense de violenter les indigènes soit pour payer les impôts, soit pour fournir un portage quelconque. . . .

On ne veut pas d'une action militaire sur la route commerciale laquelle, déjà couteuse par elle-même, tarirait les ressources de la doune et mettrait le trouble dans le budget.[59]

Whether or not Clozel acted upon the direct inspiration of the commercial community is something which requires more research to determine.[60] In any event the important point to emphasize is that there did not need to be any direct influence for the outcome to have been what it was. No 'conspiracy theory' is needed in this case to explain the progressive elaboration of policy. Given the structure of the federal and territorial budgets and the procedures for obtaining investment capital for infrastructure expansion, Clozel simply could not afford to ignore the desires of the commercial community for very long. Their interests became his predominant concern.[61] With the exception of one military campaign against the Agba in 1905 Clozel held the military in check in order to allow commerce a free hand to penetrate inland. Significantly, the Agba campaign itself was primarily undertaken as an explicit prelude to commercial penetration. According to Clozel the Agba constituted an obstacle in the projected path of the railway, and they needed to be subdued for construction to proceed.[62]

The rapid extension of European commerce inland was perhaps nowhere as dramatic as it was at Tiassalé, the traditional transit market at the southern limit of Baule country. In Tiassalé European commercial presence during the first ten years of colonial rule had been slight indeed. In the early 1890s Verdier's agent, David, operated a steam launch on the lower reaches of the Bandama, and he appears to have had some commercial relations with Etien Komenan, the chief of Tiassalé at the time of the ill-fated Voituret–Papillon expedition. Nevertheless no permanent European trading establishment existed at Tiassalé until 1895 when several European houses including the Compagnie Française de Kong, the commercial successor to Verdier's firm, set up trading posts there in the wake of the Monteil expedition. Even these ventures appear to have been short-lived, however, for in early 1897 acting Governor Bonhoure reported that all but one of the European firms were closed, and the one which still operated was inadequately provisioned. Until the turn of the century the commerce that transited Tiassalé remained firmly in the hands of the Apollonien trader community. European merchants had only a symbolic presence on the southern fringe of Baule territory, and none had penetrated into the heart of Baule country.[63]

With the rapid expansion of the export trade in raw rubber from 1898 onwards Tiassalé began to take on the appearance of a 'boom town'. The Apollonien traders and the Compagnie Française de Kong were joined in 1900 by the English firm Rider, Son and Andrew. In the following year, after the capture of Kokumbo by Colonna d'Istria, a second French firm from Bordeaux established itself: la Société Dutheil de la Rochère, de la Fournière et Cie. In July 1902 a second English firm, W. D. Woodin & Co., Ltd., installed an agent in Tiassalé to buy rubber and sell manufactures. Shortly thereafter both the Société Dutheil and the Compagnie Française de Kong extended their operations into the heart of central Baule country by establishing trading posts for the first time at Toumodi. The European commercial penetration of Baule country had begun.[64]

During Clozel's governorship the Tiassalé trade developed at an even greater pace, and European firms penetrated further into Baule territory, establishing bulking stations for raw rubber collection at Kodiokofikro and Bouaké.[65] By 1906 the Compagnie Française de l'Afrique Occidentale had agents at Tiassalé, and the local French administrator reported that there were no fewer than sixty-three trading establishments owned by forty-nine proprietors including Guinean, Senegalese, Apollonien, Sierra Leonean, Fanti, Syrian and German as well as English and French traders.[66] The number of firms continued to increase in 1907 with the addition of several new French concerns and more Senegalese traders.[67] As early as 1904 Grand Lahou, the major outlet for the Tiassalé trade, was described as 'le premier port de la Côte d'Ivoire' because of the volume of the rubber trade, and in 1905 Betsellère indicated that Tiassalé had become 'le point commercial de beaucoup le plus important de toute la colonie'.[68]

European firms were not the only ones to profit from the rubber boom. Indeed, the largest single firm in Tiassalé was that of Morgan Dougan, a Fanti merchant originally from the Gold Coast. He owned several warehouses and retail shops in Tiassalé and employed numerous other Fanti and Apollonien agents both to retail the goods he imported and to bulk the raw rubber for export. By extending loans to African traders he had succeeded in channelling their business in his direction at the expense of the European firms with considerably more capital. In 1905 he was reported to have bought and expedited seventy-five tons of raw rubber worth roughly 450,000 f. in addition to selling 328,000 f. of merchandise in his Tiassalé stores alone. His annual turnover was estimated to exceed one million francs, roughly 200,000 f. more than his largest competitor, the C.F.A.O. His recurrent expenses, however, were considerable since he owned and operated his own motor launch to link Tiassalé with Grand Lahou and employed several teams of semi-skilled and skilled labourers to serve as crew, carpenters, etc. Nevertheless, he was reputed to have made a net profit of 96,000 f. in 1905, a sum which represented more than twenty-five times the salary of a European beginning his career in the colonial service as a 'Commis des Affaires Indigènes'.[69]

Remarkable as it was, the boom in the growth of Tiassalé's trade between 1902 and 1907 appears to have had relatively little impact upon the Baule themselves. The major stimulus to commerce among the Baule was the brief reopening of the munitions trade from March 1902 until the end of November. This moved some Baule to collect rubber to offer in exchange for guns and powder, but when Clozel re-imposed the ban upon munitions sales, the Baule collection of rubber appears to have dwindled. The major areas of collection were located among the Gouro and the northern groups of Senoufo. For the most part the rubber trade merely transited Baule country, culminating in the exchange for European products at Tiassalé.[70]

Nor do the Baule appear to have been engaged as porters in the rubber trade any more than they were as producers. In its initial stages from 1898 to 1901 the Apollonien traders appear to have handled most of the business, but with the French military campaigns of 1901 and the continued trouble in Baule territory thoughout 1902, the Apollonien withdrew to concentrate their activities between Grand Lahou and Tiassalé. With French support Dyula traders replaced the Apollonien north of Tiassalé after 1901. When the Compagnie Française de Kong and the Société Dutheil extended their trading counters and bulking centres into Baule territory in 1903 it was from the Dyula communities resident in the vicinity of the French posts that they drew their porterage labour.[71] These Dyula, some of whom had settled in enclave communities in the wake of the Monteil expedition and others who were more recent arrivals, became the main African beneficiaries of the remarkable rubber boom. The Baule for their part limited their participation to the role of supplying goods and services to these alien enclaves of traders. As one observer at Tiassalé summarized the situation:

Une chose me frappe en arrivant à Tiassalé: c'est l'importance du commerce . . . Mais ce commerce n'est pas entre les mains des Baoulés qui se contentent de vendre aux commerçants de passage ou aux militaires occupant nos postes les denrées nécessaires à leur alimentation.[72]

Baule reluctance to become engaged as labourers in the emerging colonial economy can be explained partially by the recent historical experiences which they had endured. Commander Betsellère clearly understood the origins of Baule reservations:

le régime des colonnes et des répressions vigoureuses . . . avait laissé chez les indigènes l'impression que nous venions ici en conquérants; les réquisitions, les impôts et le portage exigés *manu militari* et sans discussion les avaient portés à croire que nous n'avions pas d'autre but que de les réduire en esclavage et que nous voulions inaugurer au Baoulé le système de Samory au Soudan.[73]

Given the nature of French military intervention from 1899 to 1902 this was not an implausible conclusion for the Baule to draw from events.

Even after Clozel's policies altered the particularly repressive character of French presence, however, the Baule remained aloof. The reasons for this were both social and economic. In the first place, ever since 1895 when the Baule witnessed the close collaboration between the French troops and the Dyula refugees from the Kong expedition, the Baule had come to associate work for the white man with the status of slavery. Thus any labour contract engaging the Baule to work for the white man was bound to be objectionable on these grounds alone. As Betsellère observed concerning the Baule labourer:

Il sera difficile d'en obtenir des contrats le liant à notre service pour une durée déterminée, l'engageant d'une façon formelle et qui à son avis, feraient de lui notre esclave, au même titre que nos tirailleurs, envers lesquels il use très souvent de cette epithète injurieuse.[74]

It could be argued, however, that these misgivings would not have endured for long if the salaries offered by Europeans had been sufficiently high to attract Baule labour. In the event they were not, and in this sense it is accurate to say that the Baule remained uninterested in wage employment within the colonial economy for straightforward economic reasons. The traditional industries of gold mining and cloth weaving supplemented occasionally by the collection of some raw rubber or the sale of foodstuffs or palm wine assured the Baule of an income that nearly equalled that which he could obtain by selling his services as a porter or manual labourer. Observers estimated that three Baule workers could extract an average of 1.00 to 1.50 f. worth of gold per day's work with their traditional mining technology. This amounted to a per capita daily income of roughly 0.30 f. to 0.50 f.[75] Weaving seemed to be even more lucrative. A woven robe which normally took approximately two weeks for the Baule to weave would sell locally for 7.00 f., while the more elaborate richly decorative cloth that sometimes took a month to complete would sell for 15 to 25 f. Hence those engaged in the traditional weaving industry earned the rough equivalent of 0.50 to 1.00 f. per day.[76] In terms of foodstuff production, a jar of palm wine, five kilograms of yams or a bottle of palm oil would each sell for 0.50 f. locally.[77]

Wages offered by the administration for porterage labour began at 0.50 f. per day in 1903 and rose over time to 1.00 f. in 1905, and 1.25 f. in 1911. On a monthly basis a manual labourer could expect to receive 25 f., a 'boy' (a domestic servant working for a European), 15 to 20 f., a cook, 30 f., and a 'boutiquier' (an African shopkeeper, usually either Dyula or Apollonien), 100 to 150 f.[78] In short, except for the position of 'boutiquier' the wages offered to the Baule in the colonial economy were not markedly higher than what they could expect to earn from weaving cloth, mining gold or marketing palm wine or foodstuffs. When one takes into account the social 'cost' of the humiliation involved for a freeborn Baule having to undertake work normally associated with the status of slavery, it is hardly surprising that the Baule were not eager to take up labour opportunities in the colonial economy.

Baule disdain for wage employment extended beyond the onerous porterage tasks or the positions of domestic service. When a French mining company needed labour to begin prospecting in the Toumodi region they found it impossible to recruit Baule salaried workers. Eventually they turned instead to labourers recruited in the northern Ivory coast.[79] Similarly even when the railway construction proceeded northwards into Baule country the labourers employed were not Baule but rather men from the Krou coast, Dahomeans or Ebrié.[80] Whatever labour was forthcoming from the Baule themselves was that which their slaves could accomplish, and this was absorbed by the immediate needs of the administration in the construction or repair of posts and the clearing of roads. Betsellère reported that for anything beyond this the labour needs of the administration and of commerce would have to be met by recruiting salaried workers from outside Baule territory. Even if the social stigma of working for Europeans eventually subsided among the Baule, salaries would have to increase substantially to attract the Baule to wage employment voluntarily.[81]

Clozel hoped that Baule reluctance to participate in the new structures of the colonial economy would be overcome naturally as an inevitable consequence of time without further direct administrative intrusion.

les mœurs se modifient, les besoins se développent, la production, s'accroît, avec la collaboration indispensable du temps, sous l'influence de causes multiples dont beaucoup échappent à notre action directe. Favoriser les courants naturels, les endiguer en quelques points sans les trop contrarier, c'est à quoi me paraît devoir se borner le rôle des gouvernants.[82]

This key to this strategy, however, lay in the progressive collaboration of the Baule chiefs, for it was only by heading off their potential opposition that Clozel could be assured of the peaceful conditions necessary for the gradual flowering of colonial commerce. As Clozel and his administrators were to find out, the intricacies of colonial trade and finance were relatively simple compared to the multiple complications they were to encounter in trying to elicit viable collaborators in the wake of years of intermittent warfare.

THE POLITICS OF COLLABORATION IN THE AFTERMATH OF BATTLE, 1902-1907

Given the decentralized character of the Baule pre-colonial political structures, the task of integrating legitimate chiefs into an effective system of collaboration would have been a difficult one in the best of times. The basic problem was pinpointed clearly by military officers who observed that the authority of any given chief varied considerably under different circumstances:

L'autorité d'un chef n'est acceptée que dans une seule circonstance, à la guerre . . . Mais, dès que les hostilités ont cessé et que l'on commence à discuter les conditions de la paix, chacun s'émancipe à nouveau et on se trouve alors en présence de chefs impuissants à se faire obéir.[83]

Articulating this kind of political process with the hierarchical structures of a colonial empire was bound to pose problems for even the most ardent advocate of what became known as 'la politique des races'.

To make matters worse, the pre-emptive use of military force from 1899 to 1902 raised fresh complications. By dealing brutally with chiefs in general and killing important figures like Kouamé Dié and Akafou Bulare, the impetuous junior officers had created a situation in which moderate Baule leadership was reluctant to come forward. Even those who might have been predisposed to collaborate with the French were reticent at first to identify themselves after the lessons of 1902. Akafou Bulare had been, after all, an eminently moderate chief in Baule eyes. He was the first Baule chief to welcome Marchand and he only reluctantly joined the rebels against Monteil in 1895.[84] In 1899 he tried to mediate between Captain Le Magnen and Kouadio Okou, and it was Le Magnen's impatience with his role as mediator that forced him into seclusion.[85] Even during the most heated offensives of 1900 and 1901 Akafou did not lead his partisans against the French, and in August 1901 he voluntarily presented himself to Captain Bastard and paid the tribute imposed upon him in the hopes of satisfying the French. During late 1901 and 1902 he tried once again to mediate between the dissident Kpouébo-Ngban and the French. In June 1902 he appeared to be trying to negotiate a final settlement between the Kpouébo-Ngban and Captain Bastard, but Bastard misinterpreted the gesture and imprisoned him. In addition to the humiliation of imprisonment Akafou endured repeated beatings and eventually died.[86] In the months of fighting that followed, Kakou Bla, Akafou's influential wife, was also killed. With these kinds of examples before them, it is not surprising that few chiefs beyond the immediate range of the larger military posts were eager to be known to the French.

Among the Ngban the problem became evident immediately with the cessation of hostilities in January 1903. After several pitched battles with Ngban groups around the mountain known as Orumbo Boka, Betsellère, on Clozel's suggestion, began to accept the slightest expression of compliance as a gesture of submission. On the basis of the first reports the French were led to believe that many of the influential chiefs of Ngban villages had been killed in the fighting, but subsequent information revealed that many of these chiefs were in reality still alive.[87] Over time the French succeeded in establishing contact with outlying chiefs, but only by way of slaves who were dispatched by the chiefs to deal as intermediaries. In February 1904 when Governor Clozel travelled through Baule country to survey the progress of his peace strategy, the chiefs of the Ouossou region were convoked to meet with him. The response was far from impressive. Aside from Fatou Aka, the collaborating chief from Niamwé whom Marchand had tried to install as chief of Tiassalé, and Kouadio Okou, whom the French had thoroughly defeated, only Akafou Nguessan, the daughter of the late Akafou Bulare, came forward to meet Clozel. Despite the fact that Clozel publicly accorded a pardon to Kouadio Okou, the Kpouébo-Ngban remained aloof, sending only secondary representatives to the meeting.[88] Once again in Toumodi, only Eoussou of Abli and Niango Kouadio of Toumodi itself – the two chiefs who had remained loyal to the French cause ever since the Monteil expedition – were enthusiastic in their welcome to Clozel.

The problem of finding viable collaborators was aggravated by the succession crises unleashed by French military intrusion. When Akafou Bulare and Kouamé Dié died in 1902 it was not clear who would succeed them. Both men exercised extensive influence up until their deaths, but since the office of paramount chieftaincy was not a fully institutionalized one among the pre-colonial Baule, a fixed procedure for selecting their successors was not a matter of well-established custom. Both chiefs had derived their power from the nexus of inter-village and inter-regional marriage alliances that they had built up over time, affording them the channels to recruit a sizeable following of dependants. Akafou Bulare's strategic marriage with Kakou Bla from the village of Ayérémou provided the basis of his extensive influence among the southern Ngban.[89] In addition to several marriage alliances, Kouamé Dié's power appeared to be based directly upon the large number of slave dependants that he was able to acquire from trade relations with Samory. In 1901 one officer reported that, 'Sakassou ne comprend que Kouamé Dié, ses quatre enfants dont deux en bas âge, ses femmes et environ 400 captifs.'[90]

Given the changed circumstances within Baule country since Monteil's intrusion in 1895 and the capture of Samory in 1898, it is doubtful whether individual chiefs could acquire in 1902 the same kind of broad basis for personal power that Kouamé Dié and Akafou Bulare had developed only a few years before. On the one hand, inter-village and inter-regional *atonvle* marriages had fallen into relative decline since 1895 with the influx of captives from the north. After 1898, however, this source of manpower disappeared, and in most places the Baule lost captives back to the north as the French military liberated Baule slaves. The atrophy of political marriage alliances and the decline in the number of direct dependants effectively diminished the scope of political influence by 1902. Even if chiefs had been eager to identify themselves to the French – something they were clearly not willing to do at least initially – the successors of Akafou Bulare and Kouamé Dié could not have aspired to the same degree of power as their prede-cessors. This was so not only because the French were there to curb their autonomy but also because the traditional constituents of chiefly power had been thoroughly eroded by the particular history of French intrusion. The cumulative effect of these circumstances was to eliminate paramount chieftaincy as an effective 'traditional' office among the Baule. Just as the administration came to recognize the need to collaborate with Baule paramount chiefs, the institution itself dissolved.

For the most part, Clozel failed to acknowledge the corrosive effect that French presence was having upon traditional authority. He proceeded instead to embrace the institution of paramount chieftaincy in an attempt to make it into the cornerstone of his new 'politique des races'. Among the southern Ngban the French waited expectantly for months after the end of hostilities to see who might emerge as Akafou Bulare's successor. Initially it appeared that Akafou Brou, the son of Akafou Bulare and Kakou Bla, was willing to make peace with the French on behalf of the Ngban, but in successive months Akafou Brou made it clear that despite his eminent origins he was not recognized by the other chiefs in the area as a paramount chief.[91] Other information that the French received indicated that a chief named Assiené from Kpouébo had probably been designated by Akafou Bulare before his death as his eventual successor.[92] Nevertheless the French continued to try to work through Akafou Brou and his sister Akafou N'Guessan to achieve the submission of other Ngban chiefs. Predictably the Ngban of Kpouébo refused to recognize him, suggesting instead that a chief named Kakou from the village of Moronou was the person they recognized as the legitimate successor to Akafou Bulare.[93]

Negotiations and enquiries continued without any conclusive results. At one point Fatou Aka of Niamwé apparently intervened by promising to pay the war fines to the French on behalf of the Ngban, hoping in this way to become the political heir to Akafou Bulare. His ambitions were apparent to the French, and his bid to extend his power failed.[94] To complicate matters, during June 1903 just as Akafou Brou seemed on the verge of securing the submission of several other Ngban chiefs, he became ill, and within ten days he died in circumstances which still remain obscure.[95] At the same time Captain Léonard who had been in charge of the negotiations at Ouossou handed over command to Captain Ruby. This conjuncture of events put negotiations back to the beginning again. Akafou Brou's death, like that of his father Akafou Bulare the year before, made other Ngban chiefs even more wary about coming forward. It was not so much the direct fear of the French that worried them. Rather it seems that by expressing the willingness to negotiate with the French, an Ngban chief laid himself open to severe recriminations from other chiefs who were not yet prepared to submit. The mysterious circumstances surrounding Akafou Brou's death suggested to the French that he had been poisoned, and if this was the case, it is understandable why other spokesmen did not emerge despite French gestures of conciliation.[96]

In traditional Baule custom a new paramount chief was not officially confirmed in office until the funeral and burial ceremonies of his predecessor were fully accomplished. The successor chief could legitimately claim to be the heir of the previous chief's authority only by burying the deceased chief in his own (i.e. the successor's own) village. In the event, the Ngban succession crisis dragged on for several more years. It was not until June 1906, four years after his death, that Akafou Bulare's funeral was finally held in the village of Moronou, and even then the question of his heir was not fully resolved. Nda Frété was designated as the successor, but he declined the role and Kakou Dibi was identified instead as the new paramount chief of the Ngban. In reality Kakou Dibi was incapable of exercising the authority that Akafou Bulare had known, and the outlying villages of Dida, Kpouébo, and Trétrékro seemed particularly displeased with the choice.[97]

Similar problems plagued the French in the succession crisis among the Ouarébo precipitated by Kouamé Dié's murder in February 1902. In this instance, however, the French were drawn into the intrigue more directly. Fearing the immediate repercussions which Kouamé Dié's death might have upon the population, the French tried initially to keep the death secret by announcing only that he had been wounded and was being held captive by them. They bundled the corpse from Sakassou back to Bouaké and there it remained in their possession. The ruse did not work for it was clear after the surrender of Koffi Ossou in May 1902 that the French were curious to find out who might emerge as Kouamé Dié's successor. This in itself was a sufficient index to the Baule that Kouamé Dié was clearly dead.

At first it appeared that a chief named Toto Beugré from the village of Sakabo was recognized as the natural successor to Kouamé Dié.[98] Indeed, subsequent investigations described Toto Beugré and not Kouamé Dié as the legitimate chief of the Ouarébo prior to French intrusion. According to these accounts Kouamé Dié had usurped the Ouarébo chieftaincy from Toto Beugré upon the death of Toto Dibi around the turn of the century. This may well have been the case, for Toto Beugré was the brother of Toto Dibi, and in normal Baule practice succession passes collaterally in the first instance. Whether or not Toto Beugré had a greater intrinsic claim to legitimacy than Kouamé Dié it was clear that Kouamé Dié had succeeded in asserting his authority in a dramatic fashion just before the French campaign against Sakassou. On 24 October 1901 he transferred the corpse of Toto Dibi from Mahonou where it had been to his own village of Sakassou, and there he performed new funeral ceremonies, bestowing upon himself the full prerequisites of office as successor to Toto Dibi. This political *coup* effectively displaced Toto Beugré who was exiled to the village of Sakabo.[99] Upon the death of Kouamé Dié, then, it was perhaps not unnatural that Toto Beugré once again emerged as the spokesman for the Ouarébo.

The French were pleased with the prospect of collaborating with Toto Beugré, for he appeared to be willing to come to terms with them in a more subservient manner than Kouamé Dié had. As in the case of Akafou Brou among the Ngban, however, French collaboration with Toto Beugré was short-lived. In November 1902 Beugré died in unexplained circumstances, and chiefs more openly hostile to the French appear to have gained the upper hand. Dié Lonzo, the son of Kouamé Dié, was prominent among them.[100]

Throughout 1903 the question of Kouamé Dié's successor remained unresolved. Indeed, the French inadvertently prolonged the crisis. Kouamé Dié's corpse was still in their possession and despite requests from the Ouarébo chiefs to return it to them, the French persisted in holding on to it. By a combination of miscalculation and obstinacy the French had worked themselves and the Ouarébo into an impossible situation. The administration would not return the body until the Ouarébo designated a chief and pledged their submission; the Ouarébo could not designate a successor to Kouamé Dié until his corpse had been returned and duly interred. As the French administrator at Sakassou summarized the dilemma: 'On voit que cette question du corps de Kouamé Dié est le pivot de leur politique actuelle et la pierre d'achoppement de la nôtre.'[101] The elegant principles of 'la politique des races' were reduced in this instance to an unseemly dispute over the putrifying corpse of a dead chief.

Governor Clozel tried to resolve the issue definitively during his first inspection tour through Baule country. On 14 February 1904 he arrived in Sakassou and the following day he met with a host of influential Ouarébo village chiefs and household heads. After making it clear that he wished to resolve the succession crisis he asked the elders to designate their chosen leader. There were three major contenders under consideration. First there was Yoma Boni, the designated heir to the deceased Toto Beugré and according to Delafosse the wealthiest of the three candidates.[102] Dié Lonzo, the son of Kouamé Dié, was the second contender, whom Delafosse described as the 'youngest', 'most active' and 'most intelligent' of the candidates. Thirdly, there was Kouadio Ndri, indicated as being 'l'héritier naturel' by virtue of the fact that Kouamé Dié had been his maternal uncle, and according to Delafosse the principles of matrilineal succession governed Baule inheritance practice.

Clozel was caught in a dilemma the scope of which neither he nor Delafosse fully appreciated at the time. To them the only significant question was to identify Kouamé Dié's successor in accordance with the desires of the elders and the principles of Baule legitimacy. When the elders designated Kouadio Ndri as the successor to Kouamé Dié, Clozel and Delafosse were satisfied, and they proceeded to invest him in the office in a grand ceremony, indicating at the same time that Lonzo, by virtue of his intelligence and evident leadership capabilities should be regarded as Kouadio Ndri's right-hand man. Having confirmed Kouadio Ndri as opposed to Dié Lonzo in the office, Clozel thought he was emphasizing legitimacy as opposed to competence, and he felt confident that by reinforcing legitimate chiefs in this fashion he was strengthening the French position among the Ouarébo, and by extension, among the Baule as a whole.

For the Baule, however, the significant issue at stake was not so much whether Dié Lonzo or Kouadio Ndri would be recognized by the French, but rather whether either one of these two would be chosen over the head of Yoma Boni, widely recognized as the political successor to Toto Beugré, Kouamé Dié's former political rival. In effect the French decision at Sakassou carried a significance among the Baule of which the French remained ignorant. By recognizing Kouadio Ndri as the chief of the Ouarébo, Clozel had inadvertently bestowed retro-active legitimacy upon Kouamé Dié's earlier political *coup* against Toto Beugré. Yoma Boni was not pleased; nor were large numbers of other Baule who had regarded Kouamé Dié as an illegitimate usurper of the Ouarébo paramount chieftaincy.[103] Clozel may well have thought he was confirming the principles of legitimacy, but in the eyes of many Baule he was rewarding a kind of political high-handedness that they were not prepared to tolerate. As Lieutenant Bénézet, the commander of the Sakassou post summarized the situation:

Désigner [Kouadio] Ndri comme chef des Ouarébos, c'était reconnaître l'usurpation de Kouami Dié, la consacrer en un mot; . . . les indigènes qui n'aimaient pas Kouami Dié qui n'avait regné que par la terreur, n'aiment pas non plus Ndri et reconnaissent plus volontiers l'autorité de Yoma Boni qui leur paraît plus légitime.[104]

The whole issue was thrown into dramatic relief within a few months of Clozel's intervention. As part of the Sakassou settlement in February 1904, the French agreed to return Kouamé Dié's body to the Ouarébo for burial. According to recognized practice Kouadio Ndri should have buried Kouamé Dié in Sakassou, thus symbolizing his accession to the paramount chieftaincy. But Kouadio Ndri proved incapable of accomplishing this decisive gesture. The body was taken from him, and upon the instruction of Yoma Boni, funeral ceremonies for Kouamé Dié took place on 29 May 1904 in the village of Mahonou instead of Sakassou.[105] Kouadio Ndri may have been the chief in the eyes of the French, but Yoma Boni was the legitimate chief as far as many Baule were concerned, and by conducting the funeral of Kouamé Dié in his own village, he had proved it.

The entire succession dispute had taken place within the group known as the Ouarébo-Assabou. On a broader level other problems emerged between the Ouarébo-Assabou on the one hand and the Ouarébo-Linguira on the other. The Ouarébo-Linguira had favoured the arrival of the French in 1902 as part of their effort to gain autonomy from Kouamé Dié and after his death they remained faithful collaborators with the French, supplying the fort at Sakassou with provisions when all other Ouarébo remained distant. Ngatta Blé Koffi,

Moya Ba and Okou Boni of the Ouarébo-Linguira were the closest collaborators with the French, and for their role in facilitating French intrusion they were hated by the Ouarébo-Assabou and particularly by Dié Lonzo, who considered them personally responsible for the death of his father. The latent tension between the two groups burst into the open in 1905. Dié Lonzo planned to attack Ngatta Blé Koffi in an ambush, but Ngatta Blé Koffi was warned of the scheme and avoided the proposed rendezvous.[106] Moya Ba was not so fortunate. On her way back to her village after visiting Lieutenant Bénézet at the Sakassou post, she was assassinated. As Bénézet described the incident:

Moya Ba (femme), chef du village d'Andoufoué, un des chefs les mieux disposés à notre égard a été assassinée le 5 avril 1905 à 1500 m. à peine du poste alors qu'elle venait de me rendre visite. L'assassin, N'Guessan, un des fils de Kouami Dié, l'accusait d'être la cause de notre venue dans le pays, de la guerre et par contre coup de la mort de son père. N'Guessan, j'en suis certain a été conseillé par Lonzo, qui, plus intelligent mais tout aussi vindicatif, s'est contenté de diriger l'opération sans y prendre part.[107]

The murder of Moya Ba precipitated a brief but heated fratricidal war between the Assabou and Linguira factions of the Ouarébo. The Assabou took the offensive, attacking the Linguira, but after two days of fighting the dispute reached a stalemate. The French refrained from intervening directly, but threatened reprisals against both groups if the conflict continued. An uneasy calm was restored to the region. While the French were relieved that the dispute had not turned into an open attack on themselves, they were none the less aware that their position was precarious:

Cette vengeance bien que n'étant pas dirigée contre nous nous atteint tout de même indirectement puisque les Linguiras ont toujours été nos partisans depuis notre arrivée dans le pays.[108]

Similar fratricidal disputes plagued French efforts to collaborate with Baule chiefs throughout Baule country. In addition to Moya Ba, Akafou Brou, and Toto Beugré, other Baule chiefs who had been willing to collaborate with the French also died inexplicably during Clozel's tenure as Governor. Fatou Aka, the chief of Niamwé whom Marchand had tried to install as chief of Tiassalé, died in 1905.[109] Eoussou, the chief of Abli and close friend and ally of Delafosse died the previous year.[110] Okou Boni, the third prominent chief of the Ouarébo-Linguira, died in May 1905 only a month after Moya Ba's assassination, and in 1907 Mvlan, the first Faafoué chief to come to terms with the French, died as well.[111]

Some of these chiefs were old and probably died of natural causes. Others, however, may well have been the victims of poisonings resulting from internal feuds similar to that in which Akafou Brou had lost his life among the southern Ngban. In either case the death of each chief posed renewed problems for the administration. A subservient successor could usually be found among the possible heirs, but the French were never assured that the candidate the Baule put forward to represent them was indeed a figure who could command respect in his own right. For the most part they were, as Betsellère indicated, 'des hommes de paille'.[112]

Whether or not these 'straw' chiefs were as impotent as Betsellère suggested, for the time being they were the only collaborators that the French could find. To this extent it is important to examine their understanding of and attitude toward the evolving collaborative bargain. Generally speaking the attitude of chiefs reflected on the one hand the degree of French intervention in their affairs and on the other their personal proximity to a major French military installation. Chiefs in outlying villages from whom the French attempted to collect taxes often expressed open hostility.[113] When left alone, however, these chiefs remained largely indifferent to French presence or, at most, mildly irritated by it. Often they would promise to pay taxes or provide provisions, but as they were aware that it was difficult for the French to pursue them, these promises were frequently made with no intention of ever fully honouring them. As the Ouarébo were reported to have said, 'les français . . . demandent toujours beaucoup de choses mais il suffit d'effectuer un premier compte pour qu'ils nous laissent tranquilles . . .'.[114] Since Clozel forbade the extensive use of force in collecting war fines or taxes, their assessment was largely accurate.

Chiefs who lived in close proximity to large garrisons of Senegalese troops could not afford to be so nonchalant about the colonial situation. French involvement in their affairs was both significant and sustained. To elicit the co-operation of these chiefs the French offered them the full array of administrative favours, from gunpowder permits to judicial appointments. In addition local administrators tried to emphasize the long-term advantages of collaboration, stressing that expanded commerce, new roads, and salaried labour would be in the chiefs' interest. Clozel himself elaborated these themes to Baule chiefs during his 1904 inspection tour through Baule country. At Bouaké before an assembled group of collaborating chiefs Clozel patiently explained that the taxes the French required would pay for roads, telecommunications, and the extension of the railway, all of which would benefit the Baule in the future. The response of the Baule to Clozel's speech is worth relating at length for it indicates their sober assessment of the colonial situation. When Clozel had finished his explanations, Kouassi Blé, the chief of Bouaké, asked for permission to talk on behalf of the assembled chiefs and he addressed the Governor in these terms:

Nous avons étendu tes paroles et nous en sommes satisfaits, car nous n'y avons trouvé que du bien. Mais en ce qui concerne l'impôt ce n'était pas la peine de nous donner tant d'explications. Le Blancs sont venus dans notre pays, nous leurs avons fait la guerre pour les en chasser, nous avons été battus et ils sont restés. Donc, ce sont les Blancs les plus forts et toi qui est leur chef, tu es notre maître. Par conséquent il est juste et naturel que tu réclames de nous un impôt et, tant que vous serez les plus forts, nous ne songerons jamais à vous le refuser. Tu n'as qu'à dire 'payez' et nous paierons.[115]

On the surface the misunderstanding seemed innocent enough. In Baule eyes taxes were simply tribute. As for Clozel's elaborate justifications, Kouassi Blé remained frankly sceptical:

Mais ne nous parles pas de ce que tu feras avec notre argent; nous n'avons pas besoin de savoir, c'est ton affaire et non la nôtre. Que cet argent serve à construire des routes, des chemins de fer, des lignes télégraphiques, ou qu'il serve à tout autre chose, cela est égal. Pour les routes, nous savons très bien que c'est nous qui les ferons, même après les avoir payées. Quant au chemin de fer, dont nous n'avons que vaguement entendu parler, il se peut qu'il arrive un jour jusque dans notre pays et que nous l'utilisions pour voyager; mais nous en connaissons assez pour savoir qu'il nous faudra payer lorsque nous voudrons nous en servir, même après avoir acquitté un impôt en vue de sa construction. Enfin, le télégraphe est une chose très merveilleuse, mais qui rend surtout des services aux Blancs, et si, par hasard, quelqu'un d'entre nous veut envoyer un télégramme ou parler au téléphone, il lui faut payer aussi. Ne dis donc pas qu'en échange de l'impôt versé par nous tu nous donneras des routes, un chemin de fer et des lignes télégraphiques.

En réalité, tu nous réclames de l'argent parce que tu est le maître et que le maître a le droit et le devoir de réclamer ce qu'il veut à son esclave . . .[116]

Clearly this speech reflected an assessment of the colonial situation that differed considerably from Clozel's rhetorical elaboration of 'la politique des races'. Indeed the entire structure of collaboration during his governorship was predicated upon a fundamental misunderstanding between the French and the Baule as to the goals and the duration of the colonial arrangement. The French thought the Baule would eventually come to see things their way. The Baule thought the French would eventually leave. As Bendé Kouassi, one of the administration's closest collaborators explained it to Lieutenant Buck in Bouaké:

. . . vous, vous êtes venus . . . avec de nombreux soldats; vous êtes aussi des marchands, mais, comme vous avez beaucoup de fusils, vous êtes plus exigeants. Quand vous serez fatigués de faire la guerre, vous partirez comme les autres.[117]

The mutual misunderstanding between the Baule and the French may have been fairly complete, but for the time being at least it represented an updated version of the 'working misunderstanding' that had prevailed from 1895 to 1898.[118] Tax rebates, political gifts, commercial favours, judicial prerogatives and educational opportunities for their dependants continued to offer sufficient incentives for at least some Baule chiefs to be willing to meet the minimal French demands for taxes and labour. As long as these demands did not increase too sharply, there was no reason why the 'working misunderstanding' should not continue to function for a good while to come.

CHAPTER VI

Governor Angoulvant's Development Plans and the Final Phase of Baule Resistance, 1908-1911

ECONOMIC CHANGE AND ANGOULVANT'S DEVELOPMENT PLANS, 1907–1908

At first glance Governor Clozel's economic achievements were impressive. In the four and a half years from when he first took full control of the colony in November 1902 to when he finally left in August 1907, the colony's commercial figures reached record levels, reversing the worrying dip in trade occasioned by the military campaigns of 1901 and establishing what appeared to be a climate of general expansion. A comparison of the growth in import–export totals from 1899 to 1907 reveals the measure of Clozel's achievement:[1]

1899	11,300,000 f.
1900	15,700,000
1901	12,400,000
1902	16,300,000
1903	16,700,000
1904	25,900,000
1905	21,500,000
1906	21,300,000
1907	25,200,000

What is more, Clozel succeeded in adapting the colony's budget to the new fiscal arrangements instituted in 1904. These provisions required the colonies from 1905 onwards to turn over all their customs receipts to the budget of the Government General in Dakar. A portion of this sum reverted to the Ivory Coast in the form of the Federal Government's allocations to the colony's expenses, but as the federal budgetary expenses increased in their own right, the difference between what the Ivory Coast contributed and what it received increased. The result was that the composition of the Ivory Coast budget changed markedly during Clozel's tenure in office. Through the end of 1904 customs receipts had consistently provided the overwhelming proportion of the colony's budget, but as a result of the new fiscal reforms the local budget came to depend increasingly upon internal revenues, particularly the direct head tax and the returns from patents and licences for petty traders.

A brief comparison of the structure of successive budgets from 1903 through 1908 illustrates the change that had taken place under Clozel's direction.[2]

Year	Total Ivory Coast Budget francs	Customs francs	Fed. Govt. Allocations francs	Head taxes francs	Patents, etc. francs
1903	3,125,250	1,917,193	–	546,106	106,585
1904	3,943,442	2,484,691	–	776,993	283,290
1905	2,994,946	–	1,380,000	910,778	280,183
1906	3,277,184	–	1,480,000	1,183,204	323,322
1907	3,636,393	–	1,320,000	1,438,511	441,052
1908	4,321,374	–	1,250,000	1,713,497	459,229

The fiscal reforms of 1904 had the immediate effect of reducing the colony's budget for the following year. Indeed the budget felt the impact of the reforms for several more years and it was not until 1908 that it could expand beyond the 1904 level. More significantly, the proportion of the budget derived from customs revenue declined dramatically over this period. In 1904 the total budget of just under 4 million f. consisted of nearly 2.5 millions in customs duties, a figure accounting for roughly 62 per cent of the total. By 1908, however, the Government General allocations derived from initial customs duties in the colony dropped to a level of 1.25 million f., or less than 30 per cent of the total budget of over 4.3 millions. Conversely, the proportion of the budget derived from direct taxation more than doubled from roughly 18 per cent in 1903 to nearly 40 per cent in 1908, reflecting more than a threefold increase in the total amount of head taxes collected.

In short, by 1908 the colony's budget depended heavily upon the administration's capacity to coax taxes directly from the rural chiefs. The reforms of 1904 provided the fiscal corollary to Clozel's policies of political collaboration, and it is a measure of his political skill that he was able to introduce these new fiscal measures without precipitating renewed local resistance. Essentially he had succeeded in convincing the collaborating chiefs to tolerate two burdens at once: one directly, in the form of increased contributions to the local budget; the other indirectly, in the form of the enduring customs burden which after 1904 went to support the federal administrative structures. The apparent decline in the colony's budget during most of Clozel's governorship only served to mask an overall increase in combined direct and indirect taxation of the rural masses.

Despite the decreasing importance of customs receipts in the composition of the local budget, it cannot be argued that the colony became any less dependent upon the vitality of the import-export sector. On the contrary, the budget remained highly sensitive to any shifts in commercial performance for four main reasons. In the first place, although the customs contributions (in the form of Government General allocations) declined over the period they none the less continued to provide a substantial lump of the budget, accounting for the largest single source of revenue until 1907, when they were finally displaced by head taxes. Perhaps more importantly, the customs revenues provided a direct index to the Government General of the comparative performance of the colony within the Federation as a whole. Any decline in trade would reflect itself in a corresponding decline in customs receipts which would in turn decrease the colony's contribution to the federal budget. If this were to happen, the colony's governor could expect pressure to be applied from the Governor General to ameliorate the situation. Ironically, by financing the federal budget from territorial customs duties, the new fiscal reforms multiplied the impact of the commercial interests upon the local Governor. Under the new structures both the local merchants *and* the Governor General could be expected to pounce upon any local Governor who appeared to be pursuing policies detrimental to the import-export sector, and the Governor General could influence the future career prospects of a Governor under his control in a more direct way than the commercial community ever could.

The third reason for the persistent influence of the commercial interests upon the local budget was that by deriving an increasing amount of its local income from patents and licences, the colony committed itself to stimulating petty commerce in the interior. This in turn depended directly upon the health of the large import-export concerns. Any decline in their activity would register itself directly upon the budget in the form of falling revenues from patents and licences, and this was something which the colony could not afford. Revenues from licensing combined with those from customs duties, in the form of Government General allocations, exceeded those derived from head taxes until 1908, and to this extent the budget directly reflected the vitality of commerce throughout Clozel's tenure in office.

Finally, the performance of the import-export sector impinged indirectly, but none the less significantly, upon the administration's chances of collecting the head taxes themselves. In so far as he was able, a Baule household head would avoid dipping into the reserves of gold held in his family *adya* to pay taxes. Instead, he would seek to obtain the cash to pay the tax by collecting rubber for sale, or dispatching his slaves to work as porters, or by encouraging his wives to sell foodstuffs to the local Europeans, or by increasing his own production and sale of palm wine, woven cloth, and other local manufactures. All of these activities depended to some extent upon the vitality of the import-export trade, for if this trade declined he could no longer expect to earn money by gathering rubber, producing foodstuffs or palm wine or sending his slaves to work as porters. As his cash income declined, so did his willingness to pay the required head tax. In this respect as well, then, the colony's budget remained highly vulnerable to vicissitudes of international commerce.

For all of these reasons it could be argued that Clozel's success in transforming the colony's budget without engendering further local resistance resulted as much from the expanding climate of international trade as it did from his own adroit policies of collaboration. It is difficult to establish cause and effect in this type of analysis, but it is perhaps more than a mere coincidence that Clozel's peace strategy was ushered in in the midst of an unprecedented European demand for African wild rubber.

The export figures of the Ivory Coast reveal the growing importance of the rubber 'boom' for the Ivory Coast economy:[3]

RUBBER EXPORTS FROM IVORY COAST

Year	Total exports francs	Rubber exports francs	Approx. % of Total
1896	4,400,000	440,000	10%
1897	4,700,000	580,000	12%
1898	5,000,000	1,300,000	26%
1899	5,800,000	2,900,000	49%
1900	8,000,000	4,700,000	59%
1901	6,200,000	2,800,000	45%
1902	7,100,000	3,600,000	52%
1903	7,600,000	4,600,000	61%
1904	10,300,000	6,500,000	64%
1905	7,600,000	5,300,000	69%
1906	9,600,000	6,400,000	67%
1907	10 900,000	7,000,000	60%

After an encouraging beginning in the late 1890s the importance of wild rubber dipped during the disruptive military campaigns against the Baule in 1901, but under Clozel's governorship it recovered and expanded in both absolute and relative terms, accounting for an average of nearly two-thirds of the colony's exports from 1903 to 1907.

The secondary effects of this export growth were no less important. Given the direct relationship between the availability of cash and the demand for imports on the part of African producers, the remarkable export expansion was matched by an equally impressive growth in imports over the same period. Imports which amounted to roughly 4,600,000 f. in 1896 swelled to a figure of 14,300,000 f. in 1907. Furthermore, it was largely from the income derived from the rubber boom that the rural chiefs were able to more than triple their payments in head taxes between 1903 and 1908. On the surface at least, it appeared that the fortuitous conjuncture of Clozel's collaborative policies with the concomitant rubber boom placed the Ivory Coast well on the road to colonial prosperity.

Upon closer examination, however, the apparent prosperity of the colony by the end of 1907 could be seen to have been very precarious indeed. The basic source of the colony's remarkable success was in reality the key to its imminent commercial and fiscal collapse. If the onset of the rubber boom made prosperity possible, the eclipse of that trade made disaster inevitable. By 1907 two-thirds of the colony's commercial activity could be directly or indirectly ascribed to the rubber trade, and for a combination of internal and external reasons the future of this trade was in serious doubt.

Externally, the long-term prospects for African wild rubber on the European commodity markets looked bleak. Rubber plants smuggled out of Brazil and carefully cultivated at Kew Gardens in England had given encouraging results. Large-scale plantations were established in Malaysia, and as these trees came into full production, the future of wild rubber was threatened. Plantation production provided higher quality rubber at a cheaper price and the collectors of wild rubber in West Africa could not hope to compete.[4] The eclipse of rubber collection among the Ashanti during the 1900 Kumasi campaign along with the progressive shift of production towards cocoa in that colony combined to favour Ivory Coast rubber exports for a few years after the turn of the century, but in the long run this was a passing phenomenon. Unless major innovations were introduced, West African rural collectors seemed destined to cede their importance to Malay plantation labourers in the production of European rubber supplies.

Internally, the rubber trade appeared to be in trouble for other reasons. As the pattern of commercial expansion in Baule country clearly demonstrated, the rubber boom had stimulated momentary growth without encouraging sustained development. Generally the Baule only engaged in rubber collection as an ancillary activity. For the most part they were content to let Apollonien labourers tap the reserves in their territory. The Baule derived most of their trade profits instead from the sale of goods and provision of services to the transient Dyula and Apollonien traders, although in some cases the demand for taxes encouraged the Baule to assign their slaves to gather rubber as well. The combined exploitation of the Baule forests rapidly exhausted the existing rubber plants. Tapping techniques were not well developed, and because of the urgency to obtain the maximum latex for immediate sale and payment of taxes, many of the vines and trees were totally destroyed. As the rubber boom continued, the frontier of exploitable reserves receded further and further from habitually settled areas, thus requiring more and more labour investment to obtain comparable results. By 1907 the Baule themselves were virtually out or rubber, and the transiting traffic in rubber from the northern Ivory Coast also appeared unsteady.[5] If the trade were to falter, the Baule who derived an income from providing goods and services to itinerant traders would also suffer. The collapse of the rubber trade would mean the collapse of trade in general, for the Baule were not yet engaged in producing other commodities for the European market.

To Europeans on the coast, the future prospects of the rubber trade were not immediately predictable, but ominous signs could be read in the colony's commercial figures of 1907. Despite a temporary upswing in the average local price paid to the collectors for rubber from the 1906 level of 4.20f. per kilogram to a 1907 figure of 5.10f., production dropped from 1,518,580 kg in 1906 to a level of 1,372,019 kg in 1907.[6] The price rise meant that the declared value of exported rubber actually reached unprecedented levels in the 1907 trade figures, but this merely concealed the absolute decline in production. Normally the price elasticity of supply had proved to be high with respect to rubber production – that is to say, a slight increase in price offered for rubber generally stimulated a large new outflow of the commodity. The 1907 figures suggested, however, that a production threshold had been reached. The ruinous tapping procedures had taken their toll and further expansion of rubber production would require disproportionate new labour inputs by the African collectors and traders. The 1907 statistics seemed to demonstrate that the supply of exports in this sector had reached its peak and that if in the future prices were to fall instead of rise as they had between 1906 and 1907, a major crisis in rubber production could ensue.

Signs of difficulty in the colony's economy began to multiply throughout 1907 and early 1908. As rubber became more scarce, it became increasingly difficult for the Baule to pay their taxes without dipping into their reserves of gold. The French administrator in Bouaké conceded that in return for the sum of 175,384 f. in taxes that the Baule in his region had paid over the previous three years they had received virtually nothing in return and that unless French economic policy changed, the future did not look promising. Instead of continuing to drain the country of its rapidly diminishing resources the administrator suggested a more forward programme of development for the Baule, 'une politique qui les enrichera et qui augmentera la richesse productive du sol'. The administrator was frankly criticial of Clozel's well-worn phrases concerning the efficacy of *laissez-faire* commercial expansion, and he predicted that there would be trouble from the Baule unless the administration changed its tack:

ce n'est pas par des paroles mais par des faits que nous devons aborder franchement cette politique de mise en valeur du sol. Sinon les Baoulés, qui parlent tous de notre départ prochain, en arriveront à la souhaiter plus fortement.[7]

In early 1908 the commercial community expressed its discontent with administrative policy from a different vantage point. Their specific complaint focused upon the tax levied upon petty traders in the form of licence fees. These revenues had more than quadrupled over the previous five years, and the commercial houses found them burdensome. The European merchants depended upon the petty traders in the hinterland to bulk rubber for export and retail their imported manufactured goods, and they regarded the administration's levy upon these traders as unwelcome interference with their inland operations. From their point of view the government was strangling commercial initiative at precisely the point where it needed to be more fully encouraged. The large firms required more and more traders and porters to go deeper and deeper into the bush to find rubber, and this in itself increased the costs of their operations. When the government insisted on levying licence fees that had the effect of further swelling their operating expenses, the commercial community felt it had the right to object. In addition, the merchants felt that since the immediate danger of revolt appeared to have subsided in Baule country following Clozel's conciliatory policies, they should be allowed once again to sell guns and munitions to the Baule.[8]

The commercial criticisms came at an awkward moment. Governor Clozel had left the colony, and it appeared that he was soon to be replaced. As yet, however, his successor had not been chosen, and Albert Nebout occupied the role of acting Governor. His response to the commercial interests was clear on the question of licence fees. He explained that the fees had become an important source of revenue for the colony's budget, and the administration could not simply abolish them without finding another source of income to replace them. When the merchants suggested that the head taxes could be raised to cover the difference, Nebout disagreed, indicating that the threshold of acceptable taxation had been reached in most areas and that higher head taxes might precipitate open revolt. As for guns and munitions, Nebout promised only that he would study the question further.[9]

The rising chorus of internal criticism of the administration's policies was soon reinforced by an important voice from outside the colony. The French colonial system provided for periodic inspections to be conducted of each colony. These inspection tours by independent observers served to correct the abuses of administration in local areas by compiling detailed reports on every aspect of the colony's affairs and submitting these reports to the immediate superiors of the Governor. Suggestions in these reports often served as guidelines or even blueprints for future policy. Since these inspection reports went to the Governor General and then to the Minister of Colonies, no local Governor could afford to ignore the suggestions made in them if he wished to remain on good terms with his superiors.

In February 1908 Inspector Lapalud arrived in the Ivory Coast to conduct an official inquiry, the first thorough examination the colony had undergone since the beginning of the colonial period. In the same month Gabriel Angoulvant was appointed to become Clozel's successor as the colony's Governor. Angoulvant did not arrive in the colony to assume control of the administration until late April 1908. By then Lapalud's investigations were nearly complete, and his critique of the colony's situation was sobering. Reflecting the opinions of local administrators and commercial representatives whom he had met in the course of his travels throughout the colony, Lapalud alluded in his summary report to what he called the 'désordre administratif regnant dans la colonie . . .', and emphasized that the commercial interests in the colony had been unjustifiably ignored. He acknowledged that the fiscal reforms had done considerable damage to the colony's budgets, and to help ameliorate the situation he suggested that a tax could be imposed upon all firearms and recommended in addition that the portion of tax returns allocated to the chiefs could be reduced from 10 per cent to 5 per cent. For the time being he thought it unadvisable to raise the general level of head taxes, but the possibility was not ruled out for the future. In concluding Lapalud concurred with the opinion expressed earlier by various administrators in Baule country: the future prospects of the colony depended upon a more forward economic policy designed, as he expressed it, to 'diriger l'indigène dans la voie des cultures les plus rémunératrices'.[10]

As with all inspection reports, Lapalud's findings were bound to have some impact upon the outlook of other officials. In this particular case, however, the impact was more pronounced than usual because of the combination of circumstances surrounding conditions in the Ivory Coast. In the first place, the investigations were undertaken after Clozel left the colony and before Angoulvant arrived, and in this respect they could be used to punctuate the transfer of administrative authority and signal a new departure of policy. This could have happened no matter who took control after Clozel, but the fact that Angoulvant succeeded Clozel served to enhance the importance of Lapalud's findings still further. Angoulvant, a recent graduate of the École Coloniale, was a political appointee as Governor. In marked contrast to Clozel he had little prior experience in Africa, and it was perhaps for this reason that Lapalud's reports formed such an important reference point for Angoulvant's policies in the months and years to come. In addition to the fact that these reports went to his superiors, they also served as the means by which Angoulvant learned about his own colony and West Africa in general. A more experienced administrator with years of exposure to African political and economic problems may well have regarded Lapalud's critique and suggestions as naïve or impracticable, but Angoulvant took them as gospel – a kind of inspired truth which he felt obliged to act upon as an ardent believer in France's colonial mission.

Angoulvant's début in the Ivory Coast was marked by considerable pomp and circumstance, for his arrival coincided with the first visit ever to the colony by a French minister – the Minister of Colonies, Raphaël Milliès-Lacroix. The Minister's tour underscored the importance which colonial circles in Paris were beginning to attach to the future success of the Ivory Coast, and Angoulvant was keenly aware that Ministry officials would be watching his performance closely. In comparative terms, the Ivory Coast remained among the weakest contributors to the

Government General budget, lagging far behind the colonies of Guinea, Senegal, and Niger. Its contribution was not much greater than that of Dahomey, and given the relative resources of the two colonies, colonial officials expected far more from the Ivory Coast in the future.

Comparisons between the Ivory Coast and the British colony of the Gold Coast stimulated even greater expectations for the Ivory Coast's future. The rubber boom had come and gone on the Gold Coast, but other agricultural commodities had taken its place in the first decade of the century. Coffee had already proved its export potential in the 1890s, and the rapid expansion of cocoa production was nothing short of phenomenal after 1900. The William Cadbury Company began to purchase large quantities of cocoa in 1906, and peasant producers responded by planting new trees on a massive scale throughout southern Ghana.[11] The Ivory Coast climate and soils were broadly comparable to those in the Gold Coast, and there seemed to be no reason why the same export commodities should not prosper in the Ivory Coast. If they could be grown, these crops would enable the colony to overcome its hazardous dependence upon wild rubber exports.

Angoulvant addressed himself at first to the immediate problem of balancing the 1908 budget. Expenditures were exceeding the administration's income, largely because of the recent creation of two local brigades of paramilitary forces intended eventually to replace the Senegalese troops in the country. To raise the revenue quickly Angoulvant followed one of Lapalud's suggestions and proposed to introduce a tax on firearms. The idea was initially mooted by Nebout in his role as acting Governor, and he wrote to Governor General Ponty for permission to levy the tax in April. Ponty replied that he was not opposed, but suggested that the proposal should be submitted to the Conseil d'Administration within the colony for their approval first.[12] The Conseil consisted in part of influential representatives from the commercial community, and it was in this body that the administration formally encountered the merchants' opinions on all its measures.

When Angoulvant proposed the arms tax to the Conseil in May he emphasized the commercial advantages it entailed. In order to entice gun owners to register their arms and pay the five franc tax the government intended to furnish each duly registered owner with a permit to purchase 250 grams of gunpowder. This, Angoulvant argued, would stimulate commerce, for the Baule and other groups would be eager to buy the powder which had been officially banned since 1902. The commercial community was not, however, fully satisfied with Angoulvant's proposals. M. Barthe, the Ivory Coast director of the

C.F.A.O., brought up the issue of porters' licences once again and he tried to link the approval of the arms tax with a proposal to revoke the licence fees. Angoulvant overruled Barthe, insisting that given the budgetary crisis at hand there could be no question of revoking the traders' licensing fees.[13] The arms tax was passed and became official policy with the publication of the *arrêté* of 20 July 1908.[14] Angoulvant was able to raise his much-needed revenue, but it looked as though a serious rift between the headstrong new Governor and the seasoned colonial merchants was in the making.

Among the Baule the revenue measures had far-reaching consequences. Although Baule gun owners were not pleased with the prospect of paying an additional annual tax equal to twice their existing head tax, they were none the less attracted by the possibility of purchasing more gunpowder. Under the new measures the French succeeded in collecting 131,850 f. by the end of 1908.[15] This meant that a total of 26,370 guns had been registered and that permits for a total of 6,592 kg of powder had been issued. If all this powder was purchased, as it seems likely that it was, the rural masses in the colony had received a total of 659,200 musket-charges of ammunition. It is probable that more than half of this total went into the hands of the Baule. Such a massive rearmament, while not on the same scale as that which occurred when Governor Roberdeau lifted the arms sales ban in 1902, was nevertheless significant enough to strengthen Baule confidence in their capacity to resist the French if the burdens of the colonial regime were to become much worse.

More important than the sheer quantity of gunpowder introduced into Baule country was the way in which the munitions were distributed as a result of the new measures. During Clozel's governorship sales were restricted in a blanket fashion, but exceptions were made for particularly co-operative chiefs. Clozel's policy had the effect of concentrating armament supplies in the hands of a few important chiefs, and this in turn generally consolidated their political power with respect to their subordinates. Virtually every Baule male had access to a musket, but only a few controlled adequate supplies of powder. As long as this remained the case the politics of collaboration continued to be fairly simple. Angoulvant's emergency revenue scheme, however, completely abolished the privileged position of the collaborating chief. Simply by presenting his gun, paying his tax, and receiving his permit, an individual gun holder could now obtain 250 grams of powder or the equivalent of 25 rounds of ammunition.

This created what can only be described as a potentially explosive political situation. Collaborating chiefs were irritated at the relative erosion of their privileged position, and at the same time those chiefs from outlying areas who had been disgruntled with the terms of the colonial arrangement all along now had the means to express their discontent. In the first instance this discontent did not direct itself at the French but village chiefs and household heads found it possible to assert their autonomy from the pro-French chiefs. The fragile collaborative structure carefully constructed by Clozel was poised to collapse if the pressure from above became too great.

During July and August Angoulvant toured Baule territory and began to formulate plans for the region's future development. He appeared to be oblivious to the potentially disruptive political implications of his arms tax measures, for in the following months he proceeded to issue a series of harsh and uncompromising directives to administrators in Baule country. In his 'Lettre Programme' of 16 November 1908, circulated to all his subordinates and the entire commercial community, he outlined his plans to ameliorate the colony's economic plight.[16]

Lapalud's suggestions concerning the cultivation of new export crops formed an important theme in Angoulvant's emerging development strategy. Administrators were invited to advise the Governor about the possibility of cultivating such crops as cocoa or cotton within their region. By this time the Gold Coast was well on its way to becoming the world's largest cocoa producer, and in Tiassalé the Fanti merchant, Morgan Dougan, had already begun to plant the crop on his own initiative with promising results.[17] Angoulvant saw no reason why this crop and others could not be produced on a broader scale.

To stimulate others to follow Morgan Dougan's example Angoulvant issued new land tenure regulations designed to release land to individuals intending to cultivate new crops. He did not seem to worry greatly about the reaction this might evoke from rural chiefs who customarily allocated cultivation rights. Their prerogative was simply usurped by the local French administrators who were authorized to give out land permits to whoever they judged to offer a reasonable chance of succeeding with new crops.[18] In addition the administration distributed cocoa seedlings to individuals to stimulate production. Those who benefited from both the new land tenure provisions and the governmental distribution of plants were not primarily Baule in the first instance. They consisted instead of interpreters, traders and the Dyula inhabitants of centres such as Toumodi and Tiassalé. In some cases the 'representatives' of the Baule chiefs near the French posts began to plant cocoa as well, but those individuals were for the most part Baule slaves or social subordinates, and it is understandable why they would welcome the chance to extend their cultivation rights.[19] Generally the Baule themselves remained indifferent toward these early attempts to stimulate export production in their midst.

Angoulvant intended to use the head tax as a lever with which to manœuvre the seemingly reluctant Baule into producing for the European market. In November 1908 he put forward before the Conseil d'Administration measures for raising the level of taxation with well-rehearsed justifications derived most probably from his bureaucratic training at the École Coloniale. As Angoulvant observed:

C'est un fait avéré que l'impôt joue, dans toutes les colonies, un rôle à la fois productif et moralisateur. L'indigène, qui, avant nous n'avait aucun besoin dont il ne trouve, presque sans effort, la satisfaction quasi immédiate dans les ressources à sa portée que la nature lui/prodiguées, *doit* être sollicité de produire . . . il n'est pas douteux . . . que l'obligation pour l'indigène de verser une taxe de capitation plus élevée serait extrêmement éfficace, l'impôt étant, je le répète, en l'état actuel de la mentalité indigène, le meilleur stimulant de l'énergie du natif.[20]

Angoulvant's entire rhetorical edifice rested upon pseudo-scientific racial theories feebly reinforced by a profound misreading of the African past, but for the time being this line of argument seemed to serve his purposes by justifying the raised taxes to both his administrative superiors and to the commercial community in the Ivory Coast. Not all the merchants were impressed. Barthe, the C.F.A.O. director, registered his reservations about Angoulvant's plans, but the tax increase eventually passed, only slightly modified by Barthe's criticisms.[21]

Simultaneously, Angoulvant sought to increase the colony's revenue by implementing Lapalud's suggestion to cut the tax rebates to the chiefs. Initially in 1901 the chiefs received 25 per cent of all the taxes they collected. During 1904 Clozel reduced this figure to a minimum of 10 per cent, allowing provisions for particular chiefs to receive more if their exceptional performance justified additional recompense. In 1908 Angoulvant proposed to reduce the portion to 5 per cent, and he made it clear that this represented a *maximum* figure that they could hope to receive. In reality, then, all chiefs suffered a 50 per cent cut in their rebates, and for most the decrease was even greater.[22] In addition, Angoulvant encouraged local administrators to tighten up local collection procedures by basing their tax assessments upon revised census figures rather than upon outdated estimates of population by the chiefs themselves.[23] Angoulvant's head tax measures, like those concerning the arms tax and land tenure, may have been intended to put the colony on a firm financial footing, but their effect was to strain the already fragile structures of collaboration in rural areas.

Concerning the chiefs themselves, Angoulvant made it clear that any dissent on their part would be firmly punished. In his instructions to Captain Foussat, the newly appointed administrator of the Bouaké region, Angoulvant was explicit on this point:

> Vous isolerez et éliminerez les mauvais éléments, en général seuls fauteurs de désordre. Si quelques chefs semblaient se refuser à comprendre . . . vous les punieriez aussitôt d'une façon exemplaire et, au besoin, les enverriez à Bingerville où je prendrais à leur égard telle mesure nécessaire.[24]

In subsequent instructions he made it clear that on the occasion of succession disputes, administrators should not hesitate to intervene directly to impose their favoured candidate for the office.[25] Indeed, in cases where existing chiefs proved to be ineffective or troublesome Angoulvant had no reservations about removing them from office while they were still alive.[26]

In addition to using taxation and a firm hand with chiefs, Angoulvant considered increasing rural production by imposing a form of obligatory communal labour. Noting the success that this form of labour mobilization had enjoyed in the Sudan, Angoulvant indicated that he thought it might work in the Ivory Coast not only with regard to the traditional commodities such as rubber and palm kernels which needed simply to be collected, but also in the case of the newly cultivated cash crops.[27]

To implement the entire package of reforms from the new tax measures through to the communal labour obligations Angoulvant felt that he required a new kind of authoritarian administrator at the level of the local post. Disturbed by the precarious position the colony was in when he assumed control, Angoulvant partially blamed the state of affairs upon the seemingly indulgent character of previous administrators, and he explicitly attacked the approach of men like Delafosse, Nebout, and Clozel himself:

> le chef de poste n'est pas placé dans une région, il n'est pas payé pour observer la nature et procéder à des études ethnographiques, botaniques, géologiques ou linguistiques. Il a pour mission d'administrer. Qu'on traduise ce mot . . . c'est en fin de compte . . . imposer des règlements, limiter les libertés particulières au profit de la liberté de tous, percevoir les taxes . . . nous ne pouvons supposer que

l'administrateur aura pour unique mission de plaire. Un moment viendra où il devra demander.[28]

Angoulvant's charge to his auxiliaries was simple: 'Je veux des résultats tangibles'.[29]

REACTIONS TO ANGOULVANT'S PROGRAMME, 1909-1910

Until 1908 the Baule remained largely uninvolved in production for European markets for two reasons. In the first place, the history of their previous encounters with Europeans had been a bitter and costly one, leading most freeborn Baule to regard direct participation in the colonial economy as a symbol of humiliating slave status. Thus, the pattern of French intrusion generated powerful social disincentives for the Baule to produce goods for export.

Secondly, and perhaps more important, the traditional industries of gold mining and cloth weaving were by no means defunct. On the contrary, they continued to flourish, providing the Baule with what they regarded as more attractive alternatives for investing their labour time.[30] This phenomenon created a situation in which the Baule remained aloof to the opportunities for wage employment in the colonial economy. In addition it meant that in economic terms the 'opportunity cost' to the Baule involved in adopting cash crops remained high. Planting cocoa and coffee presupposed an investment of substantial labour time before any returns were forthcoming, for it was necessary to plant the crops and tend them for several years before they began to produce. The labour time required to accomplish this was labour time which under normal circumstances could be devoted to the traditional industries of cloth weaving and gold mining.[31]

In the Baule case cash crops demanded more than the simple application of under-utilized manpower in rural areas to new tasks; instead these crops required the *diversion* of labour power from one sector in which profitable production was guaranteed to another in which, at the time, production seemed risky indeed. Some scholars have taken the remarkable expansion of cash crop production in West Africa during the early colonial period as an indication that in the pre-colonial African economies there was a high degree of 'disguised unemployment'. A. G. Hopkins suggests, for example:

it is hard to avoid the conclusion that the rise in output resulted from increased inputs of land and labour, and *therefore* that both factors had been to some extent underemployed previously.[32]

The difficulty with this generalization is that it focuses too exclusively upon the agricultural export sector as the subject for its analysis. Before the introduction of cash crops Baule labour was by no means 'underemployed', but it was engaged in sectors of production that did not register in European export figures. Gold production, jewellery manufacture and cloth weaving were industries involving large labour inputs, but the primary consumers of these commodities were the Africans themselves. Since production was for a local rather than for an export market, European administrators remained largely ignorant of the importance of these activities, and scholars ever since have tended to neglect the extent of labour inputs in these spheres. In the process they have been misled into concluding that because production of export agricultural commodities had been comparatively low in the pre-colonial period, *therefore* labour was somehow underemployed in African traditional economies. The fallacy in this reasoning is apparent once the issue of labour allocation in traditional industries is kept fully in view.

In the Baule case, at least, labour was not under-employed. On the contrary, because of the steady demand for their traditional products of gold and woven cloth, there was in effect a labour shortage among the Baule at the time of French intrusion. As far as the Baule were concerned it was the French who were inhibiting the productive potential of their economy. The only barriers to expanded production were those imposed by French presence, first because the French had cut off the supply of new slave purchases, and secondly because they were constantly trying to divert existing labour for their own porterage and construction needs. For straightforward economic reasons, then, the Baule resisted participation in the colonial economy and they hoped the French would leave so that their own systems of production could recover the autonomous prosperity that they had enjoyed before the French occupation.

Angoulvant was apparently ignorant of the economic calculation behind Baule reticence. For him their unfavourable response to the export-oriented agricultural economy was simply an index of an allegedly instinctive indolence and infantile mentality:

L'indigène . . . mène une existence indifférent, imprévoyante, sans sécurité même, paresseux autant qu'ignorant, préférant au moindre effort des privations sans nombre, il laisserait toujours inexploitées des ressources . . . si nous ne le forcions à sortir de sa torpeur, de son inertie . . . nous n'avons en aucune manière à compter sur son initiative: c'est un grand enfant retardataire dont nous devons nous faire les conseillers et les guides.[33]

With such a thoroughly misconceived analysis of the reality before him it is not surprising that Angoulvant soon encountered trouble in trying to implement his policies.

The Baule were not yet aware of the full scope of Angoulvant's paternalism, but it did not take them long to recognize that his policies constituted a wholesale assault on their own systems of production and their way of life in general. Angoulvant intended to move the colony towards what he called 'une colonisation plus scientifique . . .' the central thrust of which was to direct local labour, by force if necessary, toward producing goods for the European commodity market. Stripped of its elaborate rhetorical justifications this meant that the French administrator expected to compel the Baule to work on whatever task he assigned to them. The tasks the administration had in mind became apparent to the Baule when rubber seedlings, cocoa pods, and rice and cotton seed began to arrive in the local posts. After supervising the planting of these crops by their auxiliaries and closest collaborators in the immediate vicinity of each post, the administrators intended to extend cultivation to villages under their control by 'inviting' village chiefs and household heads to come forward and participate. The principle was that once the Baule had 'learned' how to work the new crops under the close surveillance of the local administrator, they would be expected to undertake further supervised production in their own villages.

The Baule response to these official initiatives was not overtly hostile at first. Instead the Baule simply evaded the French requests whenever possible. Administrators began to comment in early 1909 about what they called 'l'isolement des populations' - a euphemism used to describe the growing movement of Baule from the villages towards their more remote agricultural encampments.[34] The same French officers commented on the impotence of their collaborating chiefs, presumably with respect to recruiting the newly required labour.[35] Various solutions were proposed to strengthen the village as a productive unit or to reinforce the authority of the collaborating chiefs, but none of them seemed to have immediate effect.[36] Exasperated by the evasive response of the Baule and other groups to his programmes, Angoulvant began to talk in terms of renewed military operations to coerce them to work.[37]

Clozel's policy had been one of gradually diminishing the military presence in Baule country. During the final years of his governorship individual posts were transferred from military to civilian control. Four companies of Senegalese and Sudanese troops, each with a total of

130 men, remained at the time of Clozel's departure; but by September 1907 Commander Charles drew up a proposal calling for their departure and the full devolution of authority to civilian personnel. The two brigades of locally recruited 'gardes indigènes' were created in 1907[38] with the eventual intention of replacing the Senegalese troops, but the full Senegalese troop strength was maintained during the transition period between Clozel's departure and Angoulvant's installation.

When Angoulvant seemed to be firmly established, officials in Paris once again proposed to reduce the Senegalese troops. Faced with increasing unrest generated by his own policies, however, Angoulvant objected vehemently to the proposed cut in troop strength.[39] Indeed, the situation deteriorated to such an extent that forceful demonstrations of police strength were required among the Attié and the Baule-Ayaou in the early months of 1909. In late April and early May, just before leaving for Dakar to consult with Governor General Ponty, Angoulvant conducted a rapid inspection tour of the military situation among the Gouro and along the western Baule frontier.[40] The conclusions of his visit were sobering, and in Dakar he presented new proposals to the Government General requesting troop reinforcements to help face increasing local hostility to his programmes. In his request he expressed confidence that the Baule region was well in hand. The major trouble, he argued, was elsewhere, and additional troops would be needed particularly in the lagoon area near Cosrou and to extend French authority among the Gouro.[41]

Angoulvant's requests were not warmly received. On the contrary, officials had been looking forward to the long-awaited troop reduction in the Ivory Coast to ease the burden of federal expenditure in that colony. For the moment, Angoulvant's request was denied. He was told that he would be allowed to retain those forces that were still in the colony, but he should not count on more. Indeed, the Minister of Colonies, Milliès-Lacroix, had reservations about Angoulvant's performance, and he expressed his personal concern to Governor General Ponty that Angoulvant's use of force was becoming excessive.[42]

If he had been given the time, Angoulvant might well have heeded this warning and tried to moderate his approach in the future. Before he learned of the Minister's growing misgivings, however, events exploded in Baule country itself. The cumulative impact of Angoulvant's administrative measures towards the Baule finally crushed the delicate collaborative structures that Clozel had laboured to construct, and when they collapsed the French once again encountered armed Baule resistance. In reacting to the local crises at hand, Angoulvant and his subordinates committed the French to a programme of re-pression in Baule country and the colony at large which neither they, nor Governor General Ponty, nor the Minister himself could abandon without appearing to suffer a humiliating defeat.

The flashpoint of open revolt came in late June among the Baule-Akoué.[43] The Akoué were one of the few groups of Baule who by 1909 had still not engaged the French in direct combat on their own territory. Although Akoué partisans had assisted the Faafoué in the defence of Kokumbo in 1901, and although many other of their warriors came to the aid of the Ngban in their 1902 offensives, the French did nothing to retaliate against them. After establishing a post at Bonzi in late June 1901 the French seemed content to use it primarily as an observation point to monitor the trade across Baule territory toward the Gouro. Intervention in local affairs was minimal, limited to the occasional demand for porters or construction labour.

For the most part the local administrators got on well with the chief of Bonzi, Aboua Kouassi, and they had established a useful working relationship with Kouassi Ngo, the 'adopted son' of the prominent woman chief, Yabo Mousso. In 1901 the French had been led to believe that Yabo Mousso was 'la reine des Akoués'.[44] Subsequently, they learned from experience that her influence was not as extensive as they had initially thought, but they were none the less pleased for whatever help she offered them through her designated representative, Kouassi Ngo. Until Angoulvant took office French presence among the Akoué remained largely symbolic. Taxes had been the subject of a few polite requests by local administrators, but no concerted campaign of tax collection had ever been undertaken.

In 1909 the French administrator at Bonzi, an 'Adjoint des Affaires Indigènes' named Moesch, adopted a sterner approach in keeping with Angoulvant's directives. He made it clear that henceforth he intended to collect the annual head tax in full and the new arms tax as well. The Akoué for their part were more inclined to listen to Koki Yao Aounou, a forty-year-old chief from the village of Akoumiakro near Diamalabo, who was travelling throughout the Bonzi area exhorting the Akoué to withhold their taxes. The level of revenue expected from head taxes in the southern Baule region had doubled from the 1907 figure of approximately 90,000 f. to 180,000 . in 1909,[45] and in addition the arms tax represented a further heavy burden. Moreover the Akoué were struck by the anomalous situation that prevailed around them. The French had attempted to collect taxes among the neighbouring Ayaou and the Yaouré, but their efforts were a failure; these populations remained beyond the scope of control of the French posts. The Akoué, particularly those from the villages of Kami, Diamalabo, Morofé, and Kongouanou, began to regard French insistence upon collecting taxes from them as outrageous in light of the evident fact that nothing had been obtained from their Ayaou and Yaouré neighbours.

Koki Yao Aounou's campaign was well under way when Angoulvant travelled through Akoué country in the early days of June 1909, but Moesch chose to remain silent about it to the Governor. Angoulvant seemed to be morosely pre-occupied with his recent visit to Gouro country and the news of further trouble among the Attié to the south, so Moesch, not wanting to contribute to the general weight of discouraging news, said nothing.[46] Angoulvant departed with the impression that the administration of the area was under control, and this is what he confidently reported to the Governor General in Dakar on 17 June 1909. Locally, however, the situation deteriorated to the point where Marc Simon, the chief French administrator for the entire southern Baule district, felt it was necessary for him to travel from Toumodi to Bonzi to settle the issue before the tax boycott got out of hand.

On Wednesday 16 June 1909 Moesch and Simon accompanied by Kouassi Ngo, an interpreter, and seventeen Senegalese troops set off from the post at Bonzi to the village of Diamalabo to hold a meeting with recalcitrant chiefs. The encounter was short and to the point, but instead of the French imposing their point of view upon the Akoué, the tables were turned. Arriving in the village shortly before noon, Simon addressed Alou Kouassi, the chief of Diamalabo, indicating that he wanted to meet with the disgruntled chiefs in the region that evening. Alou Kouassi replied that it would be impossible to assemble the necessary people before the following day, and he designated a hut where he intended that his guests should stay the night. The Senegalese troops and the French became uneasy as they noticed that Baule warriors were beginning to gather in the village. Simon reiterated his demand to Alou Kouassi to convoke a meeting at once. Alou Kouassi retorted, 'Aujourd'hui, ce n'est plus toi qui commande; c'est moi.'[47] The Akoué warriors became increasingly belligerent, and the Baule porters from Toumodi who had accompanied Simon abandoned the group and fled. Simon and Moesch began to realize that if they stayed much longer in the village they would be fortunate to leave it alive.

Moesch advised withdrawing to Bonzi at once. As the group attempted to execute an orderly departure from the village an Akoué warrior opened fire, mortally wounding one of the Senegalese troops.

The French returned the fire as best they could in hurried retreat. They headed initially for Bonzi, but they soon realized after being ambushed in several successive villages along the route, that to continue along such a predictable path was to play into the hands of the rebels. They abandoned the route and began to cut their way through thick forest with their machetes aiming to reach Ngokro, the village of Kouassi Ngo, residence of Yabo Mousso. There Kouassi Ngo assured them they would be safe from rebel attack. Off the trail the going was slow, for the small group had suffered two killed and several wounded in the afternoon's ambush. Kouassi Ngo himself had been wounded twice, once in the head and once in the thigh as he tried to entreat the rebel villagers to let the troops pass. As night fell the pathetic company continued to cut its way deeper and deeper into the tropical undergrowth without making much forward progress. It was not until eight o'clock the next morning, 17 June, that the remaining party straggled to safety in Ngokro; they had taken eighteen hours to cover a distance of little more than five kilometres!

The incident was humiliating in the extreme, but the events which ensued were even more so. For several days the beleaguered group remained trapped in Ngokro. Reinforcements were summoned from Toumodi, and on 19 June Sergeant Niemen arrived with eighteen Senegalese soldiers. The next move according to Moesch should be to regain the Bonzi post immediately. When he and Simon left it on 16 June only seven armed guards remained behind to defend it, and Moesch feared that the Akoué would capitalize upon his evident weakness and besiege the post in his absence. Thus, no sooner had the reinforcements arrived from Toumodi than Moesch, Simon, Sergeant Niemen and the troops set out from Ngokro to relieve Bonzi.

They did not get far. Three hundred metres from the village they fell into a heavy Akoué ambush. Four soldiers were wounded instantly, and Niemen was badly hurt in the hand. Simon gave the order to retreat to Ngokro, and the rebels pursued them back to the village, wounding three more Senegalese. The French thus suffered their second major humiliation in three days.

Meanwhile at Bonzi itself, the Dyula traders resident in the area had taken refuge with the seven guards in the French post. Arming themselves with the munitions available they began firing in desperation at the Baule warriors who encircled the post in the surrounding underbrush. There were only 750 rounds of reserve ammunition when Moesch left on 16 June, and these supplies were quickly expended. Fearing imminent attack the guards, the Dyula, and their wives tried to escape towards Toumodi under cover of night. Only two of the seven guards survived; the rest, together with the Dyula men were killed while the women were captured. The Akoué under the direction of Koki Yao Aounou looted the abandoned post and uprooted the rubber and cocoa plantations which the administration had forced them to cultivate in the vicinity of the post.[48] The message was clear. The Akoué revolt was not simply a matter of discontent over excessive taxes. Their movement was a generalized uprising against the colonial arrangement that Angoulvant was trying to impose. The Akoué rejected the entire package – the Dyula trader, arms tax, cocoa seeds and all.

In the village of Ngokro, or Yamoussoukro as the French began to call it out of respect for Yabo Mousso, the situation remained critical. Akoué settlements to the south were sympathetic with Kami, Diamalabo, Morofé, and other rebel villages in the north. Simon, Moesch, and Niemen were effectively cut off from Toumodi, incapable of escaping from Yamoussoukro in any direction. Finally on 21 June Lieutenant Pelle managed to fight his way through from Toumodi to join the group at Yamoussoukro. He brought with him a motley band of reinforcements recruited in large part from the Toumodi Dyula community. Trained troops were in such short supply that Pelle was obliged to hand out rifles and cartridges to any Dyula civilians he could find willing enough to help him rescue the two administrators. The Dyula community, realizing that their own security was at stake if the Akoué revolt spread, provided thirty volunteers within a few hours and set out with Pelle to retrieve Simon and Moesch and the wounded troops. With the aid of these reinforcements and under cover of night Simon and Moesch withdrew from Yamoussoukro to Toumodi, bringing to an end the most humiliating retreat the French had experienced at the hands of the Baule since the evacuation of the Salékro post among the Nanafoué in 1902.

The Akoué revolt had an immediate impact upon neighbouring groups. Among the Ayaou, Dyula villages were attacked in July 1909, and events followed the Akoué pattern. Dyula men were killed and the women and children taken as captives.[49] Marriage alliances linked families from Kami among the Akoué with Lolobo among the Nanafoué, and in addition to possible reinforcements in battle, these alliance structures afforded some of the most rebellious Akoué with avenues of escape and refuge if the French were to launch a future counter-offensive.[50] Resistance sentiment spread as kinship ties were mobilized in preparation for defensive fighting.

In the Ouossou area south of Toumodi tensions flared up during

July between the Ngban and the resident Dyula and Senegalese groups. In this case the administration found itself in a difficult position because of its apparent alliance with the alien ethnic community. The problem began with a dispute between Ali Seck, a former Senegalese soldier, and his Baule wife, Assa Ngbin. Ali Seck married Assa Ngbin, the niece of an influential Ngban chief named Aguié Kouassi, in 1902 when he was stationed with the French occupying forces in Ouossou. Upon leaving the military Ali Seck established himself as a trader in Toumodi, and Assa Ngbin joined him there, giving birth to a child in 1904. The marriage appeared to be stable, but during June when several Dyula traders were killed in Akoué country and other Dyula and Senegalese rushed to the aid of Moesch and Simon, Assa Ngbin decided to leave Toumodi with her child and return to live with her relations in Aguiékouassikro near Ouossou.

Ali Seck was furious. He travelled from Toumodi to Ouossou and placed his complaint before the local French administrator, Lerminier, demanding that either the woman should be forced to return with the child or that the marriage payment should be reimbursed. Lerminier summoned Assa Ngbin to the post to settle the matter, but before the case could be heard Ali Seck, apparently suspecting that she had taken a Baule lover, killed her in a fit of passion. Fearing immediate retribution from the enraged Ngban, Ali Seck sought refuge in the French post. Lerminier placed him under guard, and tried to calm the angry Ngban chiefs, assuring them that Ali Seck would be brought to justice before the regional tribunal. The Ngban were not satisfied and gave Lerminier an ultimatum: if Ali Seck were not delivered to them immediately, the Ngban would declare themselves to be in open revolt. Lerminier cabled Simon in Toumodi for directions. Simon replied by authorizing the release of Ali Seck to avert what he feared would otherwise turn into a massive slaughter of Dyula and Senegalese traders throughout the entire Baule region.[51] Ali Seck was handed over to the Ngban chiefs and executed within twenty-four hours.

Simon's decision may well have prevented an imminent massacre of the Dyula in Baule country, but it also unleashed a series of other developments which further diminished the prospects for peace among the Baule. The Ali Seck 'affair', as it became known, inspired Angoulvant to take more extreme measures against the Baule. In August 1909 he outlined plans for the total disarmament of rebellious populations.[52] While this may have seemed the next logical step to take to prevent incidents like the Akoué revolt and the Ali Seck affair from occuring in the future, ultimately this decision had the effect of galvanizing Baule resistance on a scale previously unimagined.

The reasons for the rapid spread of resistance sentiment in the face of this policy decision are apparent when its local impact is taken into account. Coming only a year after the first arms tax, Angoulvant's proposals were outrageous from the Baule point of view. Many Baule had consented to pay the arms tax, but now even this did not seem to please the French. Local administrators began to demand the guns as well. The entire arms tax procedures of the previous year began to look like a cynical trick to even the most faithful of Baule collaborators. By registering the guns and issuing permits the French had succeeded in identifying by name those who were armed, and now they intended to use these tax rolls to demand the personal rendition of each individual weapon. In these circumstances those Baule who had resisted the arms tax from the outset were proven to have acted wisely. The collaborating chiefs who had dutifully complied with the French arms tax had no further grounds upon which to make a respectable political appeal to their potential followers. Some were driven into closer dependence upon the French; most moved toward more open hostility.[53]

As the local polarization of opinion became more pronounced the rebels recognized that the stakes involved in resistance were greater than ever before. Now that the price of defeat was permanent disarmament, the rebels stiffened their resolve to defend themselves. Capitulation under these circumstances would not only entail subordination to the French, but also permanent weakness before other ethnic groups within the colony who, by courting French favour, were able to retain their arms. Angoulvant's disarmament proposals threatened to upset the complex set of inter-ethnic relations by permanently disabling some groups and favouring others. The speed with which Lieutenant Pelle armed the Dyula population of Toumodi in a moment of crisis and Lerminier's apparent willingness to harbour Ali Seck proved to the Baule that the French were not impartial with respect to inter-ethnic tension. Increasingly, the Baule began to feel that their arms were their only guarantee of justice. In short, by demanding all Baule warriors to surrender their guns, Angoulvant transformed virtually all gun owners into rebels.

During July and August in a series of limited campaigns against the Akoué the French succeeded in recapturing the destroyed outpost at Bonzi. Their victory, however, was short-lived. Despite repeated assaults on Kami, the rebel stronghold, the French were unable to reduce the Akoué to submission. At the end of August the Akoué surrounded the Bonzi post, depriving it completely of supplies and reinforcements from

Toumodi. It was not until mid-November that Commander Nogués was able to break through the Akoué defences from Toumodi and reopen communications with Lieutenant Bouet and his starving garrison at Bonzi.[54]

Against this general background of retreat, defeat, and confusion in the face of Baule resistance, Angoulvant encountered heightened criticism from the commercial community. The difference of opinion between Barthe and Angoulvant during 1908 developed into a full-scale row with metropolitan repercussions during 1909 and 1910. Barthe indicated that he feared Angoulvant's policies would lead to the kind of infamous excesses characteristic of the Congo. Angoulvant tried to defend his approach, but as the metropolitan press began to cover incidents in the Ivory Coast his flowery rhetoric sounded hollow.[55]

Humanitarian circles became critical of Angoulvant's iron-fisted policies from 1909 onwards, when Dr Combe, a veteran colonial medical officer with experience in the Bouaké region, revealed startling evidence of atrocities committed by French officers among the Baule. In 1908 Captain Foussat led a particularly brutal punitive expedition against the Ayaou. During the campaign enemy corpses were decapitated and their heads were displayed by the French forces in an attempt to intimidate other groups from rebelling.[56] This was not an unusual tactic in colonial warfare, and there were earlier examples of it during the 1902 campaigns against the Baule,[57] but combined with the growing sense of outrage from the commercial community these revelations encouraged sharp criticism of Angoulvant's approach.

The Ali Seck affair provided more ammunition for Angoulvant's critics. A full page cover engraving interpreted the incident to the Paris readership of *Les Nouvelles Illustrées*, and there followed a series of articles in *La Revue Indigène* explicitly attacking the administration's action.[58] Angoulvant tried to defend his policies in general with a long self-justificatory article in the October supplement to the *Bulletin du Comité de l'Afrique Française*, but its strident tone did little to quiet his critics.[59]

The military command also became openly criticial of Angoulvant for its own reasons in late 1909. Having been denied troop reinforcements during June 1909 in Dakar, Angoulvant nevertheless obtained an emergency contingent under Commander Nogués in August for the ostensible purpose of subduing a tax revolt in Cosrou on the Ébrié lagoon. Once the troops were in the colony, Angoulvant felt he had the authority to deploy them in any way he saw fit, and during September 1909 he issued orders to Nogués to prepare for operations among the

Akoué. Noguès obliged, but simultaneously he informed his military superiors in Dakar of the subtle manœouvre Angoulvant seemed to be trying to execute to sidestep the official troop restrictions imposed upon him.

General Caudrelier, Superior Commander of French troops in West Africa, was enraged when he heard the news of Angoulvant's initiative. In Ponty's absence Caudrelier pressed acting Governor General Liotard to reprimand Angoulvant. Liotard did so, but Angoulvant defended his action. Caudrelier, ever more angry, informed Ponty who was still on leave in Paris, and Ponty directed Caudrelier to visit the Ivory Coast to conduct an official inspection. Caudrelier arrived in the colony in December, just after Noguès began the campaign against the Akoué. Angoulvant had presented him with a military *fait accompli*. Caudrelier was not pleased but he immediately recognized the gravity of the military situation. Angoulvant's orders to Noguès were no longer questioned, but because of the deteriorating situation in the colony rumours began to circulate during Caudrelier's inspection tour that Angoulvant might be replaced by a full-fledged military administration under the command of General Gouraud.[60] Criticized by the merchants and vilified by the humanitarians, Angoulvant was now mistrusted by the military. In December 1909 his position looked desperate. His job, his reputation, and his future prospects for a career were at stake, and it looked as though only an extraordinary turn in fortune could save him.

Just how Angoulvant managed to retain the governorship amidst such a universal onslaught of hostile opinion remains a mystery. Historians will have to await a serious biography of Angoulvant before the questions can be resolved satisfactorily. Doubtless his personal friendship with Governor General Ponty strengthened his position, and it is possible that his reputed membership of the Freemasons may have helped as well, for their influence was considerable in French West Africa.[61] Since he was originally a political appointee, Angoulvant must have had well-placed friends in the corridors of power in Paris, but an explanation in these terms must necessarily remain conjectural until further information can be brought to light.

Without denying the importance of each of these themes it can be argued that ultimately Angoulvant's survival in office may have been less a function of his European friends than it was of his African enemies. One more local crisis intervened to influence the decision on Angoulvant's fate, and its timing was crucial.

In early January 1910 just after Caudrelier's departure and before

Ponty's return to Dakar from Paris, warriors from various Abé villages to the south of the Baule began to advance on the railway line near Agboville. On 7 January in a co-ordinated offensive the Abé warriors attacked the railway, blew up the track in several places, looted the train carriages and killed a European agent of the C.F.A.O. named Rubino. When Angoulvant heard the alarming news, he set out immediately from the coast to try to reach Agboville with a relief train, a distance of eighty-two kilometres. From kilometre 51 onwards the train was besieged by rebels, and after several stops for repairs caused by the repeated attacks, Angoulvant was forced to order a retreat after having advanced only as far as kilometre 71, eleven kilometres short of his destination.[62]

When the news splashed in the metropolitan press, the uproar was horrendous, and superficially at least it seemed that Angoulvant's opponents now had the weapon with which to strike the *coup de grâce*.[63] In the event, however, the Abé revolt strengthened Angoulvant's position, for as his criticis became more vocal they began to cancel each other out, leaving Angoulvant to emerge as the unavoidable compromise candidate to deal with a difficult situation.

The commercial community had all along criticized Angoulvant for being too harsh with the Africans; they would have preferred a figure like Clozel whose benign approach towards Africans was more immediately beneficial to trade. Although the commercial community continued to reiterate its critique of Angoulvant after the Abé revolt, the immediate circumstances largely undercut their argument for a more restrained form of administration. By the end of January the merchants clearly recognized the necessity of avenging Rubino's assassination, restoring order and regaining control over the railway. On this issue the local commercial interests were now in favour of a more militant policy, and they probably would not have opposed Angoulvant's replacement by a military administration at least in the short run.

Formally to declare the Ivory Coast a military territory under the command of General Gouraud would, however, have created further complications on a different level. Specifically such a move would entail a public admission on the part of the Minister of Colonies that the era of military conquest was not yet over. This risked to stir up both metropolitan and international humanitarian criticism which would be detrimental to the Minister's attempts to attract commerce and encourage investment in the Ivory Coast. As long as operations in the Ivory Coast could be referred to as corrective 'police action' rather than full-scale military conquest the façade of a stable, civilized, and humane empire could be maintained. Moreover, within the colony itself the removal of Angoulvant on the heels of his humiliating retreat on the railway line may well have contributed to an African sense of victory, and this the French wanted to avoid at all costs.

With these considerations before him it is perhaps not surprising that Governor General Ponty eventually chose to support Angoulvant rather than recommend his dismissal. Upon returning from Paris to Dakar in January 1910 Ponty received the news of the Abé attack on the railway and he travelled immediately to the Ivory Coast to confer with Angoulvant on the spot. In the face of the local crisis Ponty agreed to Angoulvant's plans for repressing the wide-scale revolt within the colony, and when he returned to Dakar he publicly endorsed Angoulvant against the continued chorus of critics.[64]

THE REPRESSION AND ITS AFTERMATH, 1910-1911

To enable Angoulvant to pursue his plans for the complete 'pacification' of the Ivory Coast, Ponty authorized massive troop reinforcements. In addition to the four companies of Senegalese troops already within the colony Ponty dispatched four new companies including field artillery units. Furthermore, the combat and support strength of each of these contingents swelled enormously. In 1908 each of the four existing companies contained 130 men, providing a total of 520 in all. During 1910 the number in each company rose to 200, making a total of 1,600 Senegalese troops in the eight companies as a whole. Hence, while the number of Senegalese companies doubled, the number of troops nearly tripled within the first few months of 1910. This was not all. In 1908 Angoulvant possessed two brigades of 'gardes indigènes' of 160 men each. In 1910 two more brigades were formed, bringing the total of locally recruited troops to a figure of 640, not counting the armed militia known as the 'garde de police' whose role was to assure the stability of a region once the military offensives were complete. The result was that the total troop strength increased from a level of 840 men in 1908 to 2,240 in 1910.[65]

An analysis of the local and federal budgets indicated the degree of financial commitment to the stepped-up military offensives. The Government General allocations to the Ivory Coast budget jumped from the 1909 figure of 1,330,000 f. to a record level of 2,200,000 f. in 1910, representing an enormous increase in federal expenditure for the military campaigns.[66] This did not, however, begin to meet all the expenses involved. Angoulvant estimated that the colony would have to allocate an additional 1,000,000 f. to support the Senegalese companies with local provisions, supplies, and foodstuffs. To finance the newly created brigades of 'gardes indigènes' and the 'gardes de police' whose salaries had to be paid out of the local budget, Angoulvant estimated a further 1,450,000 f. was required for 1910. These combined expenses represented a burden of roughly 2,450,000 f. to be paid out of the local budget at a time when the total local budget, exclusive of the Government General allocations, only reached a figure of 4,821,000 f.

In short, more than half of the local budget was directed toward financing the military repression of the colony's rebels, and when the federal expenditures are considered together with the local budget, the total estimated figure for the military activity reached a level of 4,650,000 f. in 1910 alone. Angoulvant hoped to recuperate some of these expenses immediately by collecting heavy war fines, but by September 1910 he felt it was necessary to issue an appeal to the *Rapporteur du budget* in the French parliament to try to convince the Chambre to provide direct assistance to the colony's budget.[67]

With the new resources at his disposal and a series of directives from Ponty giving him ultimate authority over the deployment of troops within the colony, Angoulvant had all that was necessary to begin a systematic 'pacification' programme.[68] Numerous campaigns were waged throughout 1910 in Baule country and the rest of the colony as well. An adequate military history of the Ivory Coast campaign has yet to be written, but Angoulvant himself provided the outlines for such a history in his own book, *La Pacification de la Côte d'Ivoire*.[69] Among the Baule the major campaigns included offensives against the Akoué (October 1909-January 1910), the southern Ngban (May-June 1910), the Salé (May-July 1910), the Agba (July-December 1910), the Ouéllé in the Katiénou and Bonou regions (August-December 1910), and the Kodé, Ayaou, Yaouré and Nanafoué (January-July 1911).[70]

Each campaign ended in Baule defeat, but the results were by no means a foregone conclusion in purely military terms. Because of a series of measures halting all arms sales along the coast and tightening border controls on the frontiers with Guinea, Liberia, and the Gold Coast, the Baule were at a serious disadvantage in terms of armaments, particularly as the war dragged on,[71] but the Akoué and the Kodé learned to make their own gunpowder to stretch their dwindling supplies. It was not very powerful used on its own, but when supplemented with small quantities of European powder it enabled them to hold out a while longer.[72]

More significantly, what the Baule lacked in terms of firepower, they compensated for with superior strategy and knowledge of the terrain. In general the Baule continued to employ a purely defensive strategy, making maximum use of the techniques of ambush and surprise attack from bush cover. The most effective ambush strategy consisted of flanking both sides of a narrow path with warriors dug into trenches under cover of bush overgrowth. As a convoy of troops or supplies passed, the Baule held their fire until the end of the convoy was within range of the last of the warriors. The Baule would open fire, starting in the rear. The front of the convoy would then rush to the defence of the besieged rear, and as the forces became congested along the path, the two parallel lines of Baule warriors attacked in earnest, staggering their fire to allow one another to reload their muskets.[73]

With a few notable exceptions the Baule rarely defended their villages to any great extent. Indeed, abandoning a village in the proper manner was itself a strategy which the Baule had perfected. After placing all women, slaves, children, and valuables in one of their agricultural encampments for safe-keeping, the men of a village would return to await a French attack. When it appeared that the French assault was about to break through, the Baule would frequently set fire to the roofs of their own huts and flee to the thick underbrush surrounding the village. As the French forces penetrated the village and became enveloped in the thick smoke of the burning thatch roofs, the Baule would open fire from the surrounding bush.[74]

In isolated instances the Baule presented a determined resistance from behind elaborately constructed defences. Why they adopted this strategy is not clear. During previous campaigns the only example of entrenched strategic resistance that the French had encountered was at Kokumbo in 1901. The reasons for constructing fortifications in this case were probably related to the importance of the gold mining interests in and around Kokumbo, but no such motivation was apparent to explain why the Akoué chose to fortify Kami. The decision to do so was disastrous militarily, for in the face of French artillery no fortifications which the Baule could build out of mud and logs could hold for long. Twice the French assaulted Kami and destroyed the village, and each time the Akoué rebuilt its defences. The third assault was, however, decisive. The Kami-Akoué fled and the French proceeded to dismantle the village fortress for the last time.[75]

During the last phase of Baule resistance there is little evidence that Baule marriage alliances played a major role in enabling the Baule to develop a united defensive strategy or to launch co-ordinated offensive attacks on the French. Non-parallel marriage practices precluded the development of strong alliances between particular groups under normal circumstances. In addition, the decline of the *atonvle* form of marriage alliance and the shift toward *awlô bô* endogamy with the introduction of large numbers of slaves during the Samory era tended to increase the political isolation of each *awlô bô*. Nevertheless, some inter-group marriage alliances still existed; and although they were not strong enough to enable the Baule to mobilize large numbers of warriors for co-ordinated offensives, they continued to be important in one crucial respect: they provided the avenues of retreat for rebels on the run. A household head might fail to rally to the armed support of his in-laws in a neighbouring village, but he could not refuse them aid if they sought refuge in his village while fleeing from the French troops. Moreover, the cognatic character of Baule descent groups enabled freeborn Baule to take up residence legitimately in a variety of different social units, and Baule began to exercise this prerogative extensively as the repression became more severe.[76]

The flexibility of Baule social structures made it increasingly difficult for the French to contain the scope of the conflict, for resistance sentiment would spread as quickly as fleeing warriors took refuge among neighbouring groups. In these circumstances it became largely impossible to distinguish 'friendly' groups from 'enemy' groups. In the minds of the military officers all Baule were at least potential enemies until they proved their good will by surrendering their arms. Even if the men of a particular group were not predisposed to fight the French, they were rarely willing to give up their arms spontaneously. Most chose to evacuate their villages and live in their encampments if possible, or abandon their territory and flee to neighbouring groups if necessary.

In the face of the increasingly elusive character of the 'enemy' the French officers reverted to the search-and-destroy tactics devised by their predecessors in the earlier Baule campaigns. Clozel had prevented the military from fully implementing this strategy in 1902, largely because he feared it would destroy the productive base of the Baule economy. By 1910, however, Angoulvant endorsed these same tactics precisely because this was what he wanted to achieve. By destroying the viability of the Baule economy Angoulvant hoped to hasten the incorporation of the Baule as peasant labourers within the new structures of the export-oriented colonial economy. Food stores were confiscated, encampments were systematically burned, and newly planted crops were uprooted in an effort to bring the Baule to their knees.

Ultimately it was the cumulative impact of these measures, rather than the series of inconclusive military engagements that assured the French of victory. The Baule depended entirely upon the annual harvest of tuber crops for their sustenance, and this proved to be their undoing. In contrast to the grain-based economies of the savannah regions of West Africa, it was impossible in the Baule economy to accumulate substantial stores of transportable foodstuffs from one year to the next. Yams did not keep well, and they were too bulky to transport very far with ease. Given this circumstance all the French needed to do was to pursue an all-out search-and-destroy campaign through one growing season, and the recalcitrant Baule would be forced into submission by the threat of imminent starvation. The intensive campaigns against the Baule rebels began in January 1910 and continued throughout the planting and harvesting season for the rest of that year. The results were predictable. Where the French forces had destroyed Baule crops in the early part of the year, surrender followed in the lean months.[77]

As resisters became progressively more desperate in the face of famine, they raided the plantations of those chiefs who had remained faithful to the French. This increased the polarization between resisters and collaborators. In several cases resistance towards the French developed into a form of localized civil war between rival Baule factions.[78] The patterns of animosity generated from these encounters continued to affect Baule politics long after the French declared themselves victorious.

When individual Baule groups came forward to present their submission, the French imposed heavy sanctions upon them to ensure that their surrender was definitive. In the first instance those who gave themselves up had to hand over their arms which the French then proceeded to destroy. Among the Baule the administration collected and destroyed a total of 21,365 muskets.[79] This in itself represented the liquidation of a considerable amount of wealth. The cost of a gun varied according to the make and quality. Prices for a new gun ranged from 10 to 25 f. Assuming that an average price of 17 f. had been paid for each one of these guns, the total Baule investment destroyed by Angoulvant's disarmament measures amounted to well over 350,000 f.

In addition the French imposed heavy war fines. The purpose of this was twofold. In the first place Angoulvant counted upon the money raised in this way to meet some of the budgetary expenses involved in the pacification programme. The total burden imposed upon Baule groups reached 435,900 f. by the end of 1911. The hardest-hit groups were the southern Ngban and the Akoué who were held responsible for totals amounting to 98,000 f. and 45,850 f. respectively.[80]

Beyond the purely fiscal motivation for imposing the fines the French justified them as a means of reducing the Baule to a level of poverty that would encourage them to participate in the colonial economy. Heavy war fines, like high taxes, it was thought, would compel the Baule to dip into their household treasuries of gold, and no Baule household head could afford to do this for long without seriously weakening his own prestige.[81] In order to avoid depleting these socially important reserves administrators argued that the Baule would be obliged to become wage labourers and accept the administration's plans for growing cash crops. Lieutenant Bouet summarized the situation succinctly referring to the Akoué: 'on peut dire, à l'encontre d'un état de choses qui nous est plus familier . . . qu'ils ne seront soumis que lorsqu'ils seront pauvres'.[82]

The payment of war fines did not, of course, absolve the Baule of the responsibility to meet their annual head tax obligations, and from 1909 to 1911 the rate of taxation increased markedly throughout Baule country. The provisions of the tax reform measures of 30 December 1908 allowed Angoulvant to abandon the standard rate of 2.50 f. in favour of a sliding rate ranging from 0.50 f. to 4.50 f. depending upon the resources of the populations in particular areas. Significantly none of the Baule areas had their tax rates reduced below the previous figure of 2.50 f., and most had them raised to 3.00 f. or even 4.00 f. Thus, most Baule experienced a 20–60 per cent tax increase from 1909 to 1911 in addition to the heavy war fines.[83]

Besides these monetary burdens the Baule were also forced to submit to an obligatory resettlement scheme. Having systematically destroyed Baule villages and encampments, the military regrouped the populations in newly constructed villages within easy access to the main routes. While most of these new agglomerations retained the names of prominent pre-war villages, their composition differed radically from that of the earlier villages. Remnant populations from previously distinct groups were concentrated within one new village, forming in most cases separate *quartiers*. In this manner 312 encampments were transformed into 47 villages among the southern Ngban, and among the Akoué 217 encampments were reduced to a mere 17 new villages.[84]

The resettlement programme continued to require French vigilance to be effective. The artificial character of most of the villages meant that they had difficulty holding together as organic units on their own. As Angoulvant conceded:

il faut, pendant des années encore, rechercher et détruire les campements qui se construisent à nouveau, pour des causes diverses: disputes avec le Chef, desaccord dans le village ou tout simplement persistance des instincts ataviques d'indépendance.[85]

Village chiefs or heads of households that remained faithful to the French throughout the hostilities were installed as the political leaders of these new agglomerations even though their claims to traditional legitimacy were frequently questionable. Among the southern Ngban chiefs who emerged with French support included Kakou Dibi, Kouakou Ofite, and Akafou Nguessan, the daughter of the deceased Akafou Bulare. In addition Kimon Kouassi, Irma Nguessan and Tano Konan were singled out for special praise for their assistance in helping the French defeat the resisters.[86] Among the Akoué the French supported Okou Kouakou as the new chief of Kami and Nguessan Kouao as chief of Sarourikro, while they continued to recognize Aboua Kouassi as chief of Bonzi.[87] Because of the extraordinary devotion of Kouassi Ngo to the French throughout the entire period of Akoué resistance, the administration transferred the administrative post from Bonzi to his village of Yamoussoukro. In addition, Angoulvant rewarded Kouassi Ngo's fidelity by designating him the 'Chef de la tribu des Akoués'.[88]

In a parallel manner prominent resisters who were not killed in battle were singled out for special punishment either by the French military officers who conducted the particular campaign or by the civilian administrator in charge of the local post. Information as to which chiefs were primarily to blame for inspiring the resistance was compiled from a combination of sources, including the post's archives and previous military records, but since many of the European officers or administrators were new to their jobs, they depended heavily upon the hearsay evidence of collaborating chiefs. Lists of those to be punished were drawn up locally and then forwarded to Bingerville for approval by the Conseil d'Administration. Then the lists were subsequently endorsed by the Government General in Dakar and the sentences came into effect with the final publication of an official *Arrêté* setting out the formal terms of punishment.

The process was a long and cumbersome one in which the emphasis was upon the strict legality of every procedure. Nevertheless it is not clear that the legality of the measures guaranteed that justice was done, for it is difficult to determine the validity of the accusations brought against the resisters in the first place. In most cases the evidence offered against them was scanty indeed, and there is no record of their being granted the opportunity to defend themselves against the accusation. It is possible, indeed perhaps likely, that in the aftermath of generalized defeat, the administration was being used unwittingly by collaborating chiefs as the means by which they could settle outstanding scores with their historic rivals. Had they been aware of this, the administrators would not necessarily have objected, for their primary concern was to create the context in which their closest collaborators could affirm unchallenged authority.

Whether or not the accused were treated justly, there is no doubt that they were punished severely. Angoulvant regretted that colonial judicial practice made it illegal for him to impose the death penalty and carry out public executions.[89] Nevertheless, he had other harsh means of punishing prisoners. Measures introduced during Clozel's governorship provided Angoulvant with the legal power to condemn resisters to exile, either to a distant region within the colony or out of the colony entirely.[90] From 1909 through 1912 Angoulvant exercised this prerogative extensively against the alleged leaders of Baule resistance. During this period over 100 Baule resisters were condemned to terms of exile ranging in length from two to ten years. While some were simply incarcerated in Bingerville or in the Cavally region of the Ivory Coast itself, others were dispatched to Dahomey, Mauritania, or Senegal, where many of them died in captivity.[91]

It was with these procedures that the French finally punished the Akoué chiefs for their uprising against Simon and Moesch and their attack on the post at Bonzi. In August 1910 the French captured Koki Yao Aounou, the alleged instigator of the Akoué revolt, and in the following months they rounded up Ali Kouakou, Koffi Alani, Alani Yao, Alou Kouamé, and Tanon Konan, all reputed to have taken leading roles in the rebellion. The latter chiefs were exiled to the Cavally region for a period of five years, but the Conseil d'Administration approved Angoulvant's request to deport Koki Yao Aounou to Port Étienne in Mauritania.[92]

An exhaustive survey of the impact of French conquest upon the Baule would have to include case studies of the local political implications of deportations like these. The scores of names listed in the official edicts provide rich material for historians or anthropologists interested in doing a detailed analysis of the politics of conquest, defeat and reconstruction in localized regions. The deportation lists themselves did not, however, tell the whole story. Many of the captured chiefs never survived long enough to be deported. This appears to have been the case with Yao Guié, the alleged leader of the resistance struggle among the southern Ngban. After a series of costly battles with Commander Morel, Yao Guié surrendered to the French on 13 June 1910. During July the administrator of the Ouossou post formally requested that he be deported along with several of his followers. In October 1910 the Conseil d'Administration duly sentenced the Ngban chiefs to ten years' exile in Mauritania, but Yao Guié was not among them. His fate was not recorded, but given his history of opposition toward the French it is unlikely that they would have spared him while deporting his followers. It is more probable that he died in captivity sometime between August and October 1910 before the formal deportation sentences were delivered.[93] If so, he was not alone, for there are records indicating that several other chiefs died in captivity before they could be deported.[94]

By comparison the collaborating chiefs were fortunate, but their situation was by no means secure for several reasons. On the one hand, Angoulvant's strong-arm approach meant that they could be by-passed at will, no matter how important they had seemed during Clozel's administration. Kouadio Ndri, whom Clozel had installed as chief of the Ouarébo in February 1904, appeared to extend his power during the early months of Angoulvant's administration. During October 1908 he succeeded in recuperating the corpse of Kouamé Dié from the village of Mahonou where it had been lying in state ever since the formal funeral ceremonies that Yoma Boni had conducted in May 1904. At the time the French took this as an index of Kouadio Ndri's affirmation of authority and a symbol of their own acceptance in the area.[95]

Over the following years, however, Kouadio Ndri lost his position of pre-eminence and the French apparently withdrew their support from him. In 1911 the French dismantled their post at Sakassou and moved instead to Béoumi as part of an effort to concentrate their presence among the recalcitrant Kodé-Baule to the north of the Ouarébo. In the year following the French withdrawal Kouadio Ndri fell from power. By June 1912 the administrator at Béoumi no longer dealt with him as the legitimate chief of the Ouarébo. Instead he recognized Dié Lonzo, the son of the deceased Kouamé Dié and Kouadio Ndri's former rival.[96]

When French support for a collaborator remained constant, the individual chief concerned often faced strong recriminations from embittered Baule partisans. Kouassi Ngo, elevated by Angoulvant to the role of paramount chief of the Akoué, enjoyed full official favour, but this lasted for less than a year. On 12 December 1910 only two weeks after the rebel Akoué leader, Koki Yao Aounou, was sentenced to exile in Mauritania, Kouassi Ngo was assassinated in Yamoussoukro.[97] In a similar fashion among the Ngban, Nzoko, one of the important collaborating chiefs from the village of Moronou, was shot by Kouassi Kan, a close relation of Yao Guié.[98] As in the aftermath of the earlier periods of Baule resistance, fratricidal disputes proved in some cases to be as lethal to the collaborators as imprisonment or exile was to the captured resisters.[99]

While the direct impact of European conquest can be determined relatively easily by examining the number of armaments destroyed, the total amount of war fines and increased taxes collected, the scope of village resettlement programmes, and the combined lists of exiled rebels, it is more difficult to measure the indirect effects of conquest. The information available suggests, however, that in the wake of military conquest the Baule region suffered the effects of famine, epidemic, and wide-scale migration, reducing the Baule population to only a fraction of its former importance.[100]

Precise population figures are not available, but a comparison of successive population estimates nevertheless provides an idea of the magnitude of the devastation involved. Basing his statement upon his observations during the period of Baule prosperity from 1895 to 1899, Delafosse wrote in 1900 that the total population in the Baule region reached nearly 2,000,000.[101] On other occasions Delafosse's estimations were less generous, but he insisted that the figure of 1,300,000 represented the minimum population in the area.[102] Albert Nebout placed the number in Baule territory slightly lower at approximately 1,000,000,[103] but Captain Le Magnen suggested a higher figure of 1,500,000.[104]

Even if one takes the most conservative of these estimates as representative of the pre-1900 population, it becomes apparent that the military activity from 1900 to 1902 had a marked impact on the Baule region. Clozel estimated that the 1902 Baule population was only 642,548.[105] Angoulvant's search-and-destroy policies implemented from 1909 until 1911 inflicted further heavy losses. By 1911 the administrator of the northern Baule districts, formerly the most populous of all the Baule regions, estimated that the population level stood at 130,585.[106] If one generously doubles this figure to represent the additional population of the southern Baule regions, the total Baule figure still only reaches something in the range of 260,000 in 1911. In reality this may be an over-estimate, for the population of the Baule region by 1916 was placed at only 225,000.[107]

In short, from 1899 to 1911 the Baule population suffered an enormous decline. The precise extent of this decline is not known, but the figures available suggest that the total losses must be reckoned in tens and perhaps hundreds of thousands of people. Only a small proportion of these losses resulted directly from deaths in battle, but the ensuing famine and disease could have accounted for many more. In addition, the occupying troops liberated Baule slaves. The administration estimated that a total of 4,500 captives left various Baule regions to regain their villages of origin in the north in the wake of the military operations from 1909 to 1911.[108] Finally, perhaps the largest portion of the decline in the region's population can be accounted for in terms of Baule migration towards other regions in the colony or towards the neighbouring Gold Coast.[109]

By employing the techniques of total warfare, Angoulvant unleashed social disruption on a scale which he did not anticipate and could not really control. Nevertheless, in terms of his personal career, he managed to benefit from the havoc he had wrought. Although his strong-arm methods earned him a reputation for brutality never before equalled by a civilian administrator, his critics were effectively silenced by the upsurge in trade and production which the forced mobilization of new manpower made possible.[110] After 1911 his policy of wholesale administrative intervention in the economic affairs of the colony became a matter of simple necessity, for by this point the indigenous economy had been thoroughly shattered by the ravages of war. Henceforth, there could be no question of reverting to the less intrusive *laissez-faire* policies of Clozel. The excessive brutalities of Angoulant's policies continued to come under attack from local commercial agents,[111] but even these criticisms ceased with the onset of the First World War.[112] His administrative superiors continued to applaud his success, and when he left the colony in June 1916, he was rewarded with enlarged administrative responsibilities as acting Governor General in Dakar.[113]

Locally Angoulvant's subordinate administrators were faced with the task of reorganizing the Baule economy with the labour of the war-battered survivors. The military intervention had been brutal enough to impress upon those who remained that future resistance would be ruinous, and they were prepared to submit to French demands. As the Kodé chiefs expressed it in 1912:

les blancs sont plus forts que nous, nous en sommes maintenant sûrs et nous acceptons de faire tout ce qu'il nous commandera; lui embrasser les pieds s'il l'exige.[114]

In the aftermath of defeat the outlines of a new collaborative bargain were beginning to take shape, but this time the collaboration differed considerably from that which characterized the earlier periods. Henceforth, collaboration required Baule submission to the role of the peasant producer in the colonial export economy, and for the time being there was no question of the local Baule rejecting the imposed arrangement if they wished to survive.

CHAPTER VII

Patterns of Resistance and Collaboration

When the period from 1893 to 1911 is examined as a whole, it is posssible in retrospect to recognize several patterns in the course of Baule resistance. These patterns can help to provide the historian with a basis for analysing the Baule resistance phenomena, and it is perhaps useful to discuss each of them briefly before turning to the broader problem of interpreting Baule resistance and French conquest.

The Question of Unity

Baule resistance was never a fully unified movement. This was not surprising, given the decentralized and internally competitive nature of the Baule socio-political structures at the time of French penetration. Village groups, sub-tribes, and individual households had been engaged in trading rivalries with one another for most of the previous century, and it would have been extraordinary for these historically rooted patterns of interaction to be abruptly suspended simply because a handful of Europeans had arrived in their midst.[1]

Quite apart from the question of Baule socio-political structures, it must be emphasized that in the initial stages French encounters with the Baule were extremely localized and sporadic, and in this respect the uneven nature of French advance contributed to the fragmentation of the Baule response. Not until the later stages of the resistance period were the French perceived as a threat to the Baule people as a whole, and by then the social basis of unified action had been too far eroded to mobilize the entire population effectively. At the outset of the resistance period, the French were regarded simply as an additional factor in local politics. Understaffed and poorly supplied, the French outposts at Tiassalé, Toumodi, and Kodiokofikro hardly constituted an occupying force in the wake of the Monteil retreat. Nevertheless, the cumulative effect of their presence was to rearrange local political realities. During the years of relatively undemanding presence from 1895 to 1898, the French had a differential impact upon local groups surrounding them. When conditions among the Baule deteriorated to the point of open conflict, the groups most affected by their proximity to the French usually found themselves too compromised to join the others in open revolt. Thus in late 1894 when Asmaret, the Adioukrou chief of Lopou,[2] journeyed through Baule country to enlist united Baule support in an effort to stop the French inland advance, Fatou Aka of Tiassalé, Akafou of Ouossou, Niango Kouassi of Toumodi, Eoussou of Abli, and Kouadio Koffi of Kodiokofikro all refused to take part in the planned insurrection largely because the French had already become installed in their respective villages and integrated themselves in local exchange arrangements from which these chiefs derived a small measure of advantage. Perhaps more to the point, these chiefs realized that if a revolt were to take place, the French would be more capable of punishing them severely than the other village chiefs from outlying areas, and as a result they were more anxious to maintain at least the appearance of fidelity to the French cause. When these 'faithful' chiefs began to lose some of their following to the ranks of the more militant and disaffected chiefs of the outlying villages, some of them, like Akafou himself, were drawn into revolt to retain their chiefly status. For the most part, however, they became more closely identified with the French cause as hostilities increased.

Nebout and Delafosse sought specifically to heighten the incipient divisions between Baule groups when the local administration came under attack in 1899. Delafosse built up an alliance out of a series of personal friendships with Niango Kouadio of Toumodi, successor to Niango Kouassi, and Eoussou, chief of Abli, and in October 1899 he recruited partisans from the adherents to these 'faithful' chiefs to pursue Kouadio Okou.[3] Nebout, in replacing Delafosse, exploited the traditional antipathies between Baule groups in a similar fashion to avert an all-out Baule attack before the arrival of troop reinforcements.

The French policy of bolstering 'faithful' chiefs in or near the centres of their administrative outposts continued to divide the Baule groups from one another during the period of relative calm under Clozel's Governorship. As a result, when open revolt broke out against Angoulvant's administrative measures, the resistance movement expressed itself as a virtual civil war with a recognizable geographic pattern. Those groups which remained nearest the French outposts were considered 'pacified', for by definition the rebels had taken up residence beyond the range of French retaliation. For the French, then, the tactic became one of trying to enlarge the territory around each post and assure the communications between them. For the Baule resisters the conflict was sometimes directed as much against the fields and compounds of the collaborating chiefs as it was against the French troops.[4] In such a situation neutrality was difficult to maintain, and although those who ended up under the French sphere of influence may not have been active collaborators, their position was none the less identifiably different from those who fought to the very end. Understandably, then, the lines of conflict expressed themselves locally well after Baule armed resistance was crushed. The assassinations of Moya Ba in April 1905 and Kouassi Ngo in December 1910 were indicative of the undercurrent of continuing animosities engendered by the pattern of French conquest. As in warfare, so in peace; the Baule remained fragmented until the shared experience of colonial rule provided new grounds for collective protest in later generations.[5]

The Inter-Ethnic Dimension

Baule hostility was directed not only against the French and the collaborating chiefs, but also against the newly settled Dyula and Senegalese traders. Indeed, most of the attacks upon the French presence began with explicit acts of hostility against these alien ethnic communities. The historical roots of these animosities were apparent. For most of the pre-colonial period the Baule had excluded the northern Dyula from independent access to coastal trade.[6] This is not to suggest that individual Dyula did not enter into relations with the Baule. On the contrary, trade along the northern border was continuous, and in addition the Baule integrated large numbers of Dyula and northern Senufo into their domestic productive units, particularly when it became possible to purchase captives from Samory in the 1890s.[7]

The intrusion of the French, however, upset this pattern of interaction and assimilation. In the aftermath of the Monteil retreat the French settled communities of northern Dyula in close proximity to their administrative posts in Baule country, and successive administrators drew upon these communities for needed auxiliaries. Simultaneously they encouraged the development of Dyula trading aptitudes by employing Dyula porters to supply the network of administrative posts and later by encouraging them to act as commercial intermediaries with the Baule for the collection of wild rubber and the distribution of European manufactures.[8] For the Baule, the intrusion of these alien merchants was a direct challenge to their previous pattern of expedition trading. Furthermore, the Baule resented the *de facto* French protection of these people whom, during the pre-colonial period, they had come to regard as at least potential slaves.[9] It is perhaps understandable, then, that in their role as imposed intermediaries between the Baule and the French, these alien Dyula often became targets of the first expressions of hostility. When communities of Senegalese house-holds accompanied the occupying troops in the later stages of Baule resistance, their position was equally resented for similar reasons. It would be an exaggeration to suggest that the pattern of French intrusion created inter-ethnic animosity, but it is none the less true that French colonial rule implied a new arrangement of local inter-ethnic relations which the Baule resisted as strongly as they did the arrival of the French themselves.

Slaves and Women as Collaborators

The heaviest burden of labour within the Baule pre-colonial context fell upon the first generation captives and upon the women. There were limits to how much the Baule chiefs could exact from their slaves and subordinate women before their authority was ignored. The powers of coercion available to the head of a Baule household were restricted in normal circumstances by alternative relationships available to the woman or the dependent captive. If demands were too unreasonable, a woman would often leave her husband and rejoin her brothers who were happy to welcome any children which she might bring with her. There she would stay until conditions improved in her husband's compound. Often this type of departure could end in formal divorce. The dependent captive had no family to which he could withdraw, but escape was an alternative if conditions of exploitation became too unbearable. Most frequently this took the form of a slave seeking refuge in the entourage of another neighbouring village chief.

Insubordination of this kind was generally the exception, for in both cases there was a considerable measure of calculated risk involved on the part of either a woman or a disaffected slave. A woman's family, reluctant to repay the bride-price or rupture the marriage alliance established with her husband's village, might bring pressure upon her to return to her husband's compound, whether or not conditions there had changed. If she returned in these circumstances, she ran the risk of more pronounced abuse. Similarly an escaped captive could not always count upon a warm reception in the circle of a neighbouring chief, and if the chief decided to return him to his original master, the captive could expect severe punishment and perhaps execution. With these possibilities in mind both women and slaves would think twice before trying to escape from their husbands or masters, even when demands upon them increased.

The intrusion of the French had a twofold effect upon this complex nexus of domestic dependence and exploitation. In the first place the

the French need for porterage and provisions increased the demands of the household heads upon the women and captives in their compounds. In this respect, the exploitation of women and captives increased. Simultaneously, however, the French administrative posts provided new points of refuge for disaffected or abused slaves and women. Slaves who were mistreated or threatened with execution by their masters frequently sought refuge at the French post and obtained a measure of protection if they settled in the *village de liberté* close to the French garrison.[10] Similarly, some women soon learned to exploit the French presence to acquire a degree of personal liberty, previously unavailable to them. Baule males did not strongly oppose unions between unmarried Baule women and European auxiliaries or even the Europeans themselves, if the children of these unions were returned to be raised in the compound of the woman's household. As long as the woman's kin acquired authority over her offspring, she was allowed considerable freedom to do as she pleased, and many Baule women entered into temporary or permanent unions with the French and Senegalese men. So frequent was the custom of local concubinage that Governor Clozel felt obliged to issue instructions to limit the practice.[11]

In the occupation of Baule territory the French were significantly assisted by the collaboration of these escaped slaves and disaffected women. Both provided the French with intelligence information. In addition, these 'liberated' slaves supplied the needed manpower and often became assimilated with the resident Dyula communities around the French posts, engaging eventually in trade and sometimes coming to the armed defence of the French under attack from the Baule.[12] Women in this position provisioned the troops with foodstuffs and in time of negotiations their kin could act as valuable intermediaries with dissident factions. Just as the French policies exacerbated the divisions between different Baule groups and heightened the antagonism between the Baule and the Dyula, so too their presence upset the patterns of domestic dependence by providing an additional refuge for those disaffected with their situation under the control of authoritarian chiefs. The structure of domestic relations among the Baule thus provided the French with potential collaborators 'from within', and once the French posts were installed, it was largely a matter of time before they came forward.[13]

The Role of Paramount Chiefs

Among the Baule the *nvle kpen*, or paramount chiefs, were not usually the instigators of resistance towards the French. Their role was an ambivalent one towards the administration, but they rarely expressed outright hostility. The reason for this derived ultimately from the conservative character of traditional chieftaincy among the Baule.

In the pre-colonial context paramount chiefs were pre-eminently politico-juridical personages and not war leaders.[14] A young man could achieve distinction as a skilful warrior, but unless he could develop this reputation into the basis for obtaining a numerically important following, such a figure remained marginal, and his importance dwindled as he grew older. Chieftaincy depended upon the ability to acquire and maintain the loyalty of a following and this depended ultimately upon one's wealth. As the repositor and custodian of the descent group's *adya*, or treasury, the chief became the recipient of tribute from junior kinsmen and the source of capital for those who needed to repay debts or extend money in marriage payments. By exchanging the produce of his junior kinsmen, a skilful chief could increase his wealth in trade and translate this wealth into obtaining more dependants. These new dependants would in turn increase the productive output at his disposal.

Respected paramount chiefs settled disputes between feuding parties and acquired both wealth and power in the process, for the successful party often had to pay heavily for a chief's adjudication, and the loser frequently had to indebt himself to the paramount chief in order to pay the imposed fine. When a chief resorted to warfare, he usually did so with peace already in mind, for he was responsible for paying war indemnities to those injured in his own following, and compensation to his opponent. In either case, prolonged armed warfare was expensive, and to be avoided when possible. Typically, conflict took the form of a brief encounter followed by a period of lengthy negotiations over the terms of settlement.

In this context, successful chiefs were those who had mastered the skills of negotiation and compromise, men capable of manipulating marriage arrangements and circulating goods in such a way as to recruit a following and inspire fidelity. Such men were cautious, prudent and calculating, both by nature and experience. Furthermore, they were elderly, for by custom the *adya* treasury was transmitted collaterally to the next eldest member of a given generation before passing on to the following generation level.

Chiefs with these attributes hardly presented an aggressive threat to the French, but it took ten years for the French to realize this and adapt their strategy accordingly. Coming to Baule territory fresh from experience in the Sudan, French military officers were unfamiliar with the Baule institution of chieftaincy. They expected to encounter commanders; instead they found diplomats. The paramount chiefs regarded the French at first as simply one more element in local politics, a feature of the new situation which they would have to take into account with all others in pursuing their strategies of political manœuvre.

The French were not accustomed to being received on such tentative terms. When they made demands upon chiefs for provisions and porters, they expected results, not negotiations. They began to interpret hesitation as hostility and circumspection as conspiracy. Fear of what *might* happen distorted their perception of what *was* happening. When hostility broke out in 1894-5, military officers blamed the paramount chief of the area, Akafou, even though he probably had had little to do with the revolt. This type of misperception eventually led to the deaths of Akafou and Kouamé Dié in 1902, at the hands of two impetuous officers. In both cases, the officers expected capitulation and were deeply suspicious of Baule attempts to negotiate a settlement. The slightest incident in the course of the negotiations was perceived as a gesture of revolt, and the French dealt brutally with the paramount chiefs whom they considered responsible.

By killing Akafou and Kouamé Dié the French dealt a heavy blow to the institution of paramount chieftaincy. Clozel realized the mistake, and when he took office in 1903, he reversed the previous practice of dealing harshly with paramount chiefs and tried instead to lend administrative recognition and support to them. Advised by Maurice Delafosse, Clozel attempted to introduce what became known as 'la politique des races', an administrative procedure roughly analogous to the British practice of 'indirect rule'. The official change of heart came too late, however. The early treatment which paramount chiefs had received at the hands of the military officers sufficiently discouraged others from coming forward to take their place, and the civilian administration had difficulty in finding successors to Akafou and Kouamé Dié. Similarly when Kouadio Koffi and Kano died, no one of their stature emerged to replace them. Those who were put forward by the Baule as candidates for the paramount chieftaincies were not respected to the same degree as their predecessors, and their close association with the French administration served to discredit them further in the eyes of the Baule villagers. Kouadio N'Dri became the laughing stock of the people he was supposed to command. In effect the French intervention destroyed the institution of paramount chieftaincy first by dealing with it too brutally, and secondly by embracing it too heartily.

It would not be an exaggeration to suggest that French administrators saw themselves as occupying the role of the Baule *nvle kpen* or paramount chief.[15] Even when administrators sincerely pursued Clozel's 'politique des races' they never intended that it should lead in any way to a duality of power at the local level, with the traditional chiefs on the one hand and the French administration on the other. Delafosse specifically suggested that administrators should assimilate their role to that of the traditional paramount chief by eliciting from their subjects the forms of address appropriate to that office.

Les fonctionnaires ou officiers français en pays agni [i.e. Baule] devrait toujours exiger qu'on les appelle *nana* (ou *famye* 'chef' s'ils sont d'un grade élevé ou ont une fonction étendue); les autres appelations devraient être rejetées, car elles supposent toutes que l'interpellé n'est pas le supérieur de celui qui l'interpelle, et par conséquent constitue une impolitesse ou tout au moins un manque de déférence.[16]

In the event, Delafosse's suggestions never took hold. French administrators, whether civilian or military, were referred to as 'le commandant' and the collaborating chiefs became known as 'chefs l'impôt'.[17] There was no confusion as to where the power lay; the institution of paramount chieftaincy was virtually extinguished, and it did not re-emerge as a respected office among the Baule until late in the colonial period.

The Role of the Junior Chiefs

If the calculating disposition of the paramount chiefs did not inspire them to take the lead in resisting the French, where then did resistance activity originate? The answer seems to be that the strongest impetus for resistance came from those who might collectively be called the 'junior' chiefs. These men were 'junior' not in the generational or chronological sense of being younger, but rather in a social sense of not being quite where they aspired to be in terms of influence, wealth, and power. For the most part they were village chiefs (*klo kpenngben*) whose influence was on the verge of being recognized on a wider scale, or they were simply heads of households who aspired to achieve more autonomy by establishing a village of their own. During the period immediately before French conquest these men had just begun to consolidate their political following, and with the influx of captive slaves which they bought from Samory in the north between 1893 and 1898, they were on the way to realizing their ambitions for power and wealth.

To the extent that the period up to 1898 can be characterized as one of economic expansion for the Baule as a whole, it was primarily among this group of men that economic expectations and political aspirations were rising most rapidly.

French intrusion directly threatened the future ascendancy of these chiefs in several respects. By capturing Samory and putting an end to the southern flow of captive slaves, the French cut off a major source of new manpower, upon which these ascendant chiefs depended to a large extent, to swell the ranks of their households. Furthermore, it was mainly the households of these junior chiefs that suffered most when slaves escaped from the Baule and sought refuge at the French administrative posts. The households of the junior chiefs contained a high proportion of recently acquired slaves and these slaves were more difficult to control than the earlier generations of captives, who had been assimilated into the households of the paramount chiefs. Thus, when the occasion for escape presented itself, and especially when the French officers, from 1898 to 1903, encouraged the escape of captives, it was primarily from the households of the junior chiefs that the captives fled.

In addition, the creation of a geographically fixed administrative structure tended to crystallize a highly fluid political situation into a hierarchical system of subordination which some junior chiefs resented. Having identified those whom they thought to be the paramount chiefs by the time the Monteil expedition departed, the administration located its major posts at Ouossou, Toumodi, Kodiokofikro, and Bouaké. A problem arose, however, when the influential chiefs in these villages died, for although the household inheritance had its designated successor, the question of the successor's influence beyond his own village was another matter. The respect accorded to a *nvle kpen*, or paramount chief, was something which was as much achieved as inherited, and there was no guarantee that the successor of a paramount chief with whom the French had initially collaborated would be able to exercise the same degree of influence as his predecessor.

In short, the role of *nvle kpen* had not yet developed as a formalized institution with a prescribed pattern of recruitment by the time the French encountered the Baule, and as a result, the Baule political system remained too fluid to be easily articulated with the French administrative structures. Nevertheless, having committed themselves to particular geographic locations within Baule country, the French had a stake in reinforcing the importance of whatever chief emerged in that location upon the death of their original collaborator. This practice stood local politics on its head, for proximity to the French rather than traditional prestige became the main criterion for power. By intervening in local politics in this way the French offended the ascendant chiefs of outlying areas whose relative importance was henceforth subordinated to that of the local collaborating chief. These junior chiefs preferred to resist the French rather than endure the experience of *de facto* subordination to the newly recognized collaborating chief in the immediate vicinity of the French post. This type of pattern was dramatically exemplified in Yao Guié's refusal to acknowledge Akafou's ascendant role as a French auxiliary.[18]

While the junior chiefs of the outlying areas formed the backbone of the resistance movement, some of those near French posts became enthusiastic supporters of the French. Their decision to collaborate stemmed from the realization that the French presence could assist them in obtaining a degree of autonomy from other chiefs or enable them to project their own authority over a wider following. Niango Kouassi of Toumodi and Eoussou of Abli apparently wanted to strengthen their positions in this way, and they willingly provided volunteers to pursue Kouadio Okou after his surprise attack on the Toumodi post in 1899. Similarly, Fatou Aka, the collaborating chief of Niamwé, acted as an intermediary in the peace negotiations between the Ngban and the French in 1903 in the hopes of extending his influence over the Ngban.[19] Okou Boni and Ngata Blé Koffi of the Ouarébo-Linguiras and Moya Ba of the Andofoué are examples of chiefs who favoured the arrival of the French in order to be rid of the domination of Kouamé Dié, the paramount chief in the Sakassou area. In all these cases France found its most devoted collaborators from the ranks of these secondary chiefs who saw their particular interests being to some extent served by the French presence.[20]

In some instances a junior chief would be both a resister and a collaborator over the course of time. Kouassi Ngo of the Akoué was an interesting example of this pattern. Initially, his maternal aunt, Yabo Mousso, sent peace overtures to the French, after the fall of Kokumbo in 1902, but in the following years after the French established a post at Bonzi, both Yabo Mousso and Kouassi Ngo expressed general indifference and sometimes open hostility towards the French. In 1909, however, when Kouassi Ngo was shot in a cross-fire intended for the French administrator of the Bonzi post, he subsequently sided wholeheartedly with the French cause. Governor Angoulvant reciprocated by appointing him the 'chef de la tribu' of the Akoué, a position which he intended to be equivalent to the traditional role of paramount chief.

In addition, the French shifted the administrative centre from Bonzi to Kouassi Ngo's village of Ngokro or Yamoussoukro. Kouassi Ngo clearly decided after June 1909 that his own interests would be served more effectively by a thorough-going collaboration with the French.[21] In a similar fashion Bendé Kouassi of the Don sub-tribe and Kouassi Blé of Bouaké initially directed an attack on the Bouaké post in 1898, and again in 1900, but when they realized that the French were not dislodged, they came to terms with the administration and remained faithful collaborators for the following years. Even Kouadio Okou who initially resisted Marchand's advance and attacked Delafosse in 1899, eventually sided with the administration and tried to serve as an intermediary with recalcitrant Ngban rebels in 1910.[22]

In these instances resistance and collaboration are perhaps best described as two strategies available to the junior chiefs whose main preoccupations were grounded in the competitive nature of local politics. To the extent that the political horizons of the junior chiefs were expanding more rapidly than those of the paramount chiefs in the period just before the French intrusion, it is perhaps not surprising that they took a more active role than the paramount chiefs in both resistance and collaboration.

Kinship Structures and Baule Resistance

The cognatic character of Baule descent groups made it difficult for the French to score a resounding victory by capturing chiefs. The reason for this was that the local descent groups were not discrete and mutually exclusive social units. Any freeborn Baule was pluri-dependent – that is, potentially a dependant of several elders to whom he could trace any line of ascendant kinship. In practice this meant that the capture of a chief did not necessarily entail the capitulation of his Baule followers, for they could, and often did, relocate themselves within the descent groups of other kin.[23]

Slaves of a captured chief were not in an equally mobile position, however, for by definition they had no alternate kin. This feature of Baule social structure led to a pattern whereby slaves of a captured or killed chief would capitulate to the French more readily than the freeborn subordinates of that chief. Structurally, slaves had no choice. Whereas freeborn Baule could, at least in principle, sustain a stance of resistance from a different kin group base, slaves were uni-dependent upon their master, and when he was captured, they had little alternative but to submit to the French as well. The result was that once again in the eyes of the Baule the position of collaborator was closely associated with slave status. This encouraged freeborn Baule to persist in their resistance, for they wished to avoid being identified with the slave status of most of the collaborators. It was his potential access to alternate kin groups which distinguished the freeborn Baule from the slave, and over the several years of resistance the cognatic structure of descent groups provided the freeborn Baule with the mechanisms of escape and relocation necessary for prolonged resistance.

If the structure of Baule descent groups can be said to have facilitated prolonged resistance, the patterns of Baule marriage alliance had a more complex effect upon the organization of resistance.[24] On the one hand, the Baule prohibition of parallel marriage fostered the widest possible spread of alliances. In practice this made it virtually impossible for the French to deal with a village or indeed a whole village group in isolation. Since each localized descent group was linked in marriage to a large number of allies, every time the French struck a blow in one spot they engendered the antipathies of allied groups in a number of other places at once. In this manner, the act of repressing resistance in one area actually generated new resistance further afield. The more the French pursued their campaign, the more resistance spread, as the webs of extensive marriage alliances were mobilized in common defence. In this respect Baule marriage patterns can be said to have assisted the resistance movement.

On the other hand, the prohibition on parallel marriage and in particular the proscription of cross-cousin marriage meant that it was impossible for two Baule groups to build up a strong relationship based upon repeated marriage alliances over time. A marriage alliance was in this sense a discontinuous event – an act which once performed, precluded the replication of a similar alliance in the same direction. This kind of marriage pattern impeded the formation of enduring alliances on the basis of customary marriage exchange. In terms of the social fabric as a whole, the marriage pattern produced an alliance structure which although extensive, proved in the long run to be weak in any particular direction. Such an alliance structure was ideal for short-range defensive purposes, but as the French pressure upon the Baule wore on, the alliances crumbled. More importantly, this kind of alliance pattern never provided the Baule with the social institutions capable of mobilizing a strong offensive strategy.

In addition to the weaknesses inherent in the normal Baule alliance structures, the demise of the special *atonvle* marriage arrangement also contributed to the long-term vulnerability of the Baule. Up until the 1890s the institution of the *atonvle* marriage served to unite important chiefs from distant regions. Only men of substance could enter into these prestigious marriage arrangements, and in the absence of centralized state structures these symbolic political alliances provided the major form of inter-regional linkages. This form of marriage was virtually eclipsed, however, with the influx of large numbers of female captives during the Samory period of the mid-1890s. The strategies of paramount and junior chiefs became directed towards increasing their personal following through the purchase of captives rather than the conclusion of *atonvle* marriages, and local descent groups began to favour quasi-endogamous marriage strategies. The result was that alliance linkages between important chiefs tended to atrophy in the period just prior to French military conquest, leaving the Baule with a weak institutional framework for inter-regional resistance.[25]

Settlement Distribution and the Pattern of Defeat

Traditionally, Baule villages were not large centres of long-standing habitation. The population of Baule villages only rarely reached a figure of .1,000 or more, and most frequently the inhabitants numbered from 75 to 200. Based upon an economy of swidden agriculture the Baule tended to move their settlements over time as the soils in a particular area became exhausted. Socio-political schisms also contributed to the centrifugal pattern of Baule settlement, for when hostilities broke out between different households within a village, they often resulted in the fission of a village into two respective villages. Characteristically, the village was surrounded by a series of dispersed semi-permanent encampments or *niamwe* in which families spent several months of the year in close proximity to their fields. If tensions within the village became too pronounced, members of a household could choose to spend more of their time in their respective encampments. Over time some of these camps could develop into full-fledged villages in their own right if the founding chief could mobilize enough of a following to establish his effective independence from the parent village.

These patterns of village fission and expansive migration meant that the individual Baule spent much of his life in what might be called a state of transition from one centre of residence to another. In the normal course of events a Baule was accustomed to moving back and forth between the central village and his particular encampment, and over the period of a lifetime, both the central village and the encampment could change their locations several times. In effect, these flexible settlement patterns provided the geographic corollary to the equally flexible descent group organization characteristic of the Baule at the time of their first encounter with the French.

The French found Baule settlement patterns a source of continuous frustration. In the first instance, following the Monteil expedition in 1895 the Baule abandoned their villages along the route of French penetration and relocated them several miles to the east or west of the major trade route. As punishment for the revolt which Monteil encountered among the southern Baule, he burned several Baule villages in the immediate vicinity of the line of French supply posts, and this sufficiently discouraged the majority of Baule from resettling near the Tiassalé-Toumodi route. Only those who became collaborators with the French returned cautiously to reoccupy their villages, and even they were prepared to abandon their villages once again whenever the French demands became too unbearable.

During the period of hostility from 1899 to 1903 the French pursued the resisting Baule beyond the immediate range of the north-south trade route. Commanders Donnat, Aymerich, and Colonna d'Istria launched offensive campaigns against Kokumbo, Sakassou, Béoumi, Salékro, Yaotékro, Dida, and Baule settlements around the mountain of Orumbo Boka. Administrative posts were established in each of these villages and at Bonzi among the Akoué in order to gain more direct control over the Baule who had eluded the French authorities in the major administrative centres of Tiassalé, Toumodi, Kodiokofikro, and Bouaké.

This policy of pursuit met with only partial success, for although the French destroyed many of the outlying villages, the Baule had by this time abandoned these settlements to relocate themselves in their dispersed encampments. French military tactics were based primarily upon the strategies of assault and strategic defence, and the officers became increasingly frustrated with the inconclusive bush warfare which the Baule were forcing them to fight.

To suppress Baule resistance under these combat conditions the officers developed a full-fledged 'search-and-destroy' strategy by the end of 1902. The intention was to break the Baule will to resist by demolishing the logistic basis of their livelihood through the systematic destruction of the remote encampments. As one officer described the strategy, 'Des détachements de battue . . . sont envoyés dans les fourrés avec mission de rechercher et de détruire tous les campements qui se trouvent dans une zone déterminée aux abords du bivouac.'[26]

Governor Clozel prevented the officers from fully implementing their policy when he changed the administrative policy towards the Baule in early 1903. During his Governorship from 1903 until 1908 the Baule began to repopulate their villages and enter into sustained relations with the French in the major administrative posts. When Governor Angoulvant imposed more severe administrative measures, however, the Baule once again evaded French authority by moving to their encampments. In retaliation Angoulvant revived the policy of previous military commanders and authorized the systematic destruction of Baule encampments. Proceding from one end of a territory to the other, military detachments levelled settlements and demolished the crops of the recalcitrant Baule population. Those who capitulated were regrouped in officially created villages under the surveillance of French troops or collaborating chiefs.[27]

The search-and-destroy policy continued until the resisters had been either killed or captured, but this was not accomplished swiftly. The dispersed character of Baule settlement sustained resistance activities for several years. Eventually defeat was total, but it had not been brought about by any one decisive military engagement. Rather it resulted from the cumulative impact of destruction, impoverishment, famine, epidemics, and death. This pattern of defeat distinguished Baule resistance from the kind of warfare conducted by centralized states against European powers. Where Europeans conquered African kingdoms the productive base of the society was often left relatively unaltered by the resistance struggle itself. Among the Baule, however, the productive base became the explicit target of French military strategy, and French victory posed fundamental problems of resettlement and economic reconstruction.

The Prophetic Appeal

The encounter between the French and the Baule gave rise to intellectual as well as material problems for the Baule. French intentions were not self-evident, and over the course of time they changed in an inscrutable manner. At first the French insisted that they wanted simply to traverse Baule territory to pursue Samory, but subsequently they explained that they intended to establish permanent posts to regulate Baule trade and collect taxes. Even this arrangement did not seem to satisfy them for long, for when Angoulvant took office in 1908, he made it clear that in addition he intended to require the Baule to produce new crops for export and furnish labour for European enterprises. The remarkable change in the nature and intensity of French demands in a relatively short period of time created a situation which was for the Baule as unpredictable as it was unacceptable. Barely had they come to terms with one set of demands before a new set was imposed.

In the early stages of Baule relations with the French common sense categories of experience provided sufficient explanations for the outcome of events. If the ultimate motivation of French activity remained obscure, the immediate effects of French intrusion were far more tangible. To the extent that French presence was potentially disruptive to the customary structure of social relations from which the local chiefs derived their power, these chiefs were prepared to resist. Furthermore, they learned from experience that if they put up enough of a fight the French would reduce their demands and withdraw. It seemed to the Baule that Monteil retreated when Baule resistance proved too much to handle. Similarly, Clozel appeared to withdraw the troops and reduce his demands after the vociferous resistance of 1902. This pattern of events was both predictable and reassuring to the Baule for they still felt themselves to be masters of their own destiny. Generally, things occurred as they were expected to occur. If the French demands were too great, one resisted with force. If one resisted long and hard enough the French desisted and withdrew.

During the period of relative calm from 1903 to 1908, however, new imponderables began to emerge for the Baule. The military stalemate reached in late 1902 was susceptible to several interpretations. On the one hand, Clozel's policy of reducing military activity and abandoning the small outposts at Salékro, Yaotékro, Aondo, Guimvwé, Kokumbo, and Dida gave the Baule some reason to hope that the French would withdraw completely. Similarly, his reduction of the demand for porters and labourers supported the idea that the Baule resistance had been successful. On the other hand the central structures of French administration remained intact, and the persistent demand for taxes was not the kind of activity which the Baule expected from those who were about to withdraw.

In general the Baule adopted a tentative wait-and-see attitude towards the colonial arrangement. Most paid their taxes, and some of the chiefs who received a 10 per cent commission for collecting the revenue began to see definite advantages in the colonial system, but neither they nor the more reticent chiefs could predict with any degree of assurance what the Europeans would demand next, or how long they intended to stay. If experience was anything to go on, the Baule could reasonably expect that the Europeans would eventually leave, for over the previous sixty years every fitful French initiative on the coast had been followed by a subsequent withdrawal. Even if the French were to stay, it was not clear to the Baule where they intended to concentrate their activity or who would be in charge. So many temporary posts had been created and dismantled, and administrators had come and gone with such rapidity that for the Baule the internal rationale of French administration remained an enormous enigma.

In response to this pervasive sense of the unpredictable, Baule diviners began to emerge as important public figures. Under normal circumstances the Baule diviner, or *kômien*, was consulted in the case of personal misfortune, and he customarily diagnosed the source of an individual's trouble and prescribed a course of action for 'his client designed to assure a remedy. The social role of the *kômien* gradually shifted, however, as increasing numbers of people turned to him to clarify the enigmas of the situation at hand. To the extent that a diviner offered a diagnosis for a collective misfortune and prescribed a collective course of action to remedy the situation, he became a political figure. Increasingly, as the prominent chiefs became more and more closely associated with the colonial administration in their role as tax collectors from 1903 to 1908, political initiative among the Baule passed largely from the chiefs to the diviners.

Little is known about the precise nature of the appeal of these quasi-prophetic figures, although it is clear that they were capable of inspiring Baule resistance sentiment on a broader basis than that afforded by the narrow range of kinship ties alone. Some, known by the Baule as *amouensofue*, limited themselves to distributing charms or amulets which were supposed to bring the bearer supernatural powers. Others seemed to construct more elaborate exploratory models, and advocate departures from customary activities. In this respect they could be said to be the formulators of a new ideological framework whose scope, if not explicitly nationalistic or universalistic in orientation, was at least trans-ethnic in character. In any event, one feature common to all of these phenomena was their expressly anti-European content.

Understandably the French regarded these quasi-prophetic figures as dangerous political subversives, and the administration grew increasingly anxious about their expanding influence. Whenever possible they suppressed them brutally in an attempt to discourage the spread of their ideas. As early as 1902, for example, the administration arrested a Nanafoué diviner named Tiéfi who had created a stir in the Kokumbo area by selling a remedy which he claimed would enable his clients to rid themselves of the French post. The military commander issued orders to execute Tiéfi in public as part of an effort to discourage similar characters from emerging in the future.[28] Ironically, the Fench reaction may have contributed to the spread of this type of appeal, for while individual diviners doubtless became more circumspect in their anti-French appeals as a result of the execution, the fact that the French insisted upon executing Tiéfi only served to confirm the suggestion that his activities constituted an important threat to their position in Kokumbo. When in November 1907 the military post at Kokumbo was dismantled for reasons of economy, it is not unlikely that at least some Baule believed that Tiéfi's prophecy had finally come true.

As the conventional framework of political and kinship authority continued to collapse during the final phase of Baule resistance from 1909 to 1911, the prophetic appeal once again gained popularity. In 1910 Kouadio Boni of Mamra gained considerable influence over the Baule in the southern region. He counselled the Baule to plant no more rice and predicted that the French troops would leave if the Ngban followed his advice.[29] Kouadio Pri of Kpouébo similarly gained a significant following by providing the warriors of the southern Ngban with a charm called 'M'Bosa' which he claimed would assist them in defeating the French. The precise attributes of Kouadio Pri's charm remained a mystery to the French, but the administrator at Ouossou, Monsieur Bru, reported in April 1910 that 'tous les chefs et notables du pays vénéraient, portaient, gardaient dans leurs cases le M'Bosa, son fétiche'.[30]

The advantages of another charm called 'Abo N'Zué' were more immediately apparent. Andsoromi Taki, a diviner from Dida Moussou, claimed that the 'Abo N'Zué' charm would finally enable the Baule to drive the French away. Captain Foussat explained how Andsoromi Taki operated:

Voici comment il procédait: ses envoyés parcouraient la région annoncant que Andsoromi Taki avait enfin trouvé un fétiche qui allait débarrasser le pays de tous les blancs. Lorsqu'on avait acquis ce fétiche 'Abo N'Zué' on devenait invulnérable et il suffisait pour échapper aux balles des fusils des blancs de crier trois fois 'Abo N'Zué' pour voir les balles se changer en gouttes d'eau:

'Abo' ce qui frappe, 'N'Zué' c'est l'eau. Presque tous les villages Agbas acceptèrent 'Abo N'Zué' et les nouveaux adeptes se rendaient à Dida Moussou où ils recevaient le fameux fétiche . . .[31]

Andsoromi Taki was eventually captured by the French, but not before he had succeeded in gaining a considerable following among the northern and southern Ngban, the Agba, and the Ouéllé groups of Baule.

Inasmuch as each of these individuals limited his appeal to the provision of an instrumental device to assist the Baule in ridding themselves of the French, they essentially represented a simple extension of the traditional role of the Baule *amouensofue*. The source of their popularity was grounded in the widespread hostility to French intrusion more than it was upon a shared sense of an alternative vision of the future. In this respect the individual prophetic appeals had not yet taken on the characteristics of a full-fledged millennial movement.

There is nevertheless some evidence of the emergence of a more broadly based ideological movement in the final months of the Baule resistance. During December 1909 and January 1910 representatives of several villages in the Ouossou area travelled overland westwards through Dida territory to consult the Beugré oracle. The precise location of this oracle or the reason for its apparent authority remain obscure, but the Baule were thought to have consulted the oracle in the past during similar moments of crisis. After the murder of the two French commercial explorers, Voituret and Papillon, in 1891, for example, Etien Komenan, the king of Tiassalé, allegedly sent their remains to the Beugré oracle to determine what he should do in the face of French plans to penetrate his territory.[32] The oracle was believed to have advised Etien Komenan to resist in 1891, and the oracle's message to the Ngban representatives in early 1910 was similar. According to the administrator at Ouossou,

Ces émissaires . . . rapportaient que ce grand fétiche ordonnait de faire d'abord le vide autour de nous et ensuite la guerre et qu'il promettait la victoire. Les chefs . . . qui n'avaient aucune raison de s'écarter de nous furent demandés au Poste; ils répondirent à Irma N'Guessan notre envoyé qu'ils ne se présenteraient plus au poste, où on ne les reverrait que 'morts'. Les villages . . . suivaient le mouvement, et payaient 'l'impôt' du fétiche pour lequel il était versé 0.50 fr. par tête d'habitants.[33]

The importance of the Beugré cult for the whole southern region of the Ivory Coast is a subject which deserves further research before much can be said about it with certainty, but at least two features seem important. First, the scope of the oracle's influence was pluri-ethnic. Located in the lower Cavally region, the oracle attracted pilgrims from great distances to the east, and its influence clearly transcended several ethnic frontiers. Secondly, the oracle seemed to be capable of providing a vision of possible success and a programme for achieving that success which was sufficiently compelling to inspire the Baule to pay what the French termed 'l'impôt de fétiche'.

These aspects of the Beugré cult anticipate in a rudimentary form several features of syncretistic millennial movements which subsequently swept through these same areas in the period immediately following the final defeat of the resistance struggle.[34] It is perhaps not merely a coincidence that the renowned prophet, Harris, drew his greatest following during the First World War from the same geographic region which had previously come under the influence of the Beugré oracle. The French finally crushed the armed resistance of the Baule and other groups in the Ivory Coast, but this process itself generated the conditions in which the prophetic appeal was likely to spread.

CHAPTER VIII

French Conquest and Baule Resistance in Historical Perspective

In retrospect armed Baule resistance to the French can be seen to have been concentrated in three different periods: from 1893 to 1895; from 1898 to 1903; and from 1909 to 1911. The historical problem, then, is to discover why during these periods the Baule reaction to the French became particularly intense, while from 1895 to 1898 and again from 1903 to 1908 French–Baule relations were, if not amicable, at least not overtly hostile.

One possible approach to the problem would be to focus upon the question of leadership on both sides of the colonial encounter. From this perspective one would expect that changes in the character of French–Baule relations could be plausibly explained in terms of changes in leadership either among the Baule themselves or among the French colonial officials in charge of the colony's administration.

On the Baule side of the colonial equation this does not seem to provide a fully adequate explanation, for the simple reason that there was little demonstrable correlation between shifts in Baule resistance sentiment and changes in Baule chieftaincies. Leaders such as Akafou Bulare and Kouadio Okou were capable of being resisters at one point and collaborators at another. For the most part they and others whom the French identified as 'leaders' were merely responding to changes in the level of discontent among their followers. In short, given the essentially conservative character of Baule traditional chieftaincy and the decentralized nature of Baule political structures, it seems difficult to explain Baule resistance in leadership terms alone.[1] In this respect Baule resistance stands in marked contrast to resistance movements elsewhere in West Africa where individuals like Lat Dior, Rabah, Amadou Seku, Mamadou Lamine, and Samory assumed vital leadership roles.

Akafou Bulare's case provides a good example of the Baule pattern. To the extent that he was a 'leader' he used his position to try to conciliate between the French and more hostile Baule, but his efforts proved fruitless because on the one hand he could not mollify the resistance sentiment of junior chiefs like Yao Guié, and on the other hand the French became increasingly irritated with his persistent attempts to negotiate when they felt that outright submission was called for.[2] Thus, 'leaders' like Akafou Bulare were largely ineffectual, and to the extent that chiefs like Yao Guié gained ascendancy, it was because they became recognized spokesmen for a broadly based resistance sentiment. To account for Baule resistance, then, one must look beyond the question of leadership alone to examine the basis for the pervasive reaction against French presence.

On the European side, however, the question of changing leadership would seem to have been important in determining the type of administration the Baule experienced and reacted against. On the surface at least it would seem that during each period of difficulty between the French and the Baule the growth of Baule resistance sentiment followed the transfer of administrative initiative from civilian to military personnel. Thus, when Lieutenant-Colonel Monteil intruded into Baule country on his way to meet Samory in 1894 and 1895 he provoked the first Baule revolt. When Captain Benoît established the post at Bouaké in 1898, the results were broadly the same. Similarly, as the initiative in southern Baule regions passed from Delafosse and Nebout to men like Captain Le Magnen, Commander Donnat, Lieutenant-Colonel Aymerich, and Commander Colonna d'Istria during the period from 1899 to 1902, Baule reaction was predictably hostile. Finally, from 1909 to 1911 Baule resistance spread when effective control passed from civilian administrators like Marc Simon into the hands of Commander Noguès and his successor, Lieutenant-Colonel Lagarrue.

Following this line of reasoning it could be argued that Baule resistance was ultimately an epiphenomenon of an essentially intra-European struggle. From this perspective, the fundamental conflict was that which took place in French colonial circles between the advocates of civilian authority versus the partisans of military rule. Whenever the military partisans gained the upper hand in dealing with the Baule their approach was inevitably authoritarian, and this invariably provoked open armed conflict. On the other hand, whenever the advocates of civilian rule emerged victorious, the approach to the Baule was more explicitly political and negotiative, and collaborative relations could be established with local chiefs.[3]

At a glance this type of explanation seems to provide a reasonable gloss for the broad sweep of events. Moreover, such an interpretation would seem to fit well with the current understanding of French expansion in the rest of West Africa. Traditionally historians have depicted France's intrusion into West Africa as a classic example of military imperialism in which the primary campaigns were largely conceived and wholly executed by junior military officers. In those circumstances the economic rationale for conquest was often flimsy in the extreme. Political, military, and strategic concerns dominated the creation of the French empire, and the personal ambition of aspiring junior officers provided much of its motive force.[4] As J.D. Hargreaves has expressed it:

French expansion in West Africa . . . seems to have owed less to pressure from persons interested in the economic resources of the area than to initiatives of local military commanders and governors, taking advantage of opportunities for glory provided by changing political conditions in France.[5]

In this sense French military conquest and Baule resistance might be portrayed as merely an extension southwards of the essentially irrational and impetuous pattern of provocative conquest characteristic of the unbridled military élites in the western Sudan.

Despite its superficial plausibility, however, this explanation proves, upon closer scrutiny, to be inadequate for several reasons. In the first place, relations between the military and the Baule were not uniformly nor uniquely hostile. On the contrary, there were numerous examples of military officers who succeeded in working amicably with the Baule. Commander Betsellère, placed in charge of Baule territory at the end of 1902, managed to restore effective calm in the area throughout his period in office. The only military campaign he undertook was against the Agba in 1905, and this was on the explicit orders of Clozel, a civilian governor. Otherwise Betsellère's relations with the Baule were predicated entirely upon respect for Baule chiefs, tolerance for local customs and patience in the execution of his requests. Betsellère's successor, Commander Charles, continued his tolerant tradition in local administration with similar results. The performance of both of these men illustrated that military administration did not inevitably provoke armed Baule resistance.

Furthermore, civilian administration was by no means a guarantee of peaceful relations with the Baule. The row between Delafosse and Kouadio Okou in 1899 provided the starting point for a wide-scale revolt in southern Baule country from 1899 to 1902. Similarly, in 1909 the Commis d'Affaires Indigènes, Moesch, and the senior civilian administrator in the region, Marc Simon, managed to touch off the decisive Akoué revolt with their ill-advised visit to Diamalabo. As these events suggest, there was nothing intrinsically amicable about civilian personnel. It will be necessary to look beyond the simple dichotomy between civilian versus military leadership on the European side of the colonial equation to arrive at an understanding of Baule resistance.

The incidents involving Delafosse and Simon provide the basis for constructing a more useful explanatory model. Their respective difficulties in 1899 and 1909 suggest that there was an archetypal sequence of events leading in each period to an escalation of hostilities, and in the ensuing periods of conflict the military did not act as autonomously as it might be supposed. The typical scenarios involved *both* civilian and military personnel and normally developed along the following lines. To begin with there was a breakdown of collaborative relations between the Baule and the civilian administration. Then in the face of humiliation and retreat civilian administrators called upon the military to sort out the situation. The military officers subsequently arrived in full swagger, but they were insufficiently armed or provisioned to do anything but arouse further Baule hostility. At that point the colonial administration was presented with an embarrassing choice: either back the impatient military with all the resources necessary to suppress Baule resistance, or scale down the military presence and attempt to re-establish a basis for collaboration with the existing Baule chiefs.[6]

This general sequence of events repeated itself in each of the three periods of Baule resistance. In the first two periods the administration decided to back away from full-scale military conquest. In 1895 it was the Minister of Colonies, Émile Chautemps, who ordered Monteil to withdraw to the coast. In 1902 it was acting Governor Clozel who, after consultations with Governor General Roume, instructed the military to terminate its operations gracefully and prepare the terrain for political collaboration. Only in 1910 did the administration choose to react differently. Responding to Angoulvant's repeated request for troops and finances, Governor General Ponty finally supplied the support necessary for the total suppression of Baule resistance.

In the light of these observations, the framework for interpreting Baule resistance shifts significantly. Historical explanations based on military versus civilian leadership glide into the background. They can be seen as essentially secondary to two other questions of a more fundamental nature. First, why did the successive collaborative arrangements between the French administrators and the Baule break down in the first place? and secondly, why was it that in 1910 the colonial authorities chose to pursue full-scale repression whereas on previous occasions when faced with a similar choice they had decided to diminish the military presence?

The answers to both these questions hinge upon the crucial issue of labour. In the first instance the collaborative arrangements between the French and the Baule chiefs broke down whenever French demands for labour threatened the stability or continuity of Baule productive relations. A close examination of the incidents leading up to each period of armed struggle reveals that this was the enduring theme inspiring each phase of determined resistance. In 1894–5 French demands for porters to march to the north made it difficult for the Baule to control their newly acquired captives, and they responded by halting the French advance.[7] In 1898 when Samory had been subdued, the problem of escaping captives inspired Kouassi Blé's attack on the Bouaké post.[8] Similarly the French attempt to move the Dyula populations from the southern Baule area back to the north in 1899 provided the context for Kouadio Okou's revolt.[9] Clozel understood Baule sensitivities on the issue of disruptive labour demands, and to the extent that he initiated an era of *détente* in Franco-Baule relations it was largely because he reduced the direct demand for labour time in administrative tasks and assured Baule chiefs that he did not wish to 'liberate' their slaves.[10] Conversely, Angoulvant's insensitivity to Baule customary labour practices led him to formulate unrealistic policies aimed specifically at re-structuring the Baule labour force to suit the needs of the colonial economy.[11] Predictably his demands precipitated the final wave of Baule armed resistance.

The question of taxation contributed to Baule irritation with the French, but here again the fundamental issue involved traditional patterns of labour. As long as the level of taxation did not force the Baule to release their captives to work in realms beyond their control or oblige the Baule themselves to accept wage employment, the Baule were prepared to pay the necessary head taxes to please the French. Clozel's policy of reducing labour requirements and depending upon the chiefs for tax returns seemed to pay off handsomely. Head tax contributions to the colony's budget nearly tripled between 1903 and 1907, and the chiefs themselves showed signs of active participation in collecting taxes, particularly since they were assured of sizable rebates in the process.[12] Angoulvant's tax reforms changed all of this and provoked further Baule resistance precisely because Angoulvant clearly intended to use heavy taxation as a means of coercing the Baule to turn to wage employment and cash crop production.[13] This fundamentally challenged the organization of Baule domestic labour, and for this reason many household chiefs were prepared to resist these initiatives.

In each period, then, it was over the issue of labour that the initial collaborative relationships between the French and the Baule repeatedly collapsed, triggering the archetypal sequence of events including the appeal for troops, the preliminary military interventions, the spread of resistance activity, and the administration's awkward dilemma as to whether it should reinforce or restrain the military.

The particular importance of the labour issue in the eyes of the Baule can be explained by the state of their economy at the time of French intrusion. The Baule had not yet experienced the 'economic revolution' which many of the coastal societies had undergone earlier in the nineteenth century. Located nearly one hundred kilometres inland from the coast, the Baule remained separated from direct commercial contact with Europeans by a series of palm oil producing groups to the south. The rise in purchasing power on the part of these groups and the relatively abundant supplies of captive labour from the north meant that an archaic economy based upon gold production, cotton weaving and the transit commerce in captives remained viable among the Baule long after other areas of West Africa had been obliged to convert their economies to produce cheap agricultural commodities for European markets. Gold and woven cloth continued to be in high demand among the neighbours of the Baule, and the only barrier to increased Baule production was the availability of manpower. Their economy was, in effect, a labour-scarce one in the process of expanding at the time of French intrusion. As long as the French did not interfere with this economy and the productive relations upon which it was based, the Baule saw no reason why they should not tolerate the French; and some chiefs clearly felt it was in their interest to collaborate with them. When, however, the French presence began to challenge or subvert these productive relations, the Baule saw every reason why they should resist, and the precarious collaborative arrangements collapsed.

Just as problems concerning the disposition of labour provided the motive force behind Baule resistance sentiment, so too they explained why in 1910 the administration ultimately decided to reinforce rather than withdraw the troops as it had before in 1895 and again in 1902. In the earlier periods the structure of the colony's trade and the nature of the colonial budget permitted the administration to conduct its affairs without having to concern itself with the direct mobilization of rural labour. The administration's role was to facilitate the export of products already abundant in the colony, including palm oil, palm kernels, tropical woods and wild rubber. These products could be collected with minimal European intrusion, and the normal incentives of market exchange were sufficient to stimulate enough trade to support the colony's budget which was derived principally from customs revenues.

By 1908, however, several important changes in the composition of the colony's trade and the structure of the local and federal budgets led the administration to develop an urgent interest in African labour.[14] With the fiscal reforms of 1904 the tax burden on the rural populations increased significantly. At the same time it became apparent in 1907 that the colony could not count on the continued expansion of traditionally collected produce to assure its prosperity in the future. The limits of rubber exploitation in response to normal market incentives appeared to have been reached in 1906, and in 1907 production dwindled despite relatively high prices. Without direct intervention of the administration to coerce increased production or to introduce new cash crops, the future prosperity of the import–export sector looked precarious indeed. Moreover, the administration had committed itself to providing several hundred kilometres of railway and an expanded port facility. Unless rural production were to be increased these important capital investments would remain under-utilized while the debts incurred for their construction would inevitably have to be repaid.

These changed circumstances meant that the administration began to consider itself entitled, indeed obliged, to intervene directly to mobilize the rural labour force to respond to new cash crops and increase their production of the traditional exports. Angoulvant's plans to increase taxes, introduce plantation crops, and impose collective labour obligations were all designed to this end. In support of his approach Angoulvant invoked the theories of Lucien Hubert who summarized the situation succinctly:

De jour en jour, nous comprenons mieux que la véritable trésor dont nous devons tirer parti dans nos colonies, ce ne sont ni les richesses naturelles, ni les espaces libres, mais les races indigènes . . . c'est la population qui fait la force et la richesse d'un pays; le capital à mettre en valeur, c'est l'homme.[15]

This realization marked a significant departure from the approach under Clozel's governorship when the administration had remained generally content to leave the problem of organizing production in the hands of its collaborating chiefs while concentrating its attention upon providing the infrastructure for expanded trade.[16]

Given the increased importance of African labour for the colony's anticipated development it is not surprising that when confronted with the archetypal scenario of revolt in 1909 colonial officials reacted differently from their predecessors in earlier periods. In 1895 and again in 1902 an era of commercial expansion could be restored simply by removing the military and reviving previous collaborative arrangements with the available chiefs. By 1910 when Governor General Ponty faced the decision to reinforce or withdraw the troops in the Ivory Coast, such an alternative strategy was no longer assured. Fifteen years of French presence had eroded the authority of traditional chiefs with respect to their following, particularly in the light of widespread disaffection in the face of deteriorating economic circumstances. Collaborative arrangements with these chiefs could not be counted upon to provide the kind of submissive labour force that Angoulvant felt the colony required. In his opinion and in the opinion of Governor General Ponty as well, only total military conquest would guarantee the necessary conditions to mobilize the rural labour force in the service of the colonial economy.

The ineptitudes of military officers occasionally revived the classic civilian–military debate reminiscent of the days of the Sudanese conquest, and the final reinforcement of troops by Ponty in 1910 made it appear that the *pacification* of the Ivory Coast was merely a latter-day version of *la conquête du Soudan*. Fundamentally, however, the motive force behind the two conquests differed considerably, and so did the nature of the resistance in both cases. Whereas the capture of Samory assured the end of resistance in the northern Ivory Coast, the deaths of Kouamé Dié and Akafou Bulare had no such effect among the Baule. Individual Baule chiefs were not so much the leaders of revolt as they were the spokesmen for a pervasive resistance sentiment. The French sought to crush this sentiment on a village by village basis in order to absorb the Baule as peasant producers in the colonial economy.

In this instance, then, armed struggle was but part of a more fundamental encounter. The essential confrontation was that between a persistently viable traditional economy and a nascent colonial economy. The former was based on the household production of exports of high value-to-weight ratio; the latter depended upon the large scale production of cheap agricultural commodities of low value-to-weight ratio. Both economies were geared to produce goods for exchange, but because of the nature of their respective exports, the organization of labour in each economic system differed considerably. Between the French administration and the Baule the crucial issue at stake concerned the control over the disposition of the rural labour bound up at the time in household units of production. When the civilian administrators proved incapable of mobilizing this labour in service of the colonial economy through existing collaborative arrangements, they called upon the military to accomplish by force what they had been helpless to achieve through persuasion. In this instance military conquest was simply the means of implementing an economic policy designed by civilian authorities on the outskirts of empire.

Thus, we must reassess the view that in the era of the 'new imperialism' European conquest was essentially a reflex response by metropolitan statesmen to the phenomena of political instability on the periphery of informal empire. According to this 'peripheral' theory of imperialism, it could be maintained that the French had no fundamental economic motive for subduing the Baule people on a village by village basis; instead, they were forced to take this step only when unstable political conditions threatened to jeopardize the collaborative arrangements that supported the framework of empire.[17] As D. K. Fieldhouse has phrased it:

In the most general terms it must be concluded that Europe was pulled into imperialism by the magnetic force of the periphery . . . But economic factors did not, on their own account, necessarily or even commonly generate need or desire for formal empire . . . it would seem that empire-building occurred on the scale that it did in . . . parts of Africa, Asia and the Pacific and not other regions, because it was in . . . those places that relations between representatives of the advanced economies of Europe and other less-developed societies became fundamentally unstable.[18]

The difficulty with this kind of interpretation is that it stops short of the fundamental object of inquiry. True, colonial conquest - in the Baule case as elsewhere - occurred only when informal collaborative arrangements broke down. But surely, such a statement is a descriptive truism; it explains nothing. We are left with the enduring question: why did collaboration collapse? The answer to this question leads us directly into the realm of economic considerations, for if we are to explain political instability on the outskirts of empire in any more precise terms than simply 'the natives were restless' we must examine the changing political economy of the periphery.[19] When taxation increases, when commodity prices for customary agricultural products decline, when new cash crop production is imposed, when rival chiefs are offered differential access to new economic possibilities, and when co-operative chiefs watch their commissions cut in half, it is hardly surprising that the collaborative arrangements which previously supported the edifice of empire finally collapse under the strain of changing circumstance. It is precisely these kinds of conditions that deserve renewed attention in studies of imperialism.

It might be argued that to talk of the Baule case as if it were in the realm of imperial studies is a conceptual mistake. Imperialism had to do with the partition of Africa, the scramble for territory and the annexation of colonies in the late nineteenth century. Baule resistance and French conquest came much later, and thus they fall within the domain of colonial revolts and police actions rather than as part of imperialism itself.

The argument stems from fundamental definitions. If imperialist phenomena are to be understood strictly in terms of statesmen's decisions involving the declaration of paper claims to sovereignty over outlying regions in the tropics, then clearly the Baule case has nothing to do with imperialism. Most historians, however, would prefer to conceive the subject in broader terms. Ronald Robinson has offered a widely accepted definition: 'Imperialism in the industrial era is a process whereby agents of an expanding society gain inordinate influence over the vitals of weaker societies by 'dollar' diplomacy, ideological suasion, conquest and rule . . .'.[20]

According to this formulation, the Baule case is firmly within the purview of imperial studies, for it was only in 1911 that the French gained 'inordinate influence over the vitals' of Baule society through conquest. It is true that this process occurred well after formal annexation of the Ivory Coast as a colony in 1889, but this sequence was common in Africa. As Robinson and Gallagher have stressed: 'Imperialism was not the cause of the partition. It was the result.'[21]

On the basis of the Baule material, then, it is possible to refine the general theories of imperialism that are of interest to historians of European expansion. Colonial conquest may well have been a reflex response of the metropolitan powers to crises on the periphery of informal empire, but the crises themselves were frequently precipitated by unilateral alterations in the collaborative system introduced from Europe either through subtle market mechanisms expressed in a progressive deterioration of terms of trade or through much more explicit economic policies imposed by European agents of empire on the spot.

In this sense, the 'peripheral' theory of imperialism is a subset of a properly conceived economic theory of imperialism. Far from offering an alternative to economic explanations for European expansion, the 'peripheral' theory merely underscores the central significance of economic considerations. The range of relevant phenomena is no longer thought to include only those in Europe itself, but economic considerations nevertheless remain the essential subject-matter of the study at hand. Traditional economic theories of imperialism may well be sorely deficient if they focus too exclusively upon metropolitan industrial structures, individual European firms or aggregate capital flows, but alternate theories of imperialism fail completely if they fall short of examining in detail the changing political economy on the periphery of informal empire. As the Baule case demonstrates, careful studies of these conditions hold the key to understanding the motive force of European imperialism.

When we move beyond interpreting the motives for colonial conquest and into the realm of assessing the impact of colonial rule itself, the Baule evidence offers further insights. Judgements have differed concerning the significance of early colonial policy for the economic transformation of West Africa. During much of the colonial era observers assumed that the imposition of colonial rule marked a sharp break with the pre-colonial past in economic as well as political affairs. Characteristically, the innovations of the colonial rulers were held to be responsible for a veritable 'economic revolution' in West Africa, setting in motion a process of progressive development through which Africans were thought to have been brought into the modern world.[22]

By way of a much-needed corrective, recent scholarship has produced convincing evidence to challenge the assumed importance of the break between the pre-colonial and colonial periods. Pointing to the early and mid-nineteenth century production of groundnuts and palm oil and the massive importation of European manufactures, Colin Newbury has suggested that the break in economic terms came before the imposition of formal colonial rule: 'If "Revolution" there was (to use McPhee's term), we should look for its effects before European colonial powers were extensively established.'[23] Echoing a similar theme, A. G. Hopkins in his recent survey of West African economic history has drawn attention to African experimentation and adaptation of new forms of economic production before the colonial period and independent of European intervention.[24]

From this perspective, then, the advent of formal colonial rule did not inaugurate a radical departure in the increasing development of African production for European commodity markets. As Hopkins summarizes it, 'there are sound reasons for thinking that colonial rule itself had a less dramatic and less pervasive economic impact than was once supposed.'[25] For Hopkins the colonial endeavour is presented in economic terms as merely an effort by Europeans to facilitate the expansion of existing trade by overcoming the remaining 'constraints' to the development of commerce in the context of an 'open economy'.[26]

According to this interpretation, European economic planning in West Africa was highly restrained in the early period of colonial rule. This pattern of minimal intrusion is portrayed as characteristic of both major colonial traditions. 'As far as economic policy was concerned', Hopkins writes, 'France and Britain had more in common than is often appreciated'.[27] In both cases, it is argued:

Economic policy was limited both in its philosophy and its techniques. Governments were not envisaged as playing a central and dynamic part in developing the estates they had acquired . . . Once pacification had been achieved, government activity reverted to its traditional role: that of light administration. In economic affairs the political officers merely acted as Great White Umpires, ensuring that the rules were observed, not that they were changed.[28]

Emphasizing the political as well as the economic features of administrative restraint, Ronald Robinson elaborates this theme with specific reference to British territories in West Africa.[29] The reasons for adopting a colonial policy of limited intervention, according to Robinson, derived ultimately from the British tradition of 'empire on the cheap'. Early attempts to pursue a more forward policy in reference to the three crucial realms of taxation, land appropriation, and chiefly appointments provoked serious African resistance, and colonial authorities recognized that to suppress this resistance would be a costly proposition. Rather than incur the expenses involved in implementing a more positive policy, the administration contented itself with a programme of limited government.

In the event, Robinson argues, the relative success of African resistance movements ensured that British agents would be confined to performing necessary tasks in the service of enduring African political institutions. 'Far from west Africans being taken prisoner by British imperialism, British imperialism was the prisoner of its chiefly, west African collaborators.' In overall terms colonial administrators had a very limited impact. 'They could not transform, they only scratched the surface of Africa's historic continuities.'[30]

However appropriate these generalizations may be for large parts of the British territories, it would be misleading to accept them as adequate descriptions of colonial rule in West Africa as a whole. In the

Ivory Coast the Baule evidence suggests that in the recent literature on colonial rule the corrective swing of the scholarly pendulum may have gone too far. Colonial administrators may have preferred a limited role, but their administration was not always as 'light' as some have suggested. Moreover, colonial policy itself could and sometimes did take the form of positive intervention in the economic and political life of the rural populations. Ronald Robinson is quite right to point out that 'the advent of colonialism . . . represented not so much the construction of a new collaborative system but the extension of an old one from the coast inland . . .',[31] but it would be a mistake to minimize the significance of this achievement. For all of those populations, like the Baule, that lay beyond the realm of cash crop production throughout the nineteenth century, the extension of the coastal system into their midst demanded a fundamental reorganization of their economic and political institutions. In these regions early colonial rule involved a substantial break with patterns of pre-colonial life. Here the 'Great White Umpires' not only changed the rules; they changed the game entirely.

When circumstances and time permitted, the colonial administration could try to coax selected chiefs into reorganizing their polities by offering whatever incentives it could muster. Over a period of time, however, these collaborative arrangements could be used to effect changes only as long as the overall economic conditions continued to be buoyant enough to provide attractive incentives. In the face of deteriorating economic circumstances the collaborative mechanisms came under strain, and if administrative demands for change in these polities became ever more insistent, the collaborative system collapsed altogether. When this occurred in the Baule case the administration developed a comprehensive economic and political policy designed to reorganize and subordinate Baule labour in the service of the colonial economy.

Governor Angoulvant described the task to his junior officers in unmistakable terms:

Il faudra modifier du tout au tout la mentalité noire pour nous faire comprendre . . . Reconnaissons-le: à l'heure actuelle, l'indigène est encore détaché de nos institutions . . . De longtemps encore, il faudra donc que nos sujets viennent au progrès malgré eux . . . L'aide de l'administration a un caractère particulier . . . Elle se manifeste par une intervention spéciale de l'autorité: celle-ci s'exerce, en effet, pour amener ces indigènes au travail, dont ils n'ont pas la notion.[32]

In his imposition of cash crop production and his uncompromising repression of the ensuing Baule revolt, Angoulvant demonstrated that in its techniques as well as its philosophy colonial policy in the Ivory Coast had become thoroughly interventionist. Whatever the pattern of colonial government elsewhere in West Africa, among the Baule early colonial rule profoundly altered and irreversibly transformed customary social, economic, and political life.

It would be misleading to suggest that in the aftermath of defeat 'traditional' Baule life simply disintegrated. But over time, that which re-emerged was in a sense 'neo-traditional' because the entire context of customary practice changed as the Baule became absorbed as primary producers in the world economy. In subsequent years, much that would announce itself to the world in terms of 'traditional' African practice is perhaps best understood not as a vestigial survival of pre-colonial Baule custom but rather as part of an attempt to establish new modes of social, economic, and political legitimacy as well as spritual autonomy in the wake of this devastating period of resistance and collaboration.

Notes

NOTES TO INTRODUCTION

[1] For a thorough study of these events see: A. S. Kanya-Forstner, *The Conquest of the Western Sudan: A Study in French Military Imperialism* (Cambridge, 1969).

[2] R. E. Robinson and J. Gallagher, 'The Partition of Africa', in *New Cambridge Modern History*, XI, (Cambridge, 1962), pp. 620–21.

[3] M. Chailley, *Les Grandes Missions français en Afrique Occidentale* (Dakar, 1953), p. 90.

[4] M. Crowder, 'Introduction', in M. Crowder, (ed.) *West African Resistance: The Military Response to Colonial Occupation* (London, 1971), p. 15.

[5] R. Hallett, *Africa Since 1875* (Ann Arbor, 1974), p. 278.

NOTES TO CHAPTER I

[1] Early accounts mention the existence of the offshore whirlpools and describe a situation in which a local population is firmly in control of the export trade. See Olfert Dapper, *Description de l'Afrique* (Amsterdam, 1686), p.277. This volume is a French translation of a text originally published in Dutch in 1668. Dapper's work is a descriptive geography, and not an eyewitness account. It represents a compilation of what was known about Africa from various travellers' accounts by the mid-seventeenth century. For a similar description of the Quaqua Coast in English, see John Ogilby, *Africa, being an accurate Description* (London, 1670), pp. 416–18.

[2] Several eyewitness accounts of the population movements in the area at the end of the seventeenth century are reproduced in P. Roussier, ed., *L'Établissement d'Issiny, 1687–1702* (Paris, 1935). Studies with accounts of the settlement of this region by African populations include: R. Bouscayrol, 'Notes sur le peuple ébrié', *BIFAN* (1949), xi, 3–4, pp.383–408; C. Bonnefoy, 'Tiégba: Notes sur un village Aizi', *Ét. Éb.*, 3 (1954), pp.7–129; H. Memel-Foté, 'Le système politique des Adioukrou: une société sans état et à classes d'âge de Côte d'Ivoire' (Thèse de 3ᵉ cycle, Université de Paris, 1969); G. Niangoran-Bouah, 'Les Abouré: une société lagunaire de Côte d'Ivoire', *AUA*, Série Lettres et Sciences Humaines, i (1965), pp.37–171; and M. Augé, *Le Rivage alladian: organisation et évoltuion des villages alladian* (Paris, 1969).

[3] Established in 1701, the French fort at Assini was evacuated in the face of local hostility in 1704; see P. Roussier (ed.) *L'Étab. d'Issiny*. Further attempts to establish permanent onshore settlements were not made until the nineteenth century.

[4] Oral traditions concerning the migrations of the Akan peoples of the eastern Ivory Coast are presented in H. Mouëzy, *Histoire et coutumes du pays d'Assinie et du royaume de Krinjabo* (Paris, 1954); G. Rougerie, 'Les Pays agni du Sud-Est de la Côte d'Ivoire forestière', *Ét. Éb.*, 6 (1957), pp.7–213; L. Tauxier, *Religion, Mœurs et Coutumes des Agnis de la Côte d'Ivoire (Indénié et Sanvi)* (Paris, 1932); Ph. and M. A. de Salverte-Marnier, 'Les Étapes du peuplement', *ÉRB*, i: *Le Peuplement* (Abidjan, 1962), pp.11–58; (anon.), 'Histoire du Peuplement', *ÉRSE, La Sociologie* (Abidjan, 1967), pp.25–48.

[5] K. Y. Daaku, 'The European Traders and the Coastal States, 1630–1720', *Transactions of the Historical Society of Ghana*, viii (1965), pp.11–23; K. Y. Daaku, *Trade and Politics on the Gold Coast, 1600–1720: A study of the African Reaction to European Trade* (Oxford, 1970).

[6] Ph. and M. A. de Salverte-Marnier, 'Les étapes du peuplement'. For a discussion of the sources on this early period of Baule history and a sketch chronology, see T. C. Weiskel, 'L'histoire socio-économique des peuples baule: problèmes et perspectives de recherche', *Cahiers d'Études Africaines*, 61–2, xvi (1–2) (1976), pp.357–95.

[7] M. Delafosse, *Essai de manuel de langue Agni* (Paris, 1900), pp.159-65, 189, 200-1. Delafosse presented Baule myths of origin and warfare, transcribed in Baule, followed by a literal and a figurative translation. Earlier accounts of Baule origins exist, including: Dr R. Verneau, 'Distribution géographique des tribus dans le Baoulé, *L'Anthropologie*, vi (1895), pp.564-8; ANRCI, X-31-23, Dr Lasnet,' 'Mission du Baoulé - Notes', 12 Aug. 1896; and ANRCI, X-38-9, Capt. Le Magnen, 'Notice sur le Baoulé', [c.1900]. In each case, however, these authors appear to have derived their material from Delafosse who had been working among the Baule since 1894. Delafosse in turn was introduced to the Baule by Albert Nebout, the first French administrator to live in the area.

[8] For a development of the ideas relating to the difficulty of using Baule oral traditions see T. C. Weiskel, 'L'histoire socio-économique des peuples baoulé précoloniaux: problèmes et perspectives de recherche', paper presented at inter-university conference, Ghana-Ivory Coast, Kumasi, Ghana (Jan. 1975), and T. C. Weiskel, 'French Colonial Rule and the Baule Peoples: Resistance and Collaboration, 1889-1911' (Oxford, D. Phil. Thesis, 1977), Ch. I.

[9] Y. Person, *Samori: Une révolution Dyula* (Dakar, 1975), iii, p.1683.

[10] For an extended description of the cloth trade on the Quaqua Coast see Dapper, *Description de l'Afrique*, p.277.

[11] 'Dernier mémoire secret sur la Côte d'Afrique', M. de Bussy, attached to dispatch of 6 June 1761. This document is reproduced photographically in *Munger Africana Library Notes*, 3 (Los Angeles, 1971), where it is accompanied by introductory notes and a translation.

[12] T. E. Bowdich, *Mission from Cape Coast Castle to Ashantee* (London, 1819), p.169. Joseph Dupuis also appears to have heard of the Baule while among the Ashanti. See J. Dupuis, *Journal of a Residence in Ashantee* (London, 1824), pp.242-3.

[13] See, for example, Gilbert's *Modern Atlas* (1841); Betts, *Family Atlas* (1848); and the Society for the Diffusion of Useful Knowledge, *Atlas* (c.1848); a further discussion of the possible indications of cartographic evidence on the Baule is presented in T. C. Weiskel, 'French Colonial Rule', Ch. I.

[14] There was, of course, always a considerable delay between what was known to traders on the coast and what appeared in published sources and maps. As a result it is not surprising that maps from the middle of the nineteenth century actually represent information relating to the late eighteenth or early nineteenth centuries.

[15] W. Hutton, *A Voyage to Africa* (London, 1821), pp.36-7.

[16] G. A. Robertson, *Notes on Africa* (London, 1819), p.82.

[17] G. A. Robertson, *Notes on Africa*, pp.82-8; P. Atger, *La France en Côte d'Ivoire de 1843 à 1893: Cinquante ans d'hésitations politiques et commerciales* (Dakar, 1962), p.47; for details of the coastal trade during the 1830s and 1840s see: ANSOM, Sénégal, III, 5b, Bouët, 'Esquisse commerciale de la Côte d'Afrique depuis Galinas jusqu'au Gabon', 6 mai 1839; and É. Bouët-Willaumez, *Le Commerce et la traite des noirs à la côte occidentale d'Afrique* (Paris, 1848). This pattern of transition in economic activity is largely consistent with patterns else-where on the coast. See for example: E. Reynolds, *Trade and Economic Change on the Gold Coast, 1807-1874* (London, 1974); and A. G. Hopkins, *An Economic History of West Africa* (London, 1973), Ch. 3.

[18] For a discussion of this general pattern of the West African coast see C. W. Newbury, 'Trade and Authority in West Africa from 1850 to 1880', in L. H. Gann and P. Duignan, eds., *Colonialism in Africa 1870-1960*, vol. i (Cambridge, 1969), pp.66-100; id., 'Prices and Profitability in Early Nineteenth-Century West African Trade', in C. Meillassoux, ed., *The Development of Indigenous Trade and Markets in West Africa* (London, 1971), pp. 91-106; and id., 'Credit in Early Nineteenth-

Century West African Trade', *JAH*, 13 (1972), pp.81-95. For details on the
coastal political organization on the Ivory Coast see: M. Augé, *Le Rivage alladian*.
    [19] For details of the organization of the trade in coastal groups see: M. Augé,
'L'organisation du commerce précolonial en Basse Côte d'Ivoire et ses effets sur
l'organisation sociale des populations', in C. Meillassoux, ed., *Trade and Markets*;
id., 'Traité précoloniale, politique matrimoniale et stratégie sociale dans les
sociétés de lagunaires de Basse Côte d'Ivoire', *Cahiers ORSTOM*, viii, 2, pp.143-
52; and H. Memel-Fotê, 'Stratégie de la politique des marchés dans une société
sans état de Basse Côte d'Ivoire: Les Adioukrou' (paper presented at the Tenth
Meeting of the International African Institute, Freetown (Dec. 1969).
    [20] Vice-Amiral Fleuriot de Langle, 'Croisières à la côte d'Afrique', *Le Tour du
Monde*, xxvi, 2 (1873), p.378.
    [21] J.-P. Chauveau, 'Note sur la place du Baoulé dans l'ensemble économique
ouest-africain précolonial', mimeo. (Abidjan, 1972); 'Note sur les échanges dans
le Baoulé précolonial', paper presented to Akan Conference (Bondoukou, Ivory
Coast, Jan. 1974), mimeo.
    [22] Early colonial accounts of this movement, based on oral traditions of the
area, include: ANRCI, X-34-8, Capt. Le Magnen to Capt. Jobard, 18 Feb. 1900;
ANRCI, X-38-9, Capt. Le Magnen, 'Notice sur le Baoulé' [c.1900]; and notes by
Delafosse quoted in Dr Verneau, 'Distribution géographique des tribus', p.566.
For recent research on the subject see Salverte-Marnier, 'Les étapes du peuple-
ment', *ÉRB*, i, pp. 39-44; and especially J.-P. Chauveau, 'Note sur L'histoire du
peuplement de la région de Kokumbo', Abidjan, Centre d'ORSTOM, *Sciences
Humaines*, iv, 11 (1971); and id., 'Note sur la morphologie matrimoniale de
Kokumbo (pays Baoulé, Côte d'Ivoire), perspective historique', Abidjan,
ORSTOM, *Sciences Humaines*, vi, 3, (1973).
    [23] Although no Baule merchants had emerged, there is some evidence that
individual Apollonien traders circulated throughout Baule country prior to the
arrival of the Europeans. Known locally as 'Asoko' these traders extended their
activities into the Ivory Coast from the Gold Coast in the late part of the nineteenth century. See Ch. III below. By the 1890s a community of Apollonien had
established themselves at the village of Ahua on the lower Bandama, just south of
Baule territory, and individual Apollonien traders had commercial dealings with
Baule chiefs further in the interior. See, for example, the brief portrait of the
Apollonien named Kouamé or Angola who had apparently operated among the
Baule for twenty years by the time the French arrived: ANSOM, Afrique, III,
23c, M-30, Nebout to Lt.-Col. Monteil, 4 Mar. 1895.
    [24] J.-P. Chauveau, 'Note sur les échanges', pp. 18, 24-7. For an elaboration
of the concept of 'transit markets' see K. Arhin, 'Atebubu markets: ca. 1884-
1930', in C. Meillassoux, ed., *Trade and Markets*, pp.199-213, particularly p.207.
The Baule case seems to support Meillassoux's hypothesis that markets emerge
among peoples like the Baule not within the territory of the ethnic group but
rather on its borders, where relations of economic complementarity stimulate
exchange. Cf. C. Meillassoux, 'Introduction', *Trade and Markets*, pp.82-3.
    [25] J.-P. Chauveau, 'Note sur les échanges', pp. 25-6; and Mohamed Sékou
Bamba, 'Tiassalé et le commerce précolonial sur le Bas-Bandama', (Paris,
Mémoire de Maîtrise, Paris I, 1975), pp.67-97.
    [26] For a brief sketch of Ashanti kinship organization see M. Fortes, 'Kinship
and Marriage among the Ashanti', in A. K. Radcliffe-Brown and D. Forde, eds.,
African Systems of Kinship and Marriage (London, 1950), pp.252-84.
    [27] For Baule kin terms as they were recorded at the outset of the colonial
period see M. Delafosse, *Essai de manuel*, pp.19-20. For subsequent lists of kin
terms see G. Effimbra, *Manuel de Baoulé* (Paris, 1959), pp.33, 35-6, 38-40,
121-2, 234, 250, 258; and P. and M. Étienne, 'L'organisation sociale des Baoulé',

ÉRB, i, pp.125–8; and 'Terminologie de la parenté et de l'alliance chez les Baoulé (Côte d'Ivoire)', *L'Homme*, vii, 4 (1967), pp.50–76.

[28] Delafosse, *Essai de manuel*, pp.159–65, 189, 200–1.

[29] Delafosse, *Essai de manuel*, p.207.

[30] The following summary of Baule political structures is based on information in Delafosse, *Essai de manuel*, pp.15–21, 117–18, 207–10; Delafosse, 'Coutumes indigènes des Agnis du Baoulé', in F.-J. Clozel and R. Villamur, eds., *Les Coutumes indigènes de la Côte d'Ivoire* (Paris, 1902), pp.95–100, 138–45; M. Menalque, *Coutumes civiles des Baoulés de la région de Dimbokro* (Paris, 1933), pp.7–10; and Ph. de Salverte-Marnier, 'L'organisation politique', *ÉRB*, i. pp.195–209.

[31] P. Étienne, 'Les aspects ostentatoires du système économique baoulé (Côte d'Ivoire)', *Économies et Sociétés*, ii, 4 (1968), pp.793–817.

[32] P. Étienne, 'Le fait villageois baoulé' (Abidjan, 1971), mimeo.

[33] P. and M. Étienne, 'A qui mieux mieux, ou le mariage chez les Baoulé', *Cah. ORSTOM*, viii, 2 (1971), pp.165–86.

[34] Delafosse, 'Coutumes indigènes', pp.138–9.

[35] Ibid. 144–5.

[36] ANRCI, X-34-8, Capt. Maillard to Chef de bataillon, 14 Apr. 1903; and P. and M. Étienne, 'A qui mieux mieux', pp.172–3.

[37] ANRCI, X-34-8, Capt. Maillard to Chef de bataillon, 14 Apr. 1903; Delafosse indicated that this kind of marriage was celebrated with elaborate festivities: see Delafosse, 'Coutumes indigènes', p.102.

[38] J.-P. Chauveau, 'Note sur la morphologie', pp. 6, 27–8, 32, 37.

[39] Hierarchies existed as a result of the uneven outcome of the competition for manpower. One chief's gain was to some extent another's loss, and both gains and losses would influence a chief's future manœuvrability by determining which strategies remained open to him. In this sense, Baule society, while lacking state structures, was not a 'segmentary' society, for a chief's position was not guaranteed by virtue of an acknowledged position in a balanced genealogical structure. Instead, dominance had to be achieved, and it could be lost. At any one point hierarchies existed, giving rise to very powerful individual chiefs, but the heirs of these chiefs had to reconstitute their own following. For a discussion of the inadequacies of a segmentary model with respect to the Baule see J.-P. Chauveau, 'Société baoulé précoloniale et modèle segmentaire: le cas de la région de Kokumbo (Baoulé-sud)', paper presented to the Second Akan Conference, Kumasi, Ghana, 1975.

[40] Delafosse, *Essai de manuel*, p.207.

[41] Ibid. 202; J. de Bettignies, 'Toumodi: Étude monographique d'un centre semi-urbain' (Abidjan, 1965), p.4.

[42] ANRCI, X-30-11, C. Pobéguin, 'Rapport annexe à la carte de la rivière Bandama depuis Lahou jusqu'au Baoulé', Thiassalé, 1 Oct. 1893; and ibid., 'Rapport sur la région du Baoulé – Nov. 1893', Thiassalé, 25 Nov. 1893, Ph. and M. A. de Salverte-Marnier, 'Les étapes du peuplement', *ÉRB*, i, pp.27, 32; Bamba, 'Tiassalé et le commerce précolonial', pp.60, 94–5, 96, 108, 115–16, 120–3; and Memel-Foté, 'Stratégie de la politique des marchés'.

[43] See for example the sizeable trade figures cited in ANRCI, III-8-80, Capt. Gouriau, 'Rapport sur les établissements Français de la Côte d'Or', 23 Oct. 1862.

[44] C. Bour, Commandant particulier des établissements de la Côte d'Or, to SEMC [Apr. 1885], cited in M. Augé, *Théorie des pouvoirs et idéologie: Étude de cas en Côte d'Ivoire* (Paris, 1976), p.25.

[45] Ph. and M. A. de Salverte-Marnier, 'Les Étapes du peuplement', *ÉRB*, i, p.32; Bamba, 'Tiassalé et le commerce précolonial', pp.60, 94–5, 96, 108, 115–16, 120–3; ANSOM, Service Géographique des Colonies, Carte de la Côte d'Ivoire de

Grand Lahou à Toumodi, dressée par C. Pobéguin, 1/150 000, sheets 1–4, [*c.* 1895].

⁴⁶ Ph. and M. A. de Salverte-Marnier, 'Les étapes du peuplement', p.32.

⁴⁷ The Ahua–Niamwé trading chain was strengthened from Niamwé northwards by the commerce joining it from Dabou by way of the overland route from Dabou and the Adioukrou peoples. Similarly the commercial position of Tiassalé was reinforced by the contribution of commerce from Petit Lahou by way of Yokoboué, Goboua, Diagboua, and Giguisou among the Dida peoples to the west of the Bandama. See Map 7.

⁴⁸ de Bettignies, 'Toumodi', p.4.

⁴⁹ This is the interpretation presented by J.–P. Chauveau, as well. See Chauveau, 'Note sur l'histoire du peuplement', pp.9–11.

⁵⁰ ANRCI, XIII-45-3/36, Bastard, 'Histoire', in 'Registre de Correspondance'. See also ANRCI, XIV-34-4, Bastard, 'Rapport mensuel, Dec. 1901', Jan. 1902.

⁵¹ ANRCI, XIV-4-3, Marchand to Binger, 6 Sept. 1893; and Bamba, 'Tiassalé et le commerce précolonial', pp.94–5.

NOTES TO CHAPTER II

¹ The best account of French presence on the Ivory Coast during the precolonial period is Atger's *La France en Côte d'Ivoire*; see also B. Schnapper, *La Politique et le commerce français dans le golfe de Guinée, 1838–1871* (Paris, 1961), for a study of early French policy along the entire coast.

² For a brief account of the events leading to Régis's departure, see Atger, *La France en Côte d'Ivoire*, pp.44–58. A more detailed presentation of Régis's coastal activities is included in P. Masson, *Marseille et la colonisation française* (Marseille, 1906), Chs. 11 and 12.

³ Verdier published an autobiographical account of his activities on the Ivory Coast in which he complains about governmental indifference to French commerce in general and his ventures in particular. See A. Verdier, *Trente-cinq années de lutte aux colonies (Côte Occidentale d'Afrique)* (Paris, 1896). For an assessment of Verdier's activities, see Atger, *La France en Côte d'Ivoire*, pp.69–70, 79–96, 137–9, 171–3.

⁴ [Governor Louis Faidherbe] 'Rapport à l'Empereur', July 1863, ANSOM, Afrique, VI, 11a, cited in J. D. Hargreaves, *France and West Africa: An Anthology of Historical Documents* (London, 1969), pp.146–7; see also Hargreaves, *Prelude to the Partition of West Africa* (London, 1963), p.127.

⁵ The negotiations with Britain are usefully summarized in Hargreaves, *Prelude*, pp.125–8, 136–44, 151–65, 174–95. Verdier, still active on the coast, understandably opposed the idea of the exchange, in a pamphlet entitled *Échange de territoire colonial. Côte Occidentale d'Afrique. Gambie cédée à la France par l'Angleterre, Grand Bassam et Assinie cédés à l'Angleterre par la France* (La Rochelle, 1876).

⁶ C. W. Newbury, 'The Tariff Factor in Anglo-French West African Partition', in *France and Britain in Africa: Imperial Rivalry and Colonial Rule*, ed. P. Gifford and W. R. Louis (New Haven, 1971), p.241. See also Kanya-Forstner, *The Conquest*, pp.155–6, upon which the following summary is based.

⁷ Recent scholarship has emphasized that an appreciation of the role of the Sudan in French official thinking is essential for an adequate assessment of the French participation in the 'scramble' for African territory. See particularly, C. W. Newbury and A. S. Kanya-Forstner, 'French Policy and the Origins of the Scramble for West Africa', *JAH*, x (1969), pp.253–76. The seemingly fickle attitude of the French toward the Ivory Coast becomes intelligible when the primary importance of the Sudan is kept clearly in mind. Changes in policy

toward the coastal possessions frequently resulted from new strategies designed to secure the French position in the Sudan.

[8] For accounts of Gallieni's thinking and France's 'New African Policy', see Kanya-Fostner, *The Conquest*, Ch. 6; J. D. Hargreaves, *Prelude*, pp.340-1; and Hargreaves, *West Africa Partitioned*, vol. i, *The Loaded Pause, 1885-1889* (London, 1974), pp.85-92.

[9] L. G. Binger, *Du Niger au Golfe de Guinée par le pays de Kong et le Mossi, 1887-1889* (Paris, 1892), 2 vols. For accounts of Treich-Laplène's missions see Verdier, *Trente-cinq années*, Ch. 8; Mouëzy, *Assinie*, pp.128-53, 155-64; and Atger, *La France en Côte d'Ivoire*, pp.117-26. Original letters from Treich-Laplène were reprinted in issues of the *Revue de Géographie* during 1895 and 1896, but he died before being able to compile an autobiography of any sort. Some controversy developed in later years over the relative importance of the respective contributions of Binger and Treich-Laplène in the creation of the Ivory Coast colony. It now seems clear that although Treich-Laplène's expeditions created the essential basis for the colony locally, Binger's influence in Parisian colonial circles was crucial in committing the Ministry to a more forward policy on the coast. See J. Chaput, 'Treich-Laplène et la naissance de la Côte d'Ivoire française', *Revue d'histoire des colonies*, xxxvi (1949), pp.87-153.

[10] Treich-Laplène to Brétignère, 5 Apr. 1887, reprinted in Mouëzy, *Assinie*, p.131.

[11] Étienne's instructions to Treich-Laplène are included along with an indication of the new colonial statutes in ANSOM, Côte d'Ivoire, I, 2a; and ANRS, 5-G-38 no. 8.

[12] For a description of the coastal trading practices see Atger, *La France en Côte d'Ivoire*, pp.46-58; and Schnapper, *La Politique et le commerce*, pp.111-41.

[13] A. Hopkins, *An Economic History of West Africa*, p.133.

[14] Atger, *La France en Côte d'Ivoire*, p.155.

[15] Figure given in ibid. 139. For a detailed account of the installation of the customs posts at Half Jack and Grand Lahou see ibid. 139-44, upon which the following paragraphs are based.

[16] Treich-Laplène to Bayol, cited in Atger, *La France en Côte d'Ivoire*, p.141.

[17] The trade ounce in use on the coast at the time was equivalent to 32 grams, and one gram of gold was equivalent to approximately 3.00 f. at the time. See Delafosse, 'Les Coutumes indigènes', p.126. Hence, 750 ounces of gold represented a value of 71,000 f.

[18] See Atger, *La France en Côte d'Ivoire*, pp.142-44.

[19] Atger, *La France en Côte d'Ivoire*, pp.147, 174.

[20] The following summary of the Bandama explorations is reconstructed from the personal accounts of several participants including an interview with Émile Paluzot in *Le Soleil*, 17 June 1891 and his 'Rapport' dated 11 Apr. 1891, both conserved in ANSOM, Côte d'Ivoire, IV, 3b; also, ANSOM, Côte d'Ivoire, III, 1, P. Brisard, 'Exploration sur le Haut-Lahou', 10 May 1891; and an article, 'La mission Armand', *BCAF*, ix (Sept. 1891), pp.12-14. A summary of the explorations based on copies of dispatches sent from the Resident to the Lieut.-Gov. of Guinée is included in Atger, *La France en Côte d'Ivoire*, pp.174-5.

[21] The names given for the chief of Tiassalé in the early documents include: 'Aken' (ANRCI, VII-3-5, Désaille to Balley, 4 Aug. 1891); 'Eky' (ANRCI, XIV-4-3, de Beeckman to Bricard, 13 Apr. 1893); and 'Ki Kouassi' (ANRCI, XIV-4-3, de Beeckman to Pobéguin, 26 June 1893). The accounts make it clear that the same person is involved in each case. Atger renders the spelling 'Alhan' (*La France en Côte d'Ivoire*, p.174), but this seems to be unknown as a local proper name. Recent studies indicate that the full name of the chief whom the French referred to most frequently as 'Eky' was 'Etien Komenan'. See Sebamed, 'Traditions

orales et Histoire-V. Tiassalé et le pénétration coloniale', *Fraternité Matin* (Abidjan), 17–18 Nov. 1973.

[22] Paluzot interview, *Le Soleil*, 17 June 1891; ANSOM, Côte d'Ivoire, IV, 3b, Paluzot, 'Rapport', 11 Apr. 1891.

[23] ANRCI, VII-3-5, Désaille to Ballay, 15 June 1891.

[24] ANRCI, VII-3-5, Désaille to Ballay, 15 June 1891; ANSOM, Côte d'Ivoire, V, 1b, Lt. Staup, 'Rapport . . . sur l'expédition de la Côte d'Or', 20 May 1891.

[25] ANRCI, XII-3-8, 'Rapport sur la situation politique pendant le période du 10 février au 10 mars 1892'.

[26] ANRCI, VII-3-8, Binger to Undersecretary of Colonies, Kong, 3 June 1892; ibid., Binger to Resident, 3 June 1892; and VII-3-11, Binger to Resident, 25 July 1892. See also Marcel Monnier, *France Noire (Côte d'Ivoire et Soudan) – Mission Binger* (Paris, 1894), pp.249–54.

[27] ANRCI, VII-3-7, Bricard to Secretary General of Guinée, 17 Dec. 1892.

[28] For the correspondence referring to the prolonged negotiations see ANRCI, VII-3-5, Albéca to Désaille, 9 July 1891; ibid., Désaille to Ballay, 4 Aug. 1891; ibid., Désaille to Ballay, 30 Aug. 1891; ibid., Désaille to Ballay, 24 Nov. 1891; ANRCI, VII-3-7, Bricard to Secretary General of Guinée, 17 Dec. 1892; ANRCI, VII-3-8, 'Rapport sur la situation politique pendant la période du 10 fév. au 10 mars 1892'; ANRCI, VII-3-7, Bricard to Secretary General of Guinée, 23 Jan. 1893; and Bricard to de Beeckman, 20 Jan. 1893 cited in ANRCI, XIV-4-3, de Beeckman to Bricard, 19 June 1893. The treaty itself is found in ANSOM, Traités, V, 549, Tiassalé, 29 Dec. 1892.

[29] ANSOM, Missions, 8, Lieut. Marchand, 'Afrique Française: Bassin du Niger – Ligne Fluviale Transnigerienne', 1 Dec. 1892. Marchand was subsequently promoted to the grade of captain before undertaking his Ivory Coast explorations.

[30] For details of these campaigns see Kanya-Forstner, *The Conquest*, pp.176–95.

[31] For Étienne's affirmations in late 1891 see *JO, Déb. Parl.*, séance du 1 déc. 1891, pp.2379–81; séance du 3 déc. 1891, pp.2400–2. For Jamais's similar statements see *JO, Déb. Parl.*, séance du 7 avril 1892, pp.491–512; séance du 11 avril 1892, pp.541–80. For Delcassé's statement see *JO, Déb. Parl.*, séance du 6 fév. 1893, pp.385–7. For a discussion of parliamentary opposition to the costly Sudanese expansion from 1891 to early 1893, see Kanya-Forstner, *The Conquest*, pp.203–5.

[32] ANSOM, Missions, 8: 'Afrique française: Bassin du Niger. Ligne fluviale transnigerienne', Lt. Marchand, 1 Dec. 1892. Marchand's proposal was summarized in a lengthy article on his explorations after his return in *BCAF*, x (Oct. 1895), pp.290–8.

[33] Once he reached the coast Binger considered his mission accomplished, and he did not devote the same kind of detailed attention to trade there as he had to the regions of the interior. Concerning the Baule hinterland Binger merely quoted word for word large passages of the observations of Fleuriot de Langle published in the 1870s. See Binger, *Du Niger au Golfe*, pp.334–6.

[34] Décrêt du 10 Mars 1893, *BOCI*, (1893), p.40; Binger was named governor on 20 March.

[35] For Binger's cautious approach see ANRCI, XIV-4-3: Binger to de Beeckman, 6 June 1893; in this letter to the interim Governor of the Ivory Coast, Binger refers to an appeal (which he addressed to Marchand by the same post) to Marchand not to proceed beyond Tiassalé. For Marchand's refusal to abandon his own mission in favour of proposed coastal explorations with Binger see ANRCI, XIV-4-3, Marchand to Binger, 6 Sept. 1893.

[36] ANRCI, XIV-4-3, de Beeckman to Bricard, 13 Apr. 1893.

[37] Arrête local, 4 Apr. 1893, *BOCI*, (1893), p.66.

[38] *BCAF*, vii (July 1893), pp.4–5.

[39] *BCAF*, ix (Sept. 1893), p.5.

[40] See Ch. I, pp.27–32 for a discussion of the trade rivalries on the lower Bandama.

[41] ANRCI, VII-3-5, Désaille to Ballay, 30 Aug. 1891.

[42] ANSOM, Côte d'Ivoire, IV, 3b, Capitaine Marchand, 'Rapport de l'Expédition de Tiassalé', 20 June 1893. Important details concerning the decline of Ahua are also given by de Beeckman in a letter which accompanied Marchand's report to the Ministry. He summarized the situation succinctly: 'Ahua est un joli village qui a beaucoup souffert du voisinage de Thiassalé.' ANSOM, Côte d'Ivoire, IV, 3b, 'Rapport no. 239, de Beeckman au Sous-secrétariat d'État des Colonies', 14 June 1893.

[43] *BCAF*, ix (Sept. 1893), p.5. It is probable that Marchand learned of Baule antagonism towards Tiassalé' while in Ahuem. Those Baule whose trade traditionally followed the Nzianou–Niamwé–Ahu–Ahuem route to the coast probably resented the rise of the Tiassalé confederation from 1891 onwards, and they may well have wished to see Tiassalé subdued. But Marchand's assumption that *all* Baule groups wanted Tiassalé eliminated and would welcome French intervention only serves as an index of how little he understood about local trade and politics. See Ch. I, pp.27–32 above for a discussion of pre-colonial trading rivalries.

[44] J.-L. Triaud, 'Un cas de passage collectif à l'Islam en Basse Côte d'Ivoire: le village d'Ahua au début du siècle', *Cahiers d'Études Africaines*, 54, xvi, 2 (1974), p.320.

[45] For a detailed account of the capture of Tiassalé see ANSOM, Côte d'Ivoire, IV, 3b, Capitaine Marchand, 'Rapport de l'Expédition de Tiassalé', 20 June 1893; and ibid., 'Rapport no. 239, de Beeckman au Sous-secrétariat d'État des Colonies', 14 June 1893.

[46] *BCAF*, xi (Nov. 1893), p.5.

[47] *BCAF*, iv (Apr. 1894), p.24.

[48] For a sympathetic portrait of Fatou Aka and a description of his role in the events leading to the capture of Tiassalé see ANRCI, XIV-4-3, Marchand to Binger, 6 Sept. 1893.

[49] 'Mes efforts dans le Baoulé au point de vue commercial n'avaient pas d'autre bût que d'ouvrir la route centrale de la contrée au commerce de Lahou . . .': Letter of Marchand first printed in *La Politique Coloniale* and reprinted in *BCAF*, iv (Apr. 1894), p.24.

[50] ANRCI, XIV-4-3, Marchand to Binger, 6 Sept. 1893; see also *BCAF*, xi (Nov. 1893), p.5.

[51] ANRCI, XIV-4-3, Marchand to Binger, 6 Sept. 1893. Emphasis in original.

[52] ANRCI, XIV-4-3, Marchand to Binger, 6 Sept. 1893.

[53] ANRCI, XIV-4-3, de Beeckman to Pobéguin, 26 June 1893.

[54] For examples of this kind of praise-song see the portrait of Marchand offered by one of his most ardent admirers, Col. Baratier, in his *Épopées africaines* (Paris, 1912), p.41. Also, M. Dutrèb, *Marchand* (Paris, 1922), Ch. III. Even recent scholarship tends to accept this assessment of Marchand's first mission uncritically. See, for example, M. Michel, *La Mission Marchand (1895–1899)* (Paris, 1972), introductory sections.

[55] Excerpts of some of Marchand's letters were printed in the colonial press. See, for example, letter from Singrobo, 13 Sept. 1893, printed in *La Politique Coloniale*, 11 Nov. 1893, reprinted as well in *BCAF*, xii (Dec. 1893), p.13; and another letter is excerpted in *BCAF*, iv (Apr. 1894), pp.24–5. In addition the letters contained in the Paris and Abidjan archives will be cited below with respect to specific details.

[56] ANRCI, XIV-4-3, Marchand to Binger, 6 Sept. 1893.

[57] Ibid. Emphasis in original.

[58] Ibid. Emphasis in original.

[59] ANSOM, Missions, 8, Marchand to M.C., Rapport, 20 Dec. 1894, p.3.

[60] ANSOM, Missions, 8, Pobéguin to Gov., 7 Oct. 1893. For biographical information on Akafou see: ANRCI, XIV-34-4, Bastard, Rapport mensuel, Dec. 1901; ANRCI, XIII-45-3/36, Registre de Correspondance, 'Histoire'; and ANRCI, XIV-4-7bis, 'Tribu N'Gbans', 1 May 1904.

[61] ANSOM, Missions, 8, Marchand to M.C., Report, 20 Dec. 1894, p.3.

[62] ANRCI, XIV-4-3, Marchand to Binger, 6 Sept. 1893.

[63] We have been unable to find any letters written by Marchand between 13 Sept., when he was in Singrobo, and 23 Dec. 1893, when he had completed much of his northern Baule reconnaissances. What we know about his travels between these dates is only by way of what is mentioned in his final report, ANSOM, Missions, 8, Marchand to M.C., Report, 20 Dec. 1894.

[64] Ibid. 4.

[65] For details of these campaigns see Kanya-Forstner, *The Conquest*, pp.191–2.

[66] *BCAF*, iv (Apr. 1894), p.24.

[67] ANSOM, Missions, 8 Marchand to M.C., Report, 20 Dec. 1894, p.6.

[68] ANSOM, Missions, 8, Marchand to M.C., Report, 20 Dec. 1894, p.6.

[69] Marchand's description of his reception in Kong is contained in a postscript of 18 May 1894 added to an earlier letter of 14 Apr. 1894. ANRCI, XIV-4-3, Marchand to Binger, 14 Apr. 1894 [with postscript of 18 May 1894]. Copies of these communications are found in ANSOM, Afrique, III, 23c.

[70] ANRCI, XIV-4-3, Marchand to Binger, 23 Dec. 1893; copy in ANSOM, Missions, 8.

[71] ANRCI, XIV-4-3, Marchand to Binger, 14 Apr. 1894.

[72] For details of Ferguson's treaty-making expeditions in the Bouna area see K. Arhin (ed.), *The Papers of George Ekem Ferguson: A Fanti Official of the Government of the Gold Coast, 1890–1897* (Cambridge, 1974), Chs. VII and VIII. Moskowitz was too exhausted to continue further exploration, and he died in Kong. For a summary of French explorations in the Niger Bend area see 'Les missions françaises dans la boucle du Niger', *BCAF*, iv (Apr. 1897), pp.108 ff.

[73] ANSOM, Missions, 8, Marchand to M.C., Report, 20 Dec. 1894.

[74] ANSOM, Missions, 8, Marchand to M.C., Report, 20 Dec. 1894.

[75] ANRCI, XIV-4-3, Marchand to Binger, 23 Dec. 1893.

[76] ANSOM, Afrique, III, 23c, Marchand to Gov., 16 July 1894. Binger had departed once again on leave and was absent when this message reached Grand Bassam. Secretary General Coustier none the less cabled the gist of Marchand's urgent appeals to the Ministry in Paris and indicated confidence in the choice of the Baule route, ANSOM, Missions, 8, Telegram, Coustier to Ministry, 31 July 1894.

[77] Kanya-Forstner, *The Conquest*, p.230.

[78] Ibid. 230–1 for a discussion of the circumstances leading to the decision to send Monteil to Kong.

[79] ANSOM, Afrique, III, 19b, Delcassé to Monteil, 14 Sept. 1894; ibid., same to same, 22 Sept. 1894; ibid., same to same, Instructions, 24 Sept. 1894.

[80] See Col. Baratier, *Épopées africaines*, p.41.

[81] ANSOM, Afrique, III, 19a, Monteil to Delcassé, 27 Sept. 1894.

[82] Lt. Col. P. -L. Monteil, *La Colonne de Kong. Une page d'histoire militaire coloniale* (Paris, n.d. [1902]), p.13.

[83] ANSOM, Afrique, III, 23c, Nebout to Gov. (Kodiokofikro), 9 Sept. 1894.

[84] ANSOM, Afrique, III, 23b, Caudrelier to Monteil, 15 Oct. 1894; and ibid., Desperles to Caudrelier, 31 Oct. 1894.

[85] ANSOM, Afrique, III, 23b, Desperles to Caudrelier, 31 Oct. 1894.

[86] ANSOM, Afrique, III, 23b, Desperles to Caudrelier, 8 Nov. 1894.

[87] Ibid.

[88] The figure of 80 per cent (4/5) is included in a full-length report in ANSOM,

Afrique, III, 19a, Monteil to Minister, 'Rapport au sujet des opérations dans le Baoulé', 19 Jan. 1895. The order to suspend supply caravans was issued by Monteil on 10 Nov. 1894.

[89] For a discussion of the French relations with the Abouré, including Monteil's occupation of Akaplass see M. Samson, 'Les Abouré de Bonoua (Côte d'Ivoire): Introduction à l'ethno-histoire' (Paris, Thèse de 3e cycle, Paris V, 1971).

[90] ANSOM, Afrique, III, 23c, Nebout to Monteil, 3 Nov. 1894.

[91] ANSOM, Afrique, III, 23b, Caudrelier to Monteil, 13 Nov. 1894.

[92] For Desperles's justification of his behaviour see ANSOM, Afrique III, 23c, Desperles to Caudrelier, 25 Nov. 1894; for Nebout's warning and criticism of Desperles, see ibid., Nebout to Caudrelier, 25 Nov. 1894.

[93] ANSOM, Afrique III, 23c, Nebout to Caudrelier, 9 Nov. 1894.

[94] ANSOM, Afrique III, 23c, Nebout to Governor, 9 Sept. 1894.

[95] ANSOM, Afrique III, 23b, Desperles to Caudrelier, 8 Nov. 1894.

[96] ANSOM, Afrique III, 23c, Nebout to Caudrelier, n.d. [? Nov. 1894].

[97] ANSOM, Afrique III, 23b, Caudrelier to Monteil, 'Au sujet de la route de Dabou à Thiassalé', 15 Oct. 1894.

[98] Ibid., Desperles to Caudrelier, 17 Nov. 1894; and Ch. Monteil to Caudrelier, 27 Nov. 1894; ANSOM, Afrique, III, 23c, Desperles to Caudrelier, 25 Nov. 1894; and ibid., Nebout to Caudrelier, 25 Nov. 1894.

[99] Except where otherwise mentioned the following summary of events is based upon ANSOM, Afrique, III, 19a, Monteil, Report, 19 Jan. 1895.

[100] Col. Baratier, who at the time was serving as a lieutenant in the Monteil expedition, was the officer to go to Lt. Haye's rescue and offers a lively description of the incident in *Épopées africaines*, pp.70–3.

[101] Three separate accounts report this incident: ANSOM, Afrique, III, 23c, Nebout to Monteil, 22 Jan. 1895; and ibid., Marchand to Monteil, 22 Jan. 1895. A third account is contained in D.P., Delafosse to Ch. Monteil, 25 Jan. 1895. I am most grateful to Mme Louise Delafosse for having been granted the opportunity to consult this and other letters of her father.

[102] ANSOM, Afrique, III, 19a, Monteil Report, 19 Jan. 1895.

[103] ANSOM, Afrique, III, 19a, Nebout to Monteil, 6 Jan. 1895. Nebout sent a copy of this letter attesting to potential revolt in the northern reaches of Baule country to the Minister.

[104] ANSOM, Afrique, III, 19a, Telegram, Monteil to M.C., 4 Jan. 1895.

[105] ANSOM, Télégrammes Afrique, Soudan, 1895, Départ no. 4, Chautemps to Grodet 9 Feb. 1895; ANSOM, Afrique, III, 19b, Chautemps to Monteil, 18 Feb. 1895. In a subsequent telegram three days later Chautemps gave a longer explanation, mentioning the advice he had received from Binger's telegram of 14 Feb. 1895. See ANSOM, Afrique, III, 19c, Chautemps to Monteil, 21 Feb. 1895.

[106] On 18 February Monteil was just approaching Kodiokofikro from Toumodi, and he was still well within Baule territory.

[107] Unaware of the new instructions Monteil continued northwards and suffered heavy losses at the hands of Samory's troops above Satama. It is perhaps because of these engagements that the popular belief has arisen that Monteil was ordered to retreat because of his defeat by Samory's *sofas*. This was not, however, the reason for Monteil's recall.

NOTES TO CHAPTER III

[1] Col. Baratier, *Épopées africaines*, p.103.

[2] Ibid. 74–104.

³ ANRM, 1-N-167, 'Ordre général no. 119, Bulletin des Opérations de la Colonne du 16 fév. au 29 mars 1895', Monteil, 30 Mar. 1895.

⁴ ANSOM, Afrique III, 23c, Marchand to Monteil, 22 Jan. 1895.

⁵ ANRM, 1-N-167, 'Ordre général no. 119', Monteil, 30 Mar. 1895.

⁶ ANSOM, Afrique III, 23c, Nebout to Monteil, 4 Mar. 1895; ANSOM, Côte d'Ivoire, V, 2b, Binger to Minister, 13 Apr. 1895. The incident was subsequently reported as well in *BCAF*, v (May 1895), p.148.

⁷ Lt.-Col. P. L. Monteil, *La Colonne de Kong*, p.37.

⁸ ANSOM, Afrique III, 23c, Lt. Bourrat to Monteil, 2 Mar. 1895.

⁹ ANRCI, X-31-23, Dr Lasnet, 'Mission du Baoulé', 12 Aug. 1896.

¹⁰ Monteil, *La Colonne de Kong*, p.37; ANSOM, Afrique III, 19a, Monteil to Ministry, 30 Mar. 1895.

¹¹ ANSOM, Afrique III, 19a, Monteil to Ministry, 30 Mar. 1895, reports that during the operations from 22 Feb. to 29 Mar., 16 troops were killed and 63 wounded.

¹² French participants in this campaign appear to have been too preoccupied with the retreat to have given much precise attention to how many refugees accompanied the departing expedition. In any case, it is perhaps understandable why they would not have given much detail on this point in their contemporary accounts, for the whole affair was profoundly embarrassing to report to the Ministry. One observer who visited the northern Baule area in June 1896, however, reported that nearly 10,000 refugees began the trek southwards with the French in March 1895 but that a year later only 5,000–6,000 remained who had not been absorbed by the Baule or died from sickness. See ANRCI, X-31-23, Lasnet, 'Mission du Baoulé', 12 Aug. 1896.

¹³ ANSOM, Côte d'Ivoire, v, 2b, Binger to Minister, 13 Apr. 1895; Governor Binger stated openly that 'ce retour avait tout l'air d'une déroute'.

¹⁴ ANSOM, Afrique III, 19a, Monteil Report, 19 Jan. 1895; ANSOM, Afrique III 23c, Marchand to Monteil, 8 Feb. 1895.

¹⁵ ANSOM, Afrique III, 23c, Nebout to Monteil, 30 Mar. 1895.

¹⁶ ANRCI, VIII-1-3/86, Monteil to Nebout, 30 Mar. 1895.

¹⁷ ANSOM, Afrique III, 19a, Monteil to M.M.C., 6 Nov. 1894.

¹⁸ See ibid.; and Monteil, *La Colonne de Kong*, p.11.

¹⁹ ANSOM, Afrique III, 23c, Nebout to Monteil, 11 Feb. 1895.

²⁰ ANRCI, VIII-1-3/86, Monteil to Binger, 30 Mar. 1895. To clear his own name of any possible scandal Monteil demanded that a full-scale parliamentary inquiry be conducted into the organization and conduct of the Kong expedition. A parliamentary commission eventually met to consider the affair and after gathering information from a number of quarters submitted a report which never really fulfilled his expectations as a public acknowledgement of his own military valour. See ANSOM, Afrique III, 21d, 'Rapport présenté au nom de la Commission d'enquête sur les opérations de la colonne de Kong', Paul Disère, Prés. de la Commission, 14 Mar. 1896.

²¹ *BCAF*, ii (Feb. 1895), p.42.

²² *La Politique Coloniale*, 26 Feb. 1895; *Le Temps*, 4 Mar. 1895; *Le Figaro*, 5 Mar. 1895.

²³ *JO, Déb. Parl.*, séance du 1 mar. 1895, pp.641 ff.

²⁴ For a summary of the pro-militarist reaction to the Monteil recall see Kanya-Forstner, *The Conquest*, pp.233–4.

²⁵ ANSOM, Afrique III, 19a, Monteil to M.M.C., ? Jan. 1895 (received by the Ministry on 16 Jan. 1895).

²⁶ ANSOM, Soudan I 6a, Delcassé to Grodet, Instructions, 4 Dec. 1893. Cited in Robinson and Gallagher, 'The Partition', p.620.

²⁷ *La Patrie*, 10 Feb., 11 Feb., 25 Feb. 1894; this version was repeated in avowedly military publications: see *Le Journal des Débats*, 11 Feb. 1894; *Le Jour*,

12 Feb., 26 Feb. 1894; and *Le Matin*, 25 Feb. 1894; all cited in Kanya-Forstner, *The Conquest*, p.223 n.4.

[28] For a discussion of the Goudam massacre see Kanya-Forstner, *The Conquest*, pp.222-3.

[29] Speech of Chautemps, *JO, Déb. Parl.*, séance du 1 mar. 1895, pp.641-2.

[30] Ibid. Large excerpts from this parliamentary debate subsequently appeared in *BCAF*, iv (Apr. 1895), pp.112-13.

[31] *JO, Déb. Parl.*, séance du 4 mar. 1895, pp.693-9.

[32] For details of Grodet's role in the Monteil affair see Kanya-Forstner, *The Conquest*, pp.231-2.

[33] It is questionable whether the intervention of these troops would have made an appreciable difference in the fate of the Monteil expedition. If they had been deployed correctly they could have helped Monteil in his encounters with Samory's *sofas*, but Monteil's major problem – and the reason for his recall – was the Baule revolt to the south, and it is doubtful whether Dargélos's forces could have quelled this disturbance. Instead their additional presence may well have precipitated a full-scale Baule uprising, something which, as subsequent years proved, would require far more than a limited intervention to terminate. The fact that a realistic assessment of Sudanese assistance to Monteil was never made during the entire debate over his recall illustrates the extent to which Baule resistance was underestimated at the time. Even in histories written years after the event, when greater reflection was possible, Grodet's role and not the Baule revolt is singled out as the decisive factor in the expedition's failure. 'La raison profonde de l'échec de la marche sur Kong . . . était dans l'inaction du Soudan français pendant la période 1894-1895' (A. Terrier and Ch. Mourey, *L'Œuvre de la Troisième République en Afrique Occidentale. L'Expansion française et la formation territoriale* (Paris, 1910), p.277).

[34] For details of Grodet's dismissal see Kanya-Forstner, *The Conquest*, pp.233-4.

[35] For the reasoning behind the creation of the Government General see ANSOM, A.O.F., VII, Chautemps, 'Rapport au Président de la République', along with the decree dated 16 June 1895. For a thorough discussion of the origins and development of the Gov. Gen. see C. W. Newbury, 'The Formation of the Government General in French West Africa', *JAH*, i, 1 (1960), pp.111-28.

[36] The council was actually created by a decree of 26 Jan. 1895; see *BOCI* (1895), p.224; but the decree was not put into effect until 29 Mar. 1895.

[37] See, however, the appeals from the commercial houses to Gov. Binger in ANSOM Afrique III, 23c, particularly that of M. Moreau, L'Inspecteur de la Compagnie Verdier, 22 Dec. 1894.

[38] See Binger's Arrêté of 10 Mar. 1895, ANSOM, Afrique III, 23c; this measure cancelled the previous regulation of the arms trade instituted by Lemarie on 23 Sept. 1894; for a presentation of the British proposal to control the arms traffic in 1895 see Chautemps to Binger, 7 Mar. 1895, reprinted in Angoulvant, *La Pacification de la Côte d'Ivoire* (Paris, 1916), pp.212-13. Angoulvant criticized Binger's armaments policy in later years and portrayed it as an open capitulation to shortsighted commercial interests; see ibid. 198, 213. For the opinion of one outspoken merchant at the time of the Monteil expedition see A. Verdier, *Questions coloniales. Côte d'Ivoire: La Verité à propos de l'expédition Monteil* (Paris, 1895).

[39] ANSOM, Côte d'Ivoire, V, 2b, Binger to M.M.C., 13 Apr. 1895.

[40] ANSOM, Côte d'Ivoire, V, 2b, Binger to M.M.C., 13 Apr. 1895.

[41] Ch. Monteil went on to a distinguished career as an administrator in the Sudan; see 'Charles Monteil, 1871-1949', *NA-IFAN*, 44 (Oct. 1949). For Nebout's earlier background see *BCAF*, v (May 1892), p.3; Nebout accumulated

years of experience in the Ivory Coast and beame an adviser to successive governors, particularly with respect to Baule resistance.

⁴² Delafosse, 'Les Agni (Paï-Pi-Bri)', *L'anthropologie*, iv (1893), pp.402–45.

⁴³ Delafosse's publications on the Baule provide the foundation for any serious inquiry into Baule pre-colonial history and social organization, and although his theories do not always prove convincing, especially in the light of more recent research, the information contained in his works is of exceptional importance to the historian. In addition to his published material, his private correspondence with his family contains rich detail about early conditions among the Baule. Mme L. Delafosse is in the process of completing a much-needed biography of her father with the aid of this correspondence, and when it appears, anthropologists and historians alike will be able more fully to appreciate his significant contribution to the period.

⁴⁴ In July there remained a total of over 300 troops divided between Kodiokofikro, Toumodi, Tiassalé, and Grand Lahou, with European officers in each locality and an artillery platoon stationed at Kodiokofikro. Cf. ANRM, 1-N-173, Commandant Caudrelier, 'L'Organisation des services militaires de la Côte d'Ivoire', 18 July 1895.

⁴⁵ M. Delafosse, *L'Afrique Occidentale Française*, vol. iv of *Histoire des Colonies françaises et de l'expansion de la France dans le monde* (Paris, 1931), p.279; F.-J. Clozel, *Dix ans à la Côte d'Ivoire* (Paris, 1906), p. 273.

⁴⁶ ANSOM, Côte d'Ivoire, IV, 5c (4) Pineau, 'Notes sur la Côte d'Ivoire', 23 Sept. 1895.

⁴⁷ Ibid.

⁴⁸ ANSOM, Côte d'Ivoire, IV, 5c (3) Pineau, 'Projet d'occupation du Baoulé, 23 Sept. 1895.

⁴⁹ For details concerning the final departures see ANRM, 1-N-167, 'Troupes de la Côte d'Ivoire, Dates de l'Évacuation des postes du Baoulé', 6 Sept. 1896.

⁵⁰ For statistics over the 1890 to 1900 period see 'La situation actuelle et l'avenir de la Côte d'Ivoire', *BCAF-RCD*, iv (Apr. 1899), pp.57–64; 'La situation générale de la colonie en 1899', *BCAF*, vi (June 1900), p.249; and 'La situation générale de la Côte d'Ivoire en 1898', *BCAF-RCD*, iv (Apr. 1900), pp.71–2. Import and export figures for 1890-8 are also printed in P. Mille, *La Côte d'Ivoire* (Paris, 1900), p.30. The year 1896 represents a turning-point in the import-export value ratio. From 1890 to 1895 the value of exports consistently exceeded the value of imports, but in 1896 this was reversed, and for the next fifteen years the value of imports exceeded the value of the colony's exports.

⁵¹ 'Note sur les objets de pacotille propres aux échanges à la Côte d'Or', *Revue Maritime et Coloniale*, vol. 23 (1868), pp.999–1006; Lt. Bonneau, *La Côte d'Ivoire: Notice historique et géographique* (Paris, n.d. [1898]) p.86.

⁵² No serious study has been made of the coastal manilla currency in the Ivory Coast, but research in this realm would be instructive. Basically, it seems that as more and more of the currency was introduced it became devalued over time; this devaluation was aggravated as the price of palm oil declined. Nevertheless, the peoples of the lagoons area continued to use it, and large quantities of it remained in circulation well into the twentieth century despite French attempts to ban its use. Oddly enough its usage never penetrated inland. Like the Sudanese cowrie it was excluded from Baule and Anyi territories, where gold remained the dominant medium of exchange.

⁵³ Lt. Bonneau, *La Côte d'Ivoire*, p.87.

⁵⁴ Ibid. As yet no examination has been made of the effects of alcoholism on the Ivory Coast population during this period, but a study on the neighbouring Gold Coast suggests that the impact of the alcohol trade was far from negligible. R. Dummett, 'The Social Impact of the European Liquor Trade on the Akan of Ghana (Gold Coast and Asante), 1875-1910', *Journal of Interdisciplinary History*, v, 1 (Summer 1974), pp.69–101.

[55] Hopkins, *An Economic History*, p.133.

[56] Ibid. 134.

[57] ANSOM, Côte d'Ivoire, XIII, 1a, cited in Atger, *La France en Côte d'Ivoire*, pp.168-9.

[58] The collection of the palm produce came to be dominated progressively by European firms which employed African personnel as buying agents. Their increased control over marketing reduced competition between buyers and allowed the European houses to pass along the price cuts in European markets directly to the producers.

[59] In 1891 Ahua, on the lower Bandama, was reported to be the centre where agents from the coastal groups met those from the Baule area to purchase slaves from them. Prices for slaves varied. Women were more highly valued than men presumably because they were potential producers of more producers. One observer recorded that a boy slave could be bought for 150-200 f., whereas a girl would cost 240 f. Cf. Lt. Armand, 'La Mission Armand', *BCAF*, ix (Sept. 1891), p.13. A second member of the Armand mission reported that in the Tiassalé area he had met a slave who had cost only 48 f., but he affirmed that a good slave would be priced as high as four ounces of gold, or 385 to 400 f. See ANSOM, Côte d'Ivoire, III, 1, P. Grisard, 'Exploration sur le Haut-Lahou', 10 Mai 1891; also printed in *BCAF*, viii (Aug. 1891), pp.6-8.

[60] Armand, 'La Mission Armand', *BCAF*, ix (Sept. 1891), p.13.

[61] John Hargreaves has indicated that 'the effects on the peoples of the Ivory Coast of the "fifty years of political and commercial hesitations" after 1843 were not profound; they were confined to coastal peoples who jealously guarded their privileges as brokers or agents for a slowly changing and expanding foreign trade' (*West Africa*, p.92). The evidence concerning the interior trade in slave labour suggests that Hargreaves' assertion deserves re-examination.

[62] For the development of new export commodities see K. Dickson, *A Historical Geography of Ghana* (Cambridge, 1971), Ch. 7; R. Dummett, 'The Rubber Trade on the Gold Coast and Asante in the Nineteenth Century: African Innovation and Market Responsiveness', *JAH*, xii, 1 (1971), pp.79-101; K. Arhin 'The Ashanti Rubber Trade with the Gold Coast in the 1890s', *Africa*, xlii, 1 (1972), pp.32-41; and E. Reynolds, *Trade and Economic Change on the Gold Coast, 1807-1874* (London, 1974), pp.174-81.

[63] Prices are those paid in Freetown, cited in Y. Person, *Samori. Une révolution Dyula*, vol. ii (Dakar, 1970), p.1001 n.131. Although prices varied slightly up and down the West African coast, the increases reflected in these figures were characteristic of those on the Ivory Coast.

[64] For the Ghana timber trade see Dickson, *A Historical Geography*, pp.177-8.

[65] *BCAF-RCD*, iv (Apr. 1899), p.63; *BCAF-RCD*, iv (Apr. 1901), p.72; and *BCAF*, x (Oct. 1906), p.279.

[66] The name was used in jest by the French merchants who found it amusing that Africans educated in England should add 'Esq.' to their names.

[67] As yet no study exists of the rise of this merchant middle class on the Ivory Coast. The French referred to them by any of several names interchangeably: Nzima or Zemma, Apollonien, or simply Fanti. Although some groups known by these labels were clearly composed of peoples of heterogeneous origins, the French tended to regard them as a separate ethnic group whose specialized role had become that of the merchant middleman. R. A. Horovitz, 'Trade between Sanwi and her Neighbors: 1843-1893', paper presented at the Akan Conference, Bondoukou (Jan. 1974), pp.11-15; Atger, *La France en Côte d'Ivoire*, pp.88-92.

[68] Atger, *La France en Côte d'Ivoire*, pp.33, 35.

[69] In 1852 Hyacinthe Hecquard reported that Muslim traders from the north whom he called 'Bambara' were present at Grand Bassam and that they acted as

the intermediaries between the coast and the interior. Cf. Hecquard, 'Rapport sur un voyage d'exploration dans l'intérieur de l'Afrique', *Revue Coloniale* série II, 8 (Mar. 1851), p.195. Forty years later, however, in 1891, Armand observed: 'Les Apolloniens sont les commerçants par excellence de ces régions ... A la côte, ils achètent une pacotille et vont très loin dans la foret ... Ce sont, en somme, les seuls commerçants qui relient les différentes zones entre elles. En dehors de la côte ils avaient, jusque dans ces derniers temps, le monopole de la "traite"'. Armand, 'La Mission Armand', p.13.

[70] Ibid.

[71] Atger, *La France en Côte d'Ivoire*, pp.88–94.

[72] Considering the rise of anti-Semitic sentiment at the time in France, this appellation, given by Dr Lasnet, was perhaps more revealing than he realized. Cf. ANRCI, X-31-23, Dr Lasnet, 'Mission du Baoulé', 12 Aug. 1896.

[73] Bonneau, *La Côte d'Ivoire*, p.94.

[74] Bonneau, *La Côte d'Ivoire*, p.95.

[75] F.-J. Clozel, *Dix ans*, pp.65–72; Delafosse, *L'Afrique Occidentale Française*, pp.281–2.

[76] For a discussion of the French intentions and a frank presentation of the policy to eliminate the Apollonien, see ANSOM, Côte d'Ivoire, I, 15d, Bonhoure, 'Rapport sur la situation agricole de la Côte d'Ivoire', 23 Oct. 1898.

[77] Public Order no. 86, Sept. 1893, Freetown, Sierra Leone; cited in M. Crowder, *West Africa under Colonial Rule* (London – Evanston, Ill., 1968), p.88 n.60.

[78] Person, *Samori*, ii, p.935.

[79] W. Tordoff, 'A Note on the Relations between Samory and King Prempeh I of Ashanti', *Ghana Notes and Queries*, 3 (1961).

[80] Person, *Samori*, ii, p.935.

[81] There is only one documented case of an agent of Samory travelling through Baule country to buy arms directly at Tiassalé. Cf. ANRM, 1-N-167, Capt. Gallé, 'Rapport Confidentiel sur le trafique de la poudre et des armes', 30 Oct. 1895 (Tiassalé). This direct purchase at Tiassalé occurs after the capture of Bondoukou, and it is possible that at this point Samory could bargain with the Baule from a position of greater strength. He may have obtained permission to buy arms directly at Tiassalé by threatening to circumvent the Baule entirely in favour of newly opened routes through the Anyi kingdoms if they did not comply with his request.

[82] ANSOM, Côte d'Ivoire, IV, 5c (5) Gallé to Pineau, 24 Aug. 1895.

[83] Ibid.; ANSOM, Côte d'Ivoire, IV, 5c (4) Pineau, 'Notes sur la Côte d'Ivoire', 23 Sept. 1895.

[84] ANSOM, Côte d'Ivoire, I, 15a, Inspecteur Général des Colonies to M.C., 5 Dec. 1895.

[85] Concerning the exchanges between Samory and the Baule, see Person, *Samori*, ii, pp.928, 932, 935, 937–8, 943.

[86] S. Touré, 'Note sur une communauté nigérienne ancienne en Côte d'Ivoire: Marabadiassa' (presented by J. Rouch and E. Bernus) *NA-IFAN*, 84 (Oct. 1959); Ph. and M. A. de Salverte-Marnier, 'Les étapes du peuplement', pp.49–52; ANRCI, XIV-34-1, Capt. Lambert to Commandant Supérieur des Troupes de l'A.O.F., July 1901.

[87] Baratier, *Épopées africaines*, p.96; ANRCI, X-31-23, Dr Lasnet, 'Mission du Baoulé', 12 Aug. 1896. Samory is often portrayed as a ruthless despot for having pursued a 'scorched earth' policy during his final retreat in 1898, but in doing so he seems only to have elaborated a tactic that Monteil first employed against him in 1895. For an analysis of Samory's movements after 1895 see Person, *Samori*, iii, pp.1685–2011. Details can be found in an interesting first-hand account by Amadou Kouroubari, a resident of Dabakala whose version entitled 'Histoire de

d'Imam Samory', was transcribed by Delafosse in Kodiokofikro in 1899–1900. Delafosse first published a Dyula language transcription as part of his *Essai de manuel pratique de la langue mandé ou mandingue* (Paris, 1901), pp.143–93, and large portions of the account were later translated into French and published in *BIFAN*, xxi, No. 3–4 (1959), pp.544–71. Further information on the post-1895 period is available in 'Les Anglais et Samory', *BCAF*, vii (July 1897), pp.252–3; 'A Propos de Samory', *BCAF*, i (Jan. 1898), pp.4–8; H. Labouret, 'Les bandes de Samory dans la Haute Côte d'Ivoire', *BCAF-RCD*, viii (Aug. 1925), pp.341–55; and D. Traoré, 'Les relations de Samory et l'état de Kong', *NA-IFAN*, 47 (1950), pp.96–7.

[88] ANRCI, X-31-23, Dr Lasnet, 'Mission du Baoulé', 12 Aug. 1896.

[89] In 1894 Nebout reported: 'Les hommes libres sont rares, la population est surtout composée d'esclaves . . .' (ANSOM, Afrique III, 23c (m-8) Nebout to Caudrelier, n.d. [? Nov. 1894]).

[90] Recent surveys suggest that 20–30 per cent of the present-day northern Baule population are of direct slave origin. Cf. Ph. and M. A. de Salverte–Marnier, 'Les étapes du peuplement', p.52.

[91] ANRCI, X-43-434, Nebout, 'Réponse au questionnaire sur les renseigne-ments économiques', 2 Jan. 1898.

[92] Dr Lasnet reported that two or three barrels of powder would be used at virtually all celebrations within each village; cf. ANRCI, X-31-23, Dr Lasnet, 'Mission du Baoulé', 12 Aug. 1896.

[93] 'Le commerce des armes ne joua pourtant plus qu'un faible rôle à cette époque, et ces esclaves serviront surtout à acheter des vivres . . .', Person, *Samori*, ii, p.938.

[94] Jean-Pierre Chauveau reports that at Kokumbo, although slaves came from other sources as well, the memory of the influx of slaves during the Samory period was so dominant that it eclipsed the significance of other slave sources. When Chauveau collected traditions in Kokumbo in the early 1970s, people still remembered Katiakofikro in the north as the major slave market, and some individuals who had been sold into captivity during Samory's period were still alive. For a discussion of captive labour at Kokumbo see J.-P. Chauveau, 'Les cadres socio-historiques de la production dans la région de Kokumbo . . . La période précoloniale', *Sciences Humaines* (Abidjan) v, 7 (1972), p.23.

[95] Ibid. 14, 50–1.

[96] ANSOM, Côte d'Ivoire, V, 3, Ch. Pobéguin, 'Renseignements sur un voyage à Sikasué, Kokombo et Sahua', 25 Oct. 1896; large extracts from this report were printed subsequently in F.-J. Clozel, 'La situation économique de la Côte d'Ivoire', *BCAF*, iv (Apr. 1899), pp.67–8.

[97] Armand, 'La Mission Armand', p.13.

[98] ANRCI, X-43-434, Nebout, Réponse au questionnaire sur les renseigne-ments économiques', 2 Jan. 1898.

[99] For the importance of manpower considerations in the traditional Baule context see Ch. I, pp.20–1 above.

[100] For a discussion of *atonvle* marriage alliances see Ch. I, pp.23–4 above.

[101] Present-day baule associate the decline of *atonvle* marriage with the beginning of the colonial period, and often attribute its disappearance to an explicit French policy to forbid such marriages. Recent anthropological research demonstrates, however, that this form of marriage disappeared prior to the establishment of effective colonial administration among the Baule, and its demise coincided with the influx of slaves from Samory between 1894 and 1898. Cf. P. and M. Étienne, ' "A qui mieux mieux" ou le mariage chez les Baoulé', *Cah. ORSTOM*, viii, 2 (1971), pp.172–3.

[102] ANSOM, Afrique III, 23b, Doudoux to Monteil, 23 Dec. 1894; ANSOM,

Afrique III, 23C, Nebout to Marchand, 16 Jan. 1895, including a note added to the same letter by Marchand and sent from Marchand to Monteil on 17 Jan. 1895.
[103] ANSOM, Afrique III, 19a, Nebout to Monteil, 6 Jan. 1895; ANSOM, Afrique III, 23c, Marchand to Monteil, 11 Jan. 1895.
[104] ANSOM, Afrique III, 19a, Nebout to Monteil, 6 Jan. 1895.
[105] ANRS, 2-G-7 (26), Bonhoure to M.C., 26 Mar. 1897.
[106] Ibid.
[107] ANRM, 1-N-167, Capt. Gernard [Note on villages] 9 June 1895; ANRCI, X-31-23, Dr Lasnet, 'Mission du Baoulé', 12 Aug. 1896.
[108] ANRS, 2-G-7 (26), Bonhoure to M.C., 26 Mar. 1897.
[109] See above, Ch. II, pp.54–5.
[110] P. Étienne, 'Les Baoulé face aux rapports de salariat', Cah. ORSTOM, VIII, 3 (1971), pp.235–42.
[111] Id., 'Les Baoulé face au fait urbain' (texte provisoire) (Abidjan, ORSTOM, n.d.) p.3; see also id., 'Le fait villageois baoulé', (Abidjan, 1971).
[112] ANSOM, Missions, 8, Marchand to M.C., 23 Dec. 1893.
[113] ANSOM, Gabon I, 6b, no. 178, Fleuriot de Langle to M.M.C., 29 Oct. 1886; and Armand, 'La Mission Armand', p.13.
[114] A. Nebout, 'Note sur le Baoulé', A Travers le Monde (Supplément du Tour du Monde) (1900), p.394.
[115] 'La situation dans le Baoulé', BCAF, ix (Sept. 1896), pp.273–4.
[116] Nebout, 'Note sur le Baoulé', p.394.
[117] ANRCI, X-31-23, Dr Lasnet, 'Mission du Baoulé', 12 Aug. 1896.
[118] ANSOM, A.O.F., I, 1, Chautemps to Chaudié, Instructions, 11 Oct. 1895.
[119] ANRCI, X-31-23, Dr Lasnet, 'Mission du Baoulé', 12 Aug. 1896. Maurice Delafosse was virtually the only administrator at the time who dissented from this prevailing assessment of the Baule. See particularly his article: 'Les Libériens et les Baoulé', Les Milieux et les Races (avril–mai 1901), pp.1–37. Here he compares the Baule quite favourably with the Liberians of Monrovia whose contact with the Whites was thought by some to indicate their greater degree of civilization. It is perhaps significant that Delafosse thought he recognized 'traces' of white influence among the Baule. See his 'Sur des traces probables de civilisation égyptienne et d'hommes de race blanche à la Côte d'Ivoire', L'anthropologie, xi (1900), pp.431–51, 543–68, 677–90.

NOTES TO CHAPTER IV

[1] For an admirable summary of the complex diplomatic exchanges and military missions that determined who controlled the Niger Bend, see Kanya-Forstner, The Conquest, pp.240–9.
[2] The best study of Samory's relations with the French in the final years and months leading to his capture is in Person, Samori, iii, pp.1767–73, 1818–45, 1886–2014. In May and June 1896 a mission including Dr Lasnet, Lt. Simonet and Delafosse under the direction of Capt. Braulot travelled to Bouaké and tried unsuccessfully to meet with Samory through emissaries. Again in Oct. 1897 A. Le Filliatre and Nebout met with Samory in Dabakala, but no agreement could be reached. Information is available on the Braulot mission of 1896 in 'Rupture de négociations avec Samory', BCAF, viii (Aug. 1896), p.241; for the Nebout mission see: 'La mission Nebout chez Samory', Revue Française de l'Étranger et des Colonies, 23 (1898), pp.15–21; and 'A propos de Samory', BCAF, i (Jan. 1898), pp.4–8. The following summary of Samory's last months is largely based upon Terrier and Mourey, L'Expansion française et la formation territoriale, pp.330–8.
[3] ANSOM, Côte d Ivoire, I, 15d, Mouttet to M.C., 25 June 1898.
[4] ANRS, 2-G-1, no. 27, Administrateur du Baoulé to Gov., 8 July 1898.

[5] Ibid.

[6] Marchand recognized Baule hostility after the poisoning attempt on his life in late Dec. 1893 at Bouaké. Cf. ANSOM, Missions, 8, Marchand Report 20 Dec. 1894, p.6; other evidence of northern Baule opposition to the French emerged as the Monteil expedition tried to enter Baule territory, see letter of Mandao Ousman, cited in ANSOM, Afrique III, 19a, Monteil Report, 19 Jan. 1895.

[7] ANRM, 1-N-167, anon., 'Renseignements demandés par la lettre no. 59', Toumodi, 9 June 1895; see also ANSOM, Côte d'Ivoire, IV, 5c (2), Pineau to Gov. of Ivory Coast, 'Situation militaire du Baoulé', 27 Aug. 1895.

[8] ANSOM, Côte d'Ivoire, I, 15a, Inspecteur Gén. des Colonies to M.C., 5 Dec. 1895.

[9] D.P., Delafosse to parents, 23 May 1896.

[10] Nebout reported, 'J'ai été très bien reçu dans le village où le nouveau chef, moins craintif que son frère, paraît vouloir s'appuyer sur nous contre les Sofas . . .', Nebout, 'Extrait d'un Rapport', 16 Feb. 1897 included in ANSOM, Côte d'Ivoire, I, 15c, Gov. to M.C., 26 Mar. 1897.

[11] ANRS, 2-G-1, no. 26, Mouttet to M.C. no. 360, 25 May 1897; and Sec. Gen. Bonhoure to Gov., 30 July 1897.

[12] Pineau had earlier advocated the military occupation of Baule territory in the wake of the Monteil expedition; see p.257 n.48 above. The post which he ordered to be established at Bouaké in June 1898 thus fulfilled his long-awaited desire to bring the Baule under military control.

[13] ANSOM, Côte d'Ivoire, I, 15d, Bonhoure to M.C., 12 Sept. 1898.

[14] For a general assessment of the functioning of the 'villages de liberté' see D. Bouche, *Les Villages de liberté en Afrique noire française, 1887–1910* (Paris, 1968).

[15] ANRCI, X-34-8, Lt. Clervaux, 'Monographie historique du Secteur de Bouaké', Nov. 1904.

[16] Ibid.; see also ANRM, 1-N-173, Benoît, 'Ordre de mouvement', 14 Nov. 1898.

[17] Capt. Benoît initially mentioned only 'un acte de brigandage', but it is clear from subsequent documents that what really worried him was 'les actes continuels de brigandage commis par les Baoulés sur les refugiés . . .'. cf. ANRM, 1-N-173, Benoît to Chef de bataillon, Commandant la Région Niger–Volta, no. 98, 21 Dec. 1898; and ibid., Benoît, 'Rapport . . . sur le mouvement insurrectionel du Baoulé Nord . . .', 5 Jan. 1899.

[18] The incidents leading up to the attack and the attack itself are described in ANRM, 1-N-173, Benoît to Chef de bataillon, 21 Dec. 1898; ibid., same to same, 25 Dec. 1898; ibid., Benoît, 'Rapport sur le mouvement insurrectionel du Baoulé Nord', 5 Jan. 1899; ANRCI, X-34-8, Lt. Clervaux, 'Monographie historique du Secteur de Bouaké', Nov. 1904; and 'Les opérations militaires au Baoulé', *Alm. Ann. Mars.* (1902), pp.22–7.

[19] Benoît to Nebout, 17 Jan. 1899 cited in ANSOM, Côte d'Ivoire, I, 15e, Penel to M.C., 25 Feb. 1899.

[20] Ibid.

[21] Nebout to Gov. [n.d.], cited in ANSOM, Côte d'Ivoire, I, 15e, Penel to M.C., 25 Jan. 1899.

[22] Telegram, Nebout to Gov. [n.d.], cited in ANRS, 2-G-1, no. 28, Gov. to M.C., 25 Jan. 1899.

[23] ANSOM, Côte d'Ivoire, I, 15e, Penel to M.C., 25 Feb. 1899.

[24] Ibid.

[25] Ibid.

[26] ANSOM, Soudan I, 9d, Guillan to Gov. Gen., 'Instructions pour Trentinian', Nov. 1898.

[27] Cited in Kanya-Forstner, *The Conquest*, p.257.

²⁸ For a succinct discussion of the specific steps leading to the end of military rule see ibid. 255–62; and Newbury, 'The Formation fo the Government General', p.120; for the new decree see 'Décret réorganisant le Gouv. Gén. de l'A.O.F.', 17 Oct. 1899 *BOCI* (1899), p.812.

²⁹ ANRCI, X-34-8, Lt. Clervaux, 'Monographie historique du Secteur de Bouaké', Nov. 1904.

³⁰ ANRCI, X-34-8, Lt. Clervaux 'Monographie', Nov. 1904; see also ANRCI, X-38-9 Capt. Le Magnen, 'Notice sur le Baoulé' [n.d., *c.*Mar. 1900]; and 'Les opérations militaires au Baoulé', *Alm. Ann. Mars.* (1902), p.22.

³¹ For a thorough discussion of Baule practices involving exchanges and debt collection see Delafosse, 'Les coutumes des Agnis du Baoulé', in F.-J. Clozel and R. Villamur, eds., *Coutumes indigènes de la Côte d'Ivoire* (Paris, 1902), pp.124–33.

³² ANRCI, X-34-8, Lt. Clervaux, 'Monographie', Nov. 1904; ANRS, 5-G-41, p.92, 'Fiche de renseignements concernant le nommé Kouassi Biri Chef de la tribu Baoulé des "Faafoué"'; ANRM, 1-N-173, Lt. Telletier, 'Rapport politique du mois d'avril' (Apr. 1899); ibid., 'Rapport politique du mois de mai', 2 June 1899; ibid., Jobard, 'Rapport sur la politique générale du Territoire de Kong', 1 July 1899.

³³ D.P., Delafosse to parents, 18 Apr. 1899.

³⁴ ANRCI, XIV-34-9, Delafosse to Gov., Rapport mensuel, 1 July 1899. Excerpts of this report were subsequently published by the Gov. in *JOCI* (1 Aug. 1899), pp.3–5.

³⁵ Ibid.

³⁶ See Ch. Wondji, 'La fièvre jaune à Grand Bassam (1899–1903)', *La Revue Française d'Histoire d'Outre-Mer*, no. 215 (2e trimestre 1972).

³⁷ D.P., Delafosse to parents, 19 July 1899; ANRCI, X-30-11, Delafosse to Commandant du territoire de Kong, no. 149, 28 Sept. 1899.

³⁸ ANSOM, Côte d'Ivoire, IV, 4c, Gov. p.i. to M.C., 30 Sept. 1899.

³⁹ D.P., Delafosse to parents, 20 Aug. 1899; ANRCI, X-30-11, Delafosse to Gov., no. 111, 20 Aug. 1899.

⁴⁰ ANSOM, Côte d'Ivoire, IV, 4c, Delafosse to Gov., 1 Sept. 1899.

⁴¹ In 1895 Delafosse was among the first to give a detailed account of these incidents, and he insisted at the time upon the dangerous character of Kouadio Okou; see D.P., Delafosse to Ch. Monteil, 25 Jan. 1899; and p.64 above.

⁴² ANSOM, Côte d'Ivoire, IV, 4c, Delafosse to Gov., 1 Sept. 1899.

⁴³ According to the instructions given to Sissé Diallo and cited in Mme L. Delafosse's biography of her father (Ch. V, pp.18–19, in manuscript), Sergeant Diallo was to burn only Kouadio Okou's compound; in a seemingly contradictory note written two days later, however, Delafosse indicated 'j'ai fait brûler *entièrement* son village dans la journée du 6 courant . . .' [emphasis is mine], cf. ANRCI, X-30-11, Delafosse to Chef de poste de Tiassalé, 8 Sept. 1899. It is possible that Sergeant Diallo proved over-zealous in the execution of his orders. If this was the case, it appears that Delafosse took full responsibility for the excesses of his subordinate.

⁴⁴ L. Delafosse, MS Biography (Ch. V, p.19), cites document concerning meeting on morning of 8 Sept. 1899.

⁴⁵ ANRCI, X-30-11, Delafosse to Chef du poste de Tiassalé, 8 Sept. 1899; ibid., Delafosse to Seigland, 8 Sept. 1899.

⁴⁶ ANRCI, X-30-11, Delafosse to Gov., 15 Sept. 1899; D.P., Delafosse to parents, 14 Oct. 1899.

⁴⁷ L. Delafosse, MS Biography, Ch. V, p.16.

⁴⁸ D.P., Capt. Le Magnen to Delafosse, 20, 23, 24, 25, 26 Sept. 1899; ibid., Delafosse to parents, 14 Oct. 1899; ANRCI, X-30-11, Delafosse to Gov., 15 Sept. 1899; ibid., Delafosse to Gov. 27 Sept. 1899; ibid., Delafosse to Commandant du

territoire de Kong, no. 149, 28 Sept. 1899; ibid., telegram, Delafosse to Gov., no. 159, 10 Oct. 1899; ibid., XIV-34-9, Chef du poste de Tiassalé to Gov., 2 Oct. 1899.

[49] The Gov. Gen. at the time was Émile Chaudié, and he had built up a reputation of opposition to military ventures.

[50] Capt. Le Magnen initially instructed Delafosse to request two companies from the Sudan, see D.P., Capt. Le Magnen to Delafosse, 26 Sept. 1899; Delafosse duly requested the two Sudanese companies the following day, cf. ANRCI, X-30-X-30-11, Delafosse to Gov. no. 147, 27 Sept. 1899. In fact, acting Gov. Capest had already requested authorization for reinforcements from the M.C., but he had been informed that Senegal could spare only 50 troops, cf. ANRCI, XIV-34-9, Gov. to Chef du poste de Tiassalé, 27 Sept. 1899. Hence, even before Capest had received Delafosse's request, the answer from the M.C. was 'no'.

[51] Capest apparently employed the term 'reprisal' to describe the burning of the post in a letter to Delafosse on 7 Oct. 1899. In the letter Capest seems to have chided Delafosse for acting imprudently. It has not been possible to locate Capest's letter, but its contents can be surmised from the stiff response to it which Delafosse wrote in self-defence, cf. ANRCI, X-30-11, Delafosse to Gov., 18 Oct. 1899.

[52] Comments in margin of ANRCI, XIV-34-9, Delafosse to Gov., 15 Sept. 1899; these comments were most probably pencilled by M. Capest before Roberdeau's arrival, but since this document is a copy of the original to be found in ANRCI, X-30-11, it is possible that Roberdeau himself made these observations while informing himself of the situation.

[53] ANSOM, Côte d'Ivoire, IV, 4c, Roberdeau to Delafosse, 10 Nov. 1899.

[54] D.P., Delafosse to parents, 16 Feb. 1900.

[55] L. Delafosse, MS Biography, Ch. V, p.26.

[56] Writing to his parents Delafosse revealed his desire to leave Baule country as soon as possible and added 'les Baoulé ont baissé fortement dans mon estime . . .' cf. D.P., Delafosse to parents, 14 Oct. 1899.

[57] ANRCI, X-30-11, Delafosse to Gov., 27 Sept. 1899; for an indication of the Ngban villages that gradually lent their support to Kouadio Okou see ANRCI, XIV-4-7bis, Lt. Goeau, 'Renseignements sur l'ouest d'Ouossou, tribu des N'Gbans – Groupe de Moronou', 26 May 1901.

[58] ANRCI, X-30-11, Delafosse to Gov., 18 Oct. 1899.

[59] Ibid.

[60] D.P., Delafosse to parents, 3 Nov. 1899.

[61] ANRCI, X-30-11, Delafosse to Commandant du territoire de Kong, no. 149, 28 Sept. 1899; ibid., Delafosse to Gov., 10 Oct. 1899; ibid., same to same 18 Oct. 1899; ibid., Nebout to Sec. Gen., 18 Jan. 1900; ANSOM, Côte d'Ivoire IV, 4c, Gov. p.i. to M.C., 30 Sept. 1899; ANRCI, XIV-34-9, Nebout to Gov., 19 Jan. 1900.

For details of the earlier conflicts between Kouadio Okou and Akafou see ANRCI, XIV-34-4, Rapport mensuel, July 1901, Ouossou, 31 July 1901; ANRCI, X-34-8, Bastard, 'Rapport d'ensemble sur le secteur d'Ouossou', 19 Sept. 1901; ANRCI, XIV-34-4, Rapport mensuel, Dec. 1901, 1 Jan. 1902; ANRCI, XIII-45-3/ 36, 'Registre de Correspondance' – Histoire [of Ouossou area] July 1902.

[62] ANSOM, Côte d'Ivoire, IV, 4c, Nebout to M.C. 28 Sept. 1899; Nebout, still in France on leave, addressed these comments to the Ministry in Paris.

[63] For a list of villages which supported Delafosse see ANRCI, X-30-11, Delafosse to Gov., 15 Sept. 1899; for comments on the use of Baule allies in fighting Kouadio Okou see D.P., Delafosse to parents, 20 Nov. 1899 and 19 Dec. 1899. Delafosse was also careful to mention his use of Baule partisans in his only published comments on the Lomo revolt, see L'Afrique Occidentale, pp.283–5.

[64] ANSOM, Côte d'Ivoire, IV, 4c, Roberdeau to Gov. Gen., 16 Dec. 1899;

ANRCI, X-30-11, Nebout to Sec. Gen., 18 Jan. 1900; ANRCI, XIV-34-9, Nebout to Gov. 19 Jan. 1900; D.P., Delafosse to parents, 19 Dec. 1899.

[65] ANRS, 5-G-43, P. 90, Nebout to Gov., 25 Dec. and 30 Dec. 1899, cited in Gov. to Gov. Gen., 22 Jan. 1900.

[66] See p.119 above. Décret réorganisant le Gouvernment Général de l'A.O.F., 17 Oct. 1899, BOCI (1899), p.812.

[67] ANRCI, XIV-34-9, Gov. to Gov. Gen., 22 Jan. 1900.

[68] Gov. Gen. to Gov., 4 Feb. 1900, cited in ANSOM, Côte d'Ivoire, IV, 4c, Gov. to M.C., 23 Feb. 1900.

[69] ANRS, 5-G-43, P. 92, Combes to Gov. Gen. 2 Feb. 1900; ANRS, 5-G-43, P. 86, 'Programme des opérations militaires ayant en vue la liaison entre la Haute et la Basse Côte d'Ivoire', [signed by] Combes and É. Chaudié, 2 Feb. 1900.

[70] Ibid., P. 95, Gov. to Gov. Gen., 20 Feb. 1900.

[71] ANRS, 5-G-43, P. 95, Gov. to Gov. Gen., 20 Feb. 1900; see also ANSOM, Côte d'Ivoire, IV, 4c, Gov. to M.C., 23 Feb. 1900.

[72] ANRS, 5-G-43, P. 110, Gov. to M.C.; ibid., P. 111 [agreement signed by Nebout and Commandant Donnat, 6 Apr. 1900].

[73] ANRS, 5-G-43, P. 3, Combes to Gov. Gen., 28 Apr. 1900; ibid., P. 12, Chef de Bataillon Desbuisson to L'Inspecteur Général des Colonies, 21 June 1900; ibid., P. 15, 'Extrait du rapport mensuel du Commandant Donnat, no. 320' [copy], 20 July 1900.

[74] Arrête local No. 205 supprimant à titre temporaire l'administration civile dans le Baoulé, 27 July 1900, BOCI (1900), p.213.

[75] The Minister of Colonies, Albert Decrais, had justified the reforms of October 1899 on the basis of reducing the cost of military administration. See Kanya-Forstner, The Conquest, p.262.

[76] ANRCI, XIII-26-12/77, Registre des Ordres: 'Instructions au sujet de l'Administration et de la comptabilité dans le cercle du Baoulé', Capt. Sagols, 7 Aug. 1900.

[77] ANRCI, X-31-23, Nebout to Gov., 2 July 1900.

[78] ANRCI, X-31-23, Donnat, 'Instructions pour le Capt. Goeching, Commandant la circonscription du Baoulé-Sud', 10 Aug. 1900.

[79] ANRCI, XIV-34-3, Lt. Buck to Chef de bataillon, 17 May 1900.

[80] ANRCI, X-34-10, Donnat to Capt. Le Magnen, Ordre no. 129, 8 May 1900, cited in 'Rapport sur les opérations exécutées le 20 mai dans la tribu des N'Gbans du Nord', Capt. Le Magnen, 23 May 1900. This report includes information on the links between Akafou and the northern Ngban; see also ANRCI, X-31-23, 'Rapport militaire et politique . . . pour le mois de mai 1900', Donnat.

[81] ANRCI, X-31-23, 'Rapport politique donnant la situation pendant le mois d'octobre et jusqu'au 14 novembre', Aymerich, 14 Nov. 1900.

[82] ANRCI, X-31-23, Nebout to Gov., 2 Aug. 1900.

[83] ANRCI, X-34-10, 'Rapport sur les opérations exécutées le 20 mai dans la tribu des N'Gbans du Nord', Capt. Le Magnen, 23 May 1900.

[84] For an indication of early French policy relating to the liberation of slaves among the Baule see ANRCI, X-31-23, 'Rapport militaire et politique . . . pour le mois de mai 1900', Donnat.

[85] ANRCI, X-34-8, Lt. Clervaux, 'Monographie', Nov. 1904.

[86] ANRCI, X-31-23, Aymerich to Gov., 30 Nov. 1900.

[87] ANRCI, X-31-23, 'Rapport politique donnant la situation pendant le mois d'octobre et jusqu'au 14 novembre', Aymerich, 14 Nov. 1900; ibid., Aymerich to Gov., 30 Nov. 1900; see also P. Sirven, L'Évolution des villages suburbains de Bouaké: contribution à l'étude géographique du phénomène de croissance d'une ville africaine (Bordeaux, 1972), pp.26–30.

[88] ANRCI, X-31-23, 'Rapport mensuel du 15 novembre au 15 décembre', Aymerich; ibid., 'Rapport politique et militaire, janvier 1901', 12 Jan. 1901.

[89] ANRCI, X-31-23, Aymerich to Gov., 30 Nov. 1900; ibid., 'Rapport politique donnant la situation pendant le mois d'octobre et jusqu'au 14 novembre', Aymerich, 14 Nov. 1900; ibid., 'Rapport mensuel du 15 nov. au 15 déc.', Aymerich.

[90] ANRCI, X-31-23, 'Rapport politique donnant la situation pendant le mois d'oct. et jusqu'au 14 nov.', Aymerich, 14 Nov. 1900.

[91] ANRCI, X-34-8, Lt. Clervaux, 'Monographie historique du Secteur de Bouaké', Nov. 1904; and 'Les opérations militaires au Baoulé', *Alm. Ann. Mars.* (1902), p.24.

[92] ANRS, 5-G-43, P. 42, telegram No. 691, Aymerich to Gov., 21 Nov. 1900; ANSOM, Côte d'Ivoire, IV, 4c, telegram, Aymerich to Gov., 27 Nov. 1900.

[93] Noël Victor Ballay was named Gov. Gen. on 1 Nov. 1900. ANSOM, Côte d'Ivoire, IV, 4c, telegram, Gov. Gen. to M.C., 22 Dec. 1900; ibid., 26 Dec. 1900.

[94] ANRCI, X-34-8, Lt. Clervaux, 'Monographie', Nov. 1904; and 'Les opérations militaires au Baoulé', *Alm. Ann. Mars.*, (1902), p.25.

[95] ANRCI, X-31-23, 'Rapport politique et militaire, janvier 1901', 12 Jan. 1901; Sirven, *L'Évolution des villages*, pp.28-9.

[96] ANRCI, x-31-23, 'Rapport politique et militaire, janvier 1901', 12 Jan. 1901.

[97] ANRCL, X-31-23, 'Rapport politique et militaire, janvier 1901', 12 Jan.

[98] During Jan. fifty 'gardes frontière' arrived in Bouaké from Kong and another fifty from Touba. In addition fifty 'tirailleurs' were dispatched to reinforce the 17th and 18th Senegalese companies within the colony. See 'Les opérations militaires au Baoulé', *Alm. Ann. Mars.* (1902), p.25.

[99] ANRS, 5-G-43, P. 134, Aymerich to Combes, 10 Feb. 1901.

[100] ANRCI, X-31-23, Aymerich to Gov., 26 Feb. 1901.

[101] ANRCI, XIII-11-123/1010, 'Renseignements politiques – 7 mars palabre avec Kouri' [1901]; ANRCI, X-31-23, 'Rapport politique et militaire', Aymerich 10 Mar. 1901. Conditions imposed included requisitions for forty sheep, 100 porters, five village chiefs to act as scouts in future military campaigns, the necessary labour for the construction of garrison buildings and road maintenance, and the annual payment of taxes.

[102] Early colonial accounts that discuss the pre-colonial organization of Baule mining practices at Kokumbo include Dr Lasnet, 'Contribution à la géographie médicale. Mission du Baoulé', *Annales d'hygiène et de médecine coloniale*, i (1898), p.319; ANRCI, XIV-29-4, Sergeant Leonetti, 'Visites aux mines de Kpolessou', 27 May 1903; and H. Hubert, 'Coutumes indigènes en matière d'exploitation de gîtes aurifères en Afrique Occidentale', *Annuaires et Mémoires du Comité d'Études Historiques et Scientifiques de l'A.O.F.* (1917), pp.226-34. Extracts from these reports are reproduced and discussed in J.-P. Chauveau, 'Les cadres socio-historiques de la production dans la région de Kokumbo', pp.89-111.

[103] ANSOM, Côte d'Ivoire, V, 3, Pobéguin to Gov., 25 Oct. 1896; ANSOM, Côte d'Ivoire, III, 4d, 'Mission J. Eysséric à la Côte d'Ivoire: Rapport', J. Eysséric, 16 May 1897.

[104] ANRCI, X-31-23, 'Rapport militaire et politique pour le mois de mai 1900', Donnat.

[105] ANRCI, XIII-26-12/77, Registre des Ordres, 'Ordre particulier no. 47', Combes, 16 May 1901. Combes's orders to Colonna d'Istria were relayed by the latter to the subordinate officers attacking Kokumbo. 'La caractéristique des opérations à entreprendre sera l'offensive la plus vigoureuse: faire le plus de mal possible à l'ennemi en le bousculant partout, où on le rencontre, en le frappant jusque dans ses biens. L'ennemi sera recherché avec ardeur . . . La déstruction totale d'un groupe ennemi serait un résultat gros de conséquences heureuses'. ANRCI, XIII-26-12/77, 'Ordre de Mouvement no. 177', Colonna d'Istria, 30 May 1901.

[106] ANRCI, X-31-23, 'Rapport sur les opérations militaires chez les N'Gbans', Aymerich [June 1901]; ibid., 'Rapport du Chef de bat.', Colonna d'Istria, 16 July 1901.

[107] Groups that assisted the French included the Saafoué, traditional rivals of the Faafoué, and groups of Aïtu and Nzipri, cf. ANRCI, X-31-23, 'Rapport du Chef de Bat.', Colonna d'Istria, 16 July 1901.

[108] Ibid.; 'Les opérations militaires au Baoulé', *Alm. Ann. Mars.* (1902), pp.26–7.

[109] ANRCI, XIV-4-8, Registre des Renseignements, 'Rapport no. 111', Lt. Nodé-Langlois, 30 June 1901.

[110] A *tas* was equivalent to 50 grams and worth 150 f. Hence the tribute to be paid in gold by Kouamé Dié amounted to the equivalent of 3,000 f. By the end of Aug. 1901 he had paid 11 *tas*, or just over half of the demanded tribute. ANRCI, X-31-23, Colonna d'Istria to Gov. p.i., 17 Aug. 1901; ANRCI, XIV-4-8, Registre de Renseignements, Capt. Lambert, Lettre no. 197, 4 Aug. 1901; ANRCI, XXI-34-4, Bastard to Chef de Bat., 3 Sept. 1901.

[111] ANRCI, XIV-34-4, Rapport mensuel, Ouossou, 31 Aug. 1901; ibid., Bastard to Chef de Bataillon, 3 Sept. 1901.

[112] To get an idea of the weight of these tribute payments it is perhaps useful to keep in mind some of the local prices for consumable goods and labour at the time. One could purchase 20 pieces of manioc, or 20 cobs of maize, or one jug of palm wine for .50 f. A small goat cost 5.00 f. while an average-sized sheep cost 10.00 f. and a chicken 1.00 f. Five or six kg of yams would cost .50 f. A day's wage for porters varied between .50 f. in the north to .80 f. in the Tiassalé region. See ANRCI, X-34-4, Rapport mensuel, Ouossou, July 1901; ibid., Bastard to Chef de Bat., 3 Sept. 1901; ANRCI, X-39-9, Betsellère to Gov., 3 Oct. 1903.

[113] ANRCI, XIV-34-4, Rapport mensuel, Ouossou, 30 Sept. 1901; ibid., Rapport mensuel, Ouossou, Oct. 1901.

[114] ANRCI, XIV-4-7bis, Bastard to Chef de Bat., 19 July 1901.

[115] ANRCI, XIV-34-4, Rapport mensuel, Ouossou, 30 June 1902.

[116] Delafosse recorded that the title *Bulare* was a 'surnom donné par ses guerriers à Akafou, chef du Baoulé, à la suite de sa lutte avec la colonne de Kong 1894–95', *Essai de manuel*, p.137 n.1.

[117] ANRCI, XIV-34-3, 'Rapport du chef de Bat., Colonna d'Istria chargé des opérations militaires dans le sud', 16 July 1901.

[118] ANRCI, XIV-29-4, 'Rapport Schneiggans sur l'établissement du poste de Bonzi', 28 June 1901; a further note dated 30 June 1901 is added to this report of 28 June 1901; ibid., Tournois to Capt. commandant le secteur de Kokumbo, 7 July 1901.

[119] 'Arrêté local créant un impôt de capitation sur les indigènes de la Côte d'Ivoire', 14 May 1901 *BOCI* (1901) p.231–2; Circulaire ministerielle, 'Recensement de la population', 23 Aug. 1901 *BOCI* (1901), p.302.

[120] 'Les opérations militaires au Baoulé', *Alm. Ann. Mars.* (1902), p.25. 'Arrêté local portant organisation du Baoulé-Nord. Division en deux cercles', 3 July 1901, *BOCI* (1901), p.237.

[121] ANSOM, Côte d'Ivoire, IV, 4c, Clozel to Gov. Gen., July 1901.

[122] The influence of the Anglo-Ashanti battles of 1900 upon the resistance sentiment among other Akan groups in the Ivory Coast has not yet been studied. Further research may well reveal that there were specific linkages in the resistance movements of the two peoples and that it was more than just coincidental that both the French and the British experienced difficulties in coming to terms with the Akan in their respective colonies during 1900.

[123] ANRCI, X-34-8, Capt. Maillard to Chef de Bat., 14 Apr. 1903; ibid., 'Instructions sur la tactique au Baoulé', Capt. Maillard, June 1903 [copy].

[124] The situation prevailing on the eve of French penetration among the

Ouarébo is perhaps an exception to this generalization. Kouamé Dié appears to have had forces at his command and he appears to have collected annual tribute payments from subordinate groups as well. See ANRCI, X-34-10, 'Rapport du Capt. Lambert sur la reconnaissance faite au pays Ouarébo du 9 au 19 septembre 1901', 22 Sept. 1901; ibid., Lt. Nodé-Langlois to Capt. Lambert, 5 Jan. 1902.

[125] ANRCI, XIV-4-7bis, Capt. Bastard [Report on reconnaissance of 28 Jan. 1902]; ibid., Capt. Bastard [to Lt. Richard], 29 Jan. 1902; ANRCI, XIV-34-4, Rapport mensuel, Ouossou, 31 Jan. 1902; ANRCI, XIV-4-7bis, Capt. Bastard [to Lt. Richard], [Feb. 1902]; ibid., same to same, 2 Feb. 1902; ibid., same to Chef de Bat., 8 Feb. 1902.

[126] ANRCI, XIV-34-4, Rapport mensuel, Ouossou, 1 Mar. 1902; ibid., Rapport mensuel, Ouossou, [31] Mar. 1902; ANRCI, XIV-4-7bis, Capt. Bastard to Lt. Richard, 21 Apr. 1902; ibid., same to same, 23 Apr. 1902; ibid., Capt. Bastard to Chef de bat., 25 Apr. 1902; ANRCI, XIV-34-4, Rapport mensuel Ouossou, Apr. 1902.

[127] ANRCI, XIV-4-8, Registre des Renseignements, Lt. Nodé-Langlois, Lettre no. 102. Capt. Lambert reported from his observations in Sept. 1901: 'Koffi Oussu, chef des Faafoués [Ouarébo] et Natta Koffi chef des Languiras ainsi que tous leurs chefs de village nous sont entièrement devoués et prêts à nous servir si nous voulons créer de postes pour les soustraire à l'autorité tyrannique de Kouami Dié'. ANRCI, X-34-10, 'Rapport du Capt. Lambert sur la reconnaissance faite au pays Ouarébo', 22 Sept. 1901. See also ANRCI, XIV-4-8, Registre des Renseignements, Lettre no. 7F, Capt. Lambert, 27 Oct. 1901.

[128] ANRCI, X-34-10, Lt. Nodé-Langlois to Capt. Lambert, 5 Jan. 1902.

[129] ANRCI, X-34-10, 'Rapport du Capt. Lambert sur la reconnaissance faite au pays Ouarébo', 22 Sept. 1901.

[130] Accounts of the incident differ in detail: see particularly ANRCI, XIV-4-8, 'Sommaire des opérations en pays Ouarébos et Kodé', Colonna d'Istria, 29 Mar. 1902; ANRCI, X-31-23, 'Rapport militaire des mois de février et mars 1902', Colonna d'Istria, 16 Apr. 1902; ANRCI, X-34-8, Lt. Clervaux, 'Monographie historique', Nov. 1904. Published references to the incident include: 'Baoulé', *Alm. Ann. Mars.* (1903), p.18; [news article in] *BCAF* (1902), p.182; and Clozel, *Dix ans*, p.86.

[131] ANRCI, X-34-10, 'Rapport du Capt. Maillard sur les opérations exécutées pendant la période du 24 mai au 14 juin contre les tribus Ouarébos', 15 June 1902; ANRCI, X-31-23, 'Rapport militaire du mois de mai 1902', Colonna d'Istria, 23 June 1902; ANRCI, X-34-8, Lt. Clervaux, 'Monographie historique', Nov. 1904.

[132] The ratinale behind the 1902 provisions is discussed in G. Angoulvant, *La Pacification de la Côte d'Ivoire* (Paris, 1916), p.199.

[133] ANRCI, X-9-194, Rapport mensuel, Tiassalé, Apr. 1902.

[134] Ibid., Rapport mensuel, Tiassalé, 28 May 1902; ANSOM, Côte d'Ivoire, V, 3, Gen. Houry to Gov. Gen., 'Situation militaire pendant le 2e semestre 1902', 18 Feb. 1903.

[135] ANRCI, X-31-23, 'Rapport militaire du mois de mai 1902', Colonna d'Istria, 23 June 1902.

[136] ANRCI, XIV-4-7bis, Capt. Bastard to Lt. Richard, 27 Apr. 1902.

[137] ANRCI, XIV-4-7bis, Capt. Bastard to Lt. Richard, 28 June 1902; ANRCI, XIV-34-4, Rapport mensuel, Ouossou, 30 June 1902; ANRCI, XIV-4-7bis, Capt. Bastard to Lt. Richard, 1 July 1902; ANRCI, X-31-23, 'Rapport militaire, Juin 1902', Colonna d'Istria, 24 Jue 1902; ANRCI, XIII-45-3/36, 'Registre de Correspondance', Capt. Bastard to Commandant de la Bat., 6 July 1902; ibid., same to same, 9 July 1902.

[138] ANRCI, XIV-34-4, 'Note de Service à M.M. les Commandants de Secteur', [Colonna d'Istria], 22 July 1902.

[139] ANRCI, XIV-29-4, Tournois to Commandant du poste de Toumodi, 17 Aug. 1902; ANRCI, XIV-34-10, Capt. Garnier to Gov. 31 Mar. 1902.

[140] ANRCI, XIV-29-4, Tournois to Commandant du Poste de Toumodi, 17 Aug. 1902.

[141] ANSOM, Côte d'Ivoire, V, 3, Gen. Houry to Gov. Gen., 'Situation militaire pendant le 2e semestre 1902', 18 Feb. 1903; 'Fin des opérations au Baoulé', *Ann. Alm. Mars.* (1904), p.20.

[142] ANSOM, Côte d'Ivoire, V, 3, Gen. Houry to Gov. Gen., 'Situation militaire pendant le 2e semestre 1902', 18 Feb. 1903.

[143] 'Notes sur la guerre en pays Baoulé, d'après des notes du commandant Maillard et des Capitaines Garnier et Privey', *RTC*, iv (1905), p.317.

[144] Ibid., pp.320, 325.

[145] ANRCI, XIII-26-12/78, Gen. Combes, 'Ordre Particulier no. 189L', 27 June 1901.

[146] ANRCI, X-34-8, 'Rapport annuel du Chef de Bat., Colonna d'Istria', 31 July 1902.

[147] In the southern region for example, Capt. Bastard wanted to pursue the Baule across the Nzi river and cut off their lines of retreat, but he was prevented from doing so by his superior, Commander Colonna d'Istria. See ANRCI, XIV-4-7bis, Capt. Bastard to Commandant Chef de Bat., 1 May 1902.

NOTES TO CHAPTER V

[1] M. Delafosse, [Clozel obituary], *BCAF* (1918), pp.76-8.

[2] Clozel, *Dix ans*, particularly Chs. II and III. These two chapters were initially published as an article in the *Journal des Voyages* (1898).

[3] ANSOM, Côte d'Ivoire, IV, 4c, Clozel to Gov. Gen., July 1901.

[4] ANSOM, Côte d'Ivoire, IV, 4c, Clozel to Gov. Gen., July 1901.

[5] 'La guerre de guérillas et d'embuscades que nous faisaient les Baoulés nous avait causé des pertes sensibles, très probablement supérieures à celles que nous leur avions fait éprouver nous-mêmes' (Clozel, *Dix ans*, pp.79-80). See also ANSOM, Côte d'Ivoire, V, 3, Clozel to Gov. Gen., 3 Apr. 1903. Capt. Privey reported that 60 per cent of the French forces were killed or wounded in this period of engagements - see Privey, 'Aperçu sur la situation politique et militaire de la Côte d'Ivoire, *RTC* (1904), 2, p.320 n.

[6] Kanya-Forstner, *The Conquest*, p.241.

[7] ANSOM, Côte d'Ivoire, V, 3, Gen. Houry to Gov. Gen., 16 June 1902; ANSOM, Côte d'Ivoire, V, 3, Gov. Gen. to M.C., 24 June 1902.

[8] Décrêt réorganisant le Gouvernement Général de l'A.O.F., 1 Oct. 1902, *BOCI* (1902), p.863; Décrêt organisant le Conseil du Gouvernement de 1' A.O.F., 17 Oct. 1902, *BOCI* (1902), p.919. For a discussion of these reforms see Newbury, 'The Government General and Political Change in French West Africa', *St. Antony's Papers: African Affairs*, No. 1 (London, 1961) pp.42-3.

[9] 'Circulaire du Gouv. Gén. pour l'application du décrêt du 1 oct. 1902. Attributions du Gouverneur Général', 11 Nov. 1902, *BOCI* (1903), p.6.

[10] Newbury, 'The Formation of the Government General', p.124 no.47.

[11] ANRCI, VII-31-9, Clozel to Betsellère, 5 Dec. 1902.

[12] ANSOM, Afrique III, 23c, Nebout to Lt. Col. Monteil, 6 Jan. 1895.

[13] Nebout and Delafosse had worked closely with one another among the Baule from 1894 onwards. Clozel was a close personal friend and student of Octave Houdas, the professor of Arabic at the École des Langues Orientales and later the father-in-law of Maurice Delafosse. The extent of the friendship between these men and their mentor, Binger, is informatively discussed in Mme Louise Delafosse's forthcoming biography of her father.

[14] ANRCI, VII-31-9, Clozel to Betsellère, 5 Dec. 1902.

[15] ANSOM, Côte d'Ivoire, V, 3, Clozel to Gov. Gen., 3 Apr. 1903.

[16] ANSOM, Côte d'Ivoire, V, 3, Gen. Houry to Gov. Gen., 'Situation militaire pendant le 2e semestre 1902', 18 Feb. 1903.

[17] ANSOM, Côte d'Ivoire, V, 3, Clozel to Gov. Gen., 3 Apr. 1903.

[18] The idea was first suggested in May 1900 by Capt. Le Magnen, but it was not acted upon until late 1902. See ANRCI, X-34-10, Capt. Le Magnen, 'Rapport sur les opérations exécutées le 20 mai dans la tribu des N'Gbans du Nord', 23 mai 1900. For the newly-created corps of porters see: Arrêté du Gov. Gen. créant une compagnie de porteurs', 14 Dec. 1902', BOCI (1903), p.10; and 'Arrêté du Gouv. Gen. – Création d'une duexième compagnie de porteurs', 7 Jan. 1903, BOCI (1903), p.16.

[19] 'Arrêté Local', 25 Nov. 1902, BOCI (1902), p.939.

[20] ANSOM, Côte d'Ivoire, V, 3, Gen. Houry to Gov. Gen., 'Situation militaire pendant le 2e semestre 1902', 18 Feb. 1903.

[21] 'Notes sur la guerre en pays Baoulé', RTC, iv (1905), p.325.

[22] ANRCI, X-38-9, Betsellère to Gov., 12 Aug. 1903; ANRCI, XIV-29-5, same to same, 15 Sept. 1903; ANRCI, V-10-255, Gov. to Gov. Gen., 8 Jan. 1904.

[23] For an account of the Senegal incident which had reverberations throughout the French possessions see M'Baye Guèye, 'L'affaire Chautemps (avril 1904) et la suppression de l'esclavage de case au Sénégal', BIFAN, xxvii, 3–4 (1965).

[24] Clozel instructions cited in ANRCI, XIV-29-5, Commandant Charles to M. l'administrateur de la circonscription de Toumodi, 11 Apr. 1906.

[25] 'Arrêté local créant un impôt de capitation sur les indigènes de la Côte d'Ivoire', 14 May 1901, BOCI (1901), p.231–2. See particularly Art. 6, p.232.

[26] 'Arrêté local – Taux de la remise allouée aux chefs indigènes (10%)', 12 July 1904, BOCI (1904), p.431.

[27] ANRCI, VII-3-19, Clozel to Gov. Gen., 20 Oct. 1905.

[28] ANRCI, X-38-9, Morisson, 'Propositions de gratification à allouer à des chefs, notables ou fonctionnaires', [Feb. 1904]; 'Arrêté fixant la répartition des fonds pour cadeaux politiques dans le cercle du Baoulé', 20 Nov. 1905, JOCI (1905), p.341.

[29] ANRCI, XIII-11-123/1003, Chef de bat. à toutes circonscriptions, 29 Apr. 1907; see also: ANRCI, XIV-29-4, Commandant Charles au Capt. chargé de l'expédition des affaires du cercle à Toumodi, 27 Nov. 1905.

[30] ANRS, 2-G-6, no. 12, Gov. to Gov. Gen., 'Rapport politique de Fév. 1906', 19 Apr. 1906.

[31] D.P., Delafosse to parents, 4 Mar. 1896.

[32] Arrêté local, 13 July 1905, JOCI (1905), pp.204–5; Arrêté local, 30 Dec. 1905, JOCI (1905), p.374; Arrêté local, 29 Aug. 1906, JOCI (1906), p.288; Arrêté local, 2 May 1907, JOCI (1907), p.134; Arrêté local, 2 Dec. 1907, JOCI (1907), p.386. For Delafosse's initial description of Baule legal procedure upon which these tribunals were modelled see Delafosse, 'Coutumes indigènes des Agni du Baoulé', in Clozel and Villamur, eds., Les Coutumes indigènes de la Côte d'Ivoire, pp.95–146; and Delafosse and Villamur, Les Coutumes agni, rédigées et codifiées d'après les documents officiels les plus récents (Paris, 1904).

[33] Delafosse, 'Coutumes indigènes', p.144.

[34] See for example, Nebout's comments as acting Governor in ANRCI, XIII-34-23/135, Nebout to Chef de bat., 22 Jan. 1906.

[35] Delafosse, 'Coutumes indigènes', p.145.

[36] ANRCI, XIV-34-8, Betsellère, 'Le progrès de la pacification au Baoulé en 1904', 31 Jan. 1905; ANRS, 2-G-5, no. 14, 'Rapport politique de Jan. 1905', 21 Mar. 1905; ANRCI, X-38-10, Rapport mensuel, Bonzi, Oct. 1906.

[37] ANRCI, X-38-11, Chef de bat. Charles, Rapport, 15 Sept. 1907.

[38] ANRCI, XIV-34-8, Betsellère, 'Le progrès de la pacification au baoulé en 1904', 31 Jan. 1905.

[39] ANRS, 2-G-5, no. 14, 'Rapport politique de Jan. 1905', 21 Mar. 1905.

[40] Both Delafosse and Clozel published articles in English at the time, something which was rare and indicative of their exposure to other colonial traditions. See F.-J. Clozel, 'Land tenure among the natives of the Ivory Coast', *Journal of the African Society*, i, 3 (1902), pp.399–415; and M. Delafosse, 'The Baule People of the Ivory Coast Interior and their religious beliefs', *The West African Mail* (1904), pp.462–4, 535–7.

[41] For a general discussion of the shifting emphasis in French colonial policy around the turn of the century see R. F. Betts, *Assimilation and Association in French Colonial Theory, 1890-1914* (New York, 1961). Explicit comparisons between French and British approaches dominated the discussion of policy alternatives. See particularly É. Baillaud, *La Situation économique de l'Afrique Occidentale anglaise en française* (Paris, 1907), and *La Politique indigène de l'Angleterre en Afrique Occidentale* (Paris, 1912).

[42] ANRCI, X-34-8, 'Commandant Charles à MM. les Capitaines Administrateurs des circonscriptions', 21 Oct. 1905; ibid., Bretteonad to Charles, 28 Oct. 1905; ibid., Voland to Charles, 31 Oct. 1905; ibid., Debieuvre to Charles, 2 Nov. 1905; see also ANRCI, XVII-24-4, 'Extrait d'une lettre adressée par M. le Gouverneur au commandant du Baoulé', 19 Feb. 1904.

[43] It has been the custom in some circles to typify the British approach to colonial administration as being that of 'indirect rule', while that of the French has often been described in contrast as being that of 'direct rule'. When examined carefully these idealized descriptions often do not apply consistently to the colonial policies of either European power. For a discussion of these issues see: H. Deschamps, 'Et maintenant, Lord Lugard?', *Africa*, xxxiii (1963); and M. Crowder's response, 'Indirect rule, French and British style', *Africa*, xxxiv (1964).

The Baule case suggests that the particular style of colonial rule varied over time within any one colony as a function of the resources available to the European power in question rather than as a simple function of presumably distinct national philosophies. Colonial 'policy' was in this sense an *ex post facto* rationalization designed to make a virtue out of what had already became a necessity locally.

[44] Clozel requested ethnographic information from administrators in a circular letter on 29 Mar. 1901, issued while he was still Secretary General of the colony. See *BCAF* (1901), p.205.

Delafosse's published studies on the Baule had a significant impact upon the outlook and understanding of subsequent administrators among the Baule, so much so that later administrators often developed what might be called a 'premature sophistication' with respect to the Baule. Once they had read Delafosse's writings on Baule history and customs and memorized a few key words from his published vocabulary lists they felt sufficiently introduced to the Baule to handle administrative affairs with confidence. The general quality of independent ethnographic evidence diminished markedly once Delafosse's materials received currency, for rather than investigate local phenomena on their own, subsequent administrators tended simply to repeat, sometimes word for word, the formulations of Delafosse. As a result his works took on the quality of an 'authorized version' of Baule history and customs.

[45] Cited in Hargreaves, *France and West Africa*, p.207.

[46] ANRCI, XIV-29-5, Circulaire No. 21c à MM. les Administrateurs de Cercle au sujet de l'hospitalité accordée dans des postes à des femmes . . ., 15 Mar. 1907.

[47] For the assimilation the administrator's role with that of a 'chief' see

Delavignette, *Freedom and Authority in French West Africa* (London, 1950) [a translation of *Service Africain* (Paris, 1946)], pp.8, 31–3; and his interesting work on French administration, *Les Vrais Chefs de l'Empire* (Paris, 1939).

[48] Delafosse, *Essai de manuel*, pp.117–18.

[49] ANRCI, X-39-9, Betsellère to Gov., 26 Feb. 1904; ANRCI, XIV-38-10, Capt. Bruyère to Chef de bat., 15 May 1904.

[50] ANRCI, XIV-34-8, Clozel to Gov. Gen., 10 Feb. 1905; ANRCI, XIV-38-20, Betsellère to Gov., 15 Aug. 1904.

[51] Privey, 'Aperçu sur la situation', p.327; this is one of the few explicit indications that metropolitan public opinion may have had an effect on the policy purused in the colonies. Just what Capt. Privey meant by the phrase 'la nervosité métropolitaine' is not entirely clear, but it is perhaps significant that E. D. Morel's 'Congo Reform Movement' was beginning to gain momentum during this period, bringing colonial atrocities to the attention of a large public. The entire subject of the role of public opinion in the formation of colonial policy deserves more study.

[52] Privey, 'Aperçu sur la situation', p.323.

[53] Ibid. 318.

[54] See for example: 'Notes sur la guerre en pays Baoulé', *RTC*, iv (1905), pp.309–44.

[55] For the approach of Commander Betsellère see ANRCI, Monographies, Bouaké, Betsellère, 'Cercle du Baoulé', 2 Apr. 1905, p.1; and ANRCI, Monographies, Dimbokro, Betsellère, 'Renseignements sur le Cercle du Baoulé', 15 Mar. 1904, p.14; for Commander Charles's approach see ANRCI, X-38-9, Commandant Charles to Commandants des circonscriptions, 6 Sept. 1905.

[56] Clozel, *Dix ans*, p.6; see also pp.12 and 14.

[57] 'La jonction des lagunes' and 'Le chemin de fer et le port de la Côte d'Ivoire' in Clozel, *Dix ans*, Appendices V and VI respectively.

[58] 'Décrêt réorganisant le Gouvernement Général de l'AOF', *BOCI* (1904), p.604.

[59] ANRCI, X-34-8, Lt. Clervaux, 'Monographie historique', Nov. 1904.

[60] A 'Chambre Consultative de Commerce' was established at the end of 1903 to keep the administration regularly informed of the commercial community's opinion. See *BCAF* (1904), p.22.

[61] The only point upon which the administration would not accede to the merchants was the question of powder sales; see Nebout to Gov. Gen., 26 Jan. 1906, cited in 'La pacification de la Côte d'Ivoire: Méthodes et résultats', *BCAF-RCD*, x (1910), [off-print], p.11.

[62] ANRCI, XIV-34-8, Clozel to Gov. Gen., 10 Feb. 1905; ANRS, 2-G-5, no. 14, Clozel, Rapport politique, 1e trimestre 1905, 4 Mar. 1905; see also Clozel, *Dix ans*, pp.101–2; and C. Benoît, *Histoire militaire de l'Afrique Occidentale française* (Paris, 1931), pp.612–15.

[63] ANSOM, Côte d'Ivoire, I, 15c, Gov. to M.C., 'Rapport politique', 26 Mar. 1897; and ANRCI, XIV-29-5, Lt. Mongélous to Chef de bat., 13 Aug. 1903.

[64] ANRCI, X-38-9, Betsellère to Lt.-Col. Vimont, 6 Feb. 1903; ANRCI, XIV-29-5, Lt. Mongélous to Chef de bat., 13 Aug. 1903.

[65] ANRCI, Monographies, Dimbokro, Betsellère, 'Renseignements sur le Cercle du Baoulé', 15 Mar. 1904, p.36.

[66] ANRCI, XIV-29-5, Lt. Guese, 'Rapport sur les principales maisons de commerce de Tiassalé', 18 Apr. 1906.

[67] M. Simon, *Souvenirs de brousse*, p.54.

[68] ANRCI, XIV-34-8, Betsellère, 'Le progrès de la pacification au Baoulé en 1904', 31 Jan. 1905; see also comments on Tiassalé's rubber trade in 'La tournée de M. Clozel', *BCAF*, iv (1904), p.122.

[69] For comments on Morgan Dougan see ANRCI, XIV-29-5, Lt. Guese, 'Rapport sur les principales maisons de commerce de Tiassalé', 18 Apr. 1906;

ANRCI, Monographies, Dimbokro, Betsellère, 'Renseignements sur le Cercle du Baoulé', 15 Mar. 1904, p.37; É. Richet, *Sur les routes d'Afrique de Port-Étienne à Abomey* (Paris, n.d.), p.224; and R. P. Bedel, 'Souvenirs de voyage', Cahier II, p.37 [entry for:] 'Jeudi 16 Jan. 1902' [this unpublished manuscript by one of the first Catholic missionaries in the Ivory Coast is conserved at the Archêvêché d'Abidjan, Église du Plateau, Abidjan, Ivory Coast.]

[70] T. Terrier, 'Monographie du Cercle du Baoulé', in Clozel, *Dix ans*, pp.146–7.

[71] ANRCI, Monographies, Dimbokro, Betsellère, 'Renseignements sur le cercle du Baoulé', 15 Mar. 1904, p.37; ANRCI, X-38-9, Betsellère to Lt.–Col. Vimont, 6 Feb. 1903.

[72] Richet, *Sur les routes d'Afrique*, p.222.

[73] ANRCI, XIV-34-8, Betsellère, 'Le progrès de la pacification au Baoulé en 1904', 31 Jan. 1905.

[74] ANRCI, Monographies, Dimbokro, Betsellère, 'Renseignements sur le cercle du Baoulé', 15 Mar. 1904, p.33.

[75] ANRCI, XI-43-434, 'Rapport économique et agricole', Toumodi, Sept. 1910.

[76] ANRCI, Monographies, Bouaké, 'Monographie du cercle du Baoulé-Nord', July 1911.

[77] ANRCI, XIV-34-4, Rapport mensuel, Ouossou, July 1901; and ibid., Bastard to Chef de bat., 3 Sept. 1901.

[78] ANRCI, X-38-9, Betsellère to Gov., 3 Oct. 1903; ANRCI, XIV-4-4, Capt. Lamoureux, 'Notice sur les progrès realisés au Baoulé aux points de vue de la colonisation européenne de l'administration et la législation', Mar. 1905; and ANRCI, Monographies, Bouaké, 'Monographie du Cercle du Baoulé-Nord', July 1911.

[79] ANRCI, Monographies, Dimbokro, Betsellère, 'Renseignements sur le cercle du Baoulé', 15 Mar. 1904, p.33.

[80] 'La tournée de M. Clozel', *BCAF*, iv (1904), p.121.

[81] ANRCI, Monographies, Dimbokro, Betsellère, 'Renseignements sur le cercle du Baoulé', 15 Mar. 1904, p.33.

[82] Clozel, *Dix ans*, p.8.

[83] Privey, 'Aperçu sur la situation', p.311.

[84] At the time Monteil recognized that Akafou did not lead the revolt, but rather joined it after his efforts to mediate failed: 'incapable d'enrayer les mauvais instincts de ses administrés, Akafou se jeta avec eux dans la rébellion' (ANSOM, Afrique, III, 19a, Monteil to M.C., 'Rapport au sujet des opérations dans le Baoulé', 19 Jan. 1895). See above, Ch. II, pp.56–65.

[85] D.P., Capt. Le Magnen to Delafosse, 20 Sept. 1899; D.P., same to same, 25 Sept. 1899; D.P., same to same, 26 Sept. 1899.

[86] See Ch. IV, pp.132–3, 135–6, 137–9, above.

[87] ANRCI, XIV-4-7bis, 'Renseignements sur les chefs rebelles du secteur de Ouossou', [n.d. – c.25 Jan. 1903]; on this list of chiefs several including N'Défou, Nzoko, Assiené, Tototi, and Kouassi Aluma are indicated as having died in the battles with the French, but later reports indicate that their deaths were unconfirmed; see for example, the list of chiefs in ANRCI, XIV-4-8, 'Registre de Renseignements', where doubts are raised about the alleged death of those initially reported killed. Assiené was said to be alive, and reports in later years confirm that Nzoko and N'Défou also survived; cf. ANRCI, XIV-4-7bis, Capt. Bruyère, 'Etat de proposition pour la répartition de l'amende de guerre', 26 May 1904.

[88] 'La tournée de M. Clozel', *BCAF*, iv (1904), p.122; ANRCI, XIV-4-8, Betsellère to Commandants de secteurs, 8 Mar. 1904; Clozel, *Dix ans*, p.81.

[89] ANRCI, XIV-34-4, Rapport mensuel, Ouossou, Dec. 1901.

[90] ANRCI, X-34-10, Capt. Lambert, 'Rapport sur la reconnaissance faite au pays Ouarébo du 9 au 19 septembre 1901', 22 Sept. 1901.

[91] ANRCI, XIV-34-4, Lt. Mongélous to Chef de bat., 20 Jan. 1903.

[92] ANRCI, X-38-9, Betsellère to Gov., 25 Jan. 1903.

[93] ANRCI, XIII-45-3/36, 'Registre de Correspondance', no. 172m, 17 Apr. 1903; ibid., no. 178m, Capt. Léonard to Betsellère, 19 Apr. 1903.

[94] Ibid., no. 203m, Capt. Léonard to Betsellère, [n.d. – between 27–30 Apr. 1903].

[95] Ibid., no. 308, Capt. Ruby to Betsellère, 22 June 1903; ibid., no. 311 Capt. Ruby to Betsellère, 24 June 1903; ANRCI, X-9-194, Rapport mensuel, Tiassalé, 1 July 1903.

[96] ANRCI, X-38-9, Betsellère, 'Rapport à M. le Lt. Col. au sujet des opérations à entreprendre dans le secteur d'Ouossou', 2 July 1903.

[97] ANRCI, X-38-10, Rapport mensuel, Ouossou, June 1906; ibid., Rapport mensuel, Ouossou, July 1906.

[98] ANRCI, XIV-34-4, Bastard, Rapport mensuel, June 1902 [with notes added by Commander Colonna d'Istria].

[99] ANRCI, XIV-4-8, 'Registre des Renseignements', Capt. Lambert, Lettre no. 7F. ANRCI, XIV-34-13, Lt. Bénézet to Chef de bat., 30 May 1904; ANRCI, X-34-8, Lt. Bénézet, 'Rapport sur la situation politique de ce district', Fort Maria, Sakasso, 14 June 1905.

[100] ANSOM, Côte d'Ivoire, V, 3, Gen. Houry to Gov. Gen., 'Situation militaire pendant le 2e semestre de 1902', 18 Feb. 1903; ANRCI, X-34-8, Lt. Clervaux, 'Monographie historique', Nov. 1904.

[101] ANRCI, X-34-9, 'Rapport mensuel du Baoulé Nord, Bouaké', Nov. 1903.

[102] M. Delafosse, 'Ethnographie de la région de Bouaké: Note ethnologique et politique sur les tribus du secteur de Bouaké', in Clozel, Dix ans, Appendix II, p.281.

[103] ANRCI, XIV-34-13, Lt. Bénézet to Chef de bat., 30 May 1904; ANRCI, X-34-8, Lt. Bénézet, 'Rapport sur la situation politique de ce district', Fort Maria, Sakasso, 14 June 1905.

[104] ANRCI, XIV-34-14, Lt. Bénézet to Chef de bat., 30 May 1904.

[105] ANRCI, XIV-34-13, 'Le Chef de bat. Morrison, commandant le circonscription de Baoulé Nord, à M. le Chef de bat., Toumodi, Bouaké', 11 June 1904.

[106] ANRCI, X-34-8, Lt. Carpentier, 'Rapport sur le régime politique du district de Sakasso', Oct. 1905.

[107] ANRCI, X-34-8, Lt. Bénézet, 'Rapport sur la situation politique de ce district', Fort Maria, Sakasso, 14 June 1905.

[108] Ibid.

[109] ANRS, 2-G-5, no. 14, Gov. to Gov. Gen., 'Rapport politique de juillet 1905, no. 477', 16 Sept. 1905.

[110] ANRS, 2-G-4, no. 10, Gov. to Gov. Gen., 'Rapport politique de juin 1904', 22 Sept. 1904.

[111] ANRCI, X-38-11, Rapport mensuel, Bouaké, July 1907; ibid., Rapport mensuel Bouaké, Aug. 1907.

[112] The phrase 'hommes de paille' was used by Betsellère to describe those whom the Baule designated to replace their paramount chiefs killed by the French. Cf. ANRCI, X-38-9, Betsellère, 'Rapport au sujet des opérations à entreprendre dans le secteur d'Ouossou', 2 July 1903. For a broader discussion of the phenomenon of 'straw chiefs' in French African territories see Delavignette, Freedom and Authority, pp.71 ff.

[113] Privey, 'Aperçu sur la situation', pp.316–17, footnote; ANRCI, XIV-29-4, Lepage to M. l'administrateur de la Circonscription de Toumodi', 21 Dec. 1905.

[114] ANRCI, X-34-9, Rapport mensuel, Bouaké, Mar. 1903; ibid., 'Rapport mensuel du Baoulé Nord, Bouaké', Aug. 1903.

[115] This speech was recollected and published by Delafosse in *Broussard ou les états d'âme d'un colonial suivis de ses propos et opinions* (Paris, 1923); Delafosse accompanied Clozel on his inspection trip of 1904, and he was an eye-witness to the encounter between Clozel and Kouassi Blé. Moreover, Delafosse spoke and understood Baule well enough not to have to depend uniquely upon an interpreter, so that although the text he presented may not have been a verbatim transcription of Kouassi Blé's discourse, it is likely that it represented the gist of the speech.

[116] Delafosse, *Broussard*, pp.221-2.

[117] ANRCI, X-34-8, Lt. Clervaux, 'Monographie historique', Nov. 1904.

[118] See above, Ch. III, p. 95.

NOTES TO CHAPTER VI

[1] The commercial statistics presented here are obtained from: Ministère des Colonies. Office Colonial, *Statistiques coloniales pour l'année 1899 - Commerce*. These figures were published annually normally with a three-year lag. Thus the figures for 1899 were published in 1902; those of 1900 in 1903, etc. Unless otherwise stated all the commercial figures in the following pages are derived from these volumes for the appropriate years mentioned. Trade totals are rounded to the nearest 100,000 f.

[2] The budgetary statistics presented here are derived from: Ministère des Colonies, Office Colonial, *Statistiques des finances des colonies françaises pour les années 1898-1907* (Melun, 1908) and Ministére des Colonies, Office Colonial, *Statistiques des finances des colonies pour les années 1904-1913* (Melun, 1917). Unless otherwise stated all the budget statistics in the following pages are derived from these volumes for the appropriate years mentioned.

[3] Ministère des Colonies. Office Colonial, *Statistiques coloniales pour l'année 1896 - Commerce* (Melun and Paris, 1899-). Figures are rounded to nearest 100,000 f., and the percentages are calculated on this basis. For this reason these percentages are only approximate.

[4] For an assessment of the importance of the raw rubber commerce up to 1908 see 'La Navigation fluviale à la Côte d'Ivoire - Le Caoutchouc', *BCAF*, 5 (1909), pp.180-1. For an analysis of what became known as the 'crise du Caoutchouc' see M. Merlin, 'La crise du caoutchouc', *BCAF*, xii (1913) pp.420-8, and the article of the same title, *BCAF*, i (1914), p.56.

[5] ANRCI, XII-11-123/1003, Charles [to] toutes circonscriptions, 25 May 1907; Tellier, 'Monographie du cercle du Baoulé', in Clozel, *Dix ans*, p.147.

[6] The 'average local price' is calculated here by dividing the total value of the exported rubber by the total volume for any given year on the basis of the annual statistics reported in the *Statistiques coloniales*. These necessarily represent approximate figures, and further research will be needed on local prices to see how producers were directly affected by European price fluctuations.

[7] ANRCI, X-38-11, Rapport mensuel, Bouaké, Sept. 1907.

[8] ANRS, 10-E-4, Procès verbal, Conseil d'Administration, séance du 23 jan. 1908.

[9] Ibid.

[10] ANRS, 4-G-6, Lapalud to M.C., 'Résumé de la Mission d'Inspection', 30 May 1908, pp.11-13, 23.

[11] Dickson, *A Historical Geography of Ghana*, pp.162-71.

[12] ANRS, 10-E-4, Procès verbal, Conseil d'Administration, séance du 30 mai 1908.

[13] ANRS, 10-E-4, Procès verbal, Conseil d'Administration, séance du 30 mai 1908.

[14] 'Arrêté local – Établissement d'une taxe sur les armes à feu non perfectionnées', *BOCI* (1908), pp.609–10.

[15] Ministère des Colonies. Office Colonial, *Statistiques des finances des colonies pour les années 1904–1913*, pp.94–7.

[16] The draft manuscript of this letter is found in ANRCI, X-35-31, Angoulvant, 'Lettre Programme', [dated 26 Oct. 1908]; it was published and circulated a month later and was subsequently always referred to as the 'Lettre Programme du 26 Novembre 1908'.

[17] Simon, *Souvenirs de brousse*, pp.72–3. A detailed history of the diffusion of cocoa in the Ivory Coast has yet to be undertaken. Some authors have suggested that Angoulvant initially introduced it as a cash crop: see D. H. Urquhart, *Report on the Cocoa Industry in the French Ivory Coast* (Bourneville, 1955), p.14. In reality, however, Morgan Dougan appears to have been planting cocoa before Angoulvant arrived in the Ivory Coast, and his role might justifiably be compared to that of Tetteh Quashie in the diffusion of cocoa in Ghana twenty years earlier.

[18] 'Circulaire locale – permis d'occuper à accorder aux indigènes pour les cultures', 26 Nov. 1908, *JOCI* (1909), p.5.

[19] For comments on the process of distribution see: 'La pacification', *BCAF–RCD*, x (1910), p.328.

[20] ANRS, 10-E-4, Procès verbal, Conseil d'Administration, séance du 25 Nov. 1908, p.59.

[21] Ibid.; and Arrêté du Gov. Gen. – Taux de la taxe à la Côte d'Ivoire (de 0.50 f. à 4.50 f.) à fixer par le Lt. Gov., 30 Dec. 1908, *JOCI* (1909), p.28.

[22] ANRS, 10-E-4, 'Procès verbal, Conseil d'Administration, séance du 25 Nov. 1908, p.69; 'Arrêté concernant les remises allouées aux chefs indigènes sur le produit de l'impôt de capitation', 25 Nov. 1908, *JOCI* (1909), pp.301–2.

[23] For Angoulvant's further instructions concerning the collection of taxes see: 'Circulaire Locale – Tenue de la comptabilité des recettes en nature effectués au titre de l'impôt de capitation', 25 Nov. 1908, *JOCI* (1909), p.4.

[24] ANRCI, X-5-122, Gov. to Capt. Foussat, 10 Oct. 1908.

[25] ANRCI, X-35-31, Gov. to M. l'administrateur du Baoulé Nord, 3 Mar. 1909.

[26] 'La pacification', *BCAF–RCD*, x (1910), p.324.

[27] ANRCI, X-35-31, Angoulvant, 'Lettre Programme', 26 Nov. 1908.

[28] 'La pacification', *BCAF–RCD*, x (1910), p.315.

[29] ANRCI, X-35-31, Angoulvant, 'Lettre Programme', 26 Nov. 1908.

[30] For a discussion of Baule reactions to labour opportunities in the colonial economy see above, Ch. V, p. 159.

[31] A detailed study of the opportunity costs involved in turning to cash crops during the early colonial period has yet to be undertaken for the Baule, but the current research of Jean-Pierre Chauveau should be instructive in this regard. The aspects involved in such a study are outlined briefly in M. J. Hay, 'Coffee and Cocoa in the Ivory Coast: A Study in the Dynamics of Economic Change' (Wisconsin, M.A. thesis, 1967), pp.19–22.

[32] Hopkins, *An Economic History*, p.232. Emphasis added.

[33] ANRCI, X-35-31, Angoulvant, 'Lettre Programme', 26 Nov. 1908.

[34] ANRCI, X-35-31, 'Rapport sur l'organisation sociale', Bouaké, 15 Feb. 1909; ibid., Simon, 'Rapport sur les diverses questions traitées dans la lettre du 26 Novembre 1908', [n.d. – c.Feb. 1909].

[35] ANRCI, X-35-31, 'Rapport sur l'organisation sociale', Bouaké, 15 Feb. 1909.

[36] ANRCI, X-35-31, Simon to administrators, lettre no. 182 [8 Mar. 1909];

ibid., Moesch to Simon, 16 Mar. 1909; ibid., Susiny to Simon, 23 Mar. 1909; ibid., Lerminier to Simon, 24 Mar. 1909.

[37] ANRCI, X-5-124, Gov. to Gov. Gen., 14 Feb. 1909.

[38] 'Arrêté du Gov. Gen. – Création de deux brigades des gardes indigènes à la Côte d'Ivoire', 19 Sept. 1907, *BOCI* (1907), p.595.

[39] ANRCI, X-5-124, Gov. to Gov. Gen., 31 Dec. 1908; ibid., same to same, 14 Feb. 1909.

[40] Simon, *Souvenirs de brousse*, p.94.

[41] ANRCI, X-5-124, Gov. to Gov. Gen., 17 June 1909.

[42] ANRCI, X-31-12, M.C. to Gov. Gen., 19 June 1909.

[43] The archives of the Bonzi post among the Akoué were destroyed along with the post itself during the resistance struggle, but the following account of Akoué resistance was pieced together from the dispatches sent from Bonzi and Toumodi to the administration in Bingerville, including ANRCI, X-31-12, Simon to Angoulvant, Télégramme officiel, no. 345, 23 June 1909; ANRCI, X-5-122, Moesch, Rapport mensuel, Bonzi, 26 June 1909; ANRCI, X-31-12, [Simon] l'administrateur du cercle du Baoulé-sud to Gov., 19 July 1909. Published accounts of the incidents are presented in Simon, *Souvenirs de brousse*; Lt. Bouet, 'Quelques opérations militaires à la Côte d'Ivoire en 1909', *RTC* ix (1911), pp.134–53, 205–20, 343–70, 589–610; and 'Opérations à la Côte d'Ivoire. Colonne du commandant Noguès (octobre 1909 à avril 1910)', *RTC*, x (1911), pp.359–81.

[44] See p.133 above.

[45] ANRS, 10-E-3, Procès verbal, Conseil d'Administration, séance du 12 Janv. 1907; Simon, *Souvenirs de brousse*, p.93.

[46] Simon, *Souvenirs de brousse*, p.95. According to this account Simon instructed Moesch to keep silent about the difficulties in the Akoué area when he saw how irritated Angoulvant was with the news of a death of an administrator among the Attié.

[47] Lt. Bouet, 'Quelques opérations militaires', pp.211–12. Bouet was not an eyewitness to the events, but he arrived to direct the subsequent operations against the Akoué in July 1909. His published account of the initial incidents was most probably reconstructed from conversations with Simon and Moesch as well as Kouassi Ngo.

[48] Lt. Bouet, 'Quelques opérations militaires', pp.219–20.

[49] ANRCI, X-5-122, [Betis], Rapport mensuel, Sakassou, July 1909.

[50] ANRCI, X-5-122, Extrait du Rapport mensuel, Tiébissou, July 1909; Lt. Bouet, 'Quelques opérations militaires', p.151.

[51] ANRCI, X-31-13, Simon to Gov., lettre no. 418, 29 July 1909; ibid., Gov. Angoulvant to Simon, lettre no. 2213 G, 23 Aug. 1909; ibid., L'Administrateur de 2e classe, Carde, Secrétaire Général, p.i., to Gov. Angoulvant, 30 Sept. 1909; ibid., L'Inspecteur [Nebout] to Gov. Angoulvant, 11 Oct. 1909; and Simon, *Souvenirs de brousse*, pp.107–18.

[52] 'Circulaire locale 294 G, relative à la détention des armes à feu et la poudre par les indigènes, application de l'Arrêté 536G'. 21 Aug. 1909, *JOCI* (1909), p.358; 'Arrêté local – No. 536 G. Interdisant la détention par les indigènes des armes à feu non perfectionnées et de leur munitions dans certaines régions de la Côte d'Ivoire', 21 Aug. 1909, *JOCI* (1909), p.360.

[53] See for example, ANRCI, X-6-128, Bru, 'Rapport sur la situation politique du poste d'Ouossou pendant le mois de janv. 1910', Jan. 1910.

[54] ANRCI, X-5-122, Lt. Bouet, Rapport mensuel, Bonzi, Sept. 1909; ibid., Lt. Bouet, Rapport mensuel, Bonzi, Oct. 1909; ibid., Lt. Bouet, 'Rapport sur le blocus du poste de Bonzi du 7 août au 10 novembre 1909', 10 Nov. 1909.

[55] Concerning Angoulvant's problems with the commercial community see

ANRS, 10-E-4, Procès verbal, Conseil d'Administration, séance du 23 jan. 1908; ibid., séance du 22 avr. 1908; ibid., séance du 30 mai 1908; ANRCI, X-35-31, Angoulvant to Monsieur Bohn, Directeur de la C.F.A.O., Marseille, 26 Jan. 1909; ANRS, 10-E-5, Procès verbal, Conseil d'Administration, 25 Mar. 1909; ANRCI, XIV-33-8, L'Inspecteur [Nebout] to Gov., 3 Mar. 1910; ibid., Angoulvant to Gov. Gen., 8 Mar. 1910; ibid., L. Barthe, C.F.A.O., to Gov., 17 Mar. 1910; ibid., Angoulvant to [L. Barthe], Agent principal de la C.F.A.O. à Bassam, 4 Apr. 1910; ANRS, 10-E-6, Procès verbal, Conseil d'Administration, séance du 23 avr. 1910; ANRCI, XIV-33-8, Bohn, C.F.A.O., Paris, to Gov., 9 May 1910; ibid., L. Barthe, Agent principal de la C.F.A.O. to Gov., 21 May 1910; ibid., Bohn, C.F.A.O., to M.C., 13 July 1910; ANRCI, XIV-34-14, Lettre d'un officiel de la C.F.A.O., Marseille to M. Étienne, Vice-Président de la Chambre des Députés, 18 July 1910.

[56] For information on the atrocities see ANRCI, XIV-38-13, M. Combe to M. le chef de Santé; 23 Jan. 1909; ibid., Angoulvant to Chef du Service de Santé, 21 Feb. 1909; ibid., A. Combe to Gov., 24 Feb. 1909; ibid., Gov. to Nebout, Inspecteur des Affaires Administratives, en tournée à Dimbokro, 26 Feb. 1909; ibid., Gov. to Capt. Foussat, 24 Mar. 1909; ibid., Foussat to Nebout, 21 May 1909; ibid., Foussat to Nebout, 23 May 1909; ibid., Nebout to Gov., 12 June 1909.

[57] ANRCI, X-38-10, Lt. Dessus à M. le Commandant, no. 15, 5 Mar. 1902.

[58] Simon, *Souvenirs de brousse*, p.116.

[59] 'La pénétration de la Côte d'Ivoire', *BCAF-RCD*, x (1909), pp.193-204.

[60] ANRCI, X-34-4, Gov. Gen. p.i. to Gov. 2 Nov. 1909; ibid., Gov. to Gov. Gen. p.i., 9 Nov. 1909; ANRS, 2-G-9 no. 15, Gov. Gen. p.i. to Gov. Gen. [Ponty], Dakar to Paris, 28 Nov. 1909; see also Simon, *Souvenirs de brousse*, p.121.

[61] The influence of the Freemasons has not yet been studied, but there is evidence from a later period that the association had a very important role in determining how policy was formulated and carried out. See for example, G. Gorer, *Africa Dances: a book about West African Negroes* (New York, 1962), pp.25-6; this book, first published in 1935, relates observations of the author during a trip in French Africa in the early 1930s.

[62] 'La situation politique de la Côte d'Ivoire', *BCAF*, ii (1910), pp.60-2.

[63] For metropolitan press coverage of the deteriorating situation in the Ivory Coast see: 'Encore des combats en Afrique: le Côte d'Ivoire soulève pour ne pas payer l'impôt', *Le Matin*, 12 Dec. 1909; 'La révolte à la Côte d'Ivoire', *Paris Journal*, 10 Feb. 1910; 'La pacification de la Côte d'Ivoire', *Le Temps*, 21 Mar. 1910; 'La situation de la Côte d'Ivoire', *Les Débats*, 21 Mar. 1910; 'La vérité sur les incidents de la Côte d'Ivoire: Le rôle de M. le Gouverneur Angoulvant', *Le Siècle*, 28-9 Mar. 1910.

[64] ANRS, 5-G-47, P. 140 & 141, [Ponty], 'Rapport sur la Côte d'Ivoire, IIe partie, Critiques auxquelles ont donné lieu les procédés de répression employés à la Côte d'Ivoire et les exigences de l'Administration à l'égard des indigènes', [n.d. – c.Mar. 1910]. See also 'Les insurrections à la Côte d'Ivoire: Le Gouverneur Général Merlaud Ponty nous expose son programme', *Le Matin*, 22 Mar. 1910; and 'Une conversation avec M. Ponty sur la situation de la Côte d'Ivoire', *Le Temps*, 23 Mar. 1910.

[65] ANRCI, X-35-31, Angoulvant to Monsieur le Député, 13 Sept. 1910.

[66] See Ministère des Colonies. Office Coloniale, *Statistiques des finances des colonies pour les années 1904-1913* (Melun, 1917), pp.94-7.

[67] ANRCI, X-35-31, Angoulvant to M. le Député, 13 Sept. 1910; this letter contains an outline of the estimated expenses for repressing the revolts.

[68] ANSOM, Côte d'Ivoire, VII, 8, Gov. Gen. [Ponty] to Chef de bat., Noguès, Commandant des détachements de la Côte d'Ivoire, 18 Feb. 1910; these instructions were to have resolved the simmering dispute between Angoulvant and the military officers. In spite of these directions, however, the tension between the

officers and Angoulvant continued throughout 1910 leading eventually to Lt. Col. Lagarrue's dismissal in Aug. 1910. Thus, Angoulvant eventually won his case against the military officers who wished to have full autonomy in commanding the operations within the colony.

[69] Angoulvant, *La Pacification*, pp.268–318; in reality, this section of Angoulvant's book was written by an administrator named Chéruy.

[70] The most detailed accounts of these campaigns are to be found in the following articles: 'Opérations militaires à la Côte d'Ivoire', *Alm. Ann. Mars.* (1909), pp.31–41; 'La Soumission des Agbas', *BCAF*, xii (1910), pp.388–9; 'Opérations militaires à la Côte d'Ivoire en 1908 et 1909 et la colonne du Bandama', *Alm. Ann. Mars.* (1911), pp.45–68; 'Colonne du commandant Morel contre les Ngbans (mai-août 1910)', *RTC*, x, (1911), pp.590–1; 'Côte d'Ivoire', *Alm. Ann. Mars.* (1912), pp.15–39; 'La réoccupation de Salékro (Côte d'Ivoire), février 1911', *RTC* (1913), 2e sem., pp.316–23. For information on the Akoué represssion see above, p.277, n.43.

[71] For a summary of Angoulvant's restrictive measures on armaments see Angoulvant, *La Pacification*, pp.201–17.

[72] Lt. Bouet, 'Quelques opérations militaires', p.152.

[73] J. de la Brousse, *La Forêt vaincue*, pp.52–3, 62; for other comments on Baule fighting strategy see 'Notes sur la guerre en pays Baoulé, d'après des notes du commandant Maillard et des capitaines Garnier et Privey', *RTC*, iv (1905), pp.309–44.

[74] 'Notes sur la guerre en pays Baoulé', pp.321–2; Lt. Bouet, 'Quelques opérations militaires', p.153.

[75] ANRCI, X-31-12, telegram, Noguès to Angoulvant, 24 Nov. 1909; ibid., same to same, 1 Dec. 1909; ibid., Gov. [Angoulvant] to Gov. Gen., 20 Dec. 1909; see also: 'Opérations à la Côte d'Ivoire. Colonne de Commandant Noguès', pp.378–81; and de la Brousse, *La Forêt vaincue*, pp.57–75.

[76] Fleeing Akoué took refuge among kinsmen in Nanafoué country, cf. ANRCI, X-5-124, Noguès to Angoulvant, 3 Mar. 1910. The Ngban fled to take refuge among the Agba, cf. ANRCI, X-31-14, Carrière, 'Rapport politique et de Tournée', Ouossou, Aug. 1911. It is significant that the Anyi groups on the left bank of the Nzi refused to harbour the Ngban in the 1910 revolt, although they had been willing to do so earlier in the revolt of 1902. See for example, ANRCI, XIII-32-86/813, Gervais, 'Résumé du compte rendu à la suite de tournée en pays Agni Ahri', 24 May 1910.

[77] Most of the campaigns ended in Dec. 1910. Under normal circumstances December was a plentiful month, following shortly after the harvest of the largest yam crops, but because of the military's policy of systematically destroying the Baule plantations, the harvest was meagre in October and November 1910 and the Baule faced starvation from December onwards.

[78] ANRCI, X-5-123, Gov. Angoulvant to Lt. Col. [Lagarrue] 'Instructions politiques et administratives donnant les conditions de soumission à imposer aux N'Gbans', 30 Apr. 1910; ANRCI, XIII-32-86/813, Prouteaux, 'Notes sur les N'Gbans Assabou', 11 May 1910; ANRCI, X-5-123, Bru, 'Liste nominative des chefs Indigènes, notables meneurs, qui ont provoqué la révolte et dont l'attitude irréductiblement hostile rend leur présence dangereuse dans le pays, et dont le déportation est proposée', 12 July 1910.

[79] Angoulvant, *La Pacification*, p.217.

[80] The measures determining the war fines imposed on the Baoulé are summarized in Angoulvant, *La Pacification*, p.245.

[81] See p.20 above.

[82] ANRCI, X-6-128, Lt. [Bouet] to Capt. [Jigoudan], 31 May 1910.

[83] 'Arrêté fixant le taux de l'impôt de capitation par cercle pour l'année

1910', no. 598, 18 Sept. 1909; and the Arrêté of 15 Sept. 1910 [establishing the rate of taxation for 1911]. Both are cited and discussed in 'La pacification', *BCAF–RCD* [off-print], p.8.

[84] Angoulvant, *La Pacification*, pp.245–6. Because of this resettlement phenomenon it has become extremely difficult to trace the precise history of any one village in Baule country today. Since each present-day village represents an amalgam of the descendants of survivors from several pre-colonial villages the 'history' of the village may vary considerably depending upon which household in the village relates past events.

[85] Angoulvant, *La Pacification*, p.246.

[86] ANRCI, X-5-123, Bru, 'Indigènes du poste d'Ouossou qui se sont signalés par les services qu'ils ont rendus', 21 July 1910; ibid., 'Organisation des villages des tribus N'Gbans', Décision de M. le Gouverneur du 28 juillet 1910, 28 July 1910.

[87] ANRCI, XVII-47-2, 'Rôle primitif pour servir à la perception de l'impôt de capitation. Population fixe'. Yamoussoukro, 10 Dec. 1911.

[88] Arrêté local, 6 Jan. 1910, *JOCI* (1910), p.7; Simon, *Souvenirs de brousse*, p.96; Lt. Bouet, 'Quelques opérations', p.147.

[89] Angoulvant, *La Pacification*, pp.239–40.

[90] Décret du 21 novembre 1904; relevant excerpts from this decree are reproduced in Angoulvant, *La Pacification*, p.233.

[91] The Arrêtés condemning the various Baule chiefs to exile are summarized in Angoulvant, *La Pacification*, pp.234–7, indicating their group of origin, the date of their condemnation, the place and duration of their sentence of exile.

[92] ANRS, 10-E-6, Procès verbal, Conseil d'Administration, séance du 28 Nov. 1910; ANRCI, X-7-172, Ponty, 'Arrêté no. 630 portant internement d'indigènes originaires de la Côte d'Ivoire', 22 June 1911.

[93] ANRCI, X-5-123, Bru, 'Liste nominative des chefs indigènes . . . dont le déportation est proposée', 12 July 1910; ANRCI, XIII, 32-86/813, Commandant Morel, Colonne contre les N'Gbans, 'Rapport d'ensemble', 5 Aug. 1910; ANRCI, X-2-60, Ponty, 'Arrêté no. 1232, portant internement d'indigènes originaires de la Côte d'Ivoire', 30 Oct. 1910.

[94] ANRCI, X-7-172, Ponty, 'Arrêté no. 630 portant internement', 22 June 1911. See comments added to the original text concerning those who had died during May, June, and July 1911 in Bingerville before being sent into exile.

[95] ANRCI, XXI-17-15, Aubin, Rapport mensuel, Sakassou, Oct. 1908.

[96] ANRCI, X-38-5, 'Rapport sur la situation politique du cercle du Baoulé Nord au 30 juin 1912', 20 July 1912. Kouadio Ndri is reputed to have lived until 1925, see Guié Kouamé, 'Monographie de Sakassou', C.E.N.W.P. [n.d. – c.1945].

[97] ANRCI, X-6-128, Gervais, 'Rapport sur la situation politique du poste et les tournées effectuées pendant le mois', Yamoussoukro, Dec. 1910.

[98] ANRCI, X-5-123, L'Administrateur du cercle du Baoulé-Sud to Gov., no. 237G, 30 Apr. 1910.

[99] See pp.168–9 above. The assassinations of faithful chiefs like Kouassi Ngo and Nzoko suggests that whatever benefits were to be derived from collaborating with the French, they were perhaps enjoyed more fully by the descendants and political heirs of these collaborators than they were by the chiefs themselves. In particular those identified as heirs of collaborating chiefs were afforded preferential access to the colonial educational structures. In this context see 'Circulaire du Gov. Gen. – Fréquentation des écoles, notamment par les enfants des agents indigènes de l'administration', 2 Feb. 1910, *JOCI* (1910), p.81.

[100] ANRCI, X-31-14, Bru, 'Rapport sur la situation politique', Jan. 1911; ibid., Carrière, Rapport politique et de Tournée, Aug. 1911.

[101] Delafosse, *Essai de manuel*, p.v.

[102] ANRCI, X-30-11, Delafosse to Gov., no. 168, 18 Oct. 1899.

[103] A. Nebout, 'Note sur le Baoulé', *A Travers le Monde* (1900) 2e sem. p.393.

[104] ANRCI, X-38-9, Capt. Le Magnen, 'Notice sur le Baoulé', [n.d.-c.Jan. 1900].

[105] Clozel, 'Le Recensement de 1901 à la Côte d'Ivoire', *BCAF* (1902), p.141.

[106] ANRCI, Monographies, Bouaké, 'Monographie du cercle du Baoulé-Nord', July 1911.

[107] G. Joseph, *La Côte d'Ivoire: Le pays et ses habitants* (Paris, 1917), cited in D. Domergue-Cloarec, 'La Côte d'Ivoire de 1912 à 1920: Influence de la première Guerre Mondiale sur l'évolution politique, économique et sociale', (Thèse de 3e cycle, Toulouse le Mirail, 1974), p.13.

[108] ANRCI, IV-40-11, L'Administrateur Commandant le Cercle [Baoulé-Sud] to Gov., 2 June 1913; ibid., L'Administrateur du Cercle du Baoulé-Nord to Gov., no. 67, 10 June 1913. The information in these and other reports from various points throughout the colony was compiled by the administration to form a composite report: ANRCI, IV-40-11, Angoulvant, 'Note sur les résultats de la pacification au point de vue anti-esclavagiste', [n.d. – c.Aug. 1913]. See also ANRCI, X-13-250, 'Note sur les repercussions de la pacification de la Côte d'Ivoire (suppression de l'esclavage)', [n.d. – c.Aug. 1913]. This was subsequently printed as 'La pacification de la Côte d'Ivoire et la répression de l'esclavagisme', *BCAF-RCD*, x (1913), pp.341-6.

[109] ANRCI, X-31-14, Bru, 'Rapport sur la situation politique', Jan. 1911. The severe repression of the last wave of resistance among the Baule and their neighbours from 1908 onward unleashed a series of internal migrations which came to worry the administration: see particularly, 'L'exode des populations de la Côte d'Ivoire. Le canal de lagunes', *BCAF*, vii (1923), p.390. Migrations of the Baule toward other forest areas in the Ivory Coast began in this period, leading later to a situation in which Baule cash crop farmers established plantations and gained control over land usage rights in large areas of Dida, Bété, and Anyi country. It was primarily because of the repressive character of the 'pacification' programme within Baule country itself that Baule migrant farmers began to 'colonize' the lands of other ethnic groups to the south-west and south-east of their territory. In this context see P. and M. Étienne, 'L'émigration baoulé actuelle', *Cahiers d'Outre-Mer*, xxi (1968), pp.155-95.

[110] ANRCI, X-34-20, Angoulvant, 'Ligne politique suivie à la Côte d'Ivoire', [n.d. – c.Dec. 1910].

[111] See for example: 'Celle qu'on n'écrit pas', *La Côte d'Ivoire*, no. 86, 30 June 1913. *La Côte d'Ivoire* was a bi-weekly journal published in the Ivory Coast under the editorship of Charles Ostench. It closely reflected the opinions of the commercial community. It has been impossible to locate a complete collection of the journal, but isolated numbers are available for reference in the ANRCI.

[112] See 'Entente cordiale', *L'Indépendant de la Côte d'Ivoire*, no. 21, 25 Oct. 1914. This is an article describing the agreement reached between the commercial community and Angoulvant to keep their differences to a minimum during the duration of the war. *L'Indépendant de la Côte d'Ivoire* was a bi-weekly journal under the direction of Julien Vizioz, published in Grand Bassam. Established in 1913, it expressed the opinions of the local merchants. It has been impossible to find a complete series of the journal, but individual numbers can be consulted in the ANRCI. For an indication of how close the administration and commerce had become by the time of Angoulvant's departure see: 'Départ du Gouverneur Angoulvant pour Dakar', *L'Indépendant*, no. 180, 9 June 1916.

[113] For Ponty's praise see 'Discours prononcé au Conseil du Governement à Dakar', cf. *BCAF-RCD*, xii (1912), p.419. Angoulvant was named as acting Gov. Gen. in June 1916.

[114] ANRCI, IX-41-21, 'Rapport sur la situation politique et des tournées éffectuées, Béoumi', June 1912.

NOTES TO CHAPTER VII

[1] For a discussion of the pre-colonial rivalries see pp.25–32 above.

[2] See p.62 above.

[3] See pp.117, and 121–2 above.

[4] See pp.127 and 203 above.

[5] After the 1899–1902 hostilities and again after the 1908–1911 conflicts, fratricidal disputes among the Baule took on a heightened intensity as various groups began to blame one another for having favoured French intrusion. The disputes were often fatal for the closest French collaborators as the assassinations of Moya Ba and Kouassi Ngo had proved. In the process the French began to develop an image of themselves as benign conciliators in 'traditional' disputes between contending factions, and in part the administration justified itself in terms of bringing 'peace' to an area characterized by endemic warfare.

[6] See pp.8, 12, 28 and 55 above.

[7] See pp.86–8 above.

[8] See pp.94–5, 109–11, and 158–60 above.

[9] The level of animosity towards the Dyula community became particularly apparent at the time of the Akoué revolt of 1909 and the Ali Seck 'affair' following immediately upon it. See pp.190–5 above.

[10] See pp.103–4 above.

[11] ANRCI, XIV-29-5, Clozel, 'Circulaire No. 21c à MM. les Administrateurs de cercle au sujet de l'hospitalité accordée dans des postes à des femmes', 15 Mar. 1907. See pp.152–3 above.

[12] This was the case of the 'liberated' slaves in the Bouaké post during the siege of 1898. The Dyula at Toumodi similarly assisted Delafosse in 1899 and came to the aid of Simon and Moesch when they were confined to Yamoussoukro in the Akoué revolt of June 1909.

[13] For comments on the helpful role of women in the establishment of French control see ANRCI, X-34-8, Capt. Maillard to Chef de bat., 23b, 14 Apr. 1903.

[14] See pp.22–5 above.

[15] See p.153 above.

[16] Delafosse, *Essai de manuel*, pp.117–18. See p.22 above concerning the title, *famien*.

[17] P. Duprey, *Histoire des Ivoiriens. Naissance d'une nation* (Abidjan, 1962), p.143.

[18] See pp.135–6 and 139 above.

[19] ANRCI, XIV-34-4, Capt. Garnier to Chef de bat., 21 Mar. 1903.

[20] See pp.136–7 above.

[21] In naming Kouassi Ngo as 'chef de la tribu des Akoués' Angoulvant made provisions to pay him a monthly salary of one hundred francs. See Arrêté local no. 22, 12 Jan. 1910, *JOCI* (1910), p.9.

[22] ANRCI, X-6-128, Bru, Rapport politique, Feb. 1910; Kouadio Okou also acted as an intermediary between the French and the Souamlé, cf. ANRCI, X-6-128, Bru, Rapport mensuel, June 1910.

[23] For a description of the flexible character of Baule social structure see particularly pp.17–25 above.

[24] See pp.19 and 23–5 above.

[25] See pp.90–3 and 201–2 above.

[26] 'Notes sur la guerre en pays Baoulé', *RTC*, iv (1905), p.324. See also pp.139–41 above.

[27] See pp. 202-3 and 204-5 above.

[28] ANRCI, XIV-29-5, Lt. Gridel, 'Rapport sur le nommé Tiéfi du village de Sikassuénou (Nanafoué)', 10 Sept. 1902; ANRCI, XIII, 26-12/76, Registre des Ordres, [Colonna d'Istria], Ordre no. 0.48, 24 Sept. 1902.

[29] ANRCI, X-5-129, [Prouteau] to Gov., Lettre no. 237G, 30 Apr. 1910; and ANRCI, X-6-128, Gervais, 'Rapport sur la situation politique du poste de Toumodi', Sept. 1910.

[30] ANRCI, X-6-128, Bru, 'Rapport sur la situation politique, Ouossou', Apr. 1910.

[31] ANRCI, X-30-11, Capt. Foussat to Gov., 9 Nov. 1910.

[32] See pp.38-9 above. The role of the Beugré cult in the developing resistance of Tiassalé after the deaths of Voituret and Papillon is mentioned in Désille to Ballay, 'Rapport du 15 avril au 15 mai 1891', cited in ANRCI, VII-3-7, Bricard to Sec. Gen. of Guinée, 17 Dec. 1892.

[33] ANRCI, X-6-128, Bru, Rapport politique, Ouossou, Feb. 1910.

[34] For an account of the rise of the prophet Harris in the Ivory Coast see G. M. Haliburton, *The Prophet Harris: A Study of an African Prophet and his Mass Movement in the Ivory Coast, 1913-1915* (London, 1971).

NOTES TO CHAPTER VIII

[1] For a discussion of the role of Baule paramount chiefs see pp.215-8 above.

[2] See p.161 above.

[3] Differences between civilian and military approaches provide a theme of continuous importance in the evolution of French-Baule relations. For the tension between these two different approaches see above, pp.41-3, 69-76, 78, 105-9, 117, 123-4, 140-1, 153-5, 196-7, and 278, n.68.

[4] For critical assessments of the character of French expansion in West Africa see the works of A. S. Kanya-Forstner, including *The Conquest*, particularly pp.263-74; and 'Military Expansion in the Western Sudan – French and British Style', in Gifford and Louis, eds., *France and Britain in Africa*, pp.409-41.

[5] J. D. Hargreaves, *West Africa*, p.97.

[6] The pattern of the encounter between the French and the Baule is largely consistent with that outlined in R. Robinson, 'Non-European Foundations of European Imperialism: Sketch for a Theory of Collaboration', in Owen and Sutcliffe, eds., *Studies in the Theory of Imperialism* (London, 1972), pp.117-24.

[7] See pp.61-5 above.

[8] See pp.103-5 and 109-10 above.

[9] See pp.109 and 113 above. The question of slave emancipation was of particular importance in the numerous revolts from 1900 to 1902 as well. See pp.126-7 and 140 (quotation) above.

[10] See p.147 above.

[11] See pp.186-8 above.

[12] For Clozel's tax policies see pp.146, 147, 169-71, 173-4 above.

[13] For Angoulvant's tax policy see pp.184-5, 204.

[14] See pp.172-80 above.

[15] L. Hubert cited in 'La pénétration', *BCAF-RCD*, x (1909), [off-print], p.9.

[16] Contrast, for example, this approach to the problems of development with Clozel's own statements of policy on pp.154, 160 above.

[17] 'Peripheral explanations' of imperialism are elaborated by D. K. Fieldhouse in his work, *Economics and Empire, 1830-1914* (London, 1973), pp.76-84, 460-3. Drawing largely upon the initial insights of Professors Robinson and Gallagher, Fieldhouse contrasts the idea of a 'peripheral' explanation with what he calls the 'Eurocentric' explanations that have dominated general theories of imperialism to date.

[18] Fieldhouse, *Economics and Empire*, pp.463, 476.

[19] As Robinson points out: 'Domination is only practicable in so far as alien power is translated into terms of indigenous political economy' (R. Robinson, 'Non-European foundations', p.119). Analysing the indigenous political economies on the frontiers of empire is therefore the essential point of departure for understanding the process of expanding European domination.

[20] Robinson, 'Non-European foundations', pp.118–19.

[21] R. E. Robinson and J. Gallagher, 'The Partition of Africa', in *New Cambridge Modern History*, xi (Cambridge, 1962), p.633.

[22] In this regard see particularly Allan McPhee, *The Economic Revolution in West Africa* (London, 1926).

[23] C. W. Newbury, 'Prices and profitability in early nineteenth-century West African trade', in C. Meillassoux, ed., *The Development of Trade and Markets in West Africa* (London, 1971), p.93.

[24] A. G. Hopkins, *An Economic History*, pp.138–9.

[25] Ibid. 167.

[26] The terms are Hopkins's. See particularly ibid. 167.

[27] Ibid. 189.

[28] Ibid. 189.

[29] R. Robinson, 'European Imperialism and Indigenous Reactions in British West Africa, 1880–1914', in H. L. Wesseling, ed., *Expansion and Reaction: Essays on European Expansion and Reactions in Asia and Africa* (Leyden, 1978), p.162.

[30] R. Robinson, 'European Imperialism', p.162.

[31] Ibid.

[32] ANRCI, X-35-31, Angoulvant, Lettre Programme, 28 Oct. 1908.

Bibliography and Sources

A. MANUSCRIPT SOURCES

I. Public Archive Collections

    a) ANRCI – Archives Nationales de la République de la Côte d'Ivoire (Abidjan)

    b) ANRM – Archives Nationales de la République du Mali (Bamako)

    c) ANRS – Archives Nationales de la République du Sénégal (Dakar)

    d) ANSOM – Archives Nationales (France), Section d'Outre–Mer (Paris)

II. Private Papers

    a) D.P. – Delafosse Papers (Mme Louise Delafosse)

    b) Archevêché (Abidjan)

III. Dissertations and Unpublished Manuscripts

B. PUBLISHED SOURCES

I. Primary Sources

    a) Government Publications and Periodicals

    b) Contemporary Books, Articles, Pamphlets

II. Secondary Studies

    a) General Works and Related Studies

    b) Studies of the Baule

A. MANUSCRIPT SOURCES

I. Public Archive Collections

a) ANRCI – Archives Nationales de la République de la Côte d'Ivoire (Abidjan, Ivory Coast)

These archives provided the main material for this thesis. They contain the monthly administrative, economic, and agricultural reports as well as the military reports for most of the Baule region. They are particularly rich for the period 1900–11. The material on the Baule has in the past been scattered throughout the various files, but the administration is now beginning to organize the reports on a geographical basis. In an effort to assist other researchers interested in the Baule peoples we compiled a preliminary handlist of materials. See T. C. Weiskel, 'Répertoire préliminaire des dossiers conservés aux Archives nationales concernant l'histoire des peuples baoulé, 1893–1920', (Abidjan, 1973).

In addition to the numbered files the collection known as the 'Monographies de Cercle' (referred to in the above text simply as 'Monographies') contains numerous useful reports.

b) ANRM – Archives Nationales de la République du Mali (Bamako, Mali)

These archives are composed in part of the records of the Sudanese military command. Since the post at Bouaké was established from the Sudan in 1898 in the wake of Samory's retreat, these archives contain valuable material relating to the northern Baule areas. There are also scattered reports from military officers in the Ivory Coast written to the military command during the 1900–2 campaigns. A useful guide has been compiled for easy access to the material. See Moussa Niakaté, *Archives Nationales du Mali: répertoire, 1855–1954* (Bamako, 1974).

c) ANRS – Archives Nationales de la Répblique du Sénégal (Dakar, Senegal)

These archives contain the records of the Government General of French West Africa (A.O.F.), and they are valuable for the reports written from the administration in the Ivory Coast to the Governor General as well as for the final military reports on the various campaigns. In addition they include the records of the Ivory Coast Conseil d'Administration (série 10-E) and a series of periodic reports (série 2-G) which contain useful material. The archives are well catalogued. See J. Charpy, *Répertoire des Archives* (Rufisque, 1955). A separate catalogue exists for the periodic reports (série 2-G): Abdoulaye Gamby N'Diaye, *Rapports politiques et périodiques, série 2-G, 1895–1922* (Dakar, 1967).

d) ANSOM – Archives Nationales (France), Section d'Outre-Mer (Paris, France)

These are the archives of the former Ministère des Colonies. They are particularly useful for the early period relating to the establishment of French control along the Ivory Coast and the early exploration missions. In addition, series 'Afrique III' contains detailed documentation of the Monteil expedition leading to the first Baule revolt (1894–1895). The collection is very well catalogued. See U.N.E.S.C.O. Conseil International des archives, *Sources de l'histoire de l'Afrique au sud du Sahara dans les archives et bibliothèques françaises: volume I – Archives* (Zug, 1971).

II. Private Papers

a) D.P. – Delafosse Papers

These private papers in the custody of Mme Louise Delafosse, the daughter of Maurice Delafosse, consist principally of correspondence from Delafosse to his parents during the period from 1894 to 1900 while he was resident in Baule country and in Liberia. Mme Delafosse is in the process of publishing a biography of her father, making full use of these materials. We are particularly grateful to her for her willingness to let us consult the correspondence and the field note-books that her father kept while in Baule territory.

b) Archevêché d'Abidjan, Abidjan Église du Plateau

The Archevêché preserves the original manuscript version of Revd. Père Bedel's 'Souvenirs de Voyage'. The second notebook of the manuscript contains a brief but interesting account of Bedel's trip into Baule country during the early months of 1902.

III. Dissertations and Unpublished Manuscripts

Bamba, Mohammed Sékou, 'Tiassalé et le commerce précolonial sur le Bas–Bandama', (Paris, Mémoire de Maîtrise – Paris I, 1975).

Bettignies, J. de, 'Toumodi. Étude monographique d'un centre semi-urbain' (Abidjan, Institut de Géographie, Université d'Abidjan, 1965).

Bidou, Rév. P., 'Du peuple Gouro', typescript (1962).

Delafosse, M. 'Manuel de langue Agni (dialecte du Baoulé)', MS conserved in the Musée de l'Homme, Paris, n.d.

Domergue–Cloarec, D., 'La Côte d'Ivoire de 1912 à 1920; Influence de la première Guerre Mondiale sur l'évolution politique, économique et sociale' (Thèse de 3e cycle, Université de Toulouse le Mirail, 1974), 2 vols.

Ekanza, S.–P. M'Bra, 'Colonisation et sociétés traditionnelles. Un quart de siècle de dégradation du monde traditionnel ivoirien, 1893–1920' (Thèse de 3e cycle, Aix–Marseille I, Université de Provence, 1972), 2 vols.

Hay, M. J., 'Coffee and Cocoa in the Ivory Coast: A Study in the Dynamics of Economic Change' (History Dept., University of Wisconsin, M.A., 1967).

Horovitz, R. A., 'Trade between Sanwi and her Neighbors: 1843–1893', Paper presented to Akan Conference, Bondoukou, Ivory Coast (Jan. 1974).

Kouamé, G., 'Monographie de Sakassou', E.N.W.P., MS conserved in I.F.A.N. library, Dakar, n.d.

Launay, R. G., 'Tying the Cola: Dyula Marriage and Social Change' (Ph.D. thesis, Cambridge University, 1975).

Ravenhill, P. L., 'The Social Organization of the Wan: A Patrilineal People of the Ivory Coast' (Ph.D. thesis, The New School for Social Research, 1975).

Semi-Bi, Zan, 'La politique coloniale des Travaux Publiques en Côte d'Ivoire (1900–1940)' (Thèse de 3e cycle, Paris – Université de Paris VII, 1973).

Thurow, D. R., 'A Case Study of Tribal Economy among the Baoulé' (M.A. thesis, Dept. of Economics, University of Illinois, 1958).

Weiskel, T. C., 'French Colonial Rule and the Baule Peoples: Resistance and Collaboration, 1889–1911', (Oxford, D.Phil., 1977).

Yahaya, Diabi, 'Les survivances de la confédération Ashanti en Côte d'Ivoire: La Monarchie baoulé de Sakassou' (Mémoire de Licence, Département d'Histoire, Université d'Abidjan, 1974).

Zinsou, J. V., 'L'administration française en Côte d'Ivoire, 1890–1920', (Aix-en-Provence, Thèse de 3e cycle, 1973).

B. PUBLISHED SOURCES

I. Primary Sources

a) *Government Publications and Periodicals*
Alm. Ann. Mars. – Almanach Annuaire du Marsouin.
BCAF – Bulletin du Comitè de l'Afrique Française.
BCAF–RCD – Bulletin du Comité de l'Afrique Française – Renseignements Coloniaux et Documents (Supplément).
BOCI – Bulletin Officiel de la Côte d'Ivoire.
Gouvernement de la Côte d'Ivoire, *Rapport d'ensemble sur la situation générale de la Colonie de la Côte d'Ivoire* (Grand Bassam, 1901), 2 parts.
Gouvernement Général de l'A.O.F., la Côte d'Ivoire, *Rapport d'ensemble sur la situation générale de la Colonie de la Côte d'Ivoire* (Bingerville, 1905).
Gouvernement Général de l'A.O.F., *La Côte d'Ivoire: Notice publiées par le Gouvernement Général à l'occasion de l'Exposition Coloniale de Marseille*, (Marseille, 1906).
Gouvernement Général de l'A.O.F., *La Côte d'Ivoire brochure de propagande*, (Bingerville, 1915).
JOAOF – Journal Officiel de l'Afrique Occidentale Française.
JOCI – Journal Officiel de la Côte d'Ivoire.
JO, Déb. Parl. – Journal Officiel, Débats Parlementaires.
Ministère des Colonies, Office Colonial, *Statistiques des finances des colonies pour les années 1904–1913* (Melun, 1917).
Ministère des Colonies, Office Colonial, *Statistiques des finances des colonies françaises pour les années 1898–1907* (Melun, 1908).
Ministère des Colonies, Office Colonial, *Statistiques coloniales pour l'année [1892–1911]: Commerce* (Paris, published annually).
RTC – Revue des Troupes Coloniales.

b) *Contemporary Books, Articles, Pamphlets*
The following contemporary published material was of particular importance in the thesis research. More complete listings of publications relating to French policy in the period and the conditions in the Ivory Coast are contained in E. A. Joucla, *Bibliographie de l'Afrique Occidentale Française* (Paris, 1937), and G. Janvier, *Bibliographie de la Côte d'Ivoire. II. Sciences de l'homme* (Abidjan, 1973).

'Les Anglais et Samory', *BCAF*, vii (juillet 1897), pp.252–3.

Angoulvant, G., *La Pacification de la Côte d'Ivoire (1908-1915). Méthode et résultats* (Paris, 1916).

–– 'Les coutumes indigènes de la Côte d'Ivoire', *BCAF-RCD*, vii (July 1916), pp.211–12.

'A propos de Samory', *BCAF*, i (Jan. 1898), pp.4–9.

Arhin, K., ed., *The Papers of George Ekem Ferguson: A Fanti Official of the Government of the Gold Coast, 1890-1897* (Cambridge, 1974).

Armand, Lieutenant, 'La Mission Armand', *BCAF*, ix (Sept. 1891), pp.12–14.

Baillaud, É., *La Situation économique de l'Afrique Occidentale anglaise et française* (Paris, 1907).

–– *La Politique indigène de l'Angleterre en Afrique Occidentale* (Paris, 1912).

'Baoule', *Alm. Ann. Mars.* (1903), pp.17–18.

Baratier, Colonel, *Épopées africaines* (Paris, 1912).

–– *A travers l'Afrique* (Paris, 1914).

Barbier, L., *La Côte d'Ivoire* (Paris, 1916).

Barot, Docteur, *Guide pratique de l'européen dans l'Afrique Occidentale à l'usage des militaires, fonctionnaires, commerçants, colons et touristes* (Paris, 1902).

Betsellère, Commandant, 'Cercle du Baoulé', in Gouvernement Général d l'AOF, *La Côte d'Ivoire* (Marseille, 1906), pp.468–505.

Bonneau, Lieutenant, *La Côte d'Ivoire* (Paris, n.d. [1898]).

Bouchet, M. A., *Le Commerce de l'Afrique Occidentale Française* (Villefranche, 1921).

Bouet, J. F., 'Quelques opérations militaires à la Côte d'Ivoire en 1909', *RTC*, ix (1910) 2e sem., pp.63–80, 134–53, 205–20, 343–70, 589–610.

Bouët-Willaumez, É., *Description nautique des côtes de l'Afrique Occidentale* (Paris, 1846).

–– *Commerce et traite des Noirs aux côtes Occidentales d'Afrique* (Paris, 1848).

Bowdich, T. E., *Mission from Cape Coast Castle to Ashantee* (London, 1819).

Brisley, T., 'Some notes on the Baoulé tribe', *Journal of the African Society*, viii (1908-9), pp.296–302.

Brousse, J. de la, *La Forêt vaincue* (*récits de la Côte d'Ivoire*) (Paris, 1932).

'Celle qu'on n'écrit pas', *La Côte d'Ivoire*, 86 (30 June 1913).

'Le chemin de fer de la Côte d'Ivoire à Bouaké', *BCAF*, ix (Sept. 1912), p.377.

Clarke, J., *Specimens of dialects. Short vocabularies of languages and notes of countries and customs in Africa* (London, 1849).

Clozel, F. -J., 'La situation économique de la Côte d'Ivoire', *BCAF-RCD*, iv (1899), pp.63–71.

—— 'La recensement de 1901 à la Côte d'Ivoire', *BCAF* (1902), p.140.

—— 'Land tenure among the natives of the Ivory Coast', *Journal of the African Society*, i, 3 (1902), pp.399–415.

—— *Dix ans à la Côte d'Ivoire* (Paris, 1906).

—— and R. Villamur, eds., *Les Coutumes indigènes de la Côte d'Ivoire* (Paris, 1902).

Collieaux, A., 'Détails rétrospectifs sur l'histoire des dernières opérations contre Samory et la prise de l'Almamy (1897–1898)', *Bulletin du Comité d'Études Historiques et Scientifiques de l'AOF*, xxi, 2 (1938), pp.290–303.

'Colonne du commandant Morel contre les Ngbans (mai–août 1910)', *RTC*, x (1911), pp.590–1.

Combes, P., 'L'aire géographique des conquêtes de Samory', *Le Tour du Monde* (1899), pp.5–6.

'Le commerce en 1898', *BCAF*, ii (1900), p.59.

'Une conversation avec M. Ponty sur la situation de la Côte d'Ivoire', *Le Temps*, 23 Mar. 1910.

Cornet, Lieutenant, 'Notes sur la Côte d'Ivoire', *RTC*, iii (1904), pp.451–2.

'Côte d'Ivoire', *Alm. Ann. Mars.* (1912), pp.15–39.

'Côte d'Ivoire: Le Chemin de fer et le port', *BCAF*, i (1906), pp.16–17.

'Côte d'Ivoire: Le Nouveau Gouverneur – La Situation générale – L'Affaire d'Assikasso – Le Movement commercial', *BCAF*, x (1898), pp.346–8.

'Côte d'Ivoire: La Colonne expéditionnaire', *BCAF*, ii (1895), p.42.

Dapper, O., *Description de l'Afrique* (Amsterdam, 1686).

Debieuvre, Général, *Les Enseignements de la guerre dans les zones forestières des tropiques et de l'Équateur* (Paris, 1932).

Debrand, Lieutenant, 'Conduite des petits détachements en forêt équatoriale', *RTC* (1911) 2e sem, pp.11–29.

Delafosse, M., 'Les Agni (Paï-Pi-Bri)', *L'Anthropologie*, iv (1893), pp.402–45.

—— 'Notes anthropologiques et zoologiques sur le Baoulé', *Bulletin du Muséum d'Histoire Naturelle* (Paris), 6 (1897), pp.193–8.

—— 'Renseignements économiques', *JOCI*, 1 juillet 1899, pp.6–7.

—— 'Renseignements économiques'. Extrait d'un rapport de M. Delafosse, administrateur du Baoulé, Toumodi, 1 juillet 1899', *JOCI*, 1 aôut 1899, pp.3–5.

—— *Essai de manuel de la langue agni* (Paris, 1900).

—— 'Sur des traces probables de civilisation égyptienne et d'hommes de race blance à la Côte d'Ivoire', *L'Anthropologie*, xi (1900), pp.431–51, 543–68, 677–90.

—— *Essai de manuel pratique de la langue mandé ou mandingue* (Paris, 1901).

—— 'Les Libériens et les Baoulé', *Les Milieux et les Races* (Paris), avril-mai 1901.

—— 'Coutumes indigènes des Agni du Baoulé', in F.-J. Clozel and R. Villamur, eds., *Les Coutumes indigènes de la Côte d'Ivoire* (Paris, 1902), pp.95–146.

—— *Vocabulaires comparatifs de plus de soixante langues ou dialectes parlés à la Côte d'Ivoire* (Paris, 1904).

—— 'The Baule People of the Ivory Coast Interior and their religious beliefs', *The West African Mail*, 12 Aug. 1904, pp.462–4; 2 Sept. 1904, pp.535–7.

—— 'Ethnographie de la région de Bouaké. Note ethnologique et politique sur les tribus du secteur de Bouaké', in Clozel, *Dix ans à la Côte d'Ivoire* (Paris, 1906), Appendice II, pp.275–82.

—— 'Les états d'âme d'un colonial' (Paris, 1909).

—— 'Coutumes observées par les femmes en temps de guerre chez les Agni de la Côte d'Ivoire', *Revue d'ethnographie et de sociologie*, iv (1913), pp.266–8.

—— *Broussard ou les états d'âme d'un colonial suivis de ses propos et opinions* (Paris, 1923).

—— and R. Villamur, *Les Coutumes agni, rédigées et codifiées d'après les documents officiels les plus récents* (Paris, 1904).

Demanche, G., 'Les troubles de la Côte d'Ivoire', *Revue Française de l'Étranger et des Colonies*, 35 (1910), pp.195–204.

'Départ du Gouverneur Angoulvant pour Dakar', *L'Indépendant de la Côte d'Ivoire*, 180, 9 June 1916.

'Dernier mémoire secret sur la Côte d'Afrique', M. de Bussy [attached to dispatch of 6 June 1761] *Munger Africana Library Notes*, 3 (1971).

Desnouy, 'Les établissements français de la Côte d'Or', *Revue Maritime et Coloniale*, xviii (1865), pp.493–529.

'Discours prononcé au Conseil du Gouvernement à Dakar', *BCAF-RCD*, xii (1912), p.419.

Du Paty de Clam, A., 'Étude sur les indigènes du Baoulé' (Paris, 1899), extract from *Bulletin de Géographie historique et descriptive*, 2 (1898).

Dupuis, J., *Journal of a Residence in Ashantee* (London, 1824).

Dupuy, E., 'La pacification de la Côte d'Ivoire', *A Travers le Monde*, 17 (1911), pp.1–4.

'Encore des combats en Afrique: La Côte d'Ivoire soulève pour ne pas payer l'impôt', *Le Matin*, 12 Dec. 1909.

'Entente cordiale', *L'Indépendant de la Côte d'Ivoire*, 21, 25 Oct. 1914.

'L'exode des populations de la Côte d'Ivoire. Le canal des lagunes', *BCAF*, vii (1923), p.390.

Eysséric, J., 'Exploration du Bandama, Côte d'Ivoire', *Annales de géographie*, vii, 33 (1898), pp.273–7.

—— *Rapport sur une mission scientifique à la Côte d'Ivoire* (Paris, 1899).

—— 'Exploration et captivité chez les Gouro', *Le Tour du Monde* vi (1900), 1er sem., pp.71–108.

'Fin des opérations au Baoulé', *Alm. Ann. Mars.* (1904), pp.19–20.

Fleuriot de Langle, Vice-Amiral, 'Croisières à la Côte d'Afrique', *Le Tour du Monde*, xxvi (1873) 2e sem., pp.353–400.

Grisard, M. P., 'Une Mission commerciale sur le Lahou', *BCAF*, viii (1891), pp.6–8.

Hecquard, M., 'Rapport sur un voyage d'exploration dans l'intérieur de l'Afrique', *Revue Coloniale*, série ii, 8 (1852), pp.193–6.

—— *Voyage sur la Côte et dans l'intérieur de l'Afrique Occidentale* (Paris, 1853).

Hubert, H., 'Coutumes indigènes en matière d'exploitation de gîtes aurifères en Afrique Occidentale', *Annuaires et Mémoires du Comité d'Études Historiques et Scientifiques de l'A.O.F.* (1917), 226–43.

Hutton, W., *A Voyage to Africa; including a narrative of an embassy to one of the interior kingdoms in the year 1820* (London, 1821).

'L'inspection de M. Ponty et le nouvel emprunt', *BCAF*, iv (1911), pp.121–9.

'Les insurrections à la Côte d'Ivoire: Le Gouverneur Général Merlaud Ponty nous expose son programme', *Le Matin*, 22 Mar. 1910.

Joseph, G., *La Côte d'Ivoire: le pays – les habitants* (Paris, 1917).

Kouroubari, A., 'Alimama Samori Ko–Ma (Histoire de l'Imâm Samori)', in M. Delafosse, *Essai de manuel pratique de la langue mandé ou mandingue* (Paris, 1901).

—— 'Histoire de l'Imâm Samory', *BIFAN*, xxi, 3–4 (1959), pp.544–71.

Labouret, H., 'Notes contributives à l'étude du peuple baoulé', *Revue des Études ethnologiques et sociologiques*, 3–4 (1914), pp.83–91, 5–6, pp.187–94.

Lambert, 'Progrès de la colonisation', in Gouvernement Général de l'AOF, *La Côte d'Ivoire* (Marseille, 1906), pp.615–75.

Lamy, 'Souvenirs de la Côte d'Ivoire', *Le Tour du Monde*, nouvelle série, 11 (1905), pp.61–96.

Lasnet, Docteur, 'Notes sur le Baoulé', *A Travers le Monde*, 52 (1896), pp.409–12.

—— 'Contribution à la géographie médicale. Mission du Baoulé', *Annales d'hygiène et de médecine coloniale*, i (1898), pp.305–48.

Le Barbier, L., *La Côte d'Ivoire. Agriculture - Commerce - Industrie - Questions économiques* (Paris, 1916).

Le Herissé, R., *Voyage au Dahomey et à la Côte d'Ivoire* (Paris, 1903).

Lestideau, E., *La Question de la Main-d'œuvre dans les colonies françaises et spécialement dans celles de l'Afrique Occidentale Française* (Rennes, 1907).

'Une lettre de M. Verdier', *BCAF*, viii (1894), pp.118–19.

Levasseur, Colonel, 'Opérations sur le Haut–Bandama (Côte d'Ivoire, janvier–juillet 1911', *RTC* (1912), 2e sem., pp.1–21.

Leverson, H. A., A. L. L. Bell, and R. S. G. Gorton, *Military Report on the French West African Colonies of Senegal, Guinea, Ivory Coast and Dahomey* (London, 1903).

Merlin, M., 'La crise du Caoutchouc', *BCAF*, xii (1913), pp.420–8.

—— 'La crise du caoutchouc', *BCAF*, i (1914), p.56.

Michelet, E. and J. Clément, *La Côte d'Ivoire* (Paris, 1906).

Mille, P., *La Côte d'Ivoire. Notice pour l'exposition universelle de 1900* (Paris, 1900).

'Mission des Troupes Noires en 1910', *BCAF–RCD*, xii (Dec. 1910).

'La mission Eysséric', *BCAF*, vi (June 1897), p. 184.

'La mission Marchand et Manet', *BCAF*, vii (July 1893), p.4.

'La mission Marchand', *BCAF* (Sept. 1893), p.5.

'La mission Marchand', *BCAF*, xi (Nov. 1893), p.5.

'La mission Marchand', *BCAF*, xii (Dec. 1893), pp.13–14.

'La mission Marchand', *BCAF*, iv (Apr. 1894), pp.24–5.

'La mission Nebout chez Samory', *Revue Française de l'Étranger et des Colonies* 23 (1898), pp.5–21.

Monnier, M., *France Noire (Côte d'Ivoire et Soudan) - Mission Binger* (Paris, 1894).

'Monteil au pays de Kong. Les suites de la Mission Monteil', *A Travers le Monde*, 38 (Sept. 1895), pp.377–8.

Monteil, P. L., *La Colonne de Kong. Une page d'histoire militaire coloniale* (Paris, n.d. [1902]).

—— *Quelques feuillets d'histoire coloniale* (Paris, 1924).

'La Navigation fluviale à la Côte d'Ivoire - Le Caoutchouc', *BCAF*, v (1909), pp.180–1.

Nebout, A., 'Note sur le Baoulé', *A Travers le Monde* (1900) 2e sem., pp.393–6, 104–4, 109–12; (1901) 1er sem., pp.17–20, 35–6.

'Note sur les objets de pacotille propres aux échanges à la Côte d'Or', *Revue Maritime et Coloniale*, xxiii (1868), pp.999–1006.

'Notes sur la guerre en pays Baoulé, d'après des notes du commandant Maillard et des capitaines Garnier et Privey', *RTC*, iv (1905), pp. 309–44.

'Notice sur la colonne des Agba', *Alm. Ann. Mars.* (1909), pp.14–16.

Ogilby, J., *Africa, being an accurate description* (London, 1670).

'Opérations à la Côte d'Ivoire. Colonne du commandant Noguès (octobre 1909 à avril 1910)', *RTC*, x (1911), pp.359–81, 487–500.

'Opérations militaires à la Côte d'Ivoire', *Alm. Ann. Mars.* (1909), pp.31–41.

'Opérations militaires à la Côte d'Ivoire en 1908 et 1909 et la colonne du Bandama', *Alm. Ann. Mars.* (1911), pp.45–68.

'Les opérations militaires au Baoulé', *Alm. Ann. Mars.* (1902), pp.22–7.

'La pacification de la Côte d'Ivoire', *Le Temps*, 21 Mar. 1910.

'La pacification de la Côte d'Ivoire. Méthodes et résultats', *BCAF-RCD*, x (1910), pp.294–331.

'La pacification de la Côte d'Ivoire et la répression de l'esclavagisme', *BCAF-RCD*, xii (1913), pp.341–6.

'Le pays des Baoulés et sa pacification d'après un rapport de l'État-Major des troupes de l'AOF', *RFC*, ii (1903), 1e sem., pp.56–80, 159–90.

'La pénétration de la Côte d'Ivoire', *BCAF-RCD*, x (1909), pp.193–204.

'Pénétration par le Bandama', *BCAF* (Oct. 1894).

Pobéguin, C., 'Notes sur les lagunes de Grand-Lahou, de Fresco et les Rivières Bandama et Yocoboue', *Bulletin de la Société de Géographie*, vii, 18 (1897), pp.106–28, 230–51.

—— 'Notes sur la Côte d'Ivoire', *Bulletin de la Société de Géographie*, viii, 19 (1898), pp.328–74.

Privey, Capitaine, 'Aperçu sur la situation politique et militaire de la Côte d'Ivoire', *RTC* (1904), 2e sem., pp.309–30.

'La réoccupation de Salékro (Côte d'Ivoire), février 1911', *RTC* (1913), 2e sem., pp.316–23.

'La réorganisation de l'Afrique Occidentale et la colonne de Kong', *BCAF*, viii (1895), pp.247–55.

'La révolte à la Côte d'Ivoire', *Paris Journal*, 10 Feb. 1910.

Richaud, L. and R. Villamur, *Notre Colonie de la Côte d'Ivoire* (Paris, 1903).

Richet, E., *Sur les routes d'Afrique de Port-Étienne à Abomey* (Paris, n.d. [c.1907]).

Robertson, G. A., *Notes on Africa* (London, 1819).

Roussier, P., ed., *L'Établissement d'Issiny, 1687–1702* (Paris, 1935).

'Rupture de négociations avec Samory', *BCAF*, viii (1896), p.241.

Sarbah, J. M., *Fanti Customary Laws* (London, 1897).

Schefer, C., *Instructions générales données de 1763 à 1870 aux gouverneurs des établissements français en Afrique occidentale* (Paris, 1921).

'Sept ans d'Afrique. La Mission du Capitaine Marchand', *BCAF* (1895), pp.290–8.

Simon, M., *Souvenirs de brousse, 1905–1918* (Paris, 1965).

'La situation actuelle et l'avenir de la Côte d'Ivoire', *BCAF-RCD*, iv (1899), pp.57–64.

'La situation dans le Baoulé', *BCAF*, ix (1896), p.273.

'La situation de la Côte d'Ivoire', *Les Débats*, 21 Mar. 1910.

'La situation générale de la colonie en 1899', *BCAF*, vi (1900), p.249.

'La situation générale de la Côte d'Ivoire en 1898', *BCAF-RCD*, iv (1900), pp.71–2.

'La situation politique de la Côte d'Ivoire', *BCAF*, ii (1910), pp.60–2.

'La soumission des Agbas', *BCAF*, xii (1910), pp.388–9.

Tellier, T., 'Monographie du cercle du Baoulé', in F. -J. Clozel, *Dix ans à la Côte d'Ivoire* (Paris, 1906), pp.133–47.

Terrier, A., 'Les colonnes du Haut–Sassandra et du Haut–Bandama', *BCAF-RCD*, xii (1911), pp.292–300.

–– and Ch. Mourey, *L'Œuvre de la Troisième Republique en Afrique Occidentale. L'Expansion française et la formation territoriale* (Paris, 1910).

'La tournée de M. Clozel', *BCAF*, iv (1904), pp.121–2.

'La transnigérien. Missions du capitaine Marchand', *A Travers le Monde*, 38 (1895), pp.373–6.

'Troubles dans le Baoulé', *BCAF*, x (1899), p.343.

'Un vieil africain: la pacification de la Côte d'Ivoire', *BCAF*, xi (1910), p.338.

Verdier, A., *Échange de territoire coloniale. Côte Occidentale d'Afrique. Gambie cédée à la France par l'Angleterre. Grand–Bassam et Assinie cédés par la France* (La Rochelle, 1876).

–– *Questions coloniales. Côte d'Ivoire: La Vérité à propos de l'expédition Monteil* (Paris, 1895).

–– *Trente-cinq années de lutte aux colonies (Côte Occidentale d'Afrique)* (Paris, 1896).

'La vérité sur les incidents de la Côte d'Ivoire: Le rôle de M. le Gouverneur Angoulvant', *Le Siècle*, 28–9 Mar. 1910.

Verneau, R., 'Distribution géographique des tribus dans le Baoulé', *L'Anthropologie*, vi (1895), pp.564–8.

Villamur, R. and M. Delafosse, *Les Coutumes agni* (Paris, 1904).

–– and L. Richaud, *Notre Colonie de la Côte d'Ivoire* (Paris, 1903).

II. Secondary Studies

a) *General Works and Related Studies*

Aberle, D. F., 'Matrilineal Descent in Cross-Cultural Perspective', in K. Gough and D. Schneider, eds., *Matrilineal Kinship* (Berkeley, 1961).

Amon d'Aby, F. J., *La Côte d'Ivoire dans la Cité africaine* (Paris, 1951).

–– 'Le problème des chefferies traditionnelles en Côte d'Ivoire', *Notes et études documentaires* (Paris), 2508 (1959).

Arhin, K., 'Atebubu markets: ca. 1884–1930', in C. Meillassoux, ed., *The Development of Indigenous Trade and Markets in West Africa* (London, 1971), pp.199–213.

— — 'The Ashanti Rubber Trade with the Gold Coast in the 1890s', *Africa*, xlii, 1 (1972), pp.32–41.

Atger, P., *La France en Côte d'Ivoire de 1843 à 1893: Cinquante ans d'hésitations politiques et commerciales* (Dakar, 1962).

Augé, M., *Le Rivage alladian: organisation et évolution des villages alladian* (Paris, 1969).

— — 'Statut, pouvoir et richesse: relations lignagères, relations de dépendance et rapports de production dans la société alladian', *Cahiers d'Études Africaines*, 39 (1969).

— — 'Traite précoloniale, politique matrimoniale et stratégie sociale dans les sociétés des lagunaires de Basse Côte d'Ivoire', *Cahiers ORSTOM*, viii, 2, pp.143–52.

— — 'L'organisation du commerce précolonial en Basse Côte d'Ivoire et ses effets sur l'organisation sociale des populations', in C. Meillassoux, ed., *The Development of Indigenous Trade and Markets* (London, 1971).

— — 'Les faiseurs d'ombre: Servitude et structure lignagère dans la société alladian', in C. Meillassoux, ed., *L'Esclavage en Afrique précoloniale* (Paris, 1975), pp.455–75.

— — *Théorie des pouvoirs et idéologie: étude de cas en Côte d'Ivoire* (Paris, 1976).

Barth, F., ed., *Ethnic Groups and Boundaries: The Social Organization of Culture Difference* (Boston, 1969).

— — 'Descent and Marriage Reconsidered', in J. R. Goody, ed., *The Character of Kinship* (Cambridge, 1973), pp.3–19.

Bauer, P., *West African Trade* (Cambridge, 1954).

Benoît, C., *Histoire militaire de l'Afrique Occidentale française* (Paris, 1931).

Berge, F., *Le Sous-secrétariat et les sous-secrétaires d'État aux colonies - Histoire de l'émancipation de l'administration coloniale* (Paris, 1962).

Bernus, E., 'Un Type d'habitat ancien en Côte d'Ivoire, la maison annulaire à impluvium des Dida, Mamini', *Cahiers d'Outre-Mer*, 17, 65 (1964), pp.81–94.

— — and S. Vianes, 'Traditions sur l'origine des Dida Mamini du canton Wata (subdivision de Divo, Côte d'Ivoire)', *NA-IFAN*, 93 (1962), pp.20–3.

Betts, R. F., *Assimilation and Association in French Colonial Theory 1890-1914* (New York, 1961).

Bohannan, P., 'The Migration and Expansion of the Tiv', *Africa*, xxiv, 1 (1954).

Boni, N., *Histoire synthétique de l'Afrique résistante* (Paris, 1971).

Bonnefoy, C., 'Tiégba: notes sur un village Aizi', *Ét. Éb.*, 3 (1954), pp.7–129.

Bouche, D., *Les Villages de liberté en Afrique noire française, 1887–1910* (Paris, 1968).

Bouscayrol, R., 'Notes sur le peuple ébrié', *BIFAN*, xi, 3–4 (1949), pp.382–408.

Boutillier, J.-L., 'Les captifs en AOF (1903–1905)', *BIFAN*, xxx, 2 (1968), pp.513–35.

Bradby, B., 'The Destruction of Natural Economy', *Economy and Society*, iv, 2 (1975), pp.127–61.

Brunschwig, H., *Mythes et réalités de l'impérialisme colonial français* (Paris, 1960).

—— 'La troque et la traite', *Cahiers d'Études Africaines*, ii, 3, 7 (1962), pp.339–46.

—— 'Politique et économie dans l'Empire français d'Afrique noire, 1870–1914', *Journal of African History*, xi, 3 (1970), pp.401–17.

—— 'De la résistance africaine à l'impérialisme Européen', *JAH* xv, 1 (1974), pp.47–64.

Buxton, J. C., *Chiefs and Strangers: a Study of Political Assimilation among the Mandari* (Oxford, 1963).

—— 'Clientship among the Mandari of the Southern Sudan', in R. Cohen and J. Middleton, eds., *Comparative Political Systems* (Garden City, N.Y., 1967).

Catala, R., 'La question de l'échange de la Gambia Britannique contre les comptoirs français du Golfe de Guinée de 1866 à 1876', *Revue d'Histoire des Colonies*, xxxv (1948), pp.114–37.

Chailley, M., *Les Grandes Missions françaises en Afrique Occidentale* (Dakar, 1953).

Chaput, J., 'Treich–Laplène et la naissance de la Côte d'Ivoire française', *Revue d'Histoire des Colonies*, xxxvi (1949), pp.87–153.

'Charles Monteil, 1871–1949', *NA-IFAN*, 44 (1949).

Coquery-Vidrovitch, C., 'De la traite des esclaves à l'exportation de l'huile de palme et des palmistes au Dahomey, XIX siècle', in C. Meillassoux, ed., *The Development of Indigenous Trade and Markets in West Africa* (London, 1971).

Côte d'Ivoire, Direction des Archives, Ministère de l'Intérieur, *Assinie et sa région dans l'histoire* (Abidjan, 1973).

Crowder, M., 'Indirect rule, French and British style', *Africa*, xxxiv (1964).

—— *West Africa under Colonial Rule* (London, 1968).

Crowder, M., ed., *West African Resistance: The Military Response to Colonial Occupation* (London, 1971).

—— and O. Ikime, eds., *West African Chiefs* (Ile–Ife, 1970).

Curtin, P. D., *Economic Change in Pre-Colonial Africa: Senegambia in the Era of the Slave Trade* (Madison, Wisc., 1975).

Daaku, K. Y., 'The European Traders and the Coastal States, 1630–1720', *Transactions of the Historical Society of Ghana*, viii (1965), pp.11–23.

— — 'Aspects of Precolonial Akan Economy', *The International Journal of African Historical Studies*, v, 2 (1972), pp.235–47.

— — *Trade and Politics on the Gold Coast, 1600-1720: A Study of the African Reaction to European Trade* (Oxford, 1970).

— — 'Trade and Trading Patterns of the Akan in the Seventeenth and Eighteenth Centuries', in C. Meillassoux, ed., *The Development of Indigenous Trade and Markets in West Africa* (London, 1971).

Delafosse, L., 'Comment prit fin la carrière coloniale de Maurice Delafosse', *Revue Française d'Histoire d'Outre-Mer*, 222, lxi, 1 (1974), pp.74–115.

Delafosse, M., 'Langues du Soudan et de la Guinée', in *Les Langues du Monde*, ed. A. Meillet and M. Cohen (Paris, 1924), pp.463–560.

— — *L'Afrique Occidentale Française*, in G. Hanotaux and A. Martineau, *Histoire des colonies françaises et de l'expansion de la France dans le Monde* (Paris, 1931).

Delavignette, R., *Les Vrais Chefs de l'Empire*, (Paris, 1939).

— — *Freedom and Authority in French West Africa* (London, 1950).

Deloncle, P., *L'Afrique Occidentale Française: Découverte, pacification, mise en valeur* (Paris, 1934).

Deschamps, H., 'Et maintenant, Lord Lugard?', *Africa*, xxxiii (1963).

Diarassouba, V. C., *L'Évolution des structures agricoles du Sénégal: Destruction et reconstruction de l'économie rurale* (Paris, 1968).

Dickson, K. B., *A Historical Geography of Ghana* (Cambridge, 1969).

Douglas, M., 'Matriliny and Pawnship in Central Africa', *Africa*, xxxiv, 4 (1964), pp.301–12.

Douglas, M., 'Is Matriliny Doomed?', in M. Douglas and P. Kaberry, eds., *Man in Africa* (London, 1969), pp.123–37.

Duboc, Général, *L'Épopée coloniale en Afrique occidentale française* (Paris, 1938).

Dummett, R., 'The Rubber Trade on the Gold Coast and Asante in the Nineteenth Century: African Innovation and Market Responsiveness', *JAH*, xii, 1 (1971), pp.79–101.

— — 'The Social Impact of the European Liquor Trade on the Akan of Ghana (Gold Coast and Asante), 1875–1910', *Journal of Interdisciplinary History*, v, 1 (1974), pp.69–101.

Dupré, G., 'Le Commerce entre société lignagères: les Nzabidans, la traite à la fin du XIX siècle (Gabon–Congo)', *Cahiers d'Études Africaines*, 12, 4 (1972), pp.616–58.

— — and P. P. Rey, 'Reflections on the Pertinence of a Theory of the History of Exchange', *Economy and Society*, ii, 2 (1973), pp. 131–63.

Duprey, P., *Histoire des Ivoiriens. Naissance d'une nation* (Abidjan, 1962).

Dutrèb, M., *Marchand* (Paris, 1922).

Fieldhouse, D. K., 'The Economic Exploitation of Africa: Some British and French Comparisons', in P. Gifford and R. Louis, eds., *France and Britain in Africa: Imperial Rivalry and Colonial Rule* (New Haven, 1971), pp.593–662.

—— *Economics and Empire 1830–1914* (London, 1973).

Forlacroix, C., 'La pénétration française dans l'Indénié (1887–1901)', *Annales de l'Université d'Abidjan*, Ethno-Sociologie, F, 1 (1969), pp.91–135.

Fortes, M., 'Kinship and Marriage among the Ashanti', in A. K. Radcliffe–Brown and D. Forde, eds., *African Systems of Kinship and Marriage* (London, 1950), pp.252–84.

Gallagher, J. and R. E. Robinson, 'The Imperialism of Free Trade', *Economic History Review*, 2nd series, vi, 1 (1953).

Godelier, M., 'Le concept de tribu. Crise d'un concept ou crise des fondements empiriques de l'anthropologie?', in M. Godelier, *Horizon, trajets marxistes en anthropologie* (Paris, 1973), pp.93–131.

Goody, J., 'Ethnohistory and the Akan of Ghana', *Africa*, xxix, 1 (1959), pp.67–81.

—— 'Marriage Policy and Incorporation in Northern Ghana', in R. Cohen and J. Middleton, eds., *From Tribe to Nation in Africa* (San Francisco, 1969).

—— 'Inheritance, Social Change and the Boundary Problem', in J. Pouillon, ed., *Échanges et Communications*, i (Paris, 1970), pp.437–61.

—— *The Character of Kinship: A Collection of Essays Presented to Meyer Fortes* (Cambridge, 1973).

Gorer, G., *Africa Dances* (London, 1935, 2nd edn. 1962).

Guèye, M'Baye, 'L'Affaire Chautemps (avril 1904) et la suppression de l'esclavage de case au Sénégal', *BIFAN*, xxvii, 3–4 (1965).

Haliburton, G. M., *The Prophet Harris: A Study of an African Prophet and his Mass Movement in the Ivory Coast, 1913–1915* (London, 1971).

Hargreaves, J. D., 'Towards a History of the Partition of Africa', *JAH*, i (1960), pp.97–109.

—— *Prelude to the Partition of West Africa* (London, 1963).

—— *West Africa: The Former French States* (Englewood Cliffs, N.J., 1967).

—— *France and West Africa: An Anthrology of Historical Documents* (London, 1969).

—— 'West African States and the European Conquest', in L. H. Gann and P. Duignan, eds., *Colonialism in Africa, 1870–1960*, vol. i, *The History and Politics of Colonialism, 1870–1914* (Cambridge, 1969), pp.199–219.

—— 'British and French Imperialism in West Africa, 1885–1898', in P. Gifford and R. Louis, eds., *France and Britain in Africa* (New Haven, 1971), pp.261–82.

—— *West Africa Partitioned*, vol. i, *The Loaded Pause, 1885–1889* (London, 1974).

Hempenstall, P. J., 'Resistance in the German Pacific Empire: Towards a Theory of Early Colonial Response', *Journal of the Polynesian Society*, 84, 1 (1975), pp.5–24.

Henige, D. P., 'The Problem of Feedback in Oral Tradition: Four examples from the Fante Coastlands', *JAH*, xiv, 2 (1973), pp.223–35.

Hérault, G., ed., 'Les termes de parenté dans onze langues Kwa de Côte d'Ivoire', paper presented at Akan Conference, Bondoukou, Ivory Coast (Jan. 1974).

Hopkins, A. G., *An Economic History of West Africa* (London, 1973).

Horton, R., 'From Fishing Village to City-State: A Social History of New Calabar', in M. Douglas and P. M. Kaberry, eds., *Man in Africa* (London, 1969) pp.38–60.

—— 'Stateless Societies in the History of West Africa', in A. D. Ade Ajayi and M. Crowder, eds. *History of West Africa*, vol. i (London, 1971), pp.78–119.

Kanya–Forstner, A. S., *The Conquest of the Western Sudan. A Study in French Military Imperialism* (Cambridge, 1969).

—— 'Myths and Realities of African Resistance', *Historical Papers 1969* (The Canadian Historical Association, 1969).

—— 'Military Expansion in the Western Sudan – French and British Style', in Gifford and Louis, eds., *France and Britain in Africa* (New Haven, 1971), pp.409–41.

Kea, R. A., 'Firearms and warfare on the Gold and Slave Coasts from the sixteenth to the nineteenth centuries', *JAH*, xii, 2 (1971), pp.185–213.

Labouret, H. 'Maurice Delafosse', *Africa*, i (1928), pp.112–15.

—— 'Les bandes de Samory dans la Haute Côte d'Ivoire, La Côte d'Or et le Pays Lobi', *BCAF-RC*, viii (1925), 341–55.

—— *Monteil, explorateur et soldat* (Paris, 1957).

La Fontaine, J., 'Descent in New Guinea: an Africanist View', in J. Goody, ed. *The Character of Kinship* (Cambridge, 1973), pp.35–52.

Louis, W. R., ed., *Imperialism: The Robinson and Gallagher Controversy* (New York, 1976).

Manoukian, M., *Akan and Ga-Adangme Peoples* (London, 1950).

Masson, P., *Marseille et la colonisation française. Essai d'histoire coloniale* (Marseille, 1906).

Mauny, R., 'Contributions à la connaissance de l'archéologie préhistorique et protohistorique ivoiriennes', *AUA*, série I (Histoire), 1 (1972), pp.13–32.

McPhee, A., *The Economic Revolution in British West Africa* (London, 1926).

Meillassoux, C., 'Essai d'interprétation du phénomène économique dans les sociétés traditionnelles d'auto-subsistance', *Cahiers d'Études Africaines*, i, 4 (1960), pp.38–67.

— — 'L'économie des échanges précoloniaux en pays Gouro', *Cahiers d'Études Africaines*, iii, 12 (1963), pp.551–76.

— — *Anthropologie économique des Gouro de Côte d'Ivoire* (Paris, 1964).

— — 'Introduction', in C. Meillassoux, ed., *The Development of Indigenous Trade and Markets in West Africa* (London, 1971).

— — ed., *L'Esclavage en Afrique précoloniale: Dix-sept études* (Paris, 1975).

Memel–Fotê, H., 'Stratégie de la politique des marchés dans une société sans état de Basse Côte d'Ivoire: Les Adioukrou', paper presented at the Tenth Meeting of the International African Institute, Freetown (Dec. 1969).

— — 'Le système politique des Adioukrou: Une société sans état et à classes d'âge de Côte d'Ivoire' (Thèse de 3e cycle, Paris) (Abidjan, 1969).

'Memorial Maurice Delafosse', numéro spécial *d'Outre-Mer: Revue Générale de Colonisation*, i, 3 (1929), pp.263–85.

Michel, M., *La Mission Marchand 1895–1899* (Paris, 1972).

Murdock, G. P., 'Kin Term Patterns and Their Distribution', *Ethnology*, ix, 2 (1970), pp.165–203.

Newbury, C. W., 'The Development of French Policy on the Lower and Upper Niger, 1880–1898', *Journal of Modern History*, 31 (1959), pp.16–26.

— — 'The Formation of the Government General in French West Africa', *JAH*, i, 1 (1960), pp.111–28.

— — 'The Government General and Political Change in French West Africa', *St. Antony's Papers*, No. 10: *African Affairs*, No. 1 (London, 1961), pp.41–59.

— — 'Trade and Authority in West Africa from 1850 to 1880', in L. H. Gann and P. Duignan, eds., *Colonialism in Africa 1870–1960*, vol. i (Cambridge, 1969), pp.66–100.

— — 'Prices and Profitability in Early Nineteenth-Century West African Trade', in C. Meillassoux, ed., *The Development of Indigenous Trade and Markets in West Africa* (London, 1971), pp.91–106.

— — 'The Tariff Factor in Anglo-French West African Partition', in P. Gifford and W. R. Louis, eds., *France and Britain in Africa* (New Haven, 1971), pp.221–59.

— — 'Credit in Early Nineteenth-Century West African Trade', *JAH*, 13 (1972), pp.81–95.

—— 'Resistance and Collaboration in French Polynesia: The Tahitian War: 1844–47', *Journal of the Polynesian Society*, 82, 1 (1973), pp.5–27.

—— and A. S. Kanya-Forstner, 'French Policy and the Origins of the Scramble for West Africa', *JAH*, 10, 2 (1969), pp.253–76.

Niangoran-Bouah, G., 'Les Abouré: une société lagunaire de Côte d'Ivoire', *AUA*, Série Lettres, i (1965), pp.37–171.

Obichere, B. I., 'The African Factor in the Establishment of French Authority in West Africa, 1880–1900', in P. Gifford and W. R. Louis, eds., *France and Britain in Africa* (New Haven, 1971), pp.443–90.

Oloruntimehin, B. O., 'French colonisation and African resistance up to the First World War', *Genève-Afrique*, xii, 1 (1973), pp.5–18.

Omer-Cooper, J., 'Kingdoms and Villages: a possible new perspective in African history', *African Social Research*, 14 (1972), pp.301–10.

Person, Y., 'En quête d'une chronologie ivoirienne', in Mauny, Vansina, and Thomas, eds., *The Historian in Tropical Africa* (London, 1964), pp.322–38.

—— 'Samori and Resistance to the French', in R. Rotberg and A. Mazrui, eds., *Protest and Power in Black Africa* (London, 1970), pp.80–112.

—— 'Le Soudan Nigérien et la Guinée Occidentale', in H. Deschamps, ed., *Histoire générale de l'Afrique Noire* (Paris, 1970), vol. i, pp. 271–304.

—— 'Du Soudan Nigérien à la Côte Atlantique', in H. Deschamps, ed., *Histoire Générale de l'Afrique Noire* (Paris, 1971), vol. ii, pp85–122.

—— 'Guinea – Samory', in M. Crowder, ed., *West African Resistance* (London, 1971).

—— *Samori. Une révolution Dyula* (Dakar, vol. i, 1968; vol. ii, 1970; vol. iii, 1975).

Rattray, R. S., *Ashanti Law and Constitution* (Oxford, 1929).

Rey, P. P., *Colonialisme, néo-colonialisme et transition au capitalisme, exemple de la Comilog au Congo-Brazzaville* (Paris, 1971).

Reynolds, E., 'The Rise and Fall of an African Merchant Class on the Gold Coast, 1830–1874', *Cahiers d'Études Africaines*, 54, xiv, 2 (1974), pp.253–64.

—— *Trade and Economic Change on the Gold Coast, 1807–1874* (London, 1974).

Richards, A. I., 'Some types of family structure amongst the Central Bantu', in A. R. Radcliffe-Brown, and D. Forde, eds. *African Systems of Kinship and Marriage* (London, 1950), pp.207–51.

Roberts, S. H., *French Colonial Policy, 1870–1925* (London, 1929), 2 vols.

Robinson, R. E., 'Non-European foundations of European imperialism: sketch for a theory of collaboration', in R. Owen and B. Sutcliffe, eds., *Studies in the Theory of Imperialism* (London, 1972), pp.117–40.

—— 'European Imperialism and Indigenous Reactions in British West Africa, 1880-1914', in *Expansion and Reaction: Essays on European Expansion and Reactions in Asia and Africa*, H. L. Wesseling, ed. (Leyden, 1978), 141-63.

—— and J. Gallagher, 'The Partition of Africa', in *New Cambridge Modern History*, vol. xi (Cambridge, 1962), pp.593-640.

—— J. Gallagher with A. Denny, *Africa and the Victorians: The Climax of Imperialism in the Dark Continent* (New York, 1961).

Rodney, W., 'The Guinea Coast', in R. Gray, ed., *The Cambridge History of Africa*, vol. iv, *c.1600-1790* (Cambridge, 1975), pp.223-324.

Rougerie, G., 'Lagunaires et terriens de la Côte d'Ivoire', *Cahiers d'Outre-Mer*, xii (1950), pp.370-7.

—— 'Les pays agni du Sud-Est de la Côte d'Ivoire forestière', *Ét. Éb.*, vi (1957), pp.7-213.

Samson, M., 'Les Abouré de Bonoua (Côte d'Ivoire): Introduction à l'Ethno-Histoire' (Thèse de 3e cycle, Paris, 1971).

Schnapper, B., *La Politique et le commerce française dans le golfe de Guinée, 1838-1871* (Paris, 1961).

Schneider, D. M., 'The Distinctive Features of Matrilineal Descent Groups', in K. Gough and D. Schneider, eds., *Matrilineal Kinship* (Berkeley, 1961) pp.1-29.

Stokes, E., 'Late nineteenth-century colonial expansion and the attack on the theory of economic imperialism: a case of mistaken identity?', *Historical Journal*, xii (1969), pp.282-95.

Strathern, A., 'Kinship, Descent and Locality: Some New Guinea Examples', in J. Goody, ed., *The Character of Kinship* (Cambridge, 1973), pp.21-34.

Suret-Canale, J., *Afrique Noire:* vol. i, *Occidentale et Centrale* (Paris, 1964).

—— *Afrique Noire:* vol. ii, *L'Ère Coloniale 1900-1945* (Paris, 1964).

Tauxier, L., *Religion, Mœurs et Coutumes des Agnis de la Côte d'Ivoire (Indénié et Sanvi)* (Paris, 1932).

Terray, E., 'Commerce pré-colonial et organisation sociale chez les Dida en Côte d'Ivoire', in C. Meillassoux, ed., *The Development of Indigenous Trade and Markets in West Africa* (London, 1971), pp.145-52.

—— 'Long-distance exchange and the formation of the state: the case of the Abron Kingdom of Gyaman', *Economy and Society*, iii, 3 (1974) pp.315-45.

—— 'La captivité dans le royaume abron du Gyaman', in C. Meillassoux, ed., *L'Esclavage en Afrique précoloniale* (Paris, 1975), pp.389-453.

Tordoff, W., 'A Note on the Relations between Samory and King Prempeh I of Ashanti', *Ghana Notes and Queries*, 3 (1961).

Touré, S., 'Note sur une communauté nigérienne ancienne en Côte d'Ivoire: Marabadiassa', recueillie par J. Rouch et. Bernus, *NA-IFAN*, 84 (1959) pp.107–10.

Traoré, D., 'Les relations de Samory et de l'état de Kong', *NA-IFAN*, 47 (1950), 96–7.

Triaud, J. L., 'Un cas de passage collectif à l'Islam en Basse Côte d'Ivoire: le village d'Ahua au début du siècle', *Cahiers d'Études Africaines*, 54, xiv, 2 (1974), pp.317–37.

Urquhart, D. H., *Report on the Cocoa Industry in the French Ivory Coast* (Bournville, 1955).

Wilks, I., 'Akwamu and Otoblohum: An Eighteenth-Century Akan Marriage Arrangement', *Africa*, xxix, 4 (1959), pp.391–404.

–– *Asante in the Nineteenth Century: The Structure and Evolution of a Political Order* (Cambridge, 1975).

Wilson, M., 'Changes in social structure in southern Africa: the relevance of kinship studies to the historian', in L. Thompson, ed., *African Societies in Southern Africa* (London, 1969), pp.71–85.

Wondji, Ch., 'La fièvre jaune à Grand Bassam (1899–1903)', *La Revue Française d'Histoire d'Outre-Mer*, 215 (1972).

Yenou, A. D., 'Quelques notes historiques sur le pays alladian (Basse Côte d'Ivoire)', *NA-IFAN*, 63 (1954), pp.83–8.

b) *Studies of the Baule*

The following recent studies have been particularly useful in completing the reserarch for the thesis. More extensive listings of recent ethnographic, historical, economic, and sociological studies on the Baule can be found in J.-P. Chauveau, 'Bibliographie sur la société baoulé (histoire, anthropologie)', in V. Guerry, *La Vie quotidienne dans un village baoulé* (Abidjan, 1972), pp.223–51; and his 'Compléments à la Bibliographie sur la Société Baoulé (Histoire, anthropologie)' (Abidjan, 1973), mimeo.; as well as in G. Janvier, *Bibliographie de la Côte d'Ivoire*, ii. *Sciences de l'Homme* (Abidjan, 1973).

Amon d'Aby, F. J., *Croyances religieuses et coutumes juridques des Agnis de la Côte d'Ivoire* (Paris, 1960).

Armengaud, M., 'Autour de la culture de la cola chez les N'Gban de Mbaiakro', *NA-IFAN*, 44 (1949).

Arnaud, G., 'Mission du Yaouré et d'Hiré (Côte d'Ivoire) – Rapport technique', (Direction des Mines, AOF, Dakar, 1947), mimeo.

Benetière, J. J. and P. Pezet, 'Histoire de l'agriculture en zone baoulé', *ÉRB*, document no. 2 (Abidjan, 1962).

Bergero–Campagne, M. B., 'L'agriculture nomade de la tribu des N'dranouas en Côte d'Ivoire', in *L'Agriculture nomade*, vol. i: *Congo Belge, Côte d'Ivoire* (FAO, Rome 1956), pp.109–230.

Bettignies, J. de, 'Éléments pour une monographie du centre semi-urbain de Toumodi', *ÉRB*, document 3 (Abidjan, 1962).

Carteron, Rév. P., *Étude de la langue baoulé*, 7 booklets (Bocanda, 1972).

Chauveau, J.-P., 'Note sur l'histoire du peuplement de la région de Kokumbo', ORSTOM, *Sciences Humaines* (Abidjan), iv, 11 (1971).

—— 'Note sur la place du Baoulé dans l'ensemble économique ouest-africain précolonial', mimeo. (Abidjan, 1972).

—— 'Les cadres socio-historiques de la production dans la région de Kokumbo (pays Baoulé, Côte d'Ivoire), I – La période précoloniale', ORSTOM, *Sciences Humaines*, v, 7 (1972).

—— 'Régime foncier et organisation du travail dans la région de Kokumbo', Exposé dans le cadre de l'AVB–CFAE, mimeo. (Abidjan, 1972).

—— 'Note sur la morphologie matrimoniale de Kokumbo (pays Baoulé, Côte d'Ivoire), perspective historique', ORSTOM, *Sciences Humaines*, vi, 3 (1973).

—— 'Note sur les échanges dans le Baoulé précolonial', paper presented to Akan Conference, Bondoukou, Ivory Coast (Jan. 1974), mimeo.

—— 'Société baoulé précoloniale et modèle segmentaire: le cas de la région de Kokumbo (Baoulé-sud)', paper presented to inter-university conference of Ghana and the Ivory Coast, Kumasi, Ghana (Jan. 1975).

Effimbra, G., *Manuel de baoulé* (Paris, 1959).

Étienne, P., 'Essai de monographie d'un village de savane: Diamelassou', *ÉRB*, document 4 (Abidjan, 1962).

—— 'Structures de parenté en pays baoulé', *Bulletin de Liaison des Sciences Humaines*, ORSTOM (Paris), 2 (1965), pp.67–76.

—— 'Phénomènes religieux et facteurs socio-économiques dans un village de la région de Bouaké (Côte d'Ivoire)', *Cahiers d'Études Africaines*, 23, vi, 3 (1966), pp.367–401.

—— 'Les Baoulé face au salariat', Congrès International des Africanistes de l'Ouest, Dakar, Dec. 1967 (Abidjan, 1967), mimeo.

—— 'Les Baoulé et le temps', *Cah. ORSTOM*, v, 3 (1968), pp.17–37.

—— 'Les aspects ostentatoires du système économique baoulé (Côte d'Ivoire)', *Économies et Sociétés*, ii. 4 (1968), pp.793–817.

—— 'Les Baoulé face au fait urbain' (Abidjan, n.d.), mimeo.

—— 'Essai de représentation graphique de l'alliance matrimoniale', *L'Homme*, x, 4 (1970), pp.36–52.

—— 'Avant-propos' in 'Du mariage en Afrique Occidentale', *Cah. ORSTOM*, viii, 2 (1971), pp.131–42.

—— 'Les Baoulé face aux rapports de salariat', *Cah. ORSTOM*, viii, 3 (1971), pp.235–42.

—— 'Le fait villageois baoulé' (Abidjan, 1971), mimeo.

—— 'Les interdictions de mariage chez les Baoulé, document de travail' (Abidjan, 1972), mimeo.

—— 'L'individu et le temps chez les Baoulé. Un cas de contradiction entre la représentation d'un phénomène social et sa pratique', *Cahiers d'Études Africaines*, 52, xiii, 4, (1973). pp.631–48.

—— 'Essai d'analyse des interdictions de mariage baoulé', paper presented at Akan Conference, Bondoukou, Ivory Coast (Jan. 1974).

—— and M. Étienne, 'L'organisation sociale des Baoulé', *ÉRB*, i, pp.125–8.

—— and —— 'Les migrations modernes', *ÉRB*, i, pp.59–82.

—— and —— 'Terminologie de la parenté et de l'alliance chez les Baoulé (Côte d'Ivoire)', *L'Homme*, vii, 4 (1967), pp.50–76.

—— and —— 'L'émigration baoulé actuelle', *Cahiers d'Outre-Mer*, xxi (1968), pp.155–95.

—— and —— ' "A qui mieux mieux" ou le mariage chez les Baoulé', *Cah. ORSTOM*, viii, 2, 165–86.

Étienne, P. and J. P. Trouchaud, 'Le régime foncier', *ÉRB*, ii, pp.47–55.

Guerry, V., *La Vie quotidienne dans un village baoulé* (Abidjan, 1970).

Lafargue, F., 'Le komyen chez les Baoulé' (Abidjan, 1970), mimeo.

Marie, A., 'Parenté, échange matrimonial et réciprocité. Essai d'interprétation à partir de la société Dan et de quelques autres sociétés de Côte d'Ivoire, Part I', *L'Homme*, xii, 3 (1972); pp.6–46.

—— 'Parenté, échange matrimonial et réciprocité. Essai d'interprétation à partir de la société Dan et de quelques autres sociétés de Côte d'Ivoire', part II, *L'Homme*, xii, 4 (1972), pp.5–36.

—— 'Structures, pratiques et idéologies chez les Baoulé', *Cahiers d'Études Africaines*, xii, 2 (1973), pp.363–76.

Ménalque, M., *Coutumes civiles des Baoulé de la région de Dimbokro* (Paris, 1933).

Miège, J., 'L'agriculture baoulé', *Conférence internationale des Africanistes de l'Ouest, Dakar, 1950. Comptes Rendus* (Dakar, 1951), vol. ii, pp.47–59.

Monnier, Y., 'Il était une fois à Ayérémou . . . Un village du sud-Baoulé', *AUA*, série G, i (1969).

Mouëzy, P., *Histoire et coutumes du pays d'Assinie et du royaume de Krinjabo* (Paris, 1942).

Retord, G., 'Les différentes parleurs Agni et le Baoulé. Essai de différenciation dialectale', in Actes du 8e Congrès de la Société Linguistique de l'Afrique Occidentale, 1969, *AUA*, série H, i (1971), pp.293–310.

Salverte-Marnier, Ph. de, 'L'organisation sociale des Baoulé: les rapports entre les sexes', *ÉRB*, i, pp.159–62 (Abidjan, 1962).

—— 'L'organisation politique et la structure territoriale', *ÉRB*, i, pp.195–209 (Abidjan, 1962).

—— 'Essai de monographie d'un village de forêt: Kouadkoubroukro', *ÉRB*, document 5: l'histoire, pp.9–38; l'organisation sociale actuelle, pp.49–79 (Abidjan, 1962).

— — and M. A. de Salverte-Marnier, 'Les étapes du peuplement', *ÉRB*, i, pp.11–58 (Abidjan, 1962).

— — and J. P. Trouchaud, 'Inventaire des villages de la zone baoulé', *ÉRB* (Abidjan, 1962).

Sebamed, 'Traditions orales et histoire – V. Tiassalé et le pénétration coloniale', *Fraternité Matin* (Abidjan) 17–18 Nov. 1973.

Sirven, P., *L'Évolution des villages suburbains de Bouaké: contribution à l'étude géographique du phénomène de croissance d'une ville africaine* (Bordeaux, 1972).

Weiskel, T. C., 'L'histoire socio–économique des peuples baoulé précoloniaux: problèmes et perspectives de recherche', paper presented at inter-university conference, Ghana–Ivory Coast, Kumasi, Ghana (Jan. 1975).

— — 'Nature, Culture and Ecology in Traditional African Thought Systems', *Cultures* (UNESCO – Paris), i, 2 (1973), pp.123–44.

— — 'L'Histoire socio-économique des peuples baule: problèmes et perspectives de recherche', *Cahiers d'Études Africaines*, 61–2, xvi (1–2) (1976) pp.357–95.

— — Labor in the Emergent Periphery: From Slavery to Migrant Labor among the Baule peoples, *c.*1880–1925', in *The World-System of Capitalism: Past and Present*, W. Goldfrank (ed.), Political Economy of the World-System Annuals, II, (Beverly Hills, 1979).

— — 'Changing Perspectives on African Resistance Movements and the Case of the Baule Peoples', in *West African Culture Dynamics: Archaeological and Historical Perspectives*, R. E. Dumett and B. K. Swartz (eds.), World Anthropology Series, (The Hague, forthcoming).

— — 'The Precolonial Baule: A Reconstruction', *Cahiers d'Études Africaines* (forthcoming).

Index

Abé warriors: role in 1910 revolt
198
Abidji: refuse porterage work in
Baule country 58
Abli, Aïtu village: Eoussou chief
of 117
Abo N'Zué 228-9
Aboua Kouassi, Akoué chief of
Bonzi 190, 205
Abouré: revolt against French 60;
and Monteil expedition 64;
commodity producers 80;
French relations with 254 n.89
Adioukrou: palm oil producers 38;
attack Péan 38; attack Staup
39; Asmaret, chief of 62, 212;
trade with in 1890s 80, 249
n.47
adya (adja) 20, 175
Agba: 19; and attacks on trading
caravans 139; military campaign
against 156; Angoulvant cam-
paign against 200; success of
Andsoromi Taki among 228
Agboville, railway stop: and Abé
worriors' advance 198
Aguié Kouassi, Ngban chief: uncle
of Assa Ngbin 194
Ahari, northern Baule group:
resistance of 127
Ahua: 30, 41, 45; Nzi Aka, chief
of 45; 247 n.23; decline of
252 n.42; 258 n.59
Ahuacré 30
Ahuakro: 63; attack at 64
Ahua–Niamwé–Nzianou trading
chain 46, 50, 249 n.47
Ahuem (Ahouem) 30, 45
Aïtu (Aïtou): 19; of Abli 117;
support enlisted by Delafosse

122; 267 n.107
Akafou Brou, Ngban chief, son of
Akafou Bulare: not recognized
as paramount chief 163; mysterious death of 164, 168
Akafou Bulare, chief of Ngban:
31, 50; greets Marchand 51;
mentioned by Desperles in
pillaging of caravans 60; refusal
to join conspiracy against
French 62, 212, 273 n.84;
reluctant to reoccupy Ouossou
94; alleged force behind 1899
revolt 120; bitter rival of
Kouadio Okou 121; swears
fidelity to French cause 121;
Delafosse finds allies to fight
against 122; Nebout attempts
to dissuade from joining forces
with Kouadio Okou 123;
alliance with northern Ngban
125, 265, n.80; 'neutralized'
by Nebout 125; submission to
French 132; Bulare, 'man of
iron' 132; position as chief
and potential collaborator 133;
resorts to armed resistance
after submission 134; precarious position in relation to
Bastard 135-6; risks losing
following in face of growing
resistance to French 136; position increasingly compromised
137; presents himself at Ouossou post 139; death of 139,
144; effects of death on Ngban
139, 238; effects of death on
French collaboration policy
161; moderate chief in Baule
eyes 161; daughter of 162;

Akafou Bulare (*cont.*)
    nature of successors to 163;
    son of, with Kakou Bla 163;
    leadership of 217, 231–2
Akafou Nguessan, daughter of
    Akafou Bulare: meets Clozel
    162; sister of Akafou Brou
    163; French support of 205
Akan: commercial system in 17th
    and 18th centuries 5–6; migra-
    tion and emergence of Baule 6
Aken (Etien Komenan) 250 n.21
Akoué: 51; and establishment of
    French post at Bonzi 133; gold
    mining at Koussou 89; revolt
    191–3, 234, 277 n.43; Angoul-
    vant's campaign against 200;
    learn to make gunpowder 200;
    fortification at Kami 201;
    heavy war fines imposed upon
    204; collaborating chiefs
    praised 205; resisting chiefs
    punished 206; paramount chief,
    Kouassi Ngo 207, 220. *See also*
    Yaba Moussou, Kouassi Ngo,
    Koki Yao Aounou
Akoumiakro, Akoué village: Koki
    Yao Aounou, chief of 190
Alani Yao, Akoué chief: captured
    by French 206
Alcohol trade: effects of 79–80,
    257 n.54
Alhan (Etien Komenan) 250 n.21
Ali Kouakou, Akoué chief 206
Ali Seck, Senegalese soldier: death
    of 194; and French 195
Alladian (Jack Jacks): 30, 35; and
    European trade in 19th century
    30; supply labour during 1880s
    trading boom 80
Alou Kouamé, Akoué chief: cap-
    tured by French 206
Alou Kouassi, Akoué chief of
    Diamalabo: encounter with
    Simon 191
Amadu Seku 1, 53, 231
amouensofue: 227; French atti-
    tude toward 227
Andsoromi Taki, prophet figure

228
Anglo-French Accord of 1889
    35
Angoulvant, Governor Gabriel:
    appointed as Clozel's succes-
    sor 179; development plans of
    180–1, 183; 'Lettre Programme'
    of 183; use of head tax to
    bring Baule into market 184;
    attacks approach of Delafosse,
    Nebout, and Clozel 185; effects
    of arms tax of 185; effects of
    head taxes of 185; land tenure
    policy of 185; reactions to his
    programme 186; paternalism of
    188; plans to plant rubber,
    cocoa, rice, and cotton in Baule
    territory 188; impact upon
    Clozel's collaborative structures
    189; plans for disarmament of
    rebellious populations 194;
    criticized by humanitarian cir-
    cles 196; criticized by com-
    mercial community 196; criti-
    cized by military 197; repres-
    sion of final phase of Baule
    revolt 199–210; appeals to
    Chambre for financial help
    200; levies war fines 200;
    'pacification' programme of
    200; plans to destroy Baule
    economy 202; tax reforms of
    235; invokes theories of Lucien
    Hubert 237; problems with
    commercial community 277
    n.55; dispute with military
    officers 278 n.68; directive to
    subordinates 243
Anno region 54
Aounou, *see* Koki Yao Aounou
Aollonien: 258 n.67, 259 n.69;
    African entrepreneurs 82;
    French attitude toward 83,
    96; replaced by Hyula 94;
    similarities to Hausa with
    respect to colonial economic
    structures 97; retain control of
    Tiassalé 156; agents employed
    by Dougan in rubber export

Apollonien (*cont.*)
business 157; traders 247 n.23.
See also Nsoko; Esquires
Archinard, General Louis: 43; campaign against Samory 52; campaign against Amadu 53; Commandant Supérieur of Sudan 41; dismissal of 73
Armand, Louis: 38, 39, 43; aid to Péan 38; and expedition to interior 38; reports on slaves in Tiassalé region 81
Arms: trade between Baule and Samory's troops 52, 259 n.81; trade in 182, 256 n.38; trade and French commerce in southern Baule territory 86; Barthe's lobbying efforts for tax on 182; effect of tax on 185; tax rejected by Akoué 193; Baule attitude toward tax on 195; confiscation of 203
Ashanti: kingdom and origin myths 6; kingdom and Akan trade network 6; source of information on Baule 8; shift from rubber to cocoa production 176; kinship organization of 247 n.26; battles with British 267 n.122
Asmaret, chief of Adioukrou village of Lopou: diplomatic mission to Sakassou 62; tries to stop French advance 212
Asoko (Apollonien) 247 n.23
Assabous, northern Baule group: and Monteil Mission 68
Assa Ngbin, Ngban woman: Baule wife of Ali Seck 194
Assiené, Ngban chief: designated as probable successor to Bulare 163
Assimilation: versus 'association' policy 151, 271 n.41
Assini: 33-6; and installation of French customs personnel 35; French fort at 245 n.3
atonvle marriage: 23, 24; super-

atonvle (*cont.*)
seded by slave marriages 91; decline of 163, 202, 222, 223, 260 n.101
Atrocities: 196, 278 n.56 and n.57
Aura Poku, Queen: sister of Dakon 6; and Baule origin myths 19
Avikam 28
awlô bô (household) 17, 20-1
awlô bô endogamy: shift toward 91-2, 202
awlô kpenngben (household head) 20-1, 25, 26, 153
Ayaou: French attempts to collect tax from 190; refusal to pay French taxes 191; Angoulvant's campaign against 200
Ayérémou (Ayrémou): 31; village of Kakou Bla 162
Aymerich, Lt.-Col.: becomes Commander after Donnat 127; implements new military strategy 129; as military leader 232

Bahooree (Baule) 8
Ballay, Governor General Noël Victor 128
Bambara traders 258 n.69
Bandama River: 29-31, 35, 38; lower Bandama 247 n.23; exploration of 250 n.20
Baoure (Baule) 12
Baratier, Lt. 63, 66, 254 n.100
Barthe, L., Director of CFAO 182, 184, 196, 278 n.55
Bastard, Captain 132, 135, 137
Batéra: 39, battle of, 45
Baule (Bahooree, Baoure, Baoulé): significance of in West African History 3-4, 231-44; seventeenth- and eighteenth-century background 5-9; nineteenth-century trade and migrations 9-17; precolonial socio-political organization 17-25; pre-colonial conflict among 25-32; character assessed by French 56, 95-8

Bendé Kouassi, chief of Don: 128, 136, 148, 171, 221
Bénézet, Lt. 168
Benoît, Capt., founder of Bouaké post: 103, 104, 106, 232
Béoumi, Kodé village 207
Betsellère, Commander 145, 233
Beugré, cult of 229, 230, 283 n.32
Binger, Capt. Louis Gustave, explorer and first Governor of Ivory Coast: early reports on commerce 16-7, 251 n.33; explorations 34, 53, 250 n.9; correspondence with Marchand 43-4, 251 n.35; row with Monteil 70-1, 255 n.13; administration 76-7, 269 n.13
bloûfwe-klo (white men's villages) 95
Bony, Chief of Jacqueville 36, 40
Bonzi, French post among Akoué: 133, 190, 192, 195, 205, 277 n.43
Bori-Bani, Samory's camp: 100-1
Bouaké (Gossa, Gbuekékro): 31; 51-2; siege of in 1898 89-105; siege in 1900 128, 221
Bouna 99-100
Bouroubourou 31. *See* Broubrou
Bowdich, T.E. 8-9
Bricard, Eloi: role as Résident 40-5
Brignan 80
Brimbo 50
Britain: negotiations with 249 n.5
British: Gold Coast possessions of 34; trade goods among African merchants 35; Marchand's concerns about 53-54; colonial 151, 271 n.41 and n.43
Bros, northern Baule group 136
Broubrou (Bouroubourou) 31, 39, 45. *See also* Tiassalé
Budget: of colony under Clozel 172-3; military expenditures 199; statistics of 275 n.2
Buen Komenan 46-7
Bulare 267 n.116. *See* Akafou bulare

Captives 213, 260 n.9. *See also* Slavery; Labour
Cash crops: use of obligatory communal labour for 185; use of taxes to stimulate production 235; mobilizing labour to produce 237
Caudrelier, P.C., Commander 61-2, 66, 100, 197
Chambre des Deputés: 42; reluctance to authorize new military expenditures 57; debates on failure of Kong expeiditon 71; attack of Chautemps policy 72; reassured by Minister 107; Angoulvant appeals to for financial help 200
Charles, Commander 150, 233
Chaudié, Jean Baptiste Émile (Governor General): 97, 108, 123-4, 264 n.49
Chautemps, François Émile (Minister of Colonies): 64-5, 147, 234; attacked by Le Herissé in Parliament 72
Chauveau, J.-P. 247 n.21, n.24, and n.25 248 n.38 and n.39, 249 n.49, 260 n.94, 266 n.102 276 n.31
chef l'impôt 218. *See also* Collaborators
Chieftaincy: household heads (*awlô kpenngben*) 19-21; village chiefs (*klo kpenngben*) 21-5; 'paramount' or regional chiefs (*nvle kpen*) 22-5; pre-colonial 17-25, *passim* 248 n.39; destruction of 'paramount' 4, 215-18
Chiefs: advantages offered to collaborating chiefs 149; political authority of 161 ff.; 'straw' chiefs 169; and taxes 180; French policy toward collaborating chiefs 212; role of 'paramount' chiefs in resistance 215-18; role of 'junior' chiefs in resistance 218-21. *See also* Leadership

Civil war: between resisters and collaborators 122, 203. *See also* Fratricidal Disputes

Civilian Administration: Binger as civilian governor 43; and coastal commerce 76–98; disputes between civilian *v.* military authority 41–3, 69–76, 78, 105–9, 117, 123–4, 140–1, 153–5, 196–7, 232–3, 238, 278 n.68

Clozel, François-Joseph (administrator, later Governor of Ivory Coast): development of new military strategy 128; decision to maintain troop strength 134; policy as governor 142–55 *passim*; inspection tours through Baule country 162, 166; attempt to settle Kouame Dié succession 166; economic achievements 172–4; military criticism of 153; Angoulvant's criticism of 185; departure 180; formulation of 'la politique des races' 153, 161, 163, 166, 170, 217–18; requests ethnographic information 271 n.44; relations with Delafosse and Nebout 269 n.13

Coastal Commerce: seventeenth and eighteenth century 5–9; nineteenth century 9–17; and trading chains to interior 27–31; changes during 1890s 76–90 *passim. See also* Commerce; Trade; Trading Chains

Coastal Revolts 33–41

Cocoa: 181, 183–4, 188; beginnings in Ivory Coast 276 n.17; rejection by Akoué 193

Collaboration: politics of 145, 150, 161–71; 'les fonds pour cadeaux politiques' 148; nature of after defeat 210; attitude of 'paramount' chiefs toward 215–18; attitude of 'junior' chiefs toward, 218–21; structure of collaboration under stress 185, 189, 239, 243

Collaborators: support of administration 151; manipulation of administration by 151, 206; deaths of 168, 207–8; attacked by resisters 203; slaves and women as 214–15; freeborn Baule association of slave status with 221–2; heirs of 280 n.99

Colonial policy, British compared with French 217, 271 n.43

Colonna d'Istria, Col.: orders occupation of Kokumbo 130; imposes tribute payments on Akafou and Kouadio Okou 132; designated Commander by Clozel 133; 232; 266 n.105

Combe, Dr: reveals French atrocities among Baule 196

Combes, Col., (later General and Supreme Military Commander): attacks Samory 52; intervenes in civilian-military disputes 124; develops new military strategy with Clozel 128, 134

Commerce: in munitions, resotred by Roberdeau 138; European commerce among Baule 154–60; effect on colony's budget 175. *See also* Coastal Commerce; Trade; Trading Chains

Commodity Shift, in coastal trade 82

Companie Française de l'Afrique Occidental (CFAO): 84, 157; agent Rubino killed by Abé warriors 198. *See also* L. Barthe

Companie Française de Kong 156. *See also* Verdier

Congo atrocities: alluded to by L. Barthe, criticizing Angoulvant's policy 196

Conseil d'Administration: created 76; and firearms tax 181; called upon to approve punishment of prominent resisters 205; sentence chiefs 207

Customs duties: and Anglo-French accord of 1889 35; collection

Customs duties (*Cont.*)
accord of 1889 35; collection along coast 36, 44
Crowder, Michael: on Baule resistance 2

Dabou, Adioukrou cillage 33, 38, 39, 249 n.47
David: agent of Verdier 156
Debts: Baule practice of collection 110–11, 263 n.31
Delfosse, Louise: 254 n.101, 257 n. 43, 263 n.44 and n.47, 264 n.55; biography of father 269 n.13
Delafosse, Maurice, French administrator among Baule: 232–3, 246 n.7, 248 n.28 and n.29, 261 n.2 and n.119, 263 n.43, 269 n.13, 275 n.115; recorded origin myths of Baule 6, 246 n.7; concerning Queen Poku's first two successors 19; concerning Baule socio-political organization 25; arrival in Ivory Coast and early career 77; reports on Bouaké 102; and Lomo revolt 112–22; use of collaborative techniques 145; monographs of 152; policies attacked by Angoulvant 185; policy toward Baule group divisiveness 212; advice to Clozel 217–18; on Baule kin terms 247 n.27; on 'less Agni' 257 n.42; publications on Baule 257 n.43, 270 n.32, 271 n.44; attitude toward Baule changes 264 n.56
Delcassé, Théophile, Minister of Colonies: 42, 43, 56; intentions for Monteil expedition 57; authorizes Monteil expedition 64; replaced by Émile Chautemps as Minister of Colonies 64; hopes to inaugurate new era of commercial expansion 73; dismisses Archinard and appoints Grodet 73

Desperles, Lt.: importance in first Baule revolt 59, 254 n.92
de Tavernost, Lt., French explorer: 39, 43; and expedition to Tiassalé 38
Diallo, Sissé, Sgt., auxiliary to Delafosse: 116, 263 n.43
Diamalabo, Akoué village 193, 234
Dié Lonzo, Ouarébo chief: commands counter-attack against French 137; son of Kouamé Dié 165; contends for position of Ouarébo chieftaincy 166; hatred of Ouarébo-Linguira collaborating chiefs 168; recognized as chief of Ouarébo by French 207
Disarmament: imposed upon subdued Baule 203
Disease: and European population, 118; causes decline of Baule population 208–9
'Direct Rule' 152, 271 n.43
Diviners, *see kômien*
Djimini refugees 117
Don, northern Baule group: 148, 221; and growing influence of Kouamé Dié 136
Donnat, Commander: 232; leads troops from Sudan 124; issues orders for first attack on Baule 126
Dougan, Morgan, Fanti merchant: profits from rubber boom 157, 272 n.69, 276 n.17; plants cocoa 183
Doumergue, Gaston, Minister of Colonies 144
Dyula: 53; refugees 78, 94; enclaves in Baule territory 95; French perceptions of 96; as manpower source 97, 104, 112, 146, 183, 192; and Akoué 193, 194–5; Baule hostility toward 213–14, 282 n.12
dyula-kro (dyula-klo) 95, 104. *See* 'Villages de liberté'

'Economic revolution': of coastal

'Economic revolution' (*cont.*)
groups in 19th century 9, 80;
among Baule 236, 241
Educational opportunities: for
heirs of collaborators 280 n.99
Eky, *see* Etien Komenan
Eloumoué 28
Endogamy: of Baule household
after 1894 92
Epidemics 118, 208
Eoussou, Aitu chief of Abli 117,
162, 168, 212, 220
Esquires ('Esq.') 82, 84n, 258
n. 66. *See also* Nsoko; Apollonien
Etienne, Eugène, Undersecretary
for the Colonies 34, 35, 38, 42
Etien Komenan, King of Tiassalé
31, 39–40, 44–7, 156, 229, 250
n.21
Etienne, P. 248 n.31 and n.32, 261
n.110 and n.111; and M. 247
n.27, 248 n.33 and n.36, 260
n.101, 281 n.109
Exile: Angoulvant's punishment
for resisters 206

Faafoué, Baule group: 19, 89, 93,
112, 127, 190
famien (famye) 22, 218. *See also*
nvle kpen
Famine 208–9, 279 n.77
Fanti, 157, 183, 258 n.67. *See*
Apollonien
Fatou Aka, chief of Niamwé: 31,
46, 60, 62, 162, 164, 212, 220,
252 n.48; death of 168
Ferguson, George, Fanti agent of
British: 54, 253 n.72
Fetish priests 151, 225–30
Fieldhouse, D. K. 239, 283 n.17
Fleuriot de Langle, Vice Admiral
12, 247, n.20, 251 n.33
Foussat, Capt., Commander of
Bouaké post: and atrocities
196
Fratricidal disputes 168, 208, 282
n.5
French: conquest of central Ivory
2; in western Sudan 3; attitude
toward Ivory Coast possessions
in 19th c. 33; military expansion 34, 41; establish customs
posts 35–6; and Dyula 55; and
Apollonien 83; and 'working
misunderstanding' with Baule
95–6, 171; 'search-and-destroy'
strategy 244–6

gardes de police 200
gardes indigènes 200
Gbuèkékro *see* Bouaké
Gold, in Baule economy: 11, 13,
20, 89, 159, 175, 204, 250
n.17, 267 n.110; mining at
Kokumbo 51, 89, 130, 266
n.102. *See also* Prices
Gold Coast 34, 42, 81, 181, 183
Gossa, *see* Bouaké
Government General: 1899 reorganization of 75–6; reforms
of 1902 144; new fiscal measures 173
Grand Bassam: 33–6; and installation of French trading post
83; population devastated by
bubonic plague and yellow
fever 114
Grand Jack 36, 37
Grand Lahou 8, 29, 30, 35,
37–8, 40–1, 44, 250 n.15
Grand Lahou-Tiassalé trading
chain 28–32, 40, 47
'Great White Umpires' 242–3
Grodet, Governor Albert: 56, 73,
75; role in failure of Monteil
expedition 256 n.33; dismissal
of 75
Guns and powder: purchased by
Baule 85; restoration of commerce by Roberdeau 138; Baule
exchange rubber for 157; sales
to Baule 179; Akoué make
gunpowder 200

Half Jack: 35–7, 40–1, 250 n.15;
revolt 37–8. *See also* Jacqueville

Half-Jack–Ahua–Niamwé traiding chain 28–32, 40, 47

Hallet, Robin: on importance of Baule resistance movement 2

Hargreaves, J. D.: on role of French military 233; on pre-colonial hinterland 258 n.61

Harris, Prophet: in Ivory Coast 230

Hay, M. J.: on early cash crop production 276 n.31

Head tax: early plans for 115; Clozel introduces 133; Clozel's directives concerning 146; role in colony's budget 173–6, 179; Angoulvant's use of after defeat 204. See also Tax

hommes de paille 169, 274 n.112. See also Collaborators

Hopkins, A. G.: on pre-colonial land and labour 186; on 'Great White Umpires' 242

Hubert, Lucien: labour theories of 237

Humanitarian criticism: of Angoulvant 197; international 198

Imperialism: 'peripheral' theory of 239–40, 283 n.17; economic theory of 240–1; general theories 239; Eurocentric theories of 283 n.17

Imra Nguessan, daughter of Akafou Bulare: 205, 229

Jack-Jacks, see Alladian

Jackville, see Jacqueville

Jacqueville (Jackville) 40, 44

Judicial system: and policy of collaboration 148–50

Junior chiefs: role in resistance 218–21

Kakou Bla, wife of Akafou Bulare: 31, 161–2; Akafou Brou, son of 163

Kakou Dibi, Ngban chief: as successor to Akafou 164; French support 205

Kami, Akoué village 89, 191, 193, 195, 201, 205

Kano, woman chief of northern Faafoué 127, 217

Kasso, Faafoué chief, brother of Kouassi Blé 104, 127

Katie Kofi, chief of Katiakofikro: French execution of 104

Kimon Kouassi, Ngban chief 205

Kinship structures: marriage alliances and atonvle marriage 17–25 passim; and Baule resistance 221–3; Baule differ from Ashanti 247 n.26. See also Marriage

klô kpenngben (village chief) 22, 25–6, 153

Kodé, northern Baule group 137, 200

Kodiokofikro, Nzipri village 58, 67

Koffi Alani, Akoué chief 206

Koffi Ossou, chief of Ouarébo-Faafoué 136–8, 165, 268 n.127

Koffi Ottokou, chief of Fahari 128

Koki Yao Aounou, Akoué resistance leader 190–1, 193, 206

Kokumbo, Faafoué village: 'gold rush' and north-south migration 13; and Baule trading chains 28; mines and slave labour among Faafoué 89; pre-colonial rivalry with Saafoué 93; French plans to occupy 120–30; Baule plans to recapture 139

Komenan, Buen, see Buen Komenan

Komenan, Etien, see Etien Komenan

kômien 227

Kong: 34; tready with Binger 52, 53; Monteil expedition to aid 56; French-Samory conflicts over 100–1; region of 40, 146

Kongouanou, Akoué village 191

Kossou, Akoué gold-producing village 89

Kouadio Boni, prophet figure 228

Kouadio Koffi, Nzipri chief 212, 217, 268

Kouadio Ndri, Ouarébo-Assabou chief 166–7, 207, 217

Kouadio Okou, Ouarébo chief of Lomo: pre-colonial dispute with Akafou Bulare 31; refusal to greet Marchand 51; role in first Baule revolt 64, 77; relations with Delafosse and Lomo revolt 112–22, 233; rivalry with Akafou Bulare 121–3; submission, 131; meets Clozel and receives pardon 162; works to assist French in subduing Ngban 221

Kouadio Pri, prophet figure of Kpouébo 228

Kouakou Ofite, Ngban chief 205

Kouamé Akafou, Nzipri chief 148

Kouamé Dié (Kouamé Guié), paramount chief of Ouarébo-Assabou: early relations with French 112–13; symbolic submission of 131, 134; considered opponent of French 136–7; opposition to from Baule 136–7, 220, 268 n.127; death of 137, 217, 268 n.130; aftermath of death 162–3, 164–8, 207, 238

Kouassi Amané 148

Kouassi Blé, Faafoué chief of Bouaké: becomes chief on death of brother, Kouassi Gbuèké 102; imprisoned by Captain Benoît 104; participation in 1898 siege on Bouaké post 104, 112, 221; considers open resistance 127; indicates willingness to come to terms with French 129; appointed as member of tribunal 148; delivers speech to Clozel 170, 275 n.115

Kouassi Gbuèké, Faafoué chief of Bouaké: 52–3, 102. See Bouaké

Kouassi Ngo, Akoué chief of Ngokro (Yamoussoukro): relationship with French 190; wounded in retreat from Diamalabo 192; fidelity honored by French 205; assassinated in Yamoussoukro 207, 213; 'chef de la tribu' 220. See Yamoussoukro

Kpouébo, southern Ngban village: 116, 123, 135, 137, 139, 161–4

Kokumbo, Faafoué gold-mining centre: 51, 89, 130, 132, 139, 226, 227

Labour: scarcity of in pre-colonial period 20; competition for labour and the politics of manpower 21; source of problems during Monteil expedition 59, 61; specialization of at Kokumbo 89; importance of for Baule 110, 146; Clozel's porterage policies 146; Baule attitudes toward 158–9; Angoulvant's plans for obligatory communal labour; question of 'underemployment' 187; importance as motive for Baule revolt 235–9; wages and compensation for 159, 267, n.112. See also Slavery

Lahou, see Grand Lahou

Laissez-faire: policy of Clozel 178, 209

Land tenure policy 183, 185

Laplud, Inspector: visits Ivory Coast 179, 180, 183–4

Leadership: importance in Baule resistance 231–2; importance in character of French rule, 234–4. See also Chieftaincy; Civilian administration

Legitimacy: principles of during collaborative policies 166–8; Angoulvant's approach to in cases of succession 185. See also Chieftaincy; 'Traditional' Baule Custom, 'Neo-traditional' Baule Custom

Liberation of captives: 68, 112; role in collaboration 215; French policy toward 265 n.84. *See also* Slavery; 'Villages de Liberté'

Lomo, souther Ouarébo village: 31, 51; revolt of 112-22. *See* Kouadio Okou

Marabadiassa 28, 86

Marchand, Captain Jean-Baptiste, French explorer: proposal for 'transnigerienne' explorations 41-2; qualities as diplomat 43; failure of initial Bandama penetration; alliance with Ahua to attack Tiassalé 45, 252 n.43; captures Tiassalé 46; installs Fatou Aka as chief of Tiassalé 46-7; ignores appeal of Gov. Binger to wait on coast 251 n.35; official mythology surrounding Baule explorations 48-9; received by Akafou 50; opposed by Kouadio Okou 51; reaches Bouaké 52; encounters Baule reticence 49, 51, 52-3, 56; poor reception in Kong 53-5; alarm over Samory and British 54; plans for French–Dyula alliance 54-5; misleading cables to Ministry concerning Baule passivity 56; row with Monteil 69

Milliès-Lacroix, Raphael, Minister of Colonies; 180, 189

Monteil, Lt.-Col. Parfait-Louis, Commander of Kong Expedition: and expedition to relieve Kong 57-71; among Baule 60-4; recall by Chautemps 64-5; contacts with Samory's *sofas* 65-6; humiliating retreat 67-9; dispute with Marchand 69: insults Nebout 69; bitterness toward Binger 71; repercussions of departure 71-6

Mory Touré: and early slave trade with Baule 86-7

Moskowitz, French explorer 54, 56-7, 253 n.72

Mouttet, Gouvernor Louis 101-2

Moya Ba, woman chief of Ouarébo-Linguira: supports French 137, 168; assassination of 168, 213; reasons for collaboration 220

Mvlan, Faafoué chief 127, 129, 148, 168

nana, 218

Nanafoué, Baule group 19, 51, 89, 133, 193, 200

Nationalist historians: and resistance studies 1

Nda Frété, Ngban chief 164

Nebout, Albert, French administrator: administrator of Kodiokofikro 58-69 *passim*; background 77; among Baule 93, 96, 101-2, 106, 112, 114, 122-3; strategy of 145. 212; as acting Governor 179; policies attacked by Angoulvant 185; as civilian leader 232; first civilian administrator among Baule 246 n.7; advisor to governors 256 n.41; mission to meet with Samory 261 n.2

'Neo-traditional' Baule custom 244

'New imperialism': era of 239

Newbury, C. W.: on Roume's plan for territories 144; on 'economic revolution' 241

N'Gatta Blé Koffi, Ouarébo-Linguira chief of Niamiabo: supports French 137; appointed to tribunal 148; as collaborator 167; Dié Lonzo's plans to attack 168; reasons for collaboration 220

Ngokro (Yamoussoukro), Akoué village: and French retreat from Bonzi 192-3; shift of French post to 221. *See* Yamoussoukro

ngonda ('crossroads'): and Baule

ngonda (*cont.*)
trade 28

N'Guessan, son of Kouamé Dié: alleged assassin of Moya Ba 168

Niaba, John, chief of Lahou: 37, 40

niamwe, Baule agricultural encampments: 25-6, 188; role in resistance struggle 223-31

Niamwé, lower Bandama village: 28-31, 40, 45; Fatou Aka, chief of 46

Niango Kouadio, Ouarébo chief of Toumodi: named to tribunal 148; welcomes Clozel 162; friendship with Delafosse 212

Niango Kouassi, Ouarébo chief of Toumodi: 61, 117, 220; son of takes trip to France with Delafosse 148; refuses to take part in insurrection 212

Nsoko 82. *See also* Apollonian; Esquires

nvle kpen 22-3, 153, 215-19 *passim*. *See also* Paramount chief

Nzi Aka, chief of Ahua: 45. *See also* Ahua

Nzima, *see* Apollonien

Nzipri, northern Baule group: join attack against Monteil 68; and slave labour at Zaakro 89; wish to join French in attack on Agba-Baule 93; villages attacked by Le Magnen 126; membership on tribunal 148; assist French in attack on Kokumbo 267 n.107

Nzoko, Ngban chief of Moronou: collaborating chief, shot 208, 280 n.99

'Official mind': thinking about value of Ivory Coast possessions in Imperial circles 34; and Monteil's recall 72

Okou Boni, Ouarébo-Luinguira chief: support of French 137; collaboration 168; death of 168; conflict with Kouamé Dié 137, 220

Okou Kouakou, Akoué chief of Kami: as new chief of Kami 205

Okou N'Gatta, Ouarébo-Linguira chief: supports French 137; member of tribunal 148

Opoku Ware, Ashantihene: succession struggle with Dakon 6

Oral traditions: importance of in reconstructing Baule history xvii; of origins of Baule 6. *See also* 'Neo-traditional' Baule custom; 'Traditional' Baule custom

Osei Tutu, Ashantihene: death of 6

Ouarébo, Baule group: and origin myths 19; subdue southern Ngban 30-1; allies of Etien Komenan 31; and Kouadio Okou 51; Delafosse seeks support of southern groups 122; French fear hostility from 127; Delafosse's survey trip through northern groups 113; submission of 131; succession dispute among 164-8, 207; French dismantle post at Sakassou 207. *See also* Dié Lonzo; Kouadio Ndri; Kouadio Okou; Kouamé Dié; Moya Ba; Niango Kouadio; Toto Buegré; Yoma Boni

Ouarébo-Assabou: control by Kouamé Dié 136; succession dispute among 167; hatred toward Ouarébo-Linugira chiefs 168

Ouarébo-Faafoué: subordinated by Kouamé Dié 136

Ouarébo-Linguira: subordinated by Kouamé Dié 136; representation on tribunal 148; as collaborators with French 167-8. *See also* N'Gatta Blé Koffi; Okou N'Gatta

Ouéllé, Baule group: Angoulvant's campaign against 200; Andsoromi Taki's following among 228

Ouossou, southern Ngban village: 31, 50; Monteil's plans to convoke chiefs at 62; in first Baule revolt 63–4; tension in area of 193–4; and Ali Seck affair 194; and link with Beugré oracle 229

Palm oil: trade on Ivory Coast 9, 11, 30–3; falling prices of 35; trade during 1840s 80; Europeans displace African traders in 258 n.58
Papillon, French explorer: 38–43 passim; death of 50, 229
Paramount chief (nvle kpen, famien): 22–3; interest in negotiating peace settlement with French 134–5; first killed 137; role in Baule resistance 215; in pre-colonial context 216; situation in colonial period 162; effective discrediting of office 4, 163, 217. See also Chieftaincy
Peasant producer: Baule role as 210
Periphery: changing political economy of 239, 241, 284 n.19
Person, Yves 8, 246 n.9, 258 n.63, 259, n.78, n.80, n.85, and n.87, 261 n.2
Pobéguin, Charles, French administrator 48–50
Political organization: pre-colonial 17–25; marriage changes and fragmentation of 92
'Politique des races' 153, 161, 163, 166, 170, 217–18
Ponty, Governor General William 189, 197, 199, 234
Porterage: 58, 62, 68, 267 n.112; role in Baule resistance motivation 59–61, 146, 235
Prempeh I, Ashantihene 85
Press: metropolitan 196, 198, 278 n.63; local 281 n.111 and n.112
Prices: for slaves 87, 258 n.59; for gold 250 n.17; for labour 159,

267, n.112; for rubber 275 n.6. See also Gold; Labour; Slavery
Privey, Captain 137, 153
Prophet figures: in final stages of resistance movement 25–30
Public opinion: role in formation of colonial policy 272 n.51

Quaqua Coast: 5; and early Akan migrations 6; and Baule economy 8; early description of 245 n.1; and early cloth trade 246 n.10

Railway construction: Abidjan to Bouaké 154
Resettlement scheme: imposed upon Baule 204
Resident 35, 37, 39. See also Treich-Laplène
Resistance: first phase 31–65; second phase 99–141; economic basis of 105–12; final phase of 186–210; and the problem of unity 211–13; role of paramount chiefs in 215–18; role of 'junior' chiefs in 218–21; role of kinship organization in 221–3; archetypal scenario of events 234–8; issue of labour as motive for 235–8
Resisters: increased polarization with collaborators 203; punished by French 205–6; 'junior' chiefs as 218–21
Roberdeau, Governor Henri 106, 118, 123–4, 138, 140
Robinson, Ronald: on imperialism 240, 284 n.19; on British territories in West Africa 242; on collaborative system 243; and Gallagher on imperialism 240
Roume, Governor General Ernest 144, 234
Rubber: reason for expanded trade in 81; export trade 156; Tiassalé trade 157, 272 n.68;

Rubber (cont.)
  Ivory Coast boom 175-7;
  budget dependence on trade in
  181; Angoulvant's plans for
  planting 188

Saafoué, southern Baule group:
  war with Faafoué 93; assist
  French 267 n.107
Sakassou, principal Ouarébo village: Asmaret's mission to 62;
  French plans to attack 136-7;
  as intended burial site for
  Kouamé Dié 167; French dismantle post at 207
Salékro, Nanafoué village: Nanafoué attack French post at 139,
  193
Samory, Mandé resistance leader:
  importance as resistance leader
  1-2, 231; armament trade with
  Baule 52; French campaigns
  against 42, 52; agents among
  northern Baule 55; importance
  of in Monteil's recall 65; sofas
  attack Monteil's troops 66;
  French fear of potential alliance with Prempeh I of Ashanti
  85; retreat of an aftermath for
  northern Baule 99-105; impact
  of capture 238; and purchase
  of arms at Tiassalé 259 n.81;
  details of relations with northern Baule 259 n.85; Monteil
  and tactics of 259 n.87. See
  also Monteil; Kong
Satama, Dyula village: and Monteil's return 66
Schneiggans, Lieutenant: estab-
  lishes French post at Bonzi
  among Akoué 133
'Search and destroy': as French
  military tactic 140, 145, 202,
  224-5
Segmentary organization: Baule
  and segmentary model 248
  n.39
Senegalese traders: Simon seeks to
  avert slaughter by Ngban 194;

Baule hostility towards 213
Senegalese troops: as part of Monteil expedition 58; besieged at
  Moronou by Ngbans 63; Nebout's requests for 123; numbers of 140; Ministry proposes
  cut in numbers 189; Angoulvant requests additional 189;
  Governor General Ponty authorizes additional 199
Senior chiefs, see nvle kpen;
  Paramount chiefs
Settlement patterns: Angoulvant's
  resettlement programme 204-5;
  and organization of resistance
  223-5. See also niamwe
Sikazué, gold producing area
  among Nanafoué 89
sikéfue, agents in Tiassalé house-
  trade 15
Simon, Marc, administrator of
  southern Baule district: and
  Akoué revolt 191-3; and Ali
  Seck affair 194; as civilian administrator 232-3; and archetypal scenario of revolt 234
Singrobo, southern Ouarébo village 31, 50
Sinzénou, Souamélé village: refuge
  of Kouadio Okou 131
Slavery and trade in slaves: decline
  of slave trade on coast 9;
  Baule trade with north for
  slaves 11, 86-7; numbers of
  slaves 87, 163, 260 n.89 and
  n.90; importance of slaves for
  labour 70, 89-90, 236; price
  of slaves 87, 258 n.59, 260
  n.93; influx of slaves and Baule
  social structure 90-1, 221-3;
  emancipation and escape of
  slaves 58, 61, 103-5, 109, 113,
  126, 140, 147, 219, 265 n.84;
  impact of decline in slaves
  from north 219; role of slaves
  as collaborators 214-15, 221.
  See also Labour; Trade; Samory
Statistics: of Baule slave and armament trade 87; of colonial

Statistics (*cont.*)
import import–export values 257, n.50, 275 n.1; of colony's budgets, 275 n.2. *See also* Prices
Staup, Lieutenant 39, 40
'Straw chiefs' 274 n.112
Succession disputes 164, 185
Syncretistic millennial movements 229

tas, gold measurement 267 n.110
Tax: on exported timber and rubber to England 84; imposed upon Baule 99, 125, 135, 146–7, 152, 169, 204, 266 n.101, 267 n.119; Clozel's regulations of 1901 147; Baule understanding of 170; in form of licence fees 178; proposed on firearms 180; returns allocated to chiefs 180; role in Baule resistance motivation 235. *See also* Head tax
Telegraph communications: extension of 154
Tiassalé: important periphery transit market 15; resistance of 33–48; and rival trading groups 28–32; transformed into Dyula town 94; and European commercial presence 156–7; 249 n.47; treaty with 251 n.28; capture of 252 n.45; rubber trade 272 n.68
Tiassalé-Grand Lahou trading chain 28–32
Tiéfu, Nanafoué diviner: 227; prophecy of 228
Timber: emerges as important Ivory Coast export during 1890s 80–1
tirailleurs sénégalais, *see* Senegalese troops
Toto Beugré, Ouarébo chief of Sakabo 165, 168
Toto Dibi, Ouarébo chief 113, 165
Toumodi, southern Ouarébo village 28, 31, 109, 117

Trade: 27–32, 36, 44, 76; resurgence under civilian administration 78; boom 88, 172, 175, 237; and patterns of debt collection 110–11. *See also* Commerce
Trading chains 27–32
'Traditional' Baule custom: 164; 'neo-traditional' aspects 244. *See also* Legitimacy
traitants 35. *See* Coastal commerce
Transit markets 15, 247 n.24
Treich-Laplène, Marcel, Resident 34–7, 250 n.9
Tribunals: modeled after Baule legal procedure 148–9, 270 n.32
Tribute: 131–2; paid by paramount chiefs to hasten withdrawal of French 135
Troops *see* Senegalese troops

'Umpires', *see* 'Great White Umpires'
Under-employment: in precolonial African economies 186–7
Unity: of Baule resistance movement 211–13

Verdier, Arthur, French coastal merchant 33, 83, 86, 156, 249 n.3, 256 n.38
Village chiefs 22–3, 218
Villages de Liberté 104, 109, 215, 262 n.14
Village resettlement: after defeat 204
Vimont, Lt.-Col. 145
Voituret, French explorer: 38–43 *passim*; death of 50, 229

Wage employment: Baule disdain for 96; French attempts to force Baule into 235; payment levels 159
Wage labourers: and Dyula 95; and porters in Tiassalé region

Wage labourers (*cont.*) 267 n.112

War fines 200, 203-4

Wild rubber: value rises dramatically during 1890s 82. *See* Rubber

Women: as collaborators 214

'Working misunderstanding': between French and Baule 95-6, 171

Yabo Mousso (Yamoussou) Akoué woman chief: affirms loyalty to French 133, 220; 'la reine des Akoués' 190; harbours French administrators under attack during Akoué revolt 192-3

Yamoussoukro (Ngokro), Akoué village: 192-3, 205, 221

Yao Guié, Kodé chief of Béoumi 137

Yao Guié, Ngban chief of Kpouébo: 116-7; militancy 121, 123, 125, 136, 220, 232; surrender of and probable cause of death 207; retaliation of relative 208

Yaouré, Baule group: 89, 190-1, 200

Yellow fever epidemic 114

Yma Boni, Ouarébo chief: and Ouarébo succession dispute 166-7, 207

Zaakro 89

Zemma, *see* Apollonien